Aviation

AN ILLUSTRATED HISTORY

Aviation

AN ILLUSTRATED HISTORY

Chris Chant
and John Batchelor

BLITZ EDITIONS

Published by Blitz Editions an imprint of
Bookmart Limited
Registered Number 2372865
Trading as Bookmart Limited
Desford Road
Enderby
Leicester LE9 5AD

Cover design by Graham Beehag.
Interior design by Graham Beehag.

ISBN 1 85605 252 4

Printed in Italy

Contents

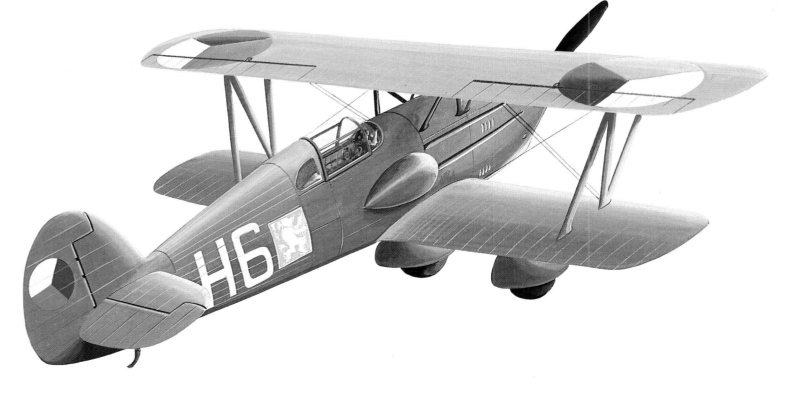

Introduction

Mankind's ability to imagine, in the widest possible sense of that word, is perhaps the most interesting factor to differentiate him from the rest of the animal world, for this ability has been of paramount importance in his evolution into a tool-user and an artist. Mankind can produce artefacts that are both useful and beautiful: many machines, and particularly some aircraft, have a certain functional beauty, and as a result they work well because they look right, and *vice versa*.

The desire to fly must be one of the oldest in human experience, and yet it has been among the most recent to be achieved. From his earliest days man has looked up into the sky and envied the birds, and from the early Egyptian period if not before, right up to the present, bird flight has won a prominent place in folklore and the arts.

Given this fascination, as strong today as it ever was despite the realization of flight as a practical science, it is hardly surprising that man has always attempted to rival the flight of birds, almost invariably with craft that resemble birds at least in their outward forms. This conviction that only aviform shapes stood a chance of flight also led to the almost universal adoption of ornithoptering, or flapping, wings on early attempts at flying machines. This was a dead end as man does not have the musculature to operate such surfaces, and no other powerplant of adequate power/weight ratio was available.

Yet despite his total lack of success, man still continued in his efforts to achieve flight. The experimenters were a strange mix : some of them, such as the great Leonardo da Vinci, were visionaries while others were fanatics or eccentrics. These pioneers followed many false leads with an enthusiasm that was often fatal, and they were almost invariably and with every justification dubbed madmen by the public. But the lure of flight remained strong, and as a result pioneer followed pioneer until the advent of the 'Age of Reason' and the application of the scientific method at last brought some real progress. Finally, in 1783, man left the earth for the first time in the hot-air balloon built by the Montgolfier brothers, and it was realized that flight was indeed possible. Shortly afterwards the eccentric and underestimated British pioneer, Sir George Cayley, formulated the problem of heavier-than-air flight and evolved the basic form of the machine that would overcome it. From this point onwards progress was relatively rapid when compared with the previous centuries, and success was inevitable once the internal combustion engine had been developed during the last quarter of the 19th century.

It is with the age of practical aviation, brought about by the genius of the Wright brothers in combining Cayley's aerodynamic ideas and Benz's engine, that this book is primarily concerned. At the heart of the text is inevitably the heavier-than-air craft, the aeroplane. But this is not an account of aircraft as such, but rather of the linked relationship of people and their flying machines. The relationship is a very direct one, and there are few people in the developed world who have not been affected by it. Men and women design, build and fly aircraft; they enjoy the benefits of air travel that allow people and goods to be moved rapidly and safely all over the globe. Unfortunately, people have also been the victims of aircraft, especially in World War II, and up to a point in the very recent part many people have lived under the threat of annihilation by nuclear weapons which can be delivered, among other means, by strategic bomber aircraft.

But while these aspects of the relationship between man and his flying machines are of the greatest economic and military importance, there are other aspects of aviation that are closer to man's original inspiration for flight: a desire to emulate the birds for no reason other than for the joy and the delight of it. Therefore just as interesting as the 'hard' relationship of economic dependence is the 'soft' relationship of sport flying, gliding, aerobatics and racing, usually undertaken by individuals, in aircraft designed, built or extensively modified by themselves or by small organizations.

As well as this direct involvement in flight, there are other aspects, like the public interest in heroes and heroines of flight such as Manfred von Richthofen, Charles Lindbergh and Amy Johnson. There is also a fascination in the drama of such events as the 1934 'MacRobertson' air race from the United Kingdom to Australia and the great waterplane races between France, Italy, the United Kingdom and the United States of America States for the Schneider Trophy in the 1920s.

The story of aviation, therefore, can be said to be a history of the relationship of mankind and aircraft in its technical, social, political, economic and emotional aspects. Thus it is a history not so much of what men arid their flying machines have done, but of why they have done it and why they have been able to do so. It is a history of motive as well as of deed.

The history of powered flight during the present century is in many respects a reflection of our civilization in both its best and its worst aspects. For the good, aviation has opened up new parts of the globe which has benefited trade and medicine, as well as leading to a higher standard of living for many. It has played a role in the general quickening of communications all over the world that has fundamentally altered mankind's attitudes to himself and the globe, and has led to the concept of 'spaceship earth'. On the other side of the coin, aviation has played a considerable part in the evolution of total war, bringing the civilian populations of the whole world within the military scope of the major warring powers. It can only be hoped that the balance has been, and will continue to be, on the side of the good; but whether marred by abuses or not, aviation has been an exiting and fascinating adventure.

The Triumph of the Wright Brothers

It is now generally accepted that the first successful flight in a heavier-than-air machine was the first of four made by the Wright brothers, Orville and Wilbur, on 17 December 1903. Indeed, there can be no doubt that this quartet of flights marked the start of the age of practical aviation, though they were also the culmination of the previous century's efforts. So the work of earlier pioneers, some of them realists and others of them simply dreamers, should not be discounted.

It was only after four years of experimental work with gliders that the Wright brothers were finally ready with their first powered heavier-than-aircraft, which was a machine driven by an engine they themselves had designed and built. The Flyer I, as this first real aeroplane is now known, was crated for transport from the Wright establishment in Dayton, Ohio, to the Kill Devil Hills in North Carolina, where the machine was reassembled in December 1903. Although it is often averred that the Wrights chose this location to ensure secrecy, in reality the brothers selected this deserted spot for its steady and moderately strong prevailing winds, which had greatly aided the brothers' gliding experiments in previous years.

effectively controlled during its flight in all three planes.

The day's historic nature was reported to the press, but received little coverage and was largely ignored. Without any fuss, however, the Wrights then disassembled the Flyer and transported it back to Dayton, where they set about the construction of a new machine that incorporated the lessons learned in North Carolina with the Flyer I.

The Wrights were the first men to fly successfully, but this should not be allowed to disguise the fact that men had indeed flown before. A succinct and generally satisfactory theory of flight's aerodynamic aspects had been evolved just over 100 years earlier by an Englishman, Sir George Cayley. In 1799 he had defined his theory about the forces acting on a body in flight and inscribed it on a silver disc. On the other side of the disc was a simple drawing of a glider containing all the elements necessary for flight. Cayley continued to work on the notion intermittently for the next 50 yards before building a full-scale model in 1849. The control surfaces had to be fixed before flight, but several short glides were made with the machine in ballast before Cayley was ready to experiment with a live passenger in the form of the son of a worker from his estate near Scarborough. Although he was only a passenger, the unknown boy has the distinction of being the first person to fly in a heavier-than-air machine. Cayley continued to work on his designs and in 1853 produced an improved design, and in this his coachman was launched across a small valley on the estate. Cayley worked on the theory of flight until 1855.

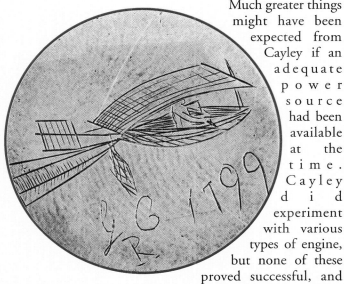

Much greater things might have been expected from Cayley if an a d e q u a t e p o w e r s o u r c e had been available at the t i m e . C a y l e y d i d experiment with various types of engine, but none of these proved successful, and Cayley was therefore limited to theory and gliding flight. This same factor bedevilled pioneers for the next quarter century until the German N. A. Otto perfected his four-stroke internal combustion engine. There followed a short phase in which the petrol engine was developed in both power and reliability, but the pioneers of flight had to wait nearly another 25 years before engine technology reached the point at which it was possible to make a powerplant offering the power/weight ratio required for the petrol engine's use in an aeroplane.

The pioneers of flight were not entirely daunted by the lack of an effective engine, though, and the drawing boards of the pioneers were littered with a host of designs characterized by varying levels of practicality and safety. A not inconsiderable proportion of these machines actually reached the hardware stage: some were built as gliders, but most of them were constructed as powered machines with a great deal of faith pinned on gas, steam or even gunpowder engines.

One of the earliest of these pioneers was a Frenchman, Felix du Temple. In 1857 he produced his first successful powered model aeroplane, and in the same year designed a full-sized monoplane which was not in the event built until

Right: In 1799 Sir George Cayley engraved a silver disc with two of the seminal thoughts about the development of heavier-than-air flight. On the reverse was an illustration of the forces acting on a body in flight, and on the obverse (illustrated) a sketch for a simple fixed-wing aeroplane.

The first attempt at a powered flight was made by Wilbur on 14 December, but the flight was unsuccessful when coarse movement of the elevator control sent the Flyer into the sand as it left its take-off trolley. Repairs were completed during the following days, and on 17 December the brothers were once again ready to continue their trials. After five local witnesses had arrived, Orville took his place prone on the lower wing of the Flyer, accelerated the engine and signalled for the machine to be released. The Flyer gathered speed down the 60-ft (18-m) rail that had been laid into the wind and, as it reached its flying speed of about 25 mph (40 km/h), lifted off the trolley and entered wingborne flight. Twelve seconds later the Flyer touched down after flying about 500 ft (150 m) through the air. The time was shortly after 10.35 in the morning. During the next 90 minutes, three more flights were made, the last of them by Wilbur. This proved the most successful flight of the day, more than 880 yards (800 m) being covered in 59 seconds.

The Wrights thus became the first men to fly a heavier-than-air machine that could take off from level ground, travel through the air under its own power, and be

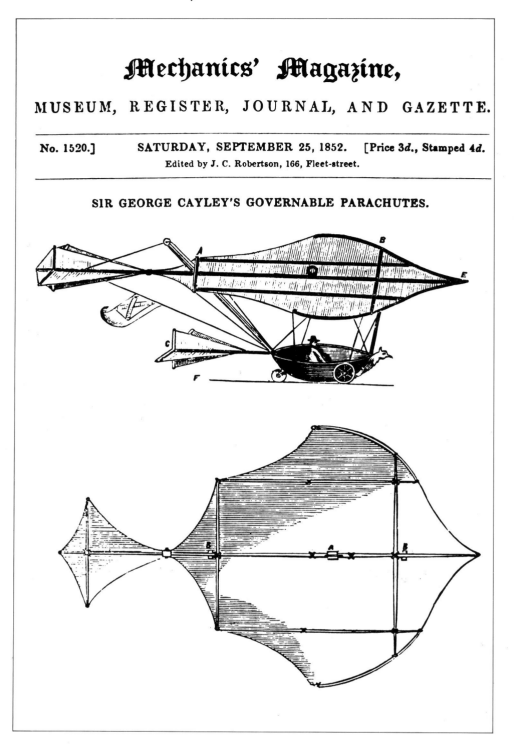

1874, when it became the first powered aeroplane to take off (if that is not too grand a term) after it had careered down a steep ramp. The aeroplane was wholly incapable of sustained flight, however, and came down almost immediately after its launch.

During 1890, some 16 years later, the first take off from level ground was made by another French aeroplane, the Eole designed by Clement Ader. This was a truly extraordinary machine configured something like a bat, with a fuselage-mounted steam engine driving a large tractor propeller. The machine took off and moved some 160 ft (50 m) through the air on 9 October 1890, but this can in no way be considered a true flight as the Eole lacked any type of control surface and was anyway incapable of sustained flight. Even so, Ader was highly encouraged by his 'success' and pressed ahead with his experiments in heavier-than-air flight with similarly configures machines.

Cayley had first developed the theory of lift through the use of cambered wing surfaces, but almost 100 years intervened before Horatio Phillips, the first great aerodynamicist, patented his theory of lift based on a differential camber between the upper and lower surfaces of the wing section. If the curvature of the upper surface of a wing is greater than that of its under surface, according to this concept, the air flows over the upper surface at a greater velocity, producing lower pressures than on the underside. Hence an upward force, 'lift', is generated as the higher pressure under the surface seeks to equalize the pressure differential with the lower-pressure air above the surface. His first patent was granted in 1884, and in 1891 Phillips made and flew a large multiplane model whose wing cellule of superimposed wings of very high aspect ratio resembled nothing so much as a venetian blind, in an effort to prove his theories. The work undertaken by Phillips was to prove invaluable to all future aircraft pioneers, for this far-sighted Englishman had paved the way into the future by his evolution of the theory of true aerodynamic lift in place of the planing lift used in kites and earlier powered aircraft efforts.

Though at times much has been claimed for the huge 'flying machine' built in 1894 by Hiram Maxim, better known as the inventor of the first true machine-gun, in reality little can be said for it. At vast expense, Maxim built a large biplane test rig to investigate the nature of lift. The test rig ran on a two-rail track, and was prevented from

Above: The *Mechanics' Magazine* of September 1852 carried these illustrations of Cayley's design for a glider that incorporated all the features of a modern aeroplane except provision for lateral control.

Right: This steam-powered aeroplane was designed in France by Félix du Temple in 1857, and in about 1874 became the first powered aeroplane to take-off. This in no way constituted a genuine flight, however, as the machine was merely released down a steep ramp and could not sustain itself in the air.

rising more than a few inches by wooden guard rails. During the course of a test run in 1894 the machine produced enough lift to rise from its supporting track and even to break through the guard rails. It then crashed, as there were no means of controlling the machine in the air. Maxim thereupon abandoned his efforts, but later attempted to secure some of the glory awarded aviation pioneers by launching extravagant claims for his rig.

In 1897 Ader produced the Avion III as his third full-sized machine. This was similar in configuration to the Eole, but had two steam engines and two propellers. Again, there was no adequate provision for controlling the machine should it have left the ground, which it did not. Nevertheless, claims for Adder to be considered the first man to fly have been made at various times since the beginning of the century.

All was not in vain during the last decade of the nineteenth century, however, for in another flight-related field great progress was being made. This was in the realm of gliding. Realizing that the non-availability of a powerplant with a suitable power/weight ratio meant almost certain failure to the pioneers concentrating on flight by means of thrust and lift, more practically minded pioneers saw that gliding flight, in which the pull of gravity replaces the thrust of the propeller as the primary motive force, offered the chance of making real advances.

Chief among these exponents of gliding was Otto Lilienthal, the great German pioneer. A practical man who believed in the scientific method, Lilienthal was content to advance by slow steps and therefore did to seek to launch anything into the air until he had fully considered all aspects of the device. In common with many other pioneers Lilienthal was fascinated by bird flight, but unlike so many of these others he did not attempt to produce mere mechanical copies of birds. Instead he analysed how birds fly and then sought to apply the same principles to a structure that was mechanically adequate to the demands that would be placed on it. In 1889 Lilienthal published his findings on bird flight in *Der Vogelflug als Grundlage der Fliegerkunst*, a book that soon became virtually the bible of future pioneers. Lilienthal built his first glider in 1891, and by 1894 had developed the monoplane standard glider that proved highly successful and appeared in so many photographs of the period. Lilienthal's gliders were not

without their faults, however: his concentration on aerofoils of parallel, rather than differential, camber was a step in the wrong direction after the tests carried out by Phillips, and his control system was adequate for his small gliders but could not be applied on anything else. Nevertheless, the important fact about Lilienthal's gliders was their success. Operating from his artificial mound in Berlin or from hilltops elsewhere in Germany, Lilienthal and his gliders proved that heavier-than-air flight, albeit of a not very practical form, was possible. This did much to increase a general enthusiasm for flight and also encouraged other pioneers to persevere in their endeavours despite their difficulties.

Lilienthal's control system was based on the movement of the glider's centre of gravity, rather than on the operation of control surfaces. This was made necessary by the light weight and relatively flimsy structure of Lilienthal's machines, which could not easily have been made to incorporate moving surfaces and their controlling cables.

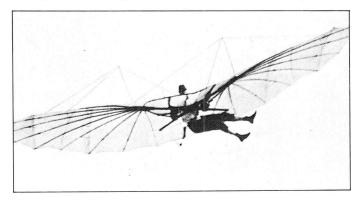

Far Right: The true precursor of modern flight, at least in terms of the aerodynamic factors involved in wingborne flight, was Otto Lilienthal. This German developed a series of lightweight but practical hang-gliders typified by the 1894 standard monoplane type (above) and the 1895 biplane (below).

Below: This is a reconstruction of the design patented in 1857 by Félix du Temple for a steam-powered tractor monoplane with forward-wing wings.

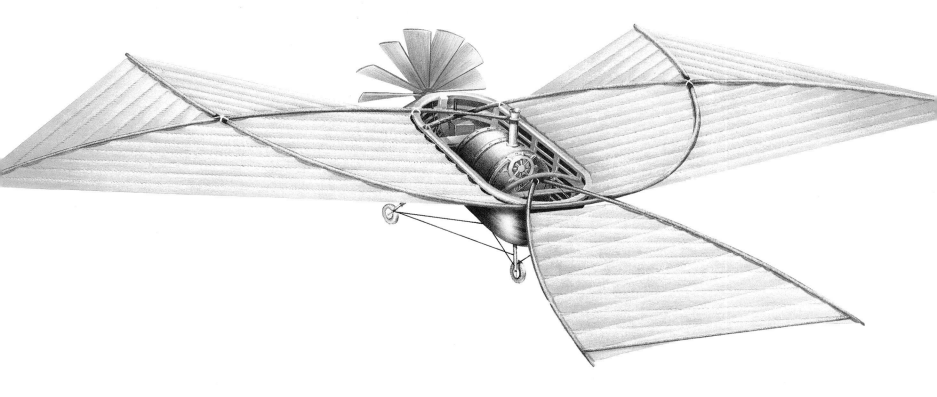

The pilot was instead suspended by his upper chest in a gap between the wings, so that his legs could swing anywhere in the hemisphere below him. The lower half of his body and his legs were then moved in the direction he wished his craft to go, the movement of the centre of gravity in that direction effecting the change. This system also obviated the need for landing gear, as the pilot merely ran down his chosen slope until he had reached flying speed and lifted off; landing was simply effected by touching down onto his feet.

Lilienthal went off at a tangent in 1896 when he started to experiment with ornithoptering (flapping) wings powered by a small gas engine. There is every reason to expect that he would have reverted without undue delay to more practical forms of propulsion, but on 9 August 1896 Lilienthal stalled during a flight, crashed and died in hospital during the following day.

Although Lilienthal was not always on the right track, his seminal importance in the history of flight cannot be denied: he was both the first man to fly in a controllable aeroplane and the source of inspiration for the next generation of pioneers, who were the men who would make powered flight a reality. From his time onwards the need for the effective means of controlling an aeroplane in the air was there for all to see. Earlier pioneers had not realized how important this factor really was, imagining perhaps that the aeroplane would somehow fly and control itself once it had risen into the air.

Lilienthal's greatness may also be gauged from the spate of imitators he inspired, principally in the United Kingdom and the United States of America. Percy Pilcher, a Scotsman, built the sturdy and practical Hawk, which had landing gear and could be towed off the ground, but this machine was still controlled in the Lilienthal 'hang-glider' fashion. Pilcher's death after a gliding accident in 1899 was a great blow to the development of British aviation, for with his demise serious experimentation came to an end for nearly 10 years. In the United States Lilienthal's imitators included Octave Chanute and A. M. Herring, the latter co-operating with Chanute in the design process and then doing most of the flying since Chanute was too old for this onerous task. The two built a few relatively successful types in 1896 and 1897, but Chanute's real importance was as a propagandist of flight. Realizing that he was too old to contribute anything but ideas to the cause, he concentrated on helping and encouraging other, younger and more dynamic designers including the Wright brothers. Chanute did, however, improve upon the structural concept of the basic Lilienthal hang-glider design by introducing the braced biplane formula, with its wing bays or cellules.

Similar progress in structures and aerodynamics was also being made at the same time by the Australian Lawrence Hargrave, who invented the box-kite in 1893. This type of flying toy gained considerable popularity in Europe and the United States in the late 1890s, and its basic shape was soon to be copied in a number of European aircraft, notably the Voisin and Farman types.

It is at this point that Orville and Wilbur Wright enter the scene as Chanute's ablest students. Determined and serious, but each characterized by a high degree of analytical and constructive imagination, the brothers belonged to a large, tight-knit family in Dayton, Ohio. Wilbur and Orville were the Wrights' third and fourth sons respectively, and in addition to two older brothers had a younger sister. From childhood the two youngest brothers displayed the energy and enthusiasms that would eventually prove profitable. Wilbur and Orville, with the latter very much the driving spirit of the team, joined forces with a friend to start a weekly newspaper. The West Side News was undertaken in its entirety by the three young men, including the printing on a press built by Orville and Wilbur, then 18 and 22 years old respectively. In 1890 the three moved into a more ambitious project, The Evening Item, but this lasted for only four months before competition with the more securely established Dayton dailies forced them out of business.

But at this time a new type of bicycle, the 'safety bicycle' with two equal-size wheels instead of one large and one small, was becoming popular and in this fact the brothers saw a good market for their undoubted engineering skills. Setting up business at first to sell bicycles, they soon expanded to the repair of damaged machines and finally the manufacture of their own 'Wright Special'. This retailed for the remarkably low price of $18 compared with the $160 Orville had paid for his first bicycle in 1892. The success of their bicycle business meant that the brothers had a secure, steady income and access to light engineering equipment and facilities. Moreover, their work with bicycles gave them an early appreciation of the value in mechanical

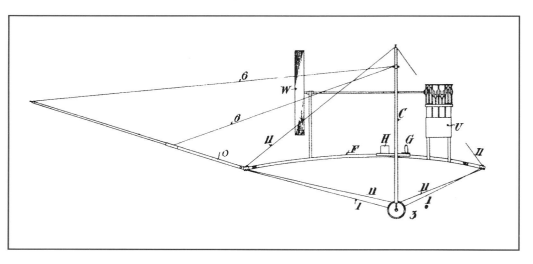

structures of lightness combined with strength, and also a keen insight into the closely allied factors of balance and control.

The brothers had been interested in flight from their youth when their father, the local bishop of the United Brethren Church, gave them a toy helicopter operated by a rubber band. Orville and Wilbur built replicas of the model, which flew successfully, but met with failure when they tried to produce scaled-up examples: after several such failures they abandoned the idea. Over the next few years, the brothers' interest in flight was limited to an appreciation of birds' soaring flight.

Wilbur later revealed that his active interest in flight was spurred by the death of Lilienthal in 1896. Orville also underwent a renewal of enthusiasm, and the two decided to evolve and build a heavier-than-air flying machine. It was the nature of the brothers, however, not to rush into a subject about which they knew next to nothing, so Orville and Wilbur set about their task with a planned method.

The brothers started by reading all that they could obtain, but took nothing as certain unless they had been able to verify it in their own experiments or through observation of soaring birds. From the first, the Wrights realized that the problem of flight was not how to get into the air, as this had been established by aviators such as Lilienthal and Chanute, and also by the engineers who were now producing more effective petrol engines. From the beginning, therefore, the brothers saw that the real problem lay in controlling the aeroplane once it had risen into the air. Control in pitch around the lateral axis was simple as it demanded only a 'horizontal rudder': now known as the elevator, this could be mounted in front of or behind the wings. A vertical rudder, too, could cope with any yawing motion round the vertical axis. But the problem of control in roll around the longitudinal axis was more difficult. Lilienthal had been experimenting with controlled wing warping, in which the wings could be twisted differentially so that the wing with its trailing edge forced down produced more lift than the other wing, with its trailing edge lifted up. The resulting differences in lift would roll the aeroplane toward the side with the lifted trailing edge, so giving a measure of control. But Lilienthal had not seen that this mechanism produced further problems: the wing with the better lift would also have more drag, and so would slew the aeroplane round in yaw once the warping was applied.

From their observation of the flight of buzzards, the Wright brothers made the same discovery of the effects of differential warping of the wingtips, and in 1899 they decided to apply the same principle to their aeroplane. After establishing how their machine could be controlled in all three planes, the brothers then decided to make a practical

beginning by the construction of a model kite-glider to test the wing warping. This first kite-glider was of 5-ft (1.52-m) span, and was ready for testing in August 1899. In it structural features the kite-glider was related to Chanute's biplane glider, and had a fixed tailplane for longitudinal stability. Control was effected by four lines, and the kite proved very successful, the wing warping in particular producing a very impressive performance. The wings had also been designed to move backwards or forwards in relation to each other to alter the centre of pressure, but this feature was not very useful and the brothers abandoned it in later models.

The Wrights' next step was clearly to build a small man-carrying glider, and this was ready by the autumn of 1900. It was similar to the 1899 kite-glider, but had a 17-ft (5.18-m) span and the elevator was located forward of the wings as the Wrights thought that this would provide a control surface that would act more rapidly and therefore more effectively. The glider lacked any fixed horizontal surfaces allied to the elevator, and had no rudder.

The Wrights selected Kitty Hawk for the tests of their new machine as there were strong, steady winds there for most of the year, and because the sand of this coastal area would help mitigate the damaging effect of any heavy landings.

Tests soon revealed that the wing area of the glider was insufficient to support the weight of a man unless the wind was quite strong. The glider was then flown mostly as a kite, when its success showed that the brothers were on the right lines. This No.1 Glider was also tested with dihedral (an angle between the wing and an imaginary horizontal so that the wing tips are higher than the wing roots). This was meant as an aid to stability, but was found to make control so difficult in the strong breezes of Kitty Hawk that the Wrights abandoned the idea almost entirely. Indeed, they went to the opposite extreme of making their machines inherently unstable by giving the wings anhedral, so that the wing tips were lower than the wing roots.

Proceeding carefully, the brothers built their No.2 Glider for further tests in 1901. Though it was similar to the No.1 Glider in basic concept, the No.2 Glider had its wing increased in span to 22 ft (6.71 m) so that its larger wing area would generate sufficient lift to carry a man aloft. Anhedral was again used, and a new warping mechanism was introduced: this latter comprised a cradle for the pilot's hips, so that when he swung his torso to the right or left as he lay on the lower wing, the wires attached to the cradle operated the warping mechanism. The new glider, flown over the Kill Devil Hills south of Kitty Hawk, proved only moderately successful, and the Wrights realized that there was still something wrong with their design.

The brothers decided that their lack of greater success indicated two major problems. Up to this point they had ignored their own strictures on the need for their own proofs and thus tended to take the figures in Lilienthal's book as gospel, but the tests of the No.2 Glider now revealed that Lilienthal had favoured too pronounced a camber for the wing section. The Wrights therefore constructed a small wind tunnel, presumably the first ever built, and during the winter of 1901-1902 undertook trials to correct Lilienthal's figures in the light of their own experience with gliders. The other problem was that of the slewing moment imparted to the glider when the wing warping

Left: Seen in the workshop after completion but before its flight trials in 1896, the Langley No.5 was the elderly designer's first successful model aeroplane, and was of the tandem-wing configuration with a small steam engine.

mechanism was used. The Wrights' first solution to this difficulty was the provision of a fixed double fin mounted on booms behind the wings to serve, the brothers hoped, as a type of stabilizing flight and so correct and correct any tendency for the aeroplane to turn toward the side of the positively warped wing.

Tests with the No.3 Glider in September 1902 showed that far from solving the problem, this in fact worsened matters as once the slewing motion started the tendency of the aeroplane to side-slip as a result of the banking caused the fins to act as a lever aiding the slewing moment. Orville and Wilbur rapidly appreciated the nature of the problem, and replaced the original fixed double fins with a single moving rudder. The control wires for this were fixed to the warp cradle so that when, for instance, right bank was applied the rudder moved automatically to the right to counteract any tendency for the machine to slew to the left. With this No.3 Glider (Modified), which was flown during October 1902, the Wright brothers had finally developed their ideas into a fully practical gliding aeroplane that could be controlled in all three planes, and this was the basis of their future success.

The Wrights devoted the winter of 1902-1903 to the building of their first powered aeroplane. The initial problem to be faced was the nature and disposition of the powerplant. The decision went in favour of two pusher propellers driven from a single engine by means of chain drives, one of them crossed so that the propellers rotated in opposite directions so that the torque of each propeller cancelled that of the other. The pilot would lie slightly to the left of the centreline with the engine marginally to the right so that the two weights would balance each other. The brothers soon realized that, as with virtually every component needed for their aircraft, they would have to make their own engine and propellers, there being no suitable units available on the commercial market. The propellers were efficient to a degree unmatched by other propellers for another six years, and the engine was an ingenious, light, but robust four-cylinder unit, which delivered 12 hp for a weight of 179 lb (81.4 kg).

The aeroplane specially built for the attempt at powered flight was similar to its predecessors in layout but somewhat larger, with a span of 40 ft 4 in (12.3 m), 8 ft 3 in (2.5 m) larger than that of the No.3 Glider. To take advantage of the propellers' greater efficiency at lower speeds these were geared down from the engine, and to avoid unnecessary complication and weight landing gear of the slid rather than wheeled type was used. This landing gear posed problems of its own, however, as a special take-off technique had to be evolved. This involved the use of a

60-ft (18.3-m) grooved wooden rail along which moved a light trolley on wheels. The aeroplane rested on the trolley and was restrained by a tethering rope while the engine was run up to full power. Once the engine had reached full power, the rope was released and the trolley-mounted aeroplane accelerated along the rail until it reached flying speed and lifted into the air. It is worth noting that detractors of the Wrights' achievement have often claimed that the brothers did not succeed in making a powered, sustained flight in 1903 because they used an accelerating device to catapult the aeroplane into the air. This was not so: it was not until 1904 that the Wrights introduced their accelerator device, and then it served only as a refinement and not as an essential component of launching.

The Wrights took their Flyer I to Kill Devil Hills in December 1903. After rehearsing their techniques on a glider, on 17 December they made the first powered, sustained and controlled flights as they took off from level ground, climbed and then descended to ground no lower than that from which they had taken off. Although the day's events were reported in the press, this momentous occasion passed almost unremarked by the public. Orville and Wilbur Wright returned to Dayton to plan their next moves. Clearly the most important matter was to improve their aeroplane and its engine, for the combination had only just been able to fly. During the winter of 1903-1904, therefore, the brothers built a new aeroplane almost identical with the Flyer I, but with reduced camber. A new engine was also built, and this could deliver an extra 4 hp.

Although not the furtive, secretive men they are sometimes labelled, the Wright brothers realized the commercial implications of their invention, and decided that their financial interests would be harmed by too much publicity before their patents had been fully secured. They therefore decided to operate their aircraft well away from large crowds. With the help of a friend named Torrence Huffman they established their flying base at the Huffman Prairie, some 10 miles (6 km) from Dayton. Here, in the second half of 1904, the Flyer II took to the air about 75 times, the best flight covering just under 3 miles (4.8 km) in 5 minutes 4 seconds. Just as important, on 20 September Wilbur Wright succeeded in flying a circle, an achievement that had eluded the brothers up to that time because their aircraft had not climbed high enough for banking.

A refinement in the Wrights' technique had been introduced earlier in September, when they started using an accelerator device for the take-off trolley. This device consisted of a heavy weight winched to the top of a derrick. Here it was attached to the tail of a rope that was led via pulleys to the front of the launching rail and then back to the trolley. The weight was released to drop to the ground so that the rope drew the trolley swiftly forwards along the rail. This device enabled the Wrights to fly on days when there was little wind, since the Flyer would have been unable to reach flying speed relative to the wind along the rail.

The brothers were seen in the air by some hundreds of people, and on two occasions reporters came to the field to investigate the reports of flight. By a quirk of nature, the engine failed to start on both of these visits, and the pressmen went away sceptical.

The next year, 1905, witnessed the emergence of the definitive, fully airworthy Wright aeroplane, the Flyer III. Again the same basic design was retained, this time with a span of 40 ft 6 in (12.35 m), but to improve the effectiveness of the elevators and the rudders they were moved farther from the wings. Some 40 flights were made between June and October, and in this period the brothers perfected their flying technique. The one problem still plaguing them was a tendency for the aeroplane to stall in turns. This was seen

Left: The Wright Flyer I is seen after its first but unsuccessful attempt at a powered flight on 14 December 1903. At the controls is Wilbur Wright, who overcorrected with the nose-mounted elevator immediately after take-off and ploughed into the sand of the Kill Devil Hills.

to be the result of the wing at the inside of the turn slowing down and losing lift. The answer was simple: merely push the nose down slightly in turns and thus keep speed up. At the same time the permanent link between the warp cradle and the rudder controls was abandoned, enabling the pilot to use the two controls separately should he so desire, or to co-ordinate them in different ratios and thus produce a greater variety of banked turns. With the engine running reliably and powerfully, the Flyer III can certainly be called the first truly practical aeroplane in history.

The considerable performance improvement of the Flyer III over the Flyer II can be gauged easily from the impressive number of flights of more than 15 minutes duration made during the summer: there were six such flights and these included two of more than 30 minutes. The year's best flight was made on 5 October, when the Flyer III was airborne for 38 minutes 3 seconds, in which time it covered more than 24 miles (38.6 km). The machine was therefore undeniably capable of sustained flight. Added to this, the fact that no major damage was done in 40 take-offs and landings bears eloquent witness to the Flyer III's sturdiness. Perhaps the most important factor, however, was that the two pilots were able to manoeuvre the aeroplane in a fully practical manner.

The confidence of the Wright brothers that they had capped six years of development work with a viable aeroplane is reflected in the fact that they offered the aeroplane to both the American and British governments. Patents for the most important elements of the Flyer were pending, and the brothers now felt that they could begin to profit from their invention. In January 1905 the brothers had offered their machine to the US Department of War, while they were still building the Flyer III: the Department turned the offer down without even considering it. The brothers then approached the British War Office. So slowly

did the administrative mills of that body grind that in October, after the performance of the Flyer III had been fully tested, the American brothers abandoned the attempt for another approach to the US Department of War. Although the Wrights made it clear that they were offering a machine with guaranteed aerial performance, the Department of War insisted on treating the offer as a request for assistance, and again turned down the offer.

The lead the United States had attained in the field of aviation can be judged by the fact that the first European aeroplane to fly, although in reality this effort was no more than a 'hop', did not take to the air for nearly another twelve months. This lead was now to be lost as a result of the shortsightedness of the government. So discouraged were the Wrights, and so fearful that their ideas might be stolen before their patents came through in 1906, that they ceased flying and development work on their aircraft for the next 30 months. The Flyer III was locked away in a shed and no one was allowed to examine it. The Wrights even refused to allow drawings of it to be made, although a fairly accurate sketch appeared in the Paris paper L'Auto on Christmas Eve 1905 after being stolen in Dayton. Nevertheless, the aeroplane remained on sale: the brothers guaranteed the performance, but would allow no one to see the machine or plans until they had bought them. So until 1908 the brothers made no future progress, although in the interval they built a few improved engines and a small number of Flyer IIIs, in the definitive form known as the Model A, against the day that either the government or commercial interests decided to consider the aeroplane seriously.

In six years these two American brothers had undertaken the research, designed and built the airframes, engines and propellers of a series of gliders and powered aircraft, culminating in the first practical aeroplane, and taught themselves to fly their machines with great proficiency. And then they stopped.

Below: The engine designed and built by the Wright brothers for their Flyer I was a masterpiece of lightweight simplicity offering what was, for the time, a high power/weight ratio. The engine was a four-cylinder inline unit with a cast aluminium body and steel cylinders, and weighed 152 lb (68.9 kg) increasing to 174 lb (78.9 kg) with its radiator and associated piping but no coolant water. The brothers had hoped for a power of 8 hp, but in fact achieved 13 hp in their initial test runs and 16 hp (reducing to 12 hp after about one minute) at Kitty Hawk.

Primitive Flying Machines

What was the rest of the aeronautical world doing whilst the Wrights were making such excellent, logical progress? The brothers' only rival in the United States was S. P. Langley, the eminent secretary of the Smithsonian Institution in Washington. Langley had developed an interest in flight as early as 1886, and soon turned his hand to the production of a series of models to test his theories. Unlike the Wright brothers, Langley was convinced that practical aircraft should have a considerable degree of inherent stability, and therefore neglected the problems of flight control. In 1896 Langley built his fifth and sixth models, both of them tandem-winged machines of considerable size. A large number of very successful flights were made with the two models, the best covering some 4,200 ft (1280 m). For this type of development work, in which the model could not be controlled after its launch in the days before the advent of radio control, inherent stability was of great significance. But Langley envisaged the same measure of stability in full-size aircraft, his feeling being that the aeroplane should be able to fly itself, leaving the pilot merely to point it in the direction desired, rather than to control it fully.

Langley's interest in flight was satisfied with the success of his models, and he intended to hand over further development to a younger man. But in 1898 the United States government asked him to build a full-size man-carrying 'Aerodrome' as Langley described his flying machines. Proceeding cautiously, Langley built a quarter-sized model in 1901, powered by a miniature petrol engine. Successful flight trials were carried out, and he then proceeded to a full-sized aeroplane, which was completed by 1903. It was a large machine, with a span of 48 ft (14.63 m), powered by the first of the classic aero engines in the form of a remarkably light radial inspired by S. M. Balzer and actually designed and built, to the permanent detriment of his eyesight, by Langley's able assistant C. M. Manly. Despite its flimsiness, the Aerodrome was structurally heavy and the machine was therefore seriously underpowered, despite the sterling performance of the Balier-Manly engine.

Langley decided that flight trials should be carried out over water, which he fondly thought would give Manly, who was to pilot the machine, a softer landing in the event of disaster. The launching platform selected was a houseboat on the River Potomac just outside Washington. To accelerate the Aerodrome to flying speed, Langley designed a catapult that could be installed on the short roof of the houseboat. On 7 October Manly attempted his first flight, but the Aerodrome fouled the launching device and crashed into the river. This accident was repeated in the second trial on 8 December, and after this failure the US government refused to sanction any further work on the Aerodrome, which was put into storage.

Left: One of the decisive moments in aviation was the first flight across the English Channel. This feat was achieved on 25 July 1909 by Louis Blériot in the Type XI monoplane of his own design.

The prescience of the government in sponsoring Langley's project makes an interesting comparison with the rebuffs received by the Wrights two years later, when they offered their Flyer III, a proven machine, to the Department of War. Langley, however, was a well-known scientist and secretary of a well-known institution. It is also interesting to compare the method employed by the two teams. The Wrights, in fact, advanced by a more scientific method than Langley: they thought about, tested and proved each aspect of flight before moving on to the next step.

In Europe, slow progress was made towards the goal of powered flight, which is surprising since the decade up to the turn of the century had been particularly fruitful, and air-mindedness was widespread. The year 1900 found only one European, Captain Ferdinand Ferber, actively pursuing the search for flight. In January 1902 Ferber, a French officer, forsook the Lilienthal type of glider with which he had been experimenting when he received information from Chanute about the Wrights' gliders. He immediately began construction of a glider patterned on the Wright type, but with only limited information on which to work his effort was a failure. One of the principal reasons for this failure was the fact that the wing surfaces were not rigid and therefore produced next to no lift. After Chanute's lecture to the Aéro-Club de France in April 1903, in which photographs and drawings of the Wrights' No.3 Glider were displayed, Ferber again set to work with renewed enthusiasm. Although he was, as usual, unsuccessful, he did initiate a design feature of considerable importance. Not satisfied with the Wrights' inherent instability, Ferber designed his 1904 glider with dihedralled wings and, more significantly, a fixed horizontal tailplane to improve longitudinal stability.

This was a major step in the right direction. But Ferber,

in common with most other Europeans, ignored the question of control in roll and instead relied in dihedralled wings for lateral stability. This was to be a stumbling block of major proportions until 1908, when Wilbur Wright demonstrated his Model A in France, and the true nature of the Wrights' skill in full lateral control was revealed. Although Chanute had given the Europeans the necessary clues for their own development of lateral control by simultaneous use of wing warping and rudder, men such as Ferber were virtually obsessed by the concept of inherent stability and still refused to see the point so clearly made by the Wrights.

The man who next took the lead in European progress was the French lawyer Ernest Archdeacon (pronounced 'arsh-deck'). Archdeacon had for some time played an important part in the Aéro-Club de France, and the Chanute lecture encouraged him to press on, both by forming an aviation committee within the club, where the main interest had always been ballooning and experimentation with dirigible airships, and by ordering a copy of the Wright glider. This copy was ready in 1904, and it was flown by Ferber and Gabriel Voisin.

Another Frenchman inspired by the Wrights was Robert Esnault-Pelterie, who decided that he could improve upon the Wrights' glider since he thought that wing warping was structurally dangerous. In common with other French experimenters, Esnault-Pelterie did not fully understand the nature of lateral control as developed by the Wrights, but he nonetheless has the distinction of being the first man to have used ailerons (rigid, movable control surfaces, hinged to operate from the rear of a rigid wing) in place of the warping used by the Americans. As with all the other French copies of the Wright glider, Esnault-Pelterie's

Below: The Langley Aerodrome is seen on its houseboat-mounted launcher catapult on the Potomac river in October 1903. The aeroplane fouled the end of the catapult and crashed into the river

was a relative failure. Yet, oddly enough, French experimenters were content to move on to powered flight without attempting even to understand, let alone correct, the shortcomings of their gliders.

In 1905 the French finally abandoned the Wright type of glider, thereby setting themselves back in the short term. The reason for this decision was a lecture given at the beginning of the year by Esnault-Pelterie, in which he stated that he had built an exact replica of the Wrights' No.3 Glider and that it would not fly in the fashion claimed by the brothers. He had then improved the design by installing ailerons, and it still would not perform adequately. The only conclusion possible, according to Esnault-Pelterie, was that the Wrights were at the least exaggerating their successes.

Some progress was made in 1905, however. Early in the year Archdeacon had another Wright-type glider built. But following the lead of Ferber, fixed vertical and horizontal tail surfaces were added. The glider was not piloted, but in two car-towed tests it seemed to behave well until there was a structural failure in the tail unit. With considerable help from Voisin, Archdeacon now built a new glider that was to introduce the Hargrave box-kite to European aviation. This was basically a Wright-type glider, fitted with a forward elevator and a two-cell box-kite mounted on booms behind the wings to provide longitudinal and directional stability. The main biplane wings were divided into three cells by 'side curtains' round each set of interplane struts. With Voisin at the controls the whole machine was mounted on floats and towed into the air over the River Seine by a motorboat. On the second flight a distance of almost 1,000 ft (300 m) was covered. Shortly afterwards, in collaboration with Louis Blériot who now entering the field of aviation and destined for a great future, Voisin produced a similar glider of smaller dimensions and improved aerodynamic qualities. On its first test, however, Voisin lost control of the glider which crashed into the River Seine and very nearly caused its pilot to drown.

In England an expatriate American, Samuel F. Cody, had also developed the Hargrave box-kite by giving its upper wings a true aerofoil, and the type had been adopted by the British army for observation purposes. Like its inventor, the method was eccentric, but it proved safe. A small kite, connected to a larger one by cable, was launched: steadily larger kites were launched under the top one until a chain of kites was airborne, capable of lifting a man under the lowest one. With the observer in a basket under the bottom kite, the whole chain was then allowed to rise to observation height. Cody also experimented with a kite-glider, but this was unsuccessful, its only notable feature being its use of ailerons.

In 1905 Ferber made his mark on history with the first 'free flight' by a powered aeroplane in Europe, and the first tractor biplane in the world. The machine in question was the Ferber VII-B, basically similar to his earlier adaptation of the Wright glider with a horizontal tail, and a 12-hp engine added between the wing leading edge and the forward elevator. Released from an overhead wire once flying speed had been reached, the Ferber VII-B could achieve only what might be described as a powered glide when it was tested on 25 May. The machine had no adequate lateral control, and Ferber still favoured a 'floating' horizontal tail, unsupported by wire bracing so that it might move up or down ill flight. Although his machine was unsuccessful, Ferber had made an extremely significant contribution to aviation with his invention of the tractor biplane layout. Once the Wright forward elevator had been abandoned in 1909, the tractor biplane was to become the basic aeroplane type for the next 20 years.

At the end of the year reports from Chanute and the Wrights themselves informed the French of the brothers' progress during the year. Yet such was the scepticism resulting from Esnault-Pelterie's lecture almost a full year before, and the widespread dissemination of the lecture as an article in the magazine L'Aérophile during June, that most people were prepared to doubt the Wrights' claims.

The brothers' claims did appear convincing, however, and most French aviation pundits were prepared to concede that there might be something in them. If this were the case, the French had been beaten in a field in which they considered themselves wholly pre-eminent; if it were not the case, it was nevertheless clear that the Wrights were further advanced than the French.

The French thought that their major task for 1906 would have to be the overtaking of the Wrights so that France would secure the honour of being the country to have made the first powered heavier-than-air flight. With the publication, in the January 1906 edition of L'Aérophile, of the major portions of the Wrights' wing warping and rudder control patent, complete with drawings, the French were for the first time in possession of the basic element of the Wrights' success, but so bound up in their own theories were the various French pioneers that the revelation was greeted with almost total indifference. Indeed, in the August number of L'Aérophile one of the more dynamic and prescient of the French pioneers, Ernest Archdeacon, issued an admonishment to his fellows on the need for a radical shake-up of the French aeronautical world. He pointed out that a suitably powerful engine, with a good power-to-weight ratio, was now available in the form of the Levavasseur Antoinette, and all that was needed to enable the French to redress the slight lead held by the Wrights was a solution to the problem of balance and control. Archdeacon gloomily stated, however, that this problem

Below: While the designers of heavier-than-aircraft craft were seeking to make their designs break the apparently intractable bonds holding them to the earth, the protagonists of light-than-air flight were enjoying a greater though shorter-lived measure of practical success. This is the Santos-Dumont No.6 dirigible airship, which achieved huge acclaim on 19 October 1901 when the intrepid designer and aeronaut won the Prix Henri Deutsch de la Meurthe for a flight from and two St Cloud via the Eiffel tower in Paris.

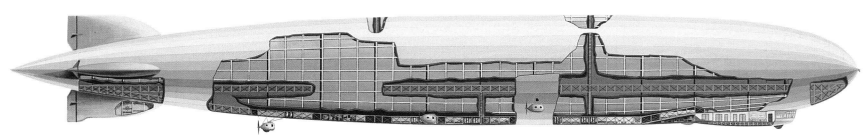

More practical airships were the creation of a German, namely Ferdinand Graf von Zeppelin. The Zeppelin airships were of the rigid type and proved reliable in service, but ultimately fell out of favour as their lifting agent was hydrogen, which is highly explosive when mixed with oxygen such as that present in the air.

was still far from solution. He had entirely overlooked the significance of the feature on the Wrights' patent in the January L'Aérophile.

As a spur to French efforts, Archdeacon again reminded his readers of the offer he had made in 1904 of a Prix Deutsch-Archdeacon for the first man to fly a circular course of 1 km (0.6 mile). Perhaps to discourage his readers from setting their sights on smaller targets, Archdeacon made no mention of the prizes that he had offered at much the same time for flights of only 25 and 100 m (27.5 and 110 yards). Nevertheless, the year 1906 was to see the winning of these last two prizes, though the third prize was to remain unclaimed until the beginning of 1908.

The engine Archdeacon had discussed in his article was designed by one of the unsung heroes of aviation, Leon Levavasseur. This man, who named his famous Antoinette engine after the daughter of Jules Gastambide, the head of his firm, originally created it in 1903 for racing motorboats. He can be said, perhaps, to have contributed more than anyone else to the final success of European aviation, and his two basic engines, of 25 hp and 50 hp, powered most of the important European types up to 1909. By the standards of the day they were reliable, and their racing heritage had given them a good power-to-weight ratio of 4.2 lb (1.9 kg)/hp. Only with the advent of the Gnome rotary, designed by Laurent Seguin in 1907 and introduced from late 1908 onwards, would the Antoinette 50-hp engine be superseded as the prime mover of European aircraft.

Notwithstanding the determined if misguided French efforts discussed above, the first man in Europe who can really be said to have flown was neither a European nor a pioneer previously interested in heavier-than-air flight. Alberto Santos-Dumont was a diminutive Brazilian whose family had become affluent through the coffee trade. He was therefore able to settle in France and pursue his love of airships before the turn of the century. Persevering despite innumerable setbacks and accidents, Santos-Dumont at last evolved a workable type of miniature dirigible. The dapper little Brazilian was often to be seen over the streets of Paris in his airships at the beginning of the century, and had

become a firm favourite of Parisians and hence of the newspapers. Indeed, to Santos-Dumont must go the lion's share of the credit for keeping Europe air-minded after the loss of Lilienthal.

Having developed an airship suitable for his own needs and interests, in 1905 Santos-Dumont became interested in heavier-than-air flying machines. His first machine, which was to be the first European aeroplane to fly, was a machine that was bizarre even by the standards of the times, and totally without further influence on the development of flight.

Perhaps inspired by Langley, Santos-Dumont described his machine as an aerodrome rather than as an avion, the word coined by Ader and now coming into general use in France. The Santos-Dumont 14-bis, as it came to be known by reason of the fact that it was tested under Santos-Dumont's No.14 airship, was designed and built near Paris in 1906. It was of canard configuration, that is with the normal positions of wings and tail assembly reversed. The control surfaces at the front of the fuselage took the form of a Hargrave box-cell mounted on a universal joint to move up and down as elevators and left and right as the rudder. The wings, spanning 37 ft 9 in (11.5 m), were attached to the rear fuselage at a considerable dihedral angle and the pilot stood in a balloon basket just in front of the wings. The landing gear consisted of a pair of narrow-track wheels under the rear fuselage and a skid under the forward control surfaces. Power was provided by a 25-hp Antoinette engine mounted at the rear of the fuselage and driving a pusher propeller.

First tests were undertaken in June 1906, the aeroplane being suspended from a wire on a pulley and towed by a donkey! It is hardly surprising that no worthwhile results were achieved. July witnessed the first air tests under the No.14 airship, and the first attempt at free flight was made on 13 September. After a hop of only 7 m (23 ft) the 14-bis came down heavily and suffered major damage. While the machine was being repaired, Santos-Dumont also changed the engine for a more powerful 50-hp Antoinette and then attempted his second flight on 23 October. This time he

One of the earliest and most successful exponents of the flying boat concept was Glenn Curtiss, a highly talented American who created an aircraft company that remained a major force in world aviation up to the end of World War II.

managed to achieve a hop of 60 m (198 ft), thereby winning the Archdeacon prize for the first flight of 25 m. Realizing that some form of lateral control was necessary, Santos-Dumont next modified the 14-bis to incorporate a pair of large ailerons, operated by a harness worn round the pilot's body, mounted between the wings in the outermost bracing bay of each pair of wings, each of which had three side-curtains.

With the aeroplane thus modified, all was ready for Santos-Dumont's greatest triumph, on 12 November 1906. After five short hops, the best of which covered 82 m (270 ft) in 7.2 seconds, Santos-Dumont finally achieved the first recognized flight in Europe by flying 220 m (722 ft) in 21.2 seconds at an altitude of some 6 m (20 ft). Although only about a third of what the Wrights had managed on their first day's flying in December 1903, this flight was enough to win Santos-Dumont wild acclaim in Paris, and warm congratulations poured in from all over the world.

There is no doubt that Santos-Dumont's achievement was a great one, for although the 14-bis was an oddity that left the ground only once again, here at last was conclusive proof that man could fly. It seemed that a new age had dawned. It is interesting to speculate what the course of aviation might have been had the Wrights' success been attended by the same acclaim in 1903.

Various sectors of the community now took an interest in aviation. Foremost among them was the champagne industry based in Reims, spearheaded by the firm of Ruinart. On 4 December 1906 this company offered a prize of 12,500 francs for the first man to fly across the English Channel. This was a very farsighted offer, and typical of the encouragement the champagne industry was to offer aviation over the next few years.

Now that Santos-Dumont had 'conquered the air', many expected to follow as though the magical influence of the Brazilian might somehow magically provide their indifferent machines with the ability to fly. In fact, during the following year only Henry Farman achieved anything like proficiency. Although of English birth, Farman had lived all his life in France and spoke virtually no English. This important pioneer took French nationality in 1937, and his first name might then have been expected to become Henri. It seems, however, that throughout his life Farman spelled his first name Henry or Henri with complete indifference.

Farman was one of the several buyers of the pusher biplanes built by the Voisin brothers. The Voisins habitually designated their machines only by the name of the customer, but as the brothers themselves played such an important part in the designs, their types should also include their own name in any realistic nomenclature. The basic Voisin aircraft was essentially a Chanute type of biplane wing with a Wright forward elevator and a Hargrave box-kite tail. This basic design, less the Wright element, was tested and refined as a hang-glider in May 1907. Little is known of the very first powered aeroplane built by the Voisins. This resulted from a commission from Henry Kapferer, basically a lighter-than-air enthusiast. Power was provided by a 25-hp Buchet engine, with which the aeroplane could not possibly have flown. In terms of basic layout the Voisin-Delagrange I seems to have been similar to what is known of the Voisin-Kapferer. The aeroplane had a shoe-shaped nacelle, or body, mounted on the lower wing, with the 50-hp Antoinette driving a pusher propeller directly at its rear. The pilot and controls were in the centre, and the biplane forward elevator was located at the front. The biplane wings had no side-curtains, and a two-cell tailplane, mounted on four booms running back from the wings, carried two rudders hinged to the rear of its outer side-curtains.

In this form the Voisin-Delagrange I took off six times in March and April 1906, but the best hop was only 60 m (198 ft). The machine was then modified at Archdeacon's suggestion, and also fitted with floats. Thus altered, the type failed to take off at all when tested on the Lac d'Enghien in spring, and was again taken in hand for modifications. The float alighting gear was replaced by wheeled landing gear, and the two rudders replaced by a single central rudder. With Delagrange replacing Charles Voisin as the pilot, the aeroplane took off twice early in November, the second of these flights proving to be the best made by a European to date, covering 500 m (1,640 ft). Unhappily, Delagrange crashed on landing and the aeroplane was destroyed.

The Voisins' third powered aeroplane set the pattern which the two brothers were to copy with increasing success up to 1910. The machine in question was built to the order of Henry Farman, and is now known as the Voisin-Farman I. Ordered in the middle of 1907, it was delivered in October. In its first form it closely resembled the Voisin-Delagrange I, with the exception of a slightly greater wing span of 10.2 m (33 ft 6 in) and a tailplane with a central rudder but with no central curtain. The machine was considerably heavier than its Delagrange counterpart, and this was probably the result of structural strengthening.

Although generally happy with the first tests, Farman instructed the Voisins to re-rig the aircraft with dihedral to increase its lateral stability, and to replace the biplane elevators with a monoplane unit. With these alterations the

Curtiss was a dedicated but practical innovator, and the use of items such as a safety wire allowed him to test aircraft without undue risk.

The experimental Hydros of 1911 paved the way for the development of the successful Curtiss series of flying boats, floatplanes and amphibians.

Voisin-Farman I flew 771 m (2,540 ft) in 52.6 seconds on 26 October. Though this was a European record, it was just one month short of four years after the Wrights' first flights, and did not even equal the time of their fourth flight. Farman, not yet satisfied with his machine, ordered that the original large tailplane be replaced by a unit of reduced span.

As the Voisin-Farman I (Modified), the aeroplane now flew well, and at last the Europeans could be said to have something approaching a practical aeroplane. The basic soundness of the Voisins' combination of Wright, Chanute and Hargrave elements, as modified by Farman, was soon proved by Farman's flight of 1030 m (3,400 ft) in a circle, in a time of 1 minute 14 seconds. This won an Archdeacon prize for a flight of more than 150 m, neither Santos-Dumont's nor Delagrange's flights having been scrutinized by the relevant officials.

Although it might seem that the greater part of the glory for these successes should go to the Voisins, in reality the man most responsible was Farman. He was the man who had seen the need for the modifications and had actually piloted the aeroplane. For the next few years Farman was to be in the vanguard of biplane development, but even he had not as yet appreciated fully the need for lateral control rather than lateral stability. The circular flight he had made on 9 November clearly demonstrated this need. To turn his aeroplane Farman had to skid it round, and at the slow speeds of only about 55 km/h (34 mph), the wing on the inside of the turn must have been very close to stalling. His low altitude would have given Farman no chance of recovering had this happened, even if he had known what to do. Because of his slow speed and extremely low altitude, however, Farman might well have been able to simply walk away from a crash as had some others.

After several years of experimentation with various types, Blèriot finally came in 1907 to adopt the tractor monoplane, the type that was to make him famous. As had been his practice with other layouts, Blèriot progressed cautiously and logically, and it was not until after he had discarded two designs that he arrived at the one now considered the definitive form, with an enclosed fuselage, tractor engine, forward-mounted wings, and empennage at the rear of the fuselage. The elevators were in fact elevons, for Blèriot had not realized that to make them efficient, ailerons must be placed as far as possible from the fuselage centreline. Power was provided by a sterling 50-hp Antoinette which enabled the Blèriot VII to take off several times at the close of 1907, two of the flights covering more than 500 m (1,640 ft). And although the Blèriot VII was not a successful type in itself, with it Blèriot had arrived at the starting point of the line of monoplanes he was to make world famous.

Other pioneers also turned their hands to tractor monoplanes in 1907, the most important of these being Esnault-Pelterie and Santos-Dumont. Toward the end of the year Esnault-Pelterie produced his interesting REP.1, powered by an excellent 30-hp air-cooled engine designed by himself. The REP.1 had no means of directional control, or even of ensuring directional stability, and the elevator was mounted at the rear of the very stumpy fuselage, where it could exert little force. Esnault-Pelterie even used a rudimentary form of Wright wing warping for lateral control, the very system he had condemned so roundly not two years before. The REP. 1 made a few hops, the most satisfactory covering some 600 m (1,970 ft) on 16 November. Without either fixed or movable vertical tail surfaces, however, the REP. I was not really a viable proposition.

Santos-Dumont, intent on exploiting his success of the previous year and improving his lead in heavier-than-air flight, also turned to the tractor monoplane, but in a form as quaint as his I4-bis had been bizarre. Being a very small man, Santos-Dumont elected to build a tiny monoplane capable of carrying only someone of his negligible weight. The result was a charming little aeroplane, the Santos-Dumont 19, which, with its successors, was given the popular name Demoiselle. On the No.19 the pilot sat under a wing spanning only 5 m (16 ft 5 in) amid the wheels of a tricycle landing gear. An angular forward elevator was intended to act in concert with the one-piece tail unit which was mounted at the end of a single bamboo pole stretching back from the wing to undertake the purposes of both elevator and rudder. Lateral control was exercised simply by the movement of the pilot's body. Power was provided by a two-cylinder Dutheil-Chalmers engine delivering 20 hp. The No.19's best hop was only 200 m (660 ft), but it set the model for the Brazilian aviator's later line of equally diminutive, but rather more successful machines.

With the de Pischoff I, built in 1907, the tractor biplane emulated the tractor monoplane and reached its definitive, if rudimentary, form. There were no control surfaces forward of the mainplanes, but there were both fixed and movable directional and longitudinal tail surfaces. In common with most other European machines of its era there was no understanding of the need for lateral control, and Alfred de Pischoff's biplane featured neither ailerons nor wing warping. Although the aeroplane failed to fly, it is still of considerable importance for, apart from introducing the tractor biplane layout, the de Pischoff I incorporated two important innovations. The more important of these was the propeller, designed and made by Lucien ChauviÉre, who also built the aeroplane: this propeller was a built-up wooden structure of considerable efficiency, and presaged the dominance of this propeller type for years to come. It was still not as advanced as the Wrights' propeller, but this deficiency would be rectified in the next two years. The de Pischoff I also introduced the 25-hp 'arrowhead' Anzani engine, in which the V of the outer two cylinders was bisected by an upright third cylinder. Blèriot's monoplanes were to take on a new lease of life with this efficient powerplant.

In England, Horatio Phillips continued a rather eccentric form of research based on a sophisticated form of lift, with little or no thought for control even in its most rudimentary form. The Phillips II, derived and amplified from the odd Phillips I of 1904, was one of the most extraordinary machines ever to leave the ground. Instead of the No.I's single 'Venetian blind' structure of very high aspect ratio wing slats, the No.II had four such structures mounted at equal distances one behind the other. Each frame of slats contained as many as 50 narrow winglets! The pilot sat perched in the middle of this structure, where his field of vision was adequate straight forward and sideways, but almost impossible in any other direction. The relatively advanced propeller was driven by a 20-hp engine, and surprisingly enough the machine seems to have made one lengthy hop into the air during the early part of 1907, but with no means of control it had no effect at all on the progress of practical flight.

Two Austrians entered the field of aviation in 1907, with important consequences for the future. Igo Etrich and Franz Wels were fascinated by bird flight, and designed an aeroplane based on a bird's wing planform. It was intended that the monoplane should be flown with an Antoinette engine, but the type was first tested with some success as a glider. Etrich, the more important of the partners, further developed this planform, and it was to become celebrated in the series of bird-like monoplanes developed in the years just before the outbreak of World War I which were extensively copied all over Europe, and were emulated especially in Germany.

At the end of 1907 then, with the lone exception of Henry Farman, European designers and aviators were still set on their own individual ways, with little objective evaluation of the problems to be faced. Farman, however, was at last beginning to point the correct way forward. As yet only in a sketchy fashion, he had at least realized that although some inherent stability was essential, so too was the need to control the aeroplane in flight, rather than merely drive it once it had been made to rise into the air. Here, for the first time since 1900, a European was beginning to grasp this fundamental aspect of flight.

It was not until 1908 that the public was first to witness aviators who could not only make small hops, but could also launch themselves into the air and stay there for · considerable periods, controlling their aircraft fully, making them climb, dive, circle, bank and otherwise perform as an expert rider might make a horse conform to his will. The general impact of this was very great; but it was greater still on the aviators and would-be aviators of Europe and America. For the first time they bad incontrovertible proof that full flight was possible, and that the key to flight was

not lift combined with inherent stability, but controllability combined with lift.

As in the previous year, it was the biplanes, mostly of the pusher variety, that led the way, although monoplanes now began to show their true worth, particularly the Blèriot and Antoinette types. And as usual there was a crop of unrealistic and hopeful machines.

Of the biplane enthusiasts, it was Delagrange and Farman who were best able to capitalize on their moderate previous successes. On 13 January 1908, Farman completed a round flight of more than 1 km (0.6 mile). Flying his Voisin-Farman I (Modified), he repeated the flight he had made at the end of 1907, witnessed this time by the requisite officials, and so collected the Grand Prix d'Aviation Deutsch-Archdeacon of 50,000 francs. The medallions due to the winning aeroplane's designers went to the Voisin brothers, Gabriel and Charles, although in light of the fact that the original Voisin-Farman had barely been able to get off the ground until modified by Henry Farman himself, this seems a somewhat dubious distinction. It is interesting to note that Farman's round trip of 1 km was in fact nearer 1.5 km (0.9 mile) for the simple reason that without lateral control he could not merely bank round the marker at the far end of his course, but rather had to skid round it in a wide curve.

Farman made several comparable flights in the next two days before taking apart his machine for the reconstruction and modification he now decided was necessary. The modified aeroplane, now designated the Voisin-Farman I-bis, was ready for flight in March. Little had been done in the way of modifying the basic airframe, but a new engine, a 50-hp Renault, had been installed and the aeroplane was completely recovered with rubberized linen to replace the silk of the Voisin-Farman I (Modified).

The Renault engine was used only once: Farman found it unsatisfactory and reverted to the original Antoinette. With the old engine once again installed the Voisin-Farman I-bis began to show its paces, unspectacular as they were soon to appear in comparison with those of Wilbur Wright's machine. On 21 March Farman flew just over 2 km (1.2

The Bristol Boxkite was one of the first genuinely successful aircraft designed in the United Kingdom, and was one of the first aircraft to be built on a 'production line' basis anywhere in the world. Notable if obsolescent features were the forward elevator, the exposed pilot's seat on the leading edge of the lower wing, and the use of an engine located behind the pilot to drive a pusher propeller turning in the gap between the four booms supporting the tail unit.

miles) in 3 minutes 31 seconds. In May, while in Ghent in Belgium, Farman took Archdeacon for two flights which constituted the first passenger flights in Europe. Farman was then invited to the United States, but his trip proved almost totally abortive for a variety of reasons, and he wasted the months of July and August. Before his departure on this venture, however, Farman succeeded in making the longest flight to date in Europe when on 6 July he stayed in the air for 20 minutes 20 seconds.

Delagrange, meanwhile, was close on Farman's heels. With his old machine virtually written off in November 1907, Delagrange ordered another machine from the Voisins. This incorporated what could be salvaged from the Voisin-Delagrange I, and emerged as the Voisin-Delagrange II. Differences between this and the Voisin-Farman I (Modified) were marginal at first, but Delagrange began to worry about lateral stability after a crash on 3 May. Consequently the aeroplane was modified as the Voisin-Delagrange III, with curtains on the two innermost sets of interplane struts. Although it made the machine look slightly strange, the curtains seem to have had the desired effect, and Delagrange managed several useful flights in Italy. The best of these flights, on 23 June, took Delagrange 14.27 km (8.87 miles) in 18 minutes 30 seconds. Like Farman, Delagrange made two passenger flights, and it is noticeable that the two pilots were closely paralleling each other in their achievements. But although their performances in the air were similar, there is no doubt that Farman was the more significant pioneer of the two, for it was his modifications to the basic Voisin aeroplane that were copied by Delagrange, not vice versa. Delagrange's use of side curtains was no more than common European practice to secure lateral stability.

These two leading European exponents of the pusher

biplane were now making flights of reasonable duration, and would continue to improve upon their performances during the late summer and autumn of 1908. Other European adherents to the biplane were not faring as well, however. In France, Ferber had joined the Antoinette concern, and his last machine was designated the Ferber IX and also Antoinette Ill. This was an extremely ungainly tractor biplane, from above resembling nothing so much as a fish skeleton since the wing ribs were uncovered on top. A forward elevator was provided, and at this stage Ferber abandoned his idea of a floating tail in favour of a fixed one. Two completely useless rudders were hinged to the outermost rear interplane struts, but they were soon changed for a more conventional one on the empennage. The Ferber IX actually rose from the ground on eight occasions, and on its last flight the machine covered 500 m (1,640 ft) before crashing. Ferber then abandoned the type.

The founding in the United States of the Aerial Experiment Association (AEA) during September 1907 by Dr Graham and Mrs Bell, with the newcomer Glenn Curtiss as its prime mover, was an event of considerable importance. During 1908, the AEA built and tested three similar biplanes, the Red Wing, the White Wing and the June Bug.

The Red Wing, designed by Lieutenant T. E. Selfridge, was powered by the first-rate Curtiss engine. The Red Wing had a span of 43 ft (13.1m) and was fitted with skids instead of wheeled landing gear as it was tested from the frozen surface of Lake Keuka. Basically a Wright type machine with tail surfaces, the Red Wing had an unusual wing layout, the lower wing having pronounced, curved dihedral, and the upper wing similarly pronounced, curved anhedral, so that the two wingtips came close to each other. The intention was presumably to get the benefit of both

The Roe IV Triplane was the last of the primitive triplanes designed by Alliott Verdon Roe, and proved modestly successful even if underpowered. After this Roe moved forward to biplane aircraft.

With his No.19 design, which was not in itself a great success and achieved only three flights in 1907, Alberto Santos-Dumont introduced the Demoiselle (dragonfly) concept that paved the way for the modern lightplane.

dihedral and a form of side curtain. Only two flights were made, with F W. Baldwin as pilot, the first on 12 March being the better, covering 319 ft (97 m).

The second effort resulted in a crash and the Red Wing was abandoned in favour of the White Wing which Baldwin designed.

The White Wing was similar to its predecessor, but had a conventional landing gear and ailerons. Five flights were made in May, the best covering 1,017 ft (310 m). But like the Red Wing before it, the White Wing was given up after a crash landing, to be replaced in turn at the centre of the AEA's attention by the June Bug, designed by Curtiss. Like the two previous aircraft, this was powered by the Curtiss engine, and retained the distinctive curved wings. But this time four ailerons were fitted, and the tail surfaces were improved by being made into a biplane structure. Flown by Curtiss himself and by J. A. McCurdy who like Baldwin was a Canadian, the June Bug proved itself far superior to the two earlier aircraft. Some 30 flights were made, the most notable being one of 2 miles (3.2 km) on 29 August. With the June Bug Curtiss won the prize offered by the Scientific American for the first flight of over 1 km (0.6 mile), with an effort of 5,090 ft (1551 m) in 1 minute 42.5 seconds. Curtiss, who had recently fallen foul of the Wright brothers because of his infringement of their 1906 warping patent, was also able to bank the June Bug round in a circle. Nevertheless, the June Bug was still a primitive machine compared with those of Delagrange and Farman, let alone those of the Wrights.

After Blèriot's introduction of the classic monoplane layout in 1907, further progress was made in 1908 towards turning this type into a viable flying machine, although complete success was to evade the two major monoplane designers until 1909. These two designers were Blèriot and Levavasseur, the latter being both chief engineer and designer of the Antoinette firm.

Blèriot quickly moved towards the finalized form of monoplane with his No.VIII, which emerged from the builder's shop in June 1908. In its first form the Blèriot VIII spanned 11 m (36 ft 1 in), but this was soon cut down to 8.5 m (27 ft 10 in). Power was provided by a 50-hp Antoinette, and although initially the fuselage was covered, the designer soon altered this, and the Blèriot VIII took on the open-fuselage form so distinctive in Blèriot monoplanes. The tail controls were conventional, except that it was the outer, rather than the rear, portions of the tail-plane that moved to give longitudinal control. With Blèriot at last on the right lines, swift progress could be expected, and Blèriot turned in a flight of 700 m (2,997 ft) on 29 June, the last day on which the Blèriot VIII was flown in its original form. The modifications envisaged by the designer involved the ailerons. On the original model these had been triangular, but Blèriot now replaced them with far more efficient rectangular units mounted as the trailing portion of each outer wing panel. The ailerons could only move downwards, so only one could be used at any one time. It was clear that Blèriot had made the right decision when flight trials with what was now designated the Blèriot VIII-bis were resumed in July, and on the 6th of that month the VIII-bis stayed up in the air for 8 minutes 24 seconds. Still not satisfied, Blèriot continued to experiment with the controls. In September he modified the No.VIII-bis into the No.VIII-ter by replacing the rectangular flap-type ailerons with differential elevons formed of the outer ends of the wings, and at the same time added a fixed horizontal tail surface. Yet again, Blèriot's modifications proved efficient, the No.VIII-ter making a 4.5-km (2.78-mile) flight on 2 October. On the 31st of the same month Blèriot made a round trip of about 28 km (17.4 miles), with two landings, in 22 minutes. One stretch of this course, about 14 km (8.7 miles) in length, was covered in 11 minutes. Still greater advances were to be expected from Blèriot in 1909. Many different types of covering were used on aircraft in the days up to 1910, but Blèriot seems to have taken the prize for the strangest: all three models of the No.VIII monoplane had their wings covered with paper.

It was in 1908, too, that Levavasseur's monoplane first appeared. Although the first Antoinettes were rather ungainly machines, Levavasseur was then to develop his basic idea into a series of extremely elegant aircraft, far excelling those of Blèriot in purely aesthetic qualities. Levavasseur's active interest in flight had begun in 1903, when he built the first petrol-engined aeroplane to be freely tested in France. The machine, of unattractive bird form, was a failure, but this fact did not deter Levavasseur. He now re-entered the field with the Gastambide-Mengin I, ordered by his employer and another member of the firm in 1907, and delivered in February 1908.

The aeroplane, although unsuccessful, was interesting in one very important respect: the aerofoil section of the wings. Up to this date most early aerofoils had consisted of parallel-sided cambered surfaces. Levavasseur, however, followed the example of Phillips, and adopted a section with considerably less camber on the under-surface. This produced as much lift as the parallel-sided aerofoils, but far less drag. Unfortunately, Levavasseur failed to appreciate that a bluff leading edge would have improved matters even further, and used a sharp one, but this does not detract from his importance as a promoter of the best type of wing section, with a high lift-to-drag ratio.

The wings of the Gastambide-Mengin I were pleasantly tapered, but the fuselage was a massive affair perched on an ungainly four-wheeled landing gear arrangement. The engine, naturally enough a 50-hp Antoinette, was mounted in the nose and drove an inefficient paddle-bladed propeller. Intended basically as a test vehicle, the aeroplane had no control surfaces at all. Only four tests were made, all 'piloted' by an Antoinette mechanic called Boyer, the best covering some 150 m (492 ft). After a crash-landing the aeroplane was reconstructed, appearing as the Gastambide-Mengin II, or more properly the Antoinette II, in July. Large triangular ailerons were added to the rear of the outer wing panels, and an elevator and twin rudders were installed. Now piloted by another member of the Société Antoinette, Welferinger, the Antoinette II proved moderately successful and its best flight during large-scale trials in July and August lasted 1 minute 36 seconds. Welferinger also took Gastambide for a flight, and completed a circle in the air, both events being firsts for monoplanes.

Levavasseur had no part, as far as is known, in the Antoinette III, otherwise designated the Ferber IX. His next aeroplane, the Antoinette IV, was the world's first truly successful monoplane. This graceful machine was completed in October 1908, and in the course of a career that was lengthy by contemporary standards, it underwent a series of modifications, especially to the landing gear. As

Pelterie's first machine, with smoother lines and larger fixed and movable rear control surfaces. Esnault-Pelterie also deemed it necessary to add an extra pair of elevators to the forward fuselage, just behind and below the engine, to improve longitudinal control. The performance of the REP. 2 appears to have been staggering by 1908 standards, attaining an altitude of 30 m (98 ft) and a speed in the region of 90 km/h (56 mph). In its first form, however, the REP. 2 was not capable of sustained flight, it being left to the REP. 2-bis of 1909 to secure this achievement for the eccentric, solitary, but undoubtedly very talented Esnault-Pelterie.

It was during 1908 that the whole tenor of European aviation was altered by one factor: the flying of Wilbur Wright in France. At the beginning of the year the Wrights' relationship with the aeronautical world took on a healthier aspect when the brothers contracted to provide an aeroplane and pilot training for the US Army's Signal Corps, and to have their aircraft built under licence in France. It was decided that while Orville conducted the Signal Corps' evaluation and acceptance trials, Wilbur should go to France to demonstrate the aeroplane already sent over in July 1907. Both the Signal Corps and French aircraft were of the batch built after the brothers had given up flying in 1905, and were of the modified Flyer III design called the Flyer Model A. Although the Wrights themselves did not use this appellation, they did call their next basic type the Flyer Model B.

Orville and Wilbur had brushed up their flying techniques on the Flyer III, modified to Model A standard by the provision of two upright seats and other refinements, during May 1908. Immediately afterward, Wilbur took ship for France to collect the crated Model A from the docks at Le Havre. He then moved on to Le Mans, where he set about assembling the Model A in a factory. Because of delays the reassembly took longer than expected, but all was ready early in August.

Naturally enough, the French aviation world had been following Wilbur's progress with interest, some with friendly anticipation but others with a gleeful feeling that their reservations about the Wrights' claims were about to be vindicated. Unruffled and methodical as ever, Wilbur was so confident in the machine and his work that he made no private test flights before announcing that he would take to the air on 8 August.

The crowd at HunaudiÈres racecourse near Le Mans on that day included many of the ablest minds in French aviation, who watched with fascination as the launching rail was laid into the wind, the aeroplane installed on the trolley, the weight hauled to the top of the derrick, and the launching rope connected. Wilbur gave the signal and the Model A accelerated smoothly down the rail and rose gracefully into the air. Wilbur climbed, circled round twice, his superb banking showing off the degree of control possible with the use of warping and rudder control, and then landed after a flight of only 1 minute 45 seconds.

The crowd was astounded, even those who had expressed a belief in the brothers' claims being overwhelmed by the magnitude of the event. It was not that Wilbur's flight had excelled in hard facts anything that the Europeans had done, but rather that it had been of a quality hitherto the subject of dreams rather than actuality. Here was a man who was not at odds with the air, but rather at one with it. Congratulations flooded in from all over Europe, and other

most attention at the time was concentrated on this machine's successor, the Antoinette V, it is impossible to trace all the modifications for lack of evidence. Nevertheless, the Antoinette IV ushered in the era of graceful Levavasseur monoplanes, the majority of them featuring a boat-shaped fuselage of triangular section, probably inspired by Levavasseur's earlier association with racing motor-boats.

One other monoplane worthy of note in 1908 was the REP. 2. This was a logical development from Esnault-

pioneers set about revising their ideas on controllability, particularly the combination of lateral and directional control. Delagrange summed up the event succinctly: 'Eh bien, nous sommes battus! Nous n'existons pas!' ('Well, we are beaten! We do not even exist!')

Wilbur continued to astonish for the next six days at HunaudiËres, and then moved to the military training ground at Camp d'Auvours, east of Le Mans. He flew from here for the rest of the year, putting in some 26 hours in the air between 8 August and the end of 1908. On 60 of his flights Wilbur took up passengers, and among other notable flights he made six lasting between one and two hours, and on the last day of the year stayed aloft for a remarkable 2 hours 20 minutes 23 seconds. He also secured the world altitude record at 110 m (361 ft). By the end of the year the Wrights' achievements in previous years had been recognized, and Wilbur Wright was a celebrity all over Europe. Indeed, other celebrities, not merely fellow aviation enthusiasts, flocked to the Camp d'Auvours to see the wonder of the year.

While Wilbur had his triumphs in Europe, Orville at first enjoyed similar acclaim in the United States. The Model A was assembled at Fort Myer outside Washington, D.C., and Orville began acceptance trials under Signal Corps' supervision on 3 September, immediately impressing all who saw him in the air with his complete mastery of flight. Progress was smooth and rapid: Orville made four flights of more than one hour, created two altitude records and took up passengers on three occasions. But on 17 September all this came to an end. Late in the afternoon, Orville had taken Lieutenant T. E. Selfridge, one of the leading lights of the AEA, on an official flight. As they circled the field, one of the blades of the starboard propeller cracked along its length: the difference in thrust now produced by the two blades caused so much vibration that the bearings of the long propeller shaft loosened, allowing the propeller to waver back and forth. The propeller thus hit and cut one of the wires bracing the rudders, and as Orville throttled back and tried to land the rudder structure collapsed, causing the aeroplane to dive into the ground. Selfridge was killed instantly, and Orville was grievously hurt. He was back on his feet fairly soon, however, and went to France to join Wilbur. Although the Fort Myer flight programme was thus cut short, Orville had impressed the Americans immensely, despite the fact that the AEA had made the first officially recognized flight in the United States only two months before. It is no exaggeration to say that Orville's work in the United States caused as much stir and enthusiasm in that country as had Wilbur's in France and Europe. Selfridge, incidentally, was the first person to be killed in a powered aeroplane, and only the fourth aviator to be killed since serious work into heavier-than-air flight had begun during the last century.

On Henry Farman's return to France from the United States, where the news of Wilbur Wright's French triumphs had overtaken him, Farman set about modifying his Voisin-Farman I-bis into the Farman I-bis (Modified) by fitting four side curtains to make individual cells of each outer wing bay. With this machine Farman now managed to make some good flights, including three lasting over 30 minutes. Being a natural airman, Farman had for some time had an inkling of what was wrong with his aircraft, and consideration of Wilbur Wright's flying made him realize suddenly that lateral control was the element missing from his Farman I-bis (Modified). Early in October, therefore, Farman installed four large ailerons, one inset into each of the outer wing panels. Although these could only move downwards, Farman had evolved the first truly efficient ailerons ever fitted. Thus improved, the aeroplane performed creditably, and on 30 October Farman made the

world's first true cross-country flight, of 27 km (16.8 miles) in 20 minutes. Still not satisfied, Farman next turned to the idea of giving his machine more lift by converting it into a sort of triplane, with a third small wing mounted above the upper wing's centre section. The extra wing proved more of a liability than an asset, however, and Farman turned to other solutions.

Farman's successes, and the Wrights' flights in France, mark the end of an era in aviation history. The experimenters, or most of them, were no longer working with a mixture of hope and desperation: they had a basis of understanding and practicality from which to develop. The sudden leap in the numbers of successes during 1909 and the sudden increase in public enthusiasm for aviation and aviation meetings were entirely due to the foundations laid in these earlier years.

Europe was stunned by the mastery of the air revealed by Wilbur Wright in the Model A during 1908, and during the first part of 1909 Wilbur and Orville Wright toured Europe giving superb demonstration flights. This is Orville in a Model A at Tempelhof near Berlin in August 1909.

200.000F. de PRIX
GRANDE
SEMAIN
Montaut
D'AVIATION DE L
REIMS DU 22 AU 29 AOÛT 1909 CHAMPAGN

The Year of the Reims Meeting

Two factors were eventually to assist European pioneers in overhauling the Wrights and taking over the lead in world aviation. Firstly, Wilbur's demonstration flying had revealed, with a clarity that was apparent to all except the blinkered Voisin brothers, that full control in all three planes was essential. Secondly, the belief of the European pioneers in their own capabilities had been greatly put out by the universal acclaim that Orville and Wilbur Wright had received. While the Europeans rarely sought to detract from the plaudits that the Wright brothers received in Europe and in the United States, they nonetheless may have felt some annoyance.

Orville and Wilbur Wright had decided right at the outset of their flying careers that inherent instability was what was needed to produce the true flying machine. The Europeans, on the other hand, had tended to the opposite view that inherent stability was essential. The Wrights wished to be able to exercise total control over their creation, while the Europeans wished to be able to drive theirs. As is so often the case, the most reasonable solution to the two camps' differences lay in the mean: the Wrights were correct to insist on control, and the Europeans were correct in wishing to ensure a measure of inherent stability. But whereas the American brothers would not budge from their preconceptions, from 1908 onwards the Europeans quickly realized that they would have a viable and safe machine if they could combine their ideas about stability with those of the Wrights on controllability. Virtually the only Europeans to fail to understand this lesson were Gabriel and Charles Voisin, whose designs went into a temporary limbo from this point onwards, even though they continued to prosper with sales of their proven but now outmoded designs.

The Wright brothers continued to play an important part in the realization of practical aviation over the next two years, but their basic Flyer design was fast approaching the end of its useful development life, and the brothers had little but drastic revisions of the original type with which to replace it. Too late they realized that they were beginning to fall from the van of aviation development, and by the end of 1909 Europe was firmly established as the centre of the aeronautical world. Aircraft of the Flyer type demanded piloting of great skill: the machine could not be left to its own devices in the air for even a few seconds, so the strain on the pilot during any but the shortest flights was considerable. Most of the emerging generation of pilots, attracted by the publicity that had attended the first European successes and Wilbur Wright's French tour, wanted to get into the air as quickly as possible. For them the Wright type of aeroplane was wholly unsuitable, and so they bought Voisin types, graduating onto less stable but fully controllable European machines once they had mastered the basic techniques.

Unfortunately for the Wrights, two basic defects with their Flyer type were now becoming increasingly apparent. Firstly, there was the problem of the forward elevator, without any fixed horizontal longitudinal control surfaces. The brothers had chosen this layout for the quick response they felt it offered, especially if the aeroplane should be in a dive. This may have been all very well for Orville and Wilbur, who had turned themselves into admirable pilots, but other men found the lack of fixed longitudinal surfaces, behind the wings in particular, produced an over sensitivity of control that could only be regarded as alarming. And it was not until too late that the brothers considered a new design to incorporate such surfaces. As usual they went by what they themselves considered to be correct, with little or no regard for the limitations of the pilots they were to train.

The other basic defect with the Flyer type was the lack of wheeled landing gear, which compelled total reliance on the launching rail and derrick weight. This system was admirable in concept and execution back in the days of the Huffman Prairie airfield, but with aviation becoming more and more a practical affair in 1909, all pilots now wanted wheeled landing gear. This allowed them to be independent of crews to assemble and prepare the rail and derrick, and also permitted the aeroplane to taxi or be moved around without use of a trolley on airfields. Yet for some strange reason best known to themselves, the brothers were loathe to add wheels to the skids of their Flyers, even when they had ample power to cope with the extra weight such wheels would have represented. It was only in 1910 that the brothers finally relented, and by then, once again, it was too late.

Wheeled landing gear had found favour in European eyes all along, and combined with controlled stability this enabled the Europeans to progress rapidly towards practical aircraft. The most important part of the Europeans' development of controlled stability was the adoption of fixed horizontal control surfaces behind the wings, together with the abandonment of control surfaces forward of the wings. Although they made rapid and precise control possible, forward control surfaces could exert no 'weathercocking', or control on pitching motion by the aeroplane, and this emphasized longitudinal instability. Trailing control surfaces, however, had quite the reverse effect, while still allowing full longitudinal controllability.

The man mainly responsible for this farsighted innovation, at least so far as biplanes were concerned, was Henry Farman. The Voisin-Farman I, in its many forms, had proved a sterling machine, but late in 1908 Farman decided that he needed a new model. Rather than commission a new one from the Voisins, he decided to try his hand at a design of his own. Despite his successes with the basic Voisin type, Farman produced an oddity, in the form of a tandem monoplane, which he designated the Farman II. He clearly had second thoughts about his machine, however, for it was abandoned even before completion. The designation was next transferred to a biplane commissioned by Farman from the Voisins, and paid for in advance.

It was this commission that produced one of the strangest and least explicable episodes in Gabriel Voisin's extraordinary career. Without informing anyone, he sold the already paid for Voisin-Farman II to an Englishman, J. T. C. Brabazon, who had bought a standard Voisin the year before. The exact date of this unsavoury double-dealing is unclear, but appears to have been either January or early February 1909. Brabazon took his new machine back to England, where in April and May he made the first flights in the United Kingdom by a Briton. Despite the special modifications in the design called for by Farman this Bird of Passage, as it was named by Brabazon, was not very successful and crashed early in May.

Quite naturally, Farman was disgusted by Gabriel Voisin's actions, but decided not to prosecute him. Instead he cut off all further contact with the Voisins, and decided to set up his own aircraft factory on the airfield at Camp de Châlons, south of Reims, where he had been flying since September 1908. This move was of great significance for aviation, at last removing Farman from the pernicious and stagnative influence of the Voisins. Farman was now entirely free to pursue an aggressive and adventurous course in the development of aviation.

The first result of Farman's split with the Voisins was the Henry Farman III, destined to be one of the great aircraft of the period up to 1912. Three things are immediately apparent on this excellent machine. Firstly, Farman had moved away from the Voisin concept of total inherent lateral stability by means of dihedral and side curtains, and had adopted four large ailerons for lateral con-

trol. This was the first time such surfaces had been incorporated in a fully practical fashion, and was an advance of considerable magnitude. Secondly, a stabilizing tailplane was added to the trailing fin and rudder assembly, although the Wright type of forward elevator was still retained. Thirdly, the cumbersome, do-or-die appearance of earlier machines was replaced by an attractive, sturdy yet practical aspect that presaged the pusher biplanes of the next few years.

Powered by a 50-hp Vivinus engine driving a primitive Voisin propeller, the aeroplane was ready in April 1909. Farman quickly set about intensive flight trials, which soon proved the new machine's practicality. He realized that the area of the ailerons was excessive, and disconnected the pair on the lower wings, locking them in place as extensions of the flying surfaces. Shortly thereafter, Farman incorporated four smaller ailerons, thus introducing the modern more balanced aileron/wing area ratio.

In its original form the Farman III was obsolete in one feature, namely its large cellular biplane tail. By August Farman had modified this to an open configuration, and in this form the Farman III reached maturity as the progenitor of the classic European biplanes. Its best flight, on 19 July, lasted 1 hour 23 minutes, and so

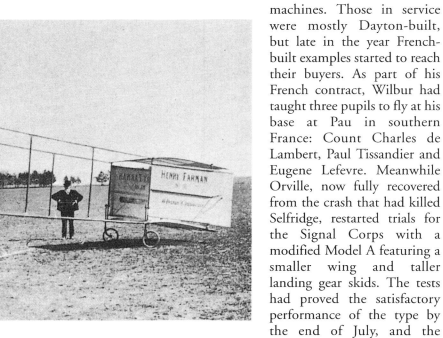

attractive was the type that two others were soon built for Roger Sommer and George Cockburn, putting Farman firmly on the scene as an aircraft manufacturer.

Despite their loss of Farman, the Voisins continued to prosper, building some 15 standard Voisins by the end of 1909. These were all conventional machines with few modifications, and several made flights in excess of two hours' duration.

The Wrights continued to fly extensively in 1909, but with few modifications to their standard Model A machines. Those in service were mostly Dayton-built, but late in the year French-built examples started to reach their buyers. As part of his French contract, Wilbur had taught three pupils to fly at his base at Pau in southern France: Count Charles de Lambert, Paul Tissandier and Eugene Lefevre. Meanwhile Orville, now fully recovered from the crash that had killed Selfridge, restarted trials for the Signal Corps with a modified Model A featuring a smaller wing and taller landing gear skids. The tests had proved the satisfactory performance of the type by the end of July, and the American government bought the machine. Wilbur remained in Europe, and continued to impress the crowds in France and Italy before returning to make demonstration flights in the United States from September to November. Wilbur's place in Europe was taken by Orville, who toured Germany in August, after the successful conclusion of the Signal Corps tests.

The practical possibilities of the monoplane had been clearly demonstrated in 1908 by the Antoinette an Blériot types, and in 1909 both lines came to maturity with a number of important designs and flights. As in the previous year, it was the Antoinette and Blériot designs which scooped the headlines, other monoplanes lagging far behind.

Levavasseur continued the work he had started with the Antoinette IV and V the year before with further revisions to these two types. The exact details are uncatalogued, but most important of all was the alteration of the aileron system. In their 1908 forms, the Antoinettes IV and V had been restricted to downward-operating ailerons only, whereby the aileron on the downward moving wing remained floating, that on the other wing doing all the work. Levavasseur now realized the inefficiency of this, and provided differentially operating ailerons for 1909.

On his next machine, the Antoinette VI, Levavasseur reverted to wing warping in place of the ailerons. This enhanced the natural beauty of the wings considerably, but to some it appears to have been a retrograde step. It should be remembered, however, that the long, narrow (high aspect ratio) wings of the Antoinettes must have suffered considerably from torsional problems no matter how well braced they were, and it seems probable that Levavasseur decided to capitalize on this factor in using controlled torsion for lateral control. It is arguable, indeed, that the provision of large ailerons on

so flexible a wing structure could be dangerous: the aileron could have operated as a servo-tab and twisted the wing to produce a bank opposite in effect to that desired.

The Antoinette VI was built for R. Demanest, but its performance was no more than average in its 15 flights between April and July 1909. Its successor, the Antoinette VII, however, was the classic of the line, and was excelled in performance only by the redoubtable Antoinette IV. Built for Hubert Latham, a Frenchman of British parentage destined to play a vital role in the popularization of flying, the machine first flew on 27 July 1909. The Antoinette VIII, built for the firm and flown for the first time on 15 August, was also a beautiful machine, but it never performed with more than the modest modest of success.

In the monoplane field, 1909 was to be Blériot's year, despite the courageous and ill-fated efforts of Latham. What was to come was foreshadowed at the Salon de l'Automobile held at the end of 1908 in Paris. In the aviation section of this exhibition, Blériot displayed his two latest machines, the Blériots IX and XI, which were all but completed.

The former of these was ready for trials early in the new year, but proved abortive. Among the most notable of its design features were the use of the much larger 100-hp Antoinette engine, a long triangular-sectioned fuselage (unique for Blériot), and a crash bar over the pilot's head and shoulders to protect him in the event of the aeroplane overturning.

The Blériot XI, however, was an altogether more successful machine, and proved the foundation of Blériot's success as an aircraft constructor. In its original form, the Blériot XI looked very odd. This was a result of the stabilizing fin mounted on pylons above the pilot's head, near the front of the fuselage. Controls were the now conventional warping, rear elevator and rudder. The Blériot XI was ready towards the end of January 1909, but two months of effort produced nothing better than one two-minute flight early in April. Blériot belatedly realized that modifications were in order and a further two months passed while the Blériot XI was transformed into the Blériot XI (Modified). The central forward fin was deleted, the rear rudder was enlarged, and, most important of all, an efficient Chauviére propeller was fitted to the 25-hp Anzani 'arrowhead' engine which replaced the earlier 30-hp REP. Results were immediately impressive, principally as a result of the far greater thrust provided by the ChauviÉre propeller. Blériot made some excellent duration and cross-country flights in this machine before turning his attention towards the English Channel. It should be noted additionally that

the Blériot XI was the first European aeroplane to utilize the Wright type of wing warping absolutely successfully.

In the spring of 1909, Blériot also determined to be the first man in history to produce a truly adequate passenger-carrying aeroplane. Accordingly he set to work and in May unveiled the Blériot XII. This was essentially a scaled-up standard Blériot type, powered at first by a 35-hp ENV engine, and later by a 60-hp unit of the same manufacture. Provision was made for one passenger and the pilot, although Blériot carried two passengers to win a special prize at the Reims aviation meeting in August. The Blériot XIII was basically similar to its predecessor, but was powered by a 40-hp Anzani instead of being powered by an ENV. On the Blériots IX, XII and XIII the designer employed a two-part tailplane: one part was an unmoving, rigidly fixed lifting surface to support the weight of the rear fuselage, while the other constituted the control and stabilizing surfaces. The success of the Blériot XI, with its conventional, or almost conventional, single tailplane, sensibly decided Blériot to abandon the two-part unit in his future designs.

The only other successful monoplane of 1909 was the last design to emerge from the drawing board of the diminutive Santos-Dumont before he was struck down by a debilitating disease. This last design, the No.20 Demoiselle was a delight, and the true progenitor of ultra-light civil aircraft. Similar to the Santos-Dumont 19, the No.20 was a small high-wing monoplane, this time with a triangular bamboo-pole fuselage and wing warping operated by wires attached to the pilot's body. The Demoiselle types were essentially oddities, and exerted no real influence on the course of aviation before World War I, but did help to increase the air-mindedness of the public, always fascinated by the activities of their dapper little favourite.

Esnault-Pelterie continued to pursue his solitary course, producing his modified REP. 2 as the REP. 2-bis at the end of 1908 and flying it during the first half of 1909. Its chief difference from its predecessor was the provision of a large tailplane well behind the wings, a belated realization by Esnault-Pelterie that his basic design was totally deficient in longitudinal stability. Although an improvement on the REP. 2, the No2-bis was still not quite right, and its best flight covered only 8 km (5 miles) on 22 May 1909. Other monoplanes of the year were even less successful, however, particularly such oddities as the Givaudan annular-wing craft, the Scottish Watson rocking-wing aeroplane and the graceful but immediately obsolete Guillebaud tandem-wing aeroplane.

Although unsuccessful in relative terms, two designs of this year were to have a profound influence on the future

Although at the Reims aviation meeting it made only three short flights, the last ending in a crash landing, the Breguet I was a technically important aeroplane. The aeroplane was the first true example of the type of tractor biplane that was soon to eclipse the monoplane as the most practical aeroplane and retain this position until well into the 1920.

Bedevilled by lack of funds, Alliott Verdon Roe was forced to rely on an obsolete JAP engine of notably low power/weight ratio and driving a hopelessly inefficient propeller for his Roe I Triplane, which nevertheless made a few 'hop' flights in 1909.

development of tractor biplanes. These were the Goupy II and Breguet I. The Goupy, designed by Ambroise Goupy and Mario Calderera and built by Blériot, was an advanced design, with staggered wings (the top wing being ahead of the lower wing) on a fuselage and empennage based on Blériot's designs. At first it was not successful, but with wing-tip elevons it started a useful career as a school aeroplane from the end of 1909. The Breguet, designed and built by Louis Breguet, was not as advanced in appearance as the Goupy II, but it played a more prominent part in the development of tractor biplanes. It was shown at the Aeronautical Show held at Olympia in London in March 1909, and was ready for flight in June. The one very unusual feature of the machine was the double use of warping: in concert as elevators and differentially as ailerons. Unlike the Goupy II, the Breguet I took part in the Reims aviation meeting where its distinctive and prophetic lines resulted in much comment.

Despite a genuine complacency, often expressed in the form of statements that they could produce an aeroplane superior to any built by the continental Europeans should they think it necessary, the United Kingdom was only now beginning to emerge from the aeronautical doldrums in which it had been languishing. Two men were principally responsible for this, and one of them, the American Cody, was not yet a British citizen. After the hesitant and minor successes of his first powered aeroplane, known as the British Army Aeroplane No.1, Cody in the last quarter of 1908 rebuilt his machine into what may be termed the Cody 2, which made some 30 flights in the first half of 1909, the best of them covering 4 miles (6.4 km). Subsequent modification turned this machine into the Cody 3, on which its flamboyant and indefatigable creator made several successful flights, the best of them covering 40 miles (64 km) in just over 60 minutes on 8 September 1909. These Cody machines were large, sturdy, but clumsy machines, and exerted no real influence on the mainstream

of aviation. They were, however, important in showing the British people that aircraft could fly, and that one designed in their own country, even if not by one of their own countrymen, could remain in the air for a considerable period. Cody's enthusiasm and determination were an encouragement to all would-be British pioneers, and helped alleviate the unconscious British fears that the 'Continentals' had stolen a march on them.

The only other British pioneer of the period to achieve anything like success was A. V. Roe, with a series of triplanes inspired by the unsuccessful Goupy I. Roe was, however, direly short of money, and could at first afford nothing better as powerplants than the 6-hp and 9-hp JAP engines, with which he could achieve nothing better than powered hops in his otherwise promising machines.

In the United States, the AEA continued its work with the Silver Wing, essentially a scaled-up version of the June Bug with a forward elevator, designed and flown by J. A. D. McCurdy. All these A.E.A. aircraft, however, were built and tested in relative isolation near the American-Canadian border, and had no direct influence on the course of aviation history apart from giving Glenn Curtiss his start in the field. Without his basic engineering and design skill, combined with his engines, it is questionable whether the AEA would have achieved even what it did.

At the beginning of 1909 Curtiss started his own aircraft business in conjunction with Augustus Herring, Chanute's associate of 10 years earlier. The firm's first machine, built for the Aeronautic Society of New York but soon lent to Curtiss, was the Gold Bug. Like the Silver Wing, this machine evolved from the June Bug and continued the basic design philosophy of the AEA, but it had parallel wings instead of the dihedral/anhedral curved wings favoured by AEA types. Powerful ailerons were installed at mid-gap, but otherwise the aeroplane was conventional by the standards of the day. The Gold Bug was making successful flights by the late spring of 1909, but by then Curtiss had decided to build a machine for himself, principally as a racing machine and record-breaker. He had clearly foreseen that public enthusiasm for aviation would soon begin to pour hard cash into the sport, and that considerable sums could be secured by the first man to develop a specialized aircraft. The Golden Flyer, as Curtiss's machine was called, was similar in layout to the Gold Bug, but was powered by a new 50-hp Curtiss engine, although for tactical reasons Curtiss often stated that the engine could deliver only 30 hp. The Golden Flyer was ready just in time for the Reims aviation meeting, and exerted a powerful influence on other designers following its great successes there. Curtiss was one of only a small handful who understood that aviation was about to burgeon into a major 'spectator sport' in the next few years, though the indications were in fact there for all to see. Most pioneers, it seems, were too wrapped up in the intricacies of their pursuit to see what was in front of them. With the Edwardian era, a lighter-hearted, more relaxed attitude now blended with the growing acceptance of new technology to produce the 'thrilling' sports of the day. Thus there was ample opportunity for quick-witted entrepreneurs to take the public's money with car, motorcycle, motorboat and, eventually, aircraft race meetings. In these meetings, the crowds were thrilled by the danger to the sportsmen involved in these various new types of transport, and also by the sheer novelty of the machines themselves.

Aviation was only one of the advances that were causing so much excitement in the first decade of the 20th century, but it was also easily the most enthralling, as the newspapers were quick to discern. The number of newspapers published and the numbers sold, especially of the 'tabloid' type, had soared throughout the world, and publishers were quick to realize that public interest in aviation could be fostered in order to boost circulation. The part played by newspapers in the growth of aviation up to World War I, therefore, was considerable, particularly after papers started to use the services of specialists of the calibre of the Daily Mail's Harry Harper, whose resourcefulness in securing aviation news often exceeded in quality the story he was after.

Two events of 1909 finally put aviation right in the public eye. Aviation, up until that year, had been considered a kind of madcap sport to be indulged in by wealthy or eccentric men with little better to do. No practical application for what had become a practical activity was envisaged by any but the most far-sighted.

But then, in July, Blériot succeeded in flying across the English Channel from France to England. The shock of this singular event was out of all proportion to the flight's significance as such, and its ripples reached out over Europe, the United States and the British Empire. For the first time people realized that a new way of life was about to break on them. The inviolability of the British Isles through its mighty navy was seen to be suddenly endangered, as there now existed in rudimentary form the means of circumventing the Royal Navy's supremacy.

The prospect of such a crossing had been in view for some time now, especially as the London newspaper, the Daily Mail, had offered a prize of £1,000 for the first man to do it. The two most likely contenders were Hubert Latham in an Antoinette, and Louis Blériot in one of his own machines. It is noteworthy that these two prime contenders both flew tractor monoplanes.

Latham was the first to make an attempt, setting out from Sangatte near Calais early on the morning of 19 July in his Antoinette IV. Unluckily for him, however, the usually reliable 50-hp Antoinette engine cut out when he was about 8 miles (12 km) out to sea, and he had to ditch the aeroplane. Thanks to the generosity of the French government, however,

the attempt had been escorted by the destroyer Harpon, which picked up both Latham and his aeroplane.

Six days later, on the 25 July, Blériot was ready to make his effort. Although still suffering from the effects of burns on one of his legs from a previous crash, Blériot set forth at the crack of dawn on his No.XI aeroplane, and landed near Dover Castle after a flight of 23.5 miles (37.8 km) in 36 minutes 30 seconds. The aeroplane was by no means suitable for the attempt, but the success was Blériot's and he received a hero's welcome in London and on his return to France. As Charles Gibbs-Smith points out, just three months earlier the British War Office had ordered the Royal Balloon Factory at Farnborough to cease work on aircraft because it was too expensive: £2,500 had been spent, at a time when a production Antoinette cost £1,000. Yet Blériot's flight had a considerable impact on the thinking of British politicians, and this decision was soon to be reversed. In more personal terms, the Channel flight ensured Blériot's financial success as an aircraft constructor, to add to his success as a motor car manufacturer, for within two days he had received orders for over 100 Blériot XI aircraft.

Latham remained determined to cross the Channel himself, and two days after Blériot's successful flight he set out again from Sangatte, this time in the Antoinette VII. All went well until he was only 1 mile (1.6 km) from England, but then the engine failed again and Latham once more came down in the sea.

The other major event of 1909 was La Grande Semaine d'Aviation de la Champagne, the first great flying meeting to be held. This grand affair attracted all the best pilots and machines in Europe, and was held on the open spaces near Bétheny outside Reims between 22 and 29 August. With many generous prizes offered by the champagne industry, the whole meeting was held under the auspices of the President of the French Republic and attended by many influential political and financial figures from all over Europe. It may truly be said that this meeting, with its plethora of events, flights and records, marked the beginning of Europe's acceptance of the aeroplane as more than just a toy.

Despite the fact that it was a pusher biplane, the Curtiss Golden Flyer revealed at the Reims aviation meeting that it was the equal of the monoplane entrants in terms of speed. The Golden Flyer took the Prix de la Vitesse at 75 km/h (46.6 mph), won the Coupe d'Aviation Gordon Bennett at 75.7 km/h (47 mph), and came second in the Prix de Tour de Piste at 76 km/h (47.25 mph).

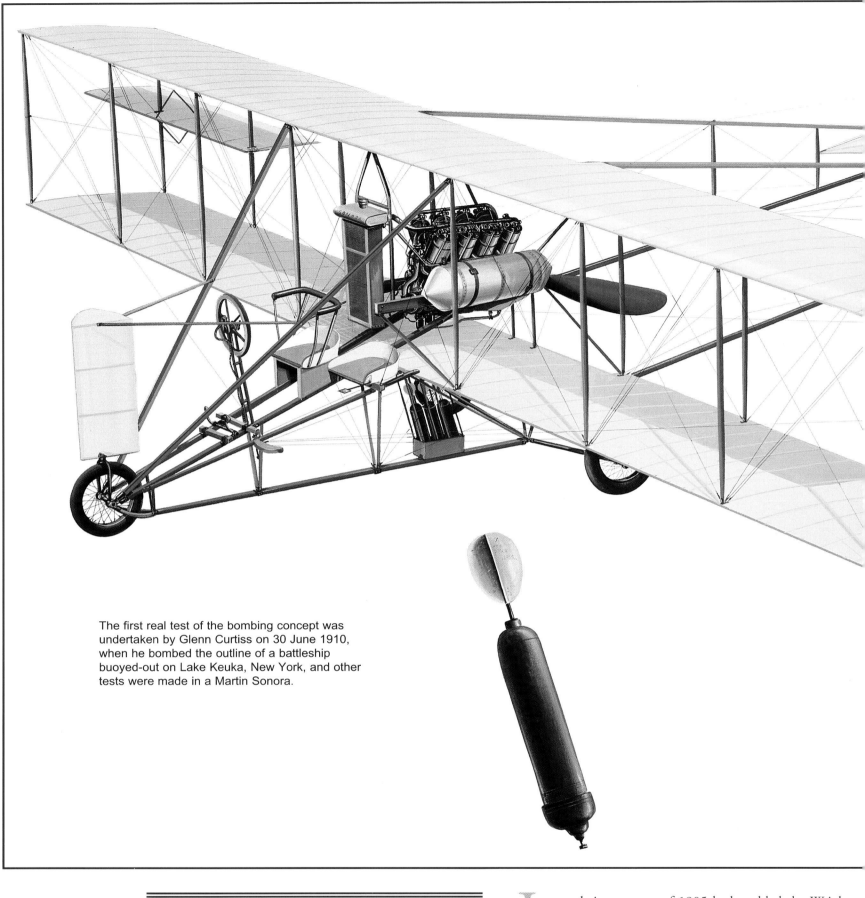

The first real test of the bombing concept was undertaken by Glenn Curtiss on 30 June 1910, when he bombed the outline of a battleship buoyed-out on Lake Keuka, New York, and other tests were made in a Martin Sonora.

Higher and Still Faster

Just as their successes of 1905 had enabled the Wright brothers to claim that not only had they produced a machine which could fly but also one that was in most respects a manoeuvrable and practical aeroplane, so the Reims meeting of 1909 had ushered in the period of practical European aviation. Although lack of clear objectives was to mean that progress was to be haphazard, even spasmodic, the future of aviation was assured, and progress was made in all aspects of the field in the course of the five years remaining before World War I. The theories of structures and stress received widespread attention, engines were improved in reliability and in performance, and aerodynamic refinements, as a result both of theoretical and of practical work, were bringing in great dividends in

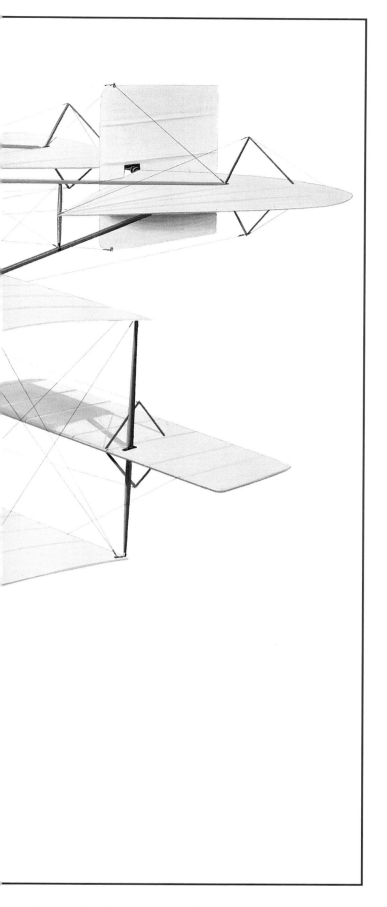

was marked more by continuous developments, no longer divided by a dependence on flying seasons into yearly stages.

Soon after the Reims meeting, a subtle alteration in attitudes was discernible. There was now an increasing tendency for the design and flying side of aviation to be separated: Blériot, for example, concentrated on the business side of his concern and entrusted the flying to the brilliant professional pilot, Adolphe Pégoud. Big business began to enter the field, and increasingly the aviation magazines and catalogues were filled with the products of such companies as the British and Colonial Aeroplane Company (soon to be changed to the Bristol Aeroplane Company) or AEG in Germany, instead of the designs of individuals. Flying was in the process of becoming big business, and prizes were now important as a means of finance rather than as an extra after the excitement and interest of a competition. This is not to deny that prize money was important to the pioneers to finance their work, but rather to emphasize that the money was now an object in itself for many companies.

There were of course exceptions to this domination by companies, men such as the celebrated T. O. M. Sopwith who entered the field in 1910 and managed to compete successfully, while at the same time designing and building. Only later did Sopwith enlarge his firm into a major aeronautical constructor.

Flying was in the process of becoming international, and nowhere was this more apparent than in the expanding number of races and competitions that took place. This internationalism lay not only in the number of places where the competitions were held, but also in the nationalities of the competitors themselves. Although most of them flew French aircraft, an increasing number of British machines was evident, marking the formal arrival of the United Kingdom onto the aeronautical scene.

Despite the paucity of American pilots and designers, entrepreneurs in the United States were quick to realize the draw that flying had become, and in January 1910 the first international competition to take place in that country was held in Los Angeles. Honours were shared between France and the United States: Louis Paulhan in a Henry Farman set a world altitude record at 1269.5 m (4,165 ft) and Curtiss established a world speed record at 88.5 km/h (55 mph) with a machine of his own design. Attendances were very large, and promoters in other cities were suddenly aware that aviation was a real money-spinner. In September there was a highly successful meeting in Boston, where most of the competitors were American and British, and the lively and dynamic figure of Claude Grahame-White dominated proceedings. Most of these competitors then moved south to New York for the meeting arranged for October in Belmont Park, again dominated by Grahame-White, who had caused a great stir by flying down to Washington before the meeting and landing in the street outside the White House to pay his respects to President Taft. America was now firmly in the grip of the flying 'bug' and races proliferated. So too did dare-devil flying, or 'barnstorming' as it came to be called, and record attempts.

The greatest of the first generation of barnstormers was Lincoln Beachey, who learned to fly at the school run by Glenn Curtiss. Opinions about his flying differed widely: some said that he was mad to attempt the feats he did while others, including no less an authority than Orville Wright, that he was the greatest pilot of all time. What is certain is that the crowds loved his stunts and flocked in great numbers to his appearances. Flying a Curtiss biplane, Beachey would perform such feats as vertical power dives and the scooping up from the ground with one of his wing-tips of a handkerchief or scarf. He also performed the remarkable feat, considering the air turbulence, of flying low over the

the way of enhanced performance. Piloting skills, too, were increasing rapidly to match the machines' superior abilities. Aircraft could be handled with greater safety and panache, the latter an important factor in keeping the interest of the public. Aviation itself was diversifying, so that while it remained basically a sport, experiments were made with other aspects of flight, such as military applications and the carriage of passengers and freight.

Progress during the earlier years in the history of aviation, dominated by the efforts of pioneers to get their various creations into the air, occurred on a seasonal basis, when the weather was good enough to allow flying. The periods of poor weather in the winter and early spring were used for construction and repair work. The post-Reims era

Niagara Falls and then under the suspension bridge just below them. Yet Beachey was no headstrong youth, but rather a man who had worked out with enormous detail the possibilities of his machine and his own skills. By pushing them to the limit, barnstorming pilots were also of great help to designers in evolving lighter and stronger structures. But, increasingly worried about the safety of the imitators of his work, Beachey retired in 1913, only to be persuaded by Pégoud's successful loop to make further appearances. In 1915, over San Francisco, the wings of his monoplane folded at 2,000 ft (610 m) and a vast crowd watched horror-struck as Beachey and his machine crashed to total destruction.

The other great person to catch the devoted attention of the American public at this time was Calbraith Rodgers, already a celebrated racer of boats, cars and horses. Late in 1911 Rodgers decided to have a stab at the $50,000 prize offered by the yellow-press magnate William Randolph Hearst for the first coast-to-coast flight across the United States in 30 days. After two months of practice on a Wright biplane, and accompanied by a chartered train carrying spares and support personnel supplied by the Vin-Fiz soft-drink firm that was sponsoring him, Rodgers set off from New York on 11 September with the intention of arriving in Pasadena, California, by 11 October. It soon became clear that the target date was impossible, but Rodgers decided that he would nonetheless continue. The journey became a heroic odyssey, and Rodgers was beset by problems the whole way: he had many crashes, souvenir-hunters stole parts of his machine, he nearly collided in mid-air with an eagle, the weather was appalling in several regions, and his engine proved very temperamental, once blowing up in the air. Yet Rodgers gamely pressed on, and finally arrived in Pasadena on 5 November. The only parts of the machine he was flying that had been with him for the whole trip were the rudder and the engine drip tray, so many times had the machine been patched up and portions replaced. Like Beachey, Rodgers also met death in the air. While stunting in April 1912 he lost control of his machine and dived to the ground.

The explosion of interest in flight after Reims was not confined to the United States. During 1910 meetings were held all over Europe: four in Italy, two in Germany, one each in Spain, Switzerland, Belgium, Denmark, Russia and Hungary, and many in the United Kingdom and France.

Crowds continued to flock to the displays and races, which steadily increased in size during the next few years. They were usually held close to large cities, sometimes on specially hired grounds and sometimes on airfields specially bought and built up by a few enterprising promoters such as Grahame-White, whose establishment of Hendon as one of the major flying areas for London is a very good example. Flying displays became a regular feature of weekend life in the cities of Europe, attended alike by the aristocracy, the middle classes and the mass of working people who could get to the field. All were catered for in separate enclosures, and large fortunes were made by the entrepreneurs who were lucky enough to have their preparations and enterprise attended by good weather.

Competitions before World War I were not restricted to aircraft alone, although they were always the centrepiece of the day's activities. The bigger displays sought to have captive hydrogen balloons on display, as well as a dirigible airship if this were possible. These would be in the air as the crowds arrived, and would remain there as people wandered around the parked aircraft, carefully roped off to prevent damage from souvenir-hunters. The flying display proper would consist of a number of races round a course marked out by pylons. The various competitors were sent off at intervals dictated by a system of handicapping, so that after the requisite number of laps the first pilot past the finishing line opposite the grandstand was the winner. If the handicapping had been well worked out, the crowds would be treated to exciting last laps as competitors raced neck and neck towards the finish. As piloting skills improved, so too did the knowledge of the aficionados as they commented knowingly on the skills of the pilot, banking or skidding round a pylon, diving or zooming in the process to set himself up for the next mark.

There were also altitude events, spot-landing competitions, dummy bombing with bags of flour on targets marked on the field, and other events. A few parachute descents, using the newly-developed 'Guardian Angel' parachute, were made from captive balloons, or in exceptional circumstances from an aeroplane. The first to achieve this difficult feat in Europe was the daring Pégoud, on 19 August 1913. Also in 1913, devotees of flying displays were treated to the world's first proper aerobatics, the first great exponent of the art being the same Pégoud,

Like the Wright Model A and the Henry Farman III, the Bristol Boxkite marked the apogee of development from the concept of the original Wright Flyer I, but was an evolutionary dead end despite its popularity. Production totalled 76 aircraft including a number rebuilt after crashes, and the several of the aircraft remained serviceable up to the eve of World War I.

Like the Bristol Boxkite, the Albatros was an unashamed copy of the Henry Farman III intended for the German market.

on a specially strengthened Blériot. Although modest by present-day standards, the aerobatics of 1913, made possible by an increasing knowledge of the aerodynamic forces acting upon a body in flight and by improved structures, were considered extremely daring. The first loop was performed in Kiev by Piotr Nesterov in a Nieuport monoplane on 20 August 1913. Nesterov was also to be the Imperial Russian Air Service's first battle casualty, and the first man in the world to destroy another aeroplane by ramming, on 26 August 1914. The man who was to make the loop his own, however, was Pégoud. His positive-g loops were marked by their almost perfect circularity, and he even went so far as to introduce negative-g, inverted, looping manoeuvres, such as the bunt in which the aeroplane is pushed down into a dive, and the down-elevator is operated until the machine is upside down. Pégoud could then fly his Blériot inverted, completing his manoeuvre with a half-roll to right his machine. Other major exponents of aerobatics were men such as Gustav Hamel, who flew a Morane-Saulnier monoplane, and B. C. Hucks, who flew Blackburn and Blériot monoplanes, both pilots specializing in looping manoeuvres. Chevillard entertained with vertical side-slips on his Henri Farman, while de Moulinais and Manton, on a MoraneSaulnier and Bristol Boxkite respectively were both excellent general aerobatic pilots. These men became household names with those who followed flying, as did other ace pilots such as Louis Paulhan, Harry Busteed, George Cockburn, André Beaumont (who flew under the pseudonym of Conneau), Geoffrey de Havilland, Bertram Dickson, Gordon England, Eustace Loraine, J. T. C. Moore-Brabazon, Harry Hawker, Howard Pixton, the Hon. C. S. Rolls, T. O. M. Sopwith and Maraca Tableau. It was men such as these, most of them flying aircraft designed by others, that brought aviation into the everyday lives of most Europeans.

Apart from their performances at air shows, these men earned their livings testing new machines, and working as instructors at the numerous flying schools which sprang up before World War I. They also flew for the sheer fun of it, their every essay into the air dutifully chronicled for an interested fellowship and public by magazines such as the Aeroplane, edited by the formidable figure, C. G. Grey, and Flight. Typical extracts of the minutiae of flying life read somewhat quaintly today, but were of considerable

importance at the time in keeping pilots in touch with what others were doing: 'On Tuesday Mr Smith Barry was piloting a biplane, banking it steeply... On Wednesday he was out for a good solo on tractor biplane No. 64. Later he flew to Fargo with Jullerot, to give help to Gordon England, who had force landed there in a machine.'

The flying displays so prominent in Europe and the United States in the period between Reims and World War I are particularly important for two reasons. Firstly, to a great extent they financed the growth and development of aviation-it was the public's money that put up the prizes and allowed manufacturers to expand their businesses, something which would have been impossible on what money they made simply from the sale of aircraft. Secondly, these displays and races provided the technical background and testing place for manufacturers to test their machines, prove their abilities in public and so sell them to the growing number of pilots in the market.

The prize money available to constructors at air displays was of course added to by that put up for special races. These included the trans-America race, the London-Manchester race for a prize of £10,000 put up by the Daily Mail and won by Paulhan in April 1910 flying a Henry Farman, the 1911 Circuit of Britain race for the Daily Mail prize of £10,000 won by André Beaumont, the 1911 Circuit of Europe race for £18,300 also won by Beaumont, the French Michelin races for distance flown with an annual prize of 20,000 francs, and the British Empire Michelin Cup races each worth £500, which were also annual races for distance flown. By the standards of the day these were very valuable prizes, and winning them made a considerable difference to the finances of most designers and constructors.

The number of constructors had grown considerably, and large companies with other basic interests were now taking an increasing share of the market. The best companies, however, were those that had got off to a sound start with aircraft that could fly in 1908 and 1909. When their own types were not selling very successfully, these companies could always undertake the building of a one-off design, or the licence-production of aircraft whose output could not keep up with demand. By 1914, therefore, the building of aircraft was in the hands of a number of small builders, producing only a few aircraft a year, and a few larger companies capable of turning out far more machines such as Bristol, Short Brothers, Blériot, Morane-Saulnier, Albatros and Caproni. These companies were to bear the brunt of the production race in the opening months of the war.

The expansion of aviation can be seen from the number of men who had entered the pilots' lists since Reims. The first woman to qualify as a pilot, Madame Ia Baronne de Laroche, received her French brevet on 8 March 1910 after qualifying on a Voisin biplane.

One of the most remarkable men to enter the field of flight at this time also had a rudely short career. A Peruvian, Georges Chavez started to learn to fly only in March 1910. In the next few months he qualified for his licence on a Farman, took part in numerous meetings with considerable distinction, and bought a Blériot monoplane on which he rose to a world altitude record of 2586.8 m (8,487 ft). Then, on 23 September, he set off on his most daring flight: a heavier-than-air crossing of the Alps from Brig to Domodossola via the Simplon Pass. Coming in to land after completing the crossing, Chavez crashed, and he died four days later in hospital. He was clearly a man of remarkable ability, and his loss to the world of aviation was a heavy blow.

One of the most remarkable flights attempted before World War I was Roland Garros' non-stop crossing of the Mediterranean in September 1913 on a Morane-Saulnier. Taking off from St Raphaîl in southern France, Garros set off south across Corsica and Sardinia, and finally landed in Bizerta late on 23 September after a flight of 729 km (453 miles) in just under 8 hours. Another notable first of a similar kind was the crossing of the North Sea by the Norwegian pilot Tryggve Gran on a Blériot monoplane on 30 July 1914, the eve of World War I.

People who would never be able to afford aircraft of their own could now take part in the adventure of flight by being passengers. The greatest passenger carriers were the five German Zeppelin airships which between 1910 and 1914 carried some 35,000 passengers over 273600 km (170,000 miles) without a single injury. But aircraft too played their part in the introduction of passenger flights, albeit in a very small way compared with the Zeppelins. One or two passengers had already been carried on a variety of aircraft when Claude Grahame-White, who always seemed to be a couple of jumps ahead of the rest of the field when assessing the future of aviation, decided that passenger flights should be added to the attractions of his displays and school at Hendon. The result was his extraordinary Charabanc, which flew for the first time late in the summer of 1913. On 2 October the type established a new world record by taking off with nine passengers and staying in the air for just under 20 minutes.

On 11 February 1914 this record was bettered by the Sikorsky Le Grand, which took 16 people up. This odd four-engined machine, which soon evolved into the world's first four-engined bomber, even had a promenade deck along the upper rear fuselage, with rails to prevent passengers falling off as the huge machine lumbered along!

But while these aircraft were amusing the audience at air displays, and while adventurous pilots were pushing forward the limits of their steadily improving machines, aircraft were gradually embroiled in warfare for the first time. The tinge of excitement felt by the spectator on the ground during an air display, watching for the half-expected misfortune to an aeroplane going through its manoeuvres, was starting its long transformation into the terror of the bomber's approach during World War II.

Uncertain as they were of the role aircraft could play in war, governments were at first hesitant to spend lavishly on the formation of air services. But the British army had used balloons regularly since 1878, and in 1907 the German army had established its Zeppelin service. It was inevitable that properly organized air services would be raised shortly after the Reims meeting had proved the practicality of aircraft to the European authorities, both civilian and military. The United States had, after all, paved the way with the purchase of a Wright biplane, named Miss Columbia, for $30,000 on 2 August 1909. In 1910 France, Germany and Russia all established air services for their armies, although the German service was not formally established until October 1912. The United Kingdom followed suit in April 1911 with the formation of the Air Battalion, Royal Engineers, expanded into the Royal Flying Corps, with Military and Naval Wings, in May 1912. In July 1914 this was split as the Royal Navy established its own Royal Naval Air Service.

The first use of aircraft in war, however, was not by one of these formally established bodies, but by the Italians, who still lacked a proper air service. The Italian army fighting the Turks in Libya used a number of aircraft provided by the Royal Aero Club of Italy, and history was made on 22 October 1911 when Captain Piazza carried out the first air reconnaissance of Turkish positions near Aziziya in a Blériot. On 1 November further history was made when Lieutenant Gavotti dropped four home-made bombs on a Turkish camp from his Etrich Taube. The Turks immediately claimed that this constituted a war crime because a hospital had been hit, although this seems unlikely. On 24 November Captain Moizo carried out the first artillery spotter flight, and on 23 February 1913 Piazza flew the world's first photographic-reconnaissance mission. Thus were born the four basic tasks to be fulfilled by aircraft in World War I. The Italians had been sufficiently impressed by the results gained by aircraft that they set up an army air service in June 1912. Further military uses for aircraft were discovered during the Balkan Wars of 1912-1913.

Other European interest in the military applications of aircraft continued in 1911 and 1912, even if it was only in a desultory fashion. In October and November of 1911 the French held the first military aircraft competition, or Concours Militaire, to find aircraft types suitable for the army air service, and experiments with armament, both bombs and machine-guns, were carried out. The first few aircraft specifically intended for war, including a two-seater Nieuport equipped with a machine-gun, also appeared.

In 1912, for the first time, armies began to consider seriously what to do with their aircraft, and thus what sort of aircraft they should have. This was partially the result of their own internal considerations, but also a result of the increasing insistence of the public. Rarely has so much public interest been shown in the weapons of war, and by 1912 the 'naval race' that had acquired great momentum

One of the most impressive aircraft to appear before World War I, the Deperdussin Monocoque was an outright racer and record-breaker. The aeroplane was a braced monoplane and was powered by a 160-hp Gnome rotary piston engine. The company pilot associated with the type was Maurice Prévost, and three times in 1913 this excellent pilot raised the world air speed record, the last figure being 203.85 km/h (126.67 mph) reached at Reims on 29 September.

after the launching of the great battleship Dreadnought by the British in 1906 had extended itself to all other aspects of military hardware. Germany was known to be building up its fleet of airships,

so the United Kingdom too must possess powerful air forces. The British public was little concerned with what these aircraft were to do, but public opinion determined that the United Kingdom should have a large number of military aircraft. Feelings in France were similar, but the French military authorities were showing a more constructive approach to the problem of aircraft and spending considerable sums on testing different types and experimenting with their tactical roles.

Although the authorities showed little interest, several interesting British designs were emerging. Roe had led the way in the development of the fully practical tractor biplane with the Avro D and E of 1911 and the F of 1912, culminating in the great Avro Type 504 of 1913. Geoffrey de Havilland, working at the Royal Aircraft Factory at Farnborough, had evolved the fully stable B.E.2 from the partially successful B.E.1 of the previous year. Most importantly, however, de Havilland had produced the B.S.1 as a fast, clean tractor biplane, the machine from which all fighters may trace their descent. But at the British Military Aircraft Competition held in August 1912, the B.E.2, as a government-sponsored machine, was not allowed to compete against private-enterprise aircraft, and Cody's extraordinary Military Trials Biplane was declared the winner, although the B.E.2, flying hors de concours, was manifestly superior. Only two of the Cody machines were ordered for the Royal Flying Corps, however, and the inherently stable B.E.2 was put into production.

Although the development and introduction of a number of standard types, such as the B.E.2 and imported Blériot Xl, as well as a variety of Avro and Sopwith types, dominated the thinking of those concerned with British military aviation in the last two years before the outbreak of World War I, there were other factors that were in the long-term of greater significance. Eugene Ely in the United States had made the first take-off and landing aboard ship, but it was the British who in many respects took the lead in the operation of wheeled aircraft from ships with a number of take-offs from the pre-Dreadnought battleships London and Hibernia while the ships were under way. Thus although Ely's feats had been considerable firsts, the British efforts paved the way for everyday operations from moving warships, and also opened up the possibility of warships designed specifically to operate aircraft at sea.

Unfortunately for aviation, 1912 had seen the partial eclipse of the monoplane. This was the result of two crashes in England, and of Blériot's doubts about the structural integrity of his basic layout. Both the British and French

armies had immediately placed a ban on the monoplane layout, and although the ban was subsequently lifted, it took monoplanes some 20 years to come back into favour.

Among the most important design advances of 1913 were the full development of the B.E.2, and the introduction of the lovely little Sopwith Tabloid side-by-side two-seater designed by Harry Hawker and Fred Sigrist. In France the fastest aircraft of the pre-war period made its appearance. This was the Deperdussin Monocoque, a beautifully streamlined monoplane capable of 203 km/h (126 mph), which looked forward to the racing aircraft of the 1920s with its monocoque (stressed 'single-shell') fuselage, enclosed engine and careful attention to the elimination of drag-producing factors.

The events of 1913, however, were notable not so much for the emergence of new types of aircraft as for the rapid development of the art of flying, and of the science of designing and building aircraft. Aerobatics came into their own, partially because there was a market for them, and daring pilots were prepared to risk their necks to exploit it, but also because thought and experimentation had led to a closer understanding of the forces acting upon an aircraft in flight. Combined with sturdier airframes and reliable engines, this enabled daring pilots to try aerobatics with some degree of safety. There were, of course, accidents, but it was only because of the activities of pilots such as Pégoud that flying advanced rapidly past the 'chauffeur' attitude towards full mastery of the air.

There were many notable flights in 1913, particularly by French pilots across the Mediterranean and through Syria and Palestine to Egypt, but there seems to have been a presentiment of what was about to happen in 1914.

The advances made in the years before the world plunged into war are best made clear through a few statistics. Since 1909, the world speed record had improved from 77 km/h (47.85 mph) to 203.86 km/h (126.67 mph), the range record had risen from 234.3 km (145.59 miles) to 1021.23 km (634.54 miles) and the altitude record had increased from 452.93 m (1,486 ft) to 6120 m (20,079 ft). But these advances were about to be utterly outstripped-

Maurice Farman was the brother of Henry Farman and also a designer of aircraft. His most important design was the MF.7 that was dubbed the Longhorn by the British. First appearing in 1912, the MF.7 was a worthy if unexceptional aeroplane that was a valuable trainer in the years immediately preceding and following the outbreak of World War I.

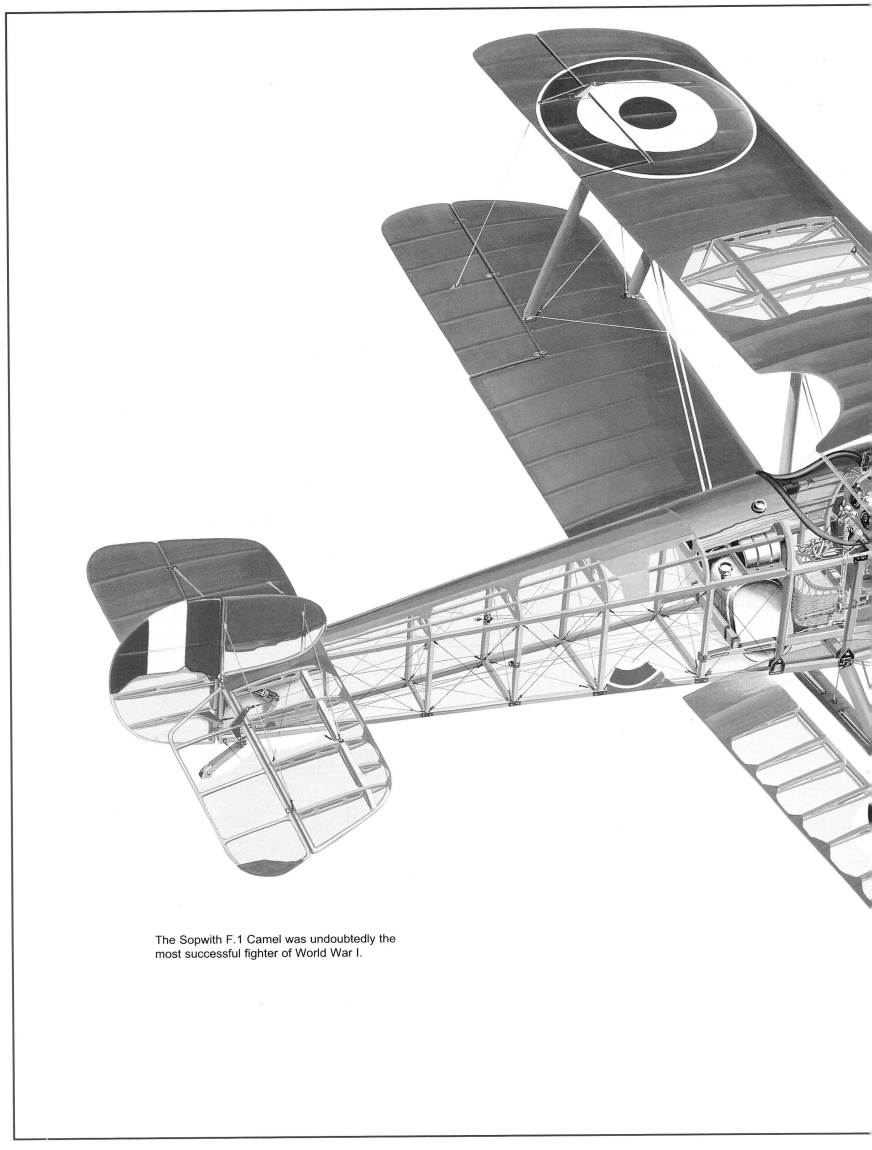

The Sopwith F.1 Camel was undoubtedly the
most successful fighter of World War I.

World War I: The Birth of Military Aviation

The widespread use of aircraft in World War I inevitably altered both the nature of aviation and public opinion about flight and fliers. Although aircraft had seen limited use as military weapons in the last few years before World War I, in 1914 most Europeans still considered flight to be the province of adventurous spirits who flew for sport and for excitement, without any real practical purpose. But by the end of the conflict aviation was very big business. Many thousands of aircraft and engines had been built in a multitude of factories, most of which had had no connection with aviation before the start of hostilities in August 1914. The air forces of the combatant nations, too, had grown into potent weapons of war, revealing to the far-sighted the potential that in World War II was to usher in the era of total war in which every man, woman and child, no matter how remote from the actual fighting front, was liable to attack.

Yet when the war started few foresaw what was about to happen, for the role of aircraft was still uncertain. Although experiments with armament, principally light machine-guns and small bombs, had been carried out before the war, general military enthusiasm for the concept of armed aircraft had been lukewarm at best. To a certain extent this was understandable as the already limited performance of most types of aircraft was seriously hampered by the addition of extra weight in the form of armament. Most generals could see little real scope for the employment of aircraft in war, and so neither could they see any purpose to be served by providing aircraft with armament to shoot at other aircraft serving in a similarly ill-defined role.

There were, however, some who realized what lay ahead. Captain Bertram Dickson, who was to die in 1913 of injuries sustained in a crash in Italy, was one such man. In 1911 he presented to the Committee of Imperial Defence an assessment of the likely role of aircraft in war, stating in part: 'In the case of a European war between two countries, both sides would be equipped with a large corps of aeroplanes, each trying to obtain information of the other, and to hide its own movements. The efforts which each would exert in order to hinder or prevent the enemy from obtaining information . . . would lead to the inevitable result of a war in the air, for the supremacy of the air, by armed aeroplanes against each other. This fight for the supremacy of the air in future wars will be of the first and greatest importance . . .' Dickson was to be proved entirely right by events.

But despite military authorities' refusal to study the benefits and disadvantages of aircraft with any insight, enthusiasts called for aircraft to take their place in the nations' armed forces. This pressure, combined with a desire not to allow any one country to take a lead in building an air force, eventually led the French, German, British and other European governments to sanction the introduction of aircraft into their military forces. Both France and Germany, the latter spurred on by the public air-mindedness engendered by the success of Ferdinand Graf von Zeppelin's great airships and the Kaiser's desire

Below: An observation type used in the early part of the war, the Aviatik B-type was designed before the outbreak of hostilities and reflected the German theory of 'chauffeur' piloting with the non-commissioned pilot located behind the commissioned observer, who was thus located in a position that hindered his fields of vision.

that his country be not outstripped in any technical way by France, soon led the field. Public indignation at this at last forced the British Government to spend more generously on their forces, and in 1913 more that £1,000,000 was allocated for the first time.

Thus the armed forces now had aircraft. But what were they to do with them? How best were the services to exploit these expensive machines and the equally expensive force of men to fly and maintain them? The only possible solution in the years immediately preceding World War I seemed to be reconnaissance of two types: firstly tactical or strategic

'[In 1910] the cavalry, in particular, were not friendly to the aeroplane, which, it was believed, would frighten the horses.' This attitude had altered little by the outbreak of war. Thus from the first, aircraft were somewhat unwelcome newcomers to the majority of conventional army officers, most of whom were also unaware of the other radical innovations made or about to be made by the weapons of modern technology: automatic weapons, efficient artillery, barbed wire, poison gas, the tank and the flamethrower.

The recruitment of pilots was relatively simple, as the new service offered a means of escape to junior officers not altogether happy with conventional regimental life. The aircraft squadrons were soon full, despite the fact that in the United Kingdom, at least, the pilots had at first to pay for their own flying training at one of the civilian flying schools that had sprung up in 1910 and 1911. Soon, however, the air forces themselves established flying schools, although these had at first to be staffed by civilian instructors.

The various military aircraft competitions held in 1911 and 1912 had been intended to produce types that could be standardized for the squadrons, thus easing procurement and maintenance problems. Yet it was one thing to select what was considered a type suitable for widespread use, and another to get it into 'mass production' and thus into widespread service. The aviation industry of the period was just not geared to mass production: most factories had experience only in the building of 'one-off' types for designers or in very limited production. The result, in military terms, was that chosen designs could not as yet be built in sufficient quantity and there could be little standardization of types within the squadrons.

reconnaissance for commanders, and secondly spotting for the artillery. In the former, it was hoped, a trained officer would be able to use the vantage point the aircraft gave him to observe and note down enemy dispositions and movements and then report them to his command. In the latter an officer could spot the fall of his battery's shot, and then issue corrections which could be delivered in a weighted container, by signalling with manoeuvres or, it was hoped, by radio once a suitably light transmitter had been developed. France and Germany, both of whom placed great reliance on artillery, were quick to adopt the role of artillery spotting for their air forces. The United Kingdom, however, still lagged behind technically and theoretically, despite the efforts of many junior officers, and until 1914 its air forces were seen as an unwanted supplement to the cavalry in the latter's traditional capacity as light reconnoitring forces. But, as was pointed out by Sir Walter Raleigh, the Royal Air Force's first official historian,

The Albatros D V was an evolutionary development of the D III intended to provide the German air arm with a fighter able to match the latest Allied equipment through refinement of an existing concept and installation of a more powerful engine.

In this respect the Germans and French were better off than the British. The Germans fielded a large number of

The Royal Aircraft Factory B.E.2 was designed before World War I with a large measure of inherent stability as an aid to safe flight, but this inhibited manoeuvrability and was therefore a major operational liability as the first fighters appeared in 1915.

Taube (dove) types derived from the experiments of Etrich and Wels, as well as units homogeneously equipped with tractor biplanes of Albatros and Aviatik design. The French had squadrons of Voisin bombers, and Blériots and Morane-Saulniers for reconnaissance work. The British, almost inevitably, went to war with several French aircraft plus a large miscellany of British types, the best of which were the Royal Aircraft Factory's Blériot Experimental (B.E.) 2, the Sopwith Tabloid, the Bristol Scout D and various marks of Avro Type 504. It is worth noting here that an odd system of nomenclature was used for Royal Aircraft Factory types. Forbidden to build aircraft so that it should not come into financial competition with the private aircraft industry, the factory resorted to a splendid ruse: allowed to repair damaged Royal Flying Corps machines, it in fact produced new types and claimed that these were merely extensive rebuilds and modifications of machines too severely damaged for conventional repair. The factory then produced a number of designs with prefixes such as B.E., F.E. (Farman Experimental), S.E. (Scouting Experimental) and R.E. (Reconnaissance Experimental). Eventually the factory got permission to build types, but by then the designations were so accepted that they were retained. Even after it had been allowed to build its designs, however, the factory's production capacity remained small, with the result that most Royal Aircraft Factory designs were built by private concerns under contract to the government.

During the first stages of the war when it finally broke out, the allied powers operated 233 aircraft (160 French and 73 British in France) against the Germans' total of 246. At first the weather was superb, but the aircraft had not been designed for intensive operations and their serviceability was low, a factor compounded by the number of different types and engines in service at a time when the Allies were in full retreat and all logistical backing was run on an extemporized basis. Yet somehow or other losses were tolerable, and from 19 August the RFC began to turn in useful reconnaissance reports. At first the high command was loathe to heed the information received from this novel source, but when British reconnaissance aircraft brought in the first news of the Germans' great left wheel to sweep down past the west side of Paris, and this information was subsequently confirmed by orthodox methods, the generals at last began to realize that in aircraft they had an important

new aid. The art of camouflage against air reconnaissance was as yet unknown, and so the observers of the 'recce-jobs' had an easy time and could turn in useful information.

It was very noticeable at this early period of the war that two entirely different styles of operational flying were in use. The Germans, on the one hand, believed that the important part of the mission, the observing, was the province of the officer, but that the aeroplane was merely his means of transport and could therefore be properly 'driven' by a non-commissioned officer. This 'chauffeur-mindedness' was hardly the best way to get the best out of machine or men, and Allied airmen were often amused by the antics of German aircrews, the officer of which could often be seen haranguing or belabouring his 'driver' for some misdemeanour. The British and French, on the other hand, believed that the pilot was as important as the observer, if not more so. The French used both NCO and officer crews from the beginning of the war, while the British preferred to entrust so valuable an item as an aeroplane only to an officer. The exigencies of the war soon led to a relaxation of the rule, however.

Although their primary tasks were reconnaissance and artillery spotting when the front was stable, the young and adventurous pilots of the day saw no reason why both sides should enjoy such benefits, when it might be possible to prevent the enemy from acquiring information by the apparently simple expedient of shooting at him and perhaps forcing him down. It was not long, therefore, before the first weapons made their appearance in the air. Initially these weapons consisted of personal equipment such as rifles and pistols. The resultant aerial duels stood little chance of inflicting mortal damage on either of the parties. More hopeful, or perhaps just less realistic, innovators tried shotguns, hand grenades, bricks and even grappling hooks on the end of lengths of cord, the last of which it was hoped would hit and destroy the enemy's propeller. Others again decided that zooming close to the enemy might cause the pilot's nerve to fail and so cause him to come down. In fact, this was the tactic used against the first aeroplane verifiably forced down in combat, when a German two-seater was brought down by the aerial antics of three pilots from No.2 Squadron, RFC, led by Lieutenant H. D. Harvey-Kelly on 25th August. On 13 August Harvey-Kelly had secured the distinction of being the first Briton to fly to the continent after the outbreak of war.

A cutaway artwork of the Albatros D Va reveals construction typical of World War I. The nicely streamlined oval-section fuselage was based on a frame of wooden formers and stringers covered in plywood for strength and durability, while the flying surface were of the standard fabric-covered largely wooden built-up construction. One of the type's major failings was its 'Vee-strutter' or sesquiplane wing cellule: the connection of the lower wing to the upper wing by a single-point attachment on each lower main spar meant that in a high-speed dive the lower wing could twist and not infrequently break away with fatal consequences.

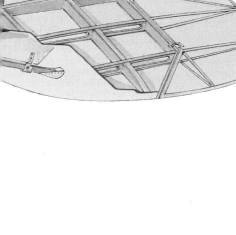

Although both the Germans and French had aircraft fitted with machine-guns at the beginning of the war, only one British aeroplane was so equipped, and even this was unofficial. The aeroplane was a Farman flown by 2nd Lieutenant L. A. Strange, with Lieutenant L. de C. Penn-Gaskell operating the Lewis light machine-gun. But, once loaded with the weight of the Lewis, the Farman could reach an altitude of only some 3,000 ft (915 m), while the German aircraft were some 2,000 ft (610 m) above them. The enterprising pair were soon ordered to remove the gun by their commanding officer, and told to get on with some useful reconnaissance work.

But it was only a matter of time before effective aerial armament began to take effect, and on 5 October a French gunner, Corporal Quénault, shot down an Aviatik two-seater with the Hotchkiss machine-gun mounted in the front of the nacelle of a Voisin bomber flown by Sergeant Joseph Frantz. From this time onwards the incidence of aerial combats, and also of aerial victories, began slowly to climb. But there remained one basic problem to be solved before air combat could reach a large scale, and this factor of interference between gun and propeller was not to be solved until 1915.

It had also occurred to various pilots early in the history of aviation that if one could fly over a target, then one could also drop missiles on it, and early in the war practical work on the development of bombing got under way. As early as 30 June 1910 the indefatigable Glenn Curtiss had dropped dummy bombs on the outline of a battleship buoyed out on Lake Keuka, New York. Bombing competitions, using bags of flour, had even become a popular feature of pre-war flying meetings. The French and Germans, particularly the former, were concerned with bombing from the beginning of the war. On 14 August the French sent two Voisins to attack the Zeppelin sheds at Metz-Frascaty, and on the 30th of the same month a German Taube dropped five small bombs on Paris, killing one civilian and injuring another two. The RFC was not at first especially interested in bombing, but its naval sister service, the Royal Naval Air Service, showed more enterprise, launching its first, and in the event abortive, raid on the Zeppelin sheds at Dusseldorf with two aircraft from Antwerp on 22 September. Another raid on the same target was launched on 8 October, and this time the Zeppelin Z.IX was destroyed.

Early bombs were extemporized affairs, usually based on an artillery shell with fins attached, and bombing sights

Left: The Voisin Type 8 was an indifferent French bomber that entered service late in 1916 when its basic concept was already outmoded.

Right: The Fokker Dr I triplane was directly inspired by a British fighter, the Sopwith Triplane, and was used by a number of aces who relished the combat advantages offered by the type's supreme agility. The Dr I's performance was not high, but the combination of low wing loading, compact overall dimensions and great structural strength conferred by the triplane wing cellule produced truly startling manoeuvrability.

Below: The rotary piston engine was largely responsible for making flight a practical reality in the period before and during World War. Offering a high power/weight ratio, the engine was based on a stationary crankshaft bolted to the airframe, and a rotating assembly of cylinders to which was attached the propeller. This is a Gnome-Rhône rotary of the type used in the first part of World War I.

were non-existent. Nevertheless the will was there, and in the autumn of 1914 the French decided to build up a major bombing force of Voisins, which were too slow and ponderous for air combat, but which had reasonable range and load-carrying capacity.

The problem that had hindered the development of true air fighting, that of the location of the machine-gun relative to the propeller, was easily solved on the older, pusher type of two-seaters. A light machine-gun, usually on a simple pillar mounting to allow easy traverse and elevation, was mounted at the front of the nacelle for the observer's use. Even on the newer tractor two-seaters, though the results were not particularly good, the observer could be provided with a light machine-gun capable of upward, rearward and lateral fire. The disadvantage of this latter system, however, was that the observer usually occupied the forward of the two seats so that the removal of his weight, on or near the aeroplane's centre of gravity, would not affect the trim of the machine on solo flights. This meant that the observer was located between the wings, which seriously curtailed his field of vision and of fire, surrounded as he was by a mass of rigging and bracing wires, many of which would be cut by bullets. One wag suggested that the way to test whether this mass of wires was intact was to place a small bird in the observer's position: if it escaped there must be a broken wire somewhere! This problem was especially acute on early models of the B.E.2, the standard British two-seater in the first period of the war. The matter was later reconsidered and improved by the reversing the positions of pilot and observer so that the observer had an improved field of fire over the aircraft's rear.

But although armament could be and was fitted to two-seaters from the earliest days of the war, two-seaters were not really suited to conversion into fighters, or

scouts as such aircraft were then designated. The two-seaters were too big, heavy, clumsy and slow. What was needed was a single-seater fighter, but tractor types were almost universal by 1915 and the problem of the position of the gun relative to the propeller became very difficult.

If the gun were fixed to fire forwards along the aeroplane's longitudinal axis and pilot's line of sight, some of the bullets fired would almost inevitably hit and damage one or more of the propeller blades. Various alternatives were tried, including the provision of guns angled out from the centreline of the aircraft by about 45° to miss the whirling propeller blades. But the sighting of such guns along such great deflection angles was so difficult as to make the expedient next to useless except for prodigiously capable men. One such was Captain Lanoe G. Hawker, the third British airman to be awarded the Victoria Cross. His award followed an occasion in July 1915 when he took on three German aircraft in one flight, forcing one down, sending the second the same way with a knocked-out engine and shooting the third down in flames, all in a Bristol Scout armed with an angled Lewis gun.

The only practical solution to the sighting problem was to fix the gun along the aeroplane's centreline, so that basically all the pilot had to do was aim his whole machine at the target and press the trigger. What was needed was a method of stopping the occasional bullet from striking the propeller blades. Experiments carried out before the war by Franz Schneider of the German LVG concern and Raymond Saulnier of the French Morane-Saulnier company had paved the way, with the invention of primitive interrupter gears which halted the action of the gun when there was a propeller blade in front of the muzzle. But both experimenters' efforts had foundered on the problem of hang-fire rounds. Here the fault lay with the manufacture of the primer and propellant for the ammunition: inconsistencies in the chemical compounds meant that occasionally bullets fired fractionally later than they should, obviating the work of the interrupter and shattering a blade. To preserve these expensive items, Saulnier had fitted the propellers he used for experiments with special steel deflectors, wedge-shaped items bolted to the back of the propeller blades in line with the gun to deflect any bullet that was heading for a blade.

The advent of war had curtailed these experiments in favour of immediate production.

Early in 1915 the idea was resurrected by Saulnier and the great pre-war stunt pilot Roland Garros, now serving with the French Aviation Militaire. Probably at the instigation of the headstrong Garros, it was soon decided by the two men that the actual interrupter gear should be omitted for the sake of lightness and simplicity, the few bullets that would hit a blade being warded off by the deflectors. Preliminary tests proved successful, and in March 1915 Garros returned to his unit with his modified Morane-Saulnier Type L parasol-wing scout. All was ready on 1 April 1915 and Garros set off in search of prey. He soon ran into four German Albatros two-seaters, which displayed no signs of fear or evasive action as the French scout closed in head-on, conventionally a safe angle. Then all of a sudden a stream of bullets flew out from the nose of the Type L and an Albatros plummeted down, its pilot dead at the controls. Before the astounded Germans could react, Garros had turned and fired at another Albatros, which immediately burst into flames and crashed. The remaining two Albatroses immediately fled, taking with them the first news of the arrival of the 'era of the true fighter aeroplane'.

German pilots, from the time of this success onwards, gave a wide berth to any Type L encountered, but in the next 17 days Garros managed to bag another three aircraft, thus becoming the world's first 'ace' fighter pilot. Although the Germans were mystified by this French success, the secret was soon to fall into their hands: on 19 April Garros was forced down behind the German lines as the result of an inevitable engine failure. In the course of almost three weeks of combat, the propeller blades of his aeroplane had been shaken many times as the deflectors forced away bullets, the consequent vibration being transmitted via the crankshaft to the already highly stressed 80-hp rotary engine. Some form of engine failure had to happen, and Garros was unlucky that the prevailing westerly wind gave him no chance of gliding back over the lines. He was captured before he could set fire to his aeroplane, and was bundled off to a prisoner of war camp. He managed to escape in January 1918 and returned to active service. Garros was not fated to survive the war, however, for on 5 October 1918 he was shot down in flames by a Fokker D VII.

Needless to say, the capture of this remarkable French aeroplane was a welcome surprise to the Germans, who immediately ordered Anthony Fokker, the enigmatic Dutch designer working for them, to copy the system on his M 5 Eindecker (monoplane) just introduced. Although a

Above: Seen here on a Morane-Saulnier Type N is the forward-firing machine gun arrangement that opened the way to the creation of the true fighter. In the absence of an effective gun interrupter system, the Morane-Saulnier company simply removed the interrupter but left on the rear of the propeller blades the wedge-shaped deflectors that prevented any bullet from hitting and fracturing the blades.

Below: The Bristol F.2B was the finest two-seat fighter of World War I, and combined good performance and agility with the extra 'sting' of a flexible machine gun.

brilliant test pilot, Fokker was at best a mediocre designer, a fact which he managed to disguise well by means of his forceful personality and brow-beating of subordinates. Reading his memoirs, one would think that on the way back to his factory at Schwerin, 200 miles (320 km) north of Berlin, Fokker himself decided not merely to copy the French idea, but to devise a proper interrupter gear so as to do away with the clumsy deflector plates. It is now clear, however, that the only part played by Fokker in the proceedings was to receive the order in Berlin. On his return to Schwerin he ordered his design team to work, and in 48 hours this able group of men had produced an efficient interrupter gear for the 7.92-mm (0.312-in) Parabellum machine-gun then in widespread use as the standard German aerial gun. (Early in 1916 the 7.92-mm/0.312-in MG 08/15 machine-gun made at Spandau near Berlin superseded the Parabellum as the standard fixed gun, hence the popular Allied misnomer of the gun as the 'Spandau'.) The Fokker interrupter, which was tested on an M 5k monoplane, redesignated E I when it entered service with armament, was very simple. Two cams on the crankshaft, exactly in line with the propeller blades, operated a pushrod which, via a mechanical linkage, prevented the gun from firing when there was a blade in front of the muzzle, regardless of whether or not the pilot's finger was on the trigger. Ordered by the German

authorities to test the design in combat himself, Fokker at first went along with the idea, but then allowed his discretion as a 'neutral' to get the better of his peremptorily ordered valour. The value of the package as a weapon, despite the mediocrity of the aeroplane in which it was installed, was nonetheless quickly realized and the type was rushed into production.

The new fighter entered service over the Western Front, and soon earned itself a fearsome reputation. Allied aircraft, which were mostly as agile and as fast as the German machine, could not cope with the technological advance of the interrupter-governed machine-gun, and for the first time in aerial warfare severe casualties began to accrue to the Allies. The press was quick to exploit the period as that of the 'Fokker Scourge', and a British Member of Parliament, Noel Pemberton-Billing (himself an aircraft designer of eccentric and spasmodic ability), soon dubbed the hapless Allied victims of the new fighter 'Fokker fodder'. The emotional controversy that resulted cast the first doubts on the way in which Allied aircraft were designed and procured, especially when no Allied counter to the Fokker was produced.

Over the front itself, the 'Fokker Scourge' was at first limited in its effect because the Germans had not evolved a tactical system to make full use of the type s impact. The E I, soon joined by the slightly larger and more powerful E II and E III, was issued to the Fliegerabteilungen (flight sections) on an ad hoc basis of one or two machines to each unit. Luckily for the Germans, prescient officers in the Bavarian air force, one of the several semi-autonomous national forces that made up the Imperial German Air Service, realized that better results would be gained by grouping into homogeneous units the presently scattered fighters. Thus was born the Kampfeinsitzerkommando (single-seater fighter unit), of which three were formed in the late summer of 1915.

The formation of these first fighter units brought prominence to two of World War I's earliest aces, Max Immelmann and Oswald Boelcke. Although represented in the German press as keen rivals in the shooting down of Allied aircraft, there seems to be little real proof of this, the two frequently co-operating until Boelcke was posted further south. Immelmann, dubbed the 'Eagle of Lille' by the press, is remembered in aviation history for the Immelmann turn named after him. This manoeuvre, intended to place the attacker once again in an advantageous position after a firing pass, consists of a half-loop followed by a half-roll immediately after breaking off the attack, the whole manoeuvre putting the attacker higher than his victim and flying in the opposite direction, from where he could either make another pass or look for new

One of the aces who flew the Fokker Dr I was Leutnant Werner Voss, whose aeroplane had a distinctive face painted on its nose. Voss ranked fourth in the list of German aces in World War I, and scored 48 victories.

propeller. The British introduced the Airco (de Havilland) D.H2, a neat pusher biplane with a Lewis gun mounted at the front of the one-man nacelle. The Bébé first achieved prominence over Verdun with Les Cigognes, an elite French formation that was basically an adaptation and expansion of Boelcke's ideas. The British, whose air forces in France were commanded by Brigadier-General Hugh Trenchard, considered it unwise to group all the best pilots into a few squadrons, leaving the majority of the squadrons to cope with mediocre and poor pilots, but instead tended to build up each fighter unit round a few pilots of excellent capabilities in the hope and expectation that their skills would rub off on the other pilots. This system in fact proved the most satisfactory of all.

After the initial period in which he had allowed his inclinations towards squadrons equipped with homogeneous aircraft to be overruled by his subordinates' desire for a mixture of types, Major-General Sir David Henderson, the RFC's first commander in France, had seen the formation of the first homogeneous squadron in July 1915, when a squadron of Vickers F.B.5 'Gunbus' two-seat fighters entered combat. This policy was now continued by Trenchard, and the first D.H.2 unit, No.24 Squadron, arrived in France in February 1916 under the command of the redoubtable Major Lanoe G. Hawker. The early British objections to homogeneous squadrons had been based on the notion that the RFC's real work was observation, reconnaissance and photographic work, so each squadron should be equipped with types suitable for such work. When the overwhelming desirability of fighter aircraft for protection became apparent, most junior commanders were of the opinion that each squadron should have a few fighters that could be sent out with the squadron's two-seaters. The high-intensity offensive operations insisted upon by Trenchard throughout the 'Fokker Scourge' had killed any lingering beliefs in this system, and the British were now wholehearted supporters of the homogeneous squadron.

Side by side, the D.H.2s and Nieuport Type 11s of the RFC and Aviation Militaire gradually wrested command of the air from the Germans, first allowing their own two-seaters to work more effectively against the German land forces, and their taking the air war effectively to the Germans, driving the latters' observation machines virtually from the air. The 'Fokker Scourge' was defeated by April, and the Allies quickly exploited their command of the air by pushing several new types into action in the second half of the year. At least interrupter gears were making a widespread appearance on the Allied side, on such excellent types as the Nieuport Type17 and SPAD S.7, both French, and the British Sopwith 1-Strutter and Sopwith Pup. All four aircraft were fitted with a fixed, forward-firing, 0.303-in (7.7-mm) Vickers gun, and the 1-Strutter, so named for its single sets of interplane struts and 'half' struts supporting the centre section, also had a Lewis gun for the observer. Much to the annoyance of RFC officialdom, the Pup received its nickname from its scaled-down family likeness to the 1-Strutter, and despite strenuous efforts to

victims. Immelmann was a 'loner' who reached a score of 15 victories before he fell to the gunner of a British F.E.2b in June 1916.

Boelcke is an altogether more important figure, one of the seminal influences in the development of combat flying and organization. Like Immelmann he was a successful individual pilot, but unlike this other early German ace Boelcke swiftly realized that he could be of greater importance than he would be simply as an ace, if he analysed the reasons for his successes and failures and imparted them to his fellow pilots. So good was he at this that he was given command of Jagdstaffel Nr 2 (2nd Fighter Squadron) when these larger units were formed, principally as a result of Boelcke's work, in August 1916. But Boelcke was not to live long to see the fruits of his labours, for after scoring the remarkable total of 40 victories by this early stage of the air war, he lost his life in October 1916. He was to the last undefeated in the air, and was killed when he and a colleague swerved to avoid colliding with a British aeroplane: the wheels of his comrade's aeroplane ripped open the top wing of the great German ace's Albatros fighter, which spun out of control to the ground below. It is hard to overestimate Boelcke's importance. He led by classic example, but his analytical teaching methods meant that no longer would pilots merely close in on the enemy from any angle before opening fire. Now they attempted to stalk their prey from a higher altitude or from 'up-sun' position, and then swooped down to deliver the killing burst before retiring to safety again.

The Fokkers ruled supreme in the autumn and winter of 1915, with the Allies apparently loathe to copy the German interrupter gear. Instead a variety of expedients were tried, with the result that the inferior German fighters continued to dominate the skies during the crucial early stages of the Battle of Verdun, that military and emotional bastion of France where the Germans had determined to 'bleed France white'.

But at last, in the spring of 1916, the Allies began to make headway, albeit still without an interrupter gear. The French produced the delightful Nieuport Type 11 Bébé (baby) sesquiplane, with a Lewis gun firing over the top wing to clear the upper arc of the disc swept by the

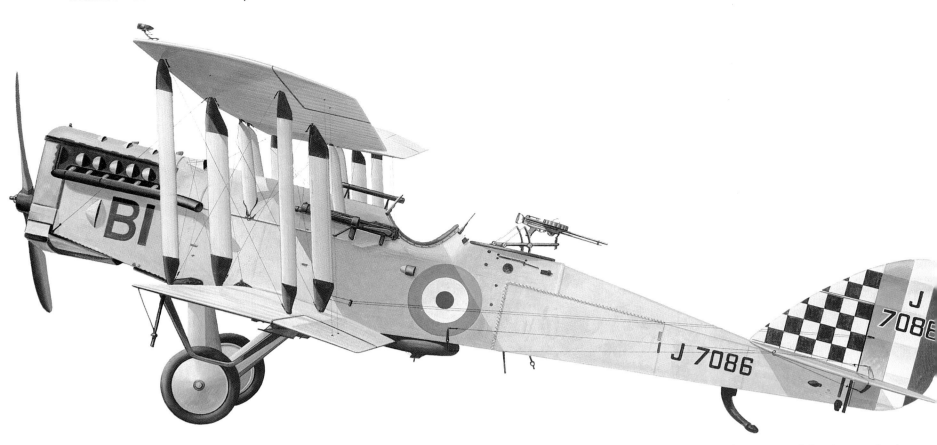

Above: The Airco D.H.9A was the definitive member of the light bomber family that started with the D.H.4. The D.H.4 had excellent performance but was tactically hampered by the separation of its two crew members by the fuel tank, the D.H.9 introduced a revised fuselage accommodating the two crew members close together but was underpowered, and the D.H.9A raised performance once more by the introduction of a more powerful engine.

Below: The AEG G IV was one of Germany most important bombers of World War I, and was an evolutionary development from the earlier AEG bombers with greater power, increased bomb load, and balanced control surfaces to improve handling.

dissuade pilots from using the nickname, 'Pup' stuck and the authorities were at last forced to accept it as official. The Pup was in many respects the first adequate fighter. Its performance was excellent, it had a fixed machine-gun with interrupter gear, and its agility was phenomenal. Unlike many other aircraft, however, the Pup's manoeuvrability was not secured at the expense of other factors, and the type lives in the memory of those who have flown it as one of the most tractable and delightful aircraft ever built. Its control response was smooth, clean and swift, allowing the pilot to place his machine exactly as he wished.

Despite the arrival of new aircraft, and despite the clear ascendancy over the German air force enjoyed by the Allies during the summer and autumn of 1916, these were not happy times for the pilots and observers of the RFC and Aviation Militaire. The terrible battle for Verdun had been followed almost immediately by the equally ghastly Battle of the Somme, and Allied aircrews had been operating at full stretch over these two sectors for over six months. Whereas the 'Fokker Scourge' had taxed the Allies mostly in a technological sense, the intensity of air operations in 1916 taxed them both technologically and in morale. For weeks on end, until they collapsed, were wounded or killed, pilots

rose at dawn and during the course of the day put in three or more patrols each of 90 minutes or more. The first of these patrols might consist of a high-altitude close-escort job at 12,000 to 15,000 ft (3660 to 4570 m) for a photo-reconnaissance aircraft working over the German front line and the areas immediately behind it. Here anti-aircraft fire, or 'Archie' as it was called in the RFC, was a constant inducement to keep as high as possible, and there was always the threat of German fighters coming out of the rising sun in the east.

After the aircraft had been refuelled and rearmed, the late morning patrol might consist of an offensive patrol over the German lines. Trenchard was particularly concerned that the war be taken to the Germans, and this meant that British pilots usually operated on the other side of the lines, harrying German two-seaters such as the Albatros C VII and LFG (Roland) C II entering service in the second half of 1916. The purpose was to prevent German single-seaters from reaching the Allied side of the lines, where artillery-spotting aircraft and balloons were playing their part in bringing down a holocaust of Allied artillery fire on the German trench lines. These offensive patrols proved very costly to the British, but Trenchard rightly insisted that they be kept up to relieve pressure on the more important two-seaters. Operating on the German side of the lines was doubly difficult for the RFC. Firstly, ground observers could see where the British aircraft were operating, thus allowing the Germans to send up the right numbers of aircraft to intercept. The German interceptors could then climb to secure the advantage of altitude and get up-sun from the Allied fighters. Secondly, damaged aircraft, or aircraft with the engine trouble that was so prevalent in these early types, were faced with the long haul back over their own lines against the prevailing west wind-many aircraft might just have got home but for the wind. Other aircraft had lost so much altitude by the time they reached the lines that they could be finally dispatched by machine-gun and rifle fire from the ground, crashing in no-man's land between the lines and immediately being shelled by the enemy's artillery.

The third type of patrol might be undertaken late in the afternoon. This was the contact patrol instituted in the opening stages of the Battle of the Somme. Commanders, who all too frequently lost touch with their attacking ground forces almost immediately after the initial assault had gone in, were desperate to find out how far their forces had advanced, and then to help them with artillery fire. But radio sets of the period were too heavy to be carried into battle, telephone lines were very often cut by enemy

totally unsuited to combat conditions where they had to fly machines few of them had ever seen before reaching their squadrons. The life expectancy of these innocents was in the region of minutes rather than hours. Even experienced pilots could expect a combat life of only a few weeks. With most of their attention devoted to the problems of flying and keeping in formation with their unit commanders, these green pilots were easy prey for the elite German pilots, many of whom began to run up high victory tallies. The burden on the Allied pilots was enormous. Novice pilots were already half defeated by their fear before they took off for their first combat patrol, and the survivors were demoralized by the continuous stream of losses and replacements. The pressure on the survivors, moreover, was increased by their natural desire to minimize losses by aiding the inexperienced in combat.

The real culprit here was the totally inadequate system of training used by the RFC. Appalled by the losses suffered as a result of this failing, Robert Smith Barry took it upon himself to reform the system. Smith Barry remains a shadowy figure to this day, but there can be little doubting Trenchard's assessment that he was 'the man who taught the world to fly'. An eccentric, gifted man, Smith Barry had learned to fly in the great days before World War I, and had also devoted very considerable thought to the nature and problems of flight. After badgering Trenchard on the

The Gotha G V was the primary twin-engined bomber operated by the Germans for longer-range missions, and could carry up to 500 kg (1,102 lb) of bombs on sorties lasting up to 5 hours 30 minutes. There were single defensive machine guns in the nose and dorsal positions.

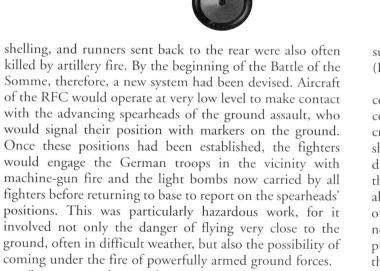

shelling, and runners sent back to the rear were also often killed by artillery fire. By the beginning of the Battle of the Somme, therefore, a new system had been devised. Aircraft of the RFC would operate at very low level to make contact with the advancing spearheads of the ground assault, who would signal their position with markers on the ground. Once these positions had been established, the fighters would engage the German troops in the vicinity with machine-gun fire and the light bombs now carried by all fighters before returning to base to report on the spearheads' positions. This was particularly hazardous work, for it involved not only the danger of flying very close to the ground, often in difficult weather, but also the possibility of coming under the fire of powerfully armed ground forces.

So great was the casualty rate in the opening weeks of this sustained campaign that replacements to hand in France were insufficient, and the training schools in Britain were called upon to send out pilots who had barely finished their training.

These green pilots were trained in a haphazard system on old machines such as the Maurice Farman M.F.7 'Longhorn' and M.F.11 'Shorthorn' and by pilots who were considered unsuitable for front-line duties or who were waiting to return to the front. They were usually capable of just managing to fly their training machines, and were

subject of training, Smith Barry was at last given No.1 (Reserve) squadron at Gosport with which to experiment.

The system already in operation used aircraft considered too old for other purposes and any officers who could be found as instructors. Teaching methods were crude: the pupil sat behind the instructor, reaching over his shoulders to rest his hand on the control column and duplicating the instructor's movements until he was thought to have learned enough, parrot-fashion, to be allowed to fly solo. If the pupil survived this, he advanced onto faster types, receiving any instruction thought to be necessary while still on the ground. During his training, the pupil might have several instructors as each was posted to the front or other 'more important' duties. Smith Barry's system, on the other hand, was simple and comprehensive. He used good aircraft and full-time skilled instructors to teach pupils who had already had background training. The machines were fitted with dual controls so that the pupil might sit in the pilot's seat with the instructor behind him. The aeroplane Smith Barry selected as the ideal training aircraft was the Type 504, already four years old as a design when Smith Barry's system got under way in 1917. 'Gosport tubes' were installed between the two cockpits so that the pupil and his instructor could speak to each other in the air, a radical innovation at the time. Results were

Above: The Rumpler C II was typical of the German air arm's C-series armed biplanes, which were general-purpose machines used mainly for armed reconnaissance and artillery spotting.

the RFC, is that no one had previously thought it necessary to rationalize and standardize flying training, so that pilots might be tested according to established methods laid down in training manuals. Yet when it was decided that some such system was necessary, Smith Barry came up with the right solution almost immediately without any fuss and with little prior experimentation; it was essentially a very simple idea.

It is indicative of Smith Barry's genius that the aeroplane he settled upon as the right training aircraft was the Type 504. Fitted with a variety of rotary engines, this was an admirable machine without vices, yet possessed of full aerobatic capabilities and reasonable performance. The type remained in Royal Air Force service until 1933, so suitable for the training role was it. Once he had learned to fly adequately on this first-class machine, the trainee pilot could then safely be entrusted with one of the advanced combat types used by the air fighting and gunnery schools attended by all combat pilots before they were posted to the front.

Towards the end of 1916 the inexorable see-saw of technological advance over the front had swung the balance in favour of Germany once again. Realizing that the Allies would produce a counter to the Eindecker by the middle of 1916, the Germans had set about developing a new generation of aircraft late in 1915. By the last months of 1916 these were beginning to enter the fray for the Deutsche Luftstreitkrafte or German air force, formed in October 1916 from the earlier hotchpotch of flying units. At the heart of this resurgence in German air superiority was the series of Albatros single-seat fighters, starting with the D I, II and Ill, the last of which entered service early in 1917. These sleek, shark-like biplanes with their plywood fuselages and well-cowled engines were capable of very good performance. Most importantly of all, however, they were armed with two machine-guns, and in the spring of 1917 this gave them twice the firepower of Allied types.

immediately impressive, not only in basic flying skills, which the pupils picked up quickly with the aid of good aircraft and instructors, but also in aerobatics, at the time discouraged as flamboyant and dangerous by the RFC authorities. Smith Barry, however, encouraged all his command, instructors and pupils alike, to fly as much as possible and to practise aerobatics for enjoyment. This produced a great increase in skills and command in the air, invaluable combat aids in France.

The Gosport system was soon adopted throughout the RFC and it is now, mutatis mutandis, the basis of the flying training used by almost every air force in the world. The flying world's debt to Smith Barry is very great, but what is most remarkable, especially in a 'hierarchical' force such as

Above and right: The Handley Page O/400 was the best British heavy bomber of World War I, and resulted from a naval request for a 'bloody paralyser' of a bomber. The type could carry up to 2,000 lb (907 kg) of bombs on sorties lasting as long as 8 hours.

The immediate consequence of the arrival of these new German fighters was total command of the air, and what became known in the RFC as 'Bloody April', when the British suffered losses in aircrews and aircraft of some 30 per cent, their highest losses of the entire war. Most tragic of all, from the long-term point of view, was the loss of many of the survivors of the previous year's hard times. With these men went most of the practical experience in how to fight an air war so crucial in helping the new pilots. Smith Barry's training programme had not yet begun to yield useful new pilots and the men posted straight from flying school to the front were shot down in droves by the 'Albatri' or 'Vee-strutters' as they were known in the slang of the RFC. The life expectancy of RFC subalterns on the Western Front in the 'Bloody April' period was between 11 days and three weeks. Bearing in mind that experienced pilots stood considerably more chance of survival, the life expectancy of new arrivals must have been a matter of hours, or at best days. Losses were almost inevitable for the RFC as Trenchard still insisted on offensive patrols and aggressive work even by two-seaters, most of which were by now the newer Armstrong Whitworth F.K.8 and Royal Aircraft Factory R.E.8. Both of these were large biplanes, and the R.E.8 had acquired an unenviable reputation as a 'deathtrap', largely undeserved. The fault really lay with the tactical employment of the type, in steady artillery spotting work, where it was particularly vulnerable to German fighter attack.

Combined with the superiority of the new generation of German fighters, the RFC's offensive tactics served to take 'trade' to the Germans, who were quite content to wait on their own side of the lines. It was the Allies who were attempting to use their strategic initiative at the time, so the German tactics were quite correct. It can be said that the aggressive British tactics, too, were basically correct despite the enormous losses entailed. Throughout the war, on the other hand, the French kept a much lower profile, like the Germans restricting the amount of offensive work done by fighters. Instead they concentrated on offensive work by reconnaissance, spotter and bomber aircraft, which could more profitably take the war to the Germans. The fighters were on the whole used to escort offensive machines, and to prevent incursions by German aircraft into French airspace.

There was also another way in which French tactics

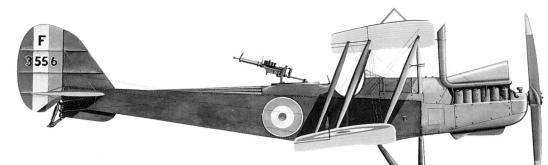

Above: Much maligned during and after World War I as a wholly indifferent aeroplane, the Royal Aircraft Factory R.E.8 was nonetheless a highly effective tactical reconnaissance and artillery spotting type whose high losses reflected the especially dangerous nature of its role rather than any inherent failing of the design.

resembled those of the Germans. Whereas the British kept squadrons posted along the length of the front, only reinforcing sectors under real threat or where a major offensive was to go in, the French and Germans instead based their air defence on a smaller number of élite units. These were used as 'fire brigades', being shuttled about from area to area as the local situation demanded. The French 'fire brigade', called Les Cigognes (the storks), was a group of fighter squadrons that varied in number considerably from period to period, but which always enjoyed priority in the receipt of the latest equipment and the best pilots. After early teething problems, the Lafayette Escadrille of Americans fighting for the French began to enjoy much the same reputation and priorities. This proved particularly important for the Americans, for when their country entered the war in April 1917 they were returned to their own national air force where they were able to bring a considerable leavening of combat experience to the otherwise totally raw crews of the American Expeditionary Force of 1918.

On the German side, the Jagdstaffeln filled a similar, if smaller, position to that held by Les Cigognes in the first half of 1917. But in June of that year a reorganization led to the formation of Jagdgeschwader Nr I (1st Fighter Wing) under the command of the redoubtable Rittmeister Manfred, Freiherr von Richthofen. The Jagdgeschwader was made up of four Jastas, as the Jagdstaffeln were usually abbreviated, and soon became known to the Allies as the 'Richthofen Circus' for the gaudy colouring of its aircraft. With a few notable exceptions, such as Charles Nungesser, the third ranking French ace with 45 victories who decorated his aeroplane with such emblems of death as coffins, skull and crossbones and funereal candles, the Allies were strict in their refusal to allow personal markings to prevail over officially ordained markings and camouflage systems. The Germans, on the other hand, allowed

Often known as the 'Star-strutter' because of its unusual and distinctive interplane bracing, the Hansa-Brandenburg D I was of German designed but built and operated by Austria-Hungary.

Below: The Caproni Ca 3 was the most important Italian heavy bomber of World War I, and could carry up to 1,000 lb (454 kg) of bombs on sorties lasting up to 3 hours 30 minutes. The powerplant comprised three inline piston engines, two of them disposed as tractor units at the front of the booms supporting the tail unit, and the third as a pusher unit at the rear of the central nacelle with a defensive machine gun above it.

considerable latitude in this matter, with the result that the more successful and flamboyant aces sported the most bizarre colour schemes of aviation history. The best known of these, and the most frequently misrepresented, was the basically red scheme of von Richthofen, leading to his epithet 'The Red Baron' in the popular press. Discovering that his eleventh victim had been the celebrated British ace Lanoe Hawker, Richthofen celebrated by having his Albatros painted blood red overall. On later machines the colour scheme was altered to a predominantly red finish.

In terms of confirmed victories von Richthofen was the most successful fighter pilot of World War I, with 80 'kills'. A protégé of Boelcke, Richthofen was a regular army officer of Silesian landed descent, and had at first shown little ability in combat or as a pilot. He achieved his first victory in September 1916, and then moved from strength to strength, his flying displaying the upmost aggression combined with superb shooting. Like many other pilots of World War I, von Richthofen was a loner in his attacks, and contributed little to the science of air fighting. A morbid man who awarded himself little silver cups for his victories and tried to secure souvenirs from each of his victims where possible, von Richthofen was a fighter ace whose chief importance was as an example to others and as a potent instrument of morale at home, where he was lionized by the press, the authorities and society. As in the case of so many pilots, the exact cause of von Richthofen's death on 21 April 1918 is uncertain, credit for it having been claimed both by

a Canadian pilot and by an Australian machine-gunner firing from the ground.

Von Richthofen's only serious contestants for the title of the greatest ace of World War I are the British ace, Edward 'Mick' Mannock with 73 victories, and the Frenchman René Fonck with 75 victories. Although little recognized until after the end of the war, when the award of the Victoria Cross to him was gazetted, Mannock was an important figure in the history of air fighting. Repatriated by Turkey when that country entered the war in November 1914, Mannock managed to get into the RFC despite astigmatism in one eye. Possessed of an intense hatred of the Germans, Mannock remarked on hearing of von Richthofen's death, when others were talking of the death of a gallant opponent, 'I hope he burns in hell!' An excellent pilot and shot in his own right, Mannock's real importance lies in his altruistic approach to combat flying, especially at the flight and squadron level. He analysed previous lessons carefully, and always briefed his pilots comprehensively before setting out on a patrol. He was especially solicitous of new pilots, often setting up 'kills' for them and then letting them finish off the aeroplane he had himself crippled. If Boelcke was the father of the theory of air fighting, Mannock was the pilot who brought the art of patrol flying to its peak during World War I. Mannock's real victory tally must have been well over 100 aircraft when account is taken of the victories he credited to novices, or set up for inexperienced pilots.

There is little doubt that Fonck was the greatest fighter pilot of World War I, however. A loner among loners, his

losses in machines and comrades, and the increasing impersonality of the air war were leading to attitudes in which the best that could be said of the enemy was that he was a fellow sufferer, and the worst that he was a barbarian: the latter was very much Mannock's attitude.

The second quarter of 1917 found both sides exhausted by 'Bloody April', the only success of which had been, from the British point of view, the success of the handful of Sopwith Triplanes, or 'Tripehounds' as they were nicknamed, operated by the Royal Naval Air Service. Although armed with only one machine-gun, these were clean aircraft that could combat the 'Albatri' by means of their remarkable rate of climb and their general agility, both functions of the large wing area contained within the small overall dimensions of a triplane layout. So impressed were the Germans that orders for triplane designs were immediately issued. The type ordered into production was the Fokker Dr I, the aeroplane flown by von Richthofen at the time of his death. Although very manoeuvrable, the Dr I in fact appeared after the epoch of the triplane, and lacked the performance to make it a fighter suitable for any but the most experienced of pilots.

Yet there was some hope on the horizon for the Allies during 'Bloody April', in the form of new aircraft types. First to arrive, late in April, was the Royal Aircraft Factory S.E.5. This, and its higher-powered S.E.5a variant, introduced two-gun armament to Allied fighters and thus equalled the firepower of German types, at the same time improving upon their performance. The ruggedness and steadiness of the S.E.5, which did not have the inherent stability of the B.E.2 series, made it an excellent combat

Above: This cutaway artwork reveals the major structural features of the Caproni Ca 2 bomber.

Below: The LFG (ROland) C II was an impressive armed two-seater with plank-type interplane struts and a deep oval-section fuselage that completely filled the interplane gap. The aeroplane was nicknamed Walfisch (whale) in German service.

Bottom: The Caudron R.11 was an elegant three-seater flown by the French air service in the bomber, reconnaissance and escort fighter roles.

tally was in all probability well over 120, but his individual successes often came in areas where no confirmation was possible. A cold figure, not particularly liked by his fellows, Fonck was a supreme marksman, practising on the ground with any weapon he could find, and constantly adjusting and improving the armament of his fighter. Fonck often returned to base with so few rounds fired that no one would believe his claims until confirmation came in. He was a master of deflection shooting, closing in on his prey until he could place the few rounds necessary 'as if by hand', in his own words. Fonck survived the war, but Mannock was killed by an unknown German infantryman who put a bullet through his heart on 26 July 1918.

By the 'Bloody April' of 1917 air combats had grown into massive affairs of up to 100 aircraft or more, a far cry from the individual combats of 1915 and early 1916. The skies over the Western Front were now dominated by huge, swirling dog-fights impossible to follow from the ground except when a crippled machine staggered out of the fray out of control or an aeroplane which had taken a bullet in the unprotected fuel system plunged down like a fiery comet, trailing flame and black oily smoke until it crashed into the ground and exploded.

There were still loners, however, such as the introspective British ace Albert Ball who was the first man to receive wide coverage in the English press, and the frail-looking Frenchman Georges Guynemer, the darling of French propaganda. These men delighted in stalking their prey through cloud and in the blind angle of the sun, but their style made out of date by the use of mass tactics where weight of numbers and skills learned in training counted more than personal genius. Air combat was at this time rapidly becoming more and more frantic. The feeling of chivalry that had dominated the early stages of the war was fading; the horrors of the ground war, the appalling

type, probably the best gun platform of the war. Oddly enough, at a time when other two-gun types were appearing with twin interrupted Vickers guns, the S.E.5/5a had only a single Vickers gun in the forward fuselage, the other gun being an uninterrupted Lewis firing over the top wing. Unfortunately, this gun had to be pulled back

Right: Production line methods were not very advanced in World War I, but nonetheless managed to ensure the delivery of large numbers of aircraft.

Below: The Australian crew of a Royal Aircraft Factory R.E.8 prepare to depart on a nocturnal mission. Such a sortie was not unduly dangerous in clear weather conditions, but a change of weather once the aeroplane was airborne could be disastrous as there were no blind-flying instruments.

along a quadrant to bring the breech within reach of the pilot so that he could change the ammunition drum when necessary. It is hard to see why this clumsy arrangement was continued: the idea was originally invented to allow Allied fighters to have a fixed forward-firing gun before the invention of an interrupter gear. The only novel use of this arrangement had been by Ball, whose favourite tactic was to close up underneath and slightly behind his unsuspecting opponent, pull back the gun so that it fired upwards and forwards at 45∞, and dispatch the German at point-blank range. Late in May the S.E.5 was joined by the French SPAD S.13, an improved version of the S.7 with more power and two guns. Fast and rugged, the S.13 was the best French fighter of the war, and was also used extensively by the Italians and Americans.

Both the S.E.5 and S.13 were fitted with powerful inline engines, but the third new Allied fighter that brought about the eclipse of the German air force in the middle of 1917 was the ultimate expression of the classic rotary-engined design philosophy. This was the Sopwith Camel, which appeared in July 1917. Bearing a strong resemblance to the Pup, the Camel lacked the earlier type's lightness of appearance, featuring instead a slightly squat, pugnacious belligerence emphasized by the 'hump' over the breeches of the twin Vickers guns that led to the type's nickname, later officially adopted. With the propeller, engine, fuel, oil, guns, ammunition and pilot all squeezed into the front 7 ft (2.13 m) of the fuselage, where their inertia would least interfere with manoeuvrability, the Camel was supremely agile, especially in right-hand turns, where the torque of the rotary complemented the turning moment of rudder and ailerons. The Camel's only fault was the result of this compactness and the torque of the rotary: pilots unused to the new fighter were liable to allow the turn to become a spin, which at low altitudes was often a fatal mistake. In the hands of a skilled pilot, however, the Camel was a superlative fighter, and the type accounted for a credited 1,294 enemy aircraft before the end of the war, though its real total was considerably higher as revealed by later research.

The fourth fighter to end German dominance of the air, a role it played for the rest of the war, was the Bristol F.2B Fighter which entered service in the summer of 1917. Originally intended as a standard two-seater to supplement the RFC's F.K.8s and R.E.8s, the F.2A version of the aircraft, which had entered service in April 1917, had sustained a rough baptism of fire at the hands of Richthofen's Jagdgeschwader Nr I, four of six F.2As failing to return. But pilots soon realized what a machine they had in the Fighter, with the performance and agility of a single-seater combined with the 'sting in the tail' of the two-seater. Once this lesson had been absorbed and the implications worked out, the Fighter became a formidable weapon.

The Germans were taken slightly unawares by the arrival of these latest Allied aircraft, and were slow to respond. Firstly a new version of the Albatros appeared, the D V and D Va, with improved aerodynamics and a more powerful engine, but this machine proved entirely incapable of wresting from the Allies the superiority they enjoyed by the summer of 1917. Urgent requests for improved types were sent out, and in January 1918 the Fokker D VII was selected for quantity production. This was the war's best fighter, and the acme of the designs of Reinhold Platz, Fokker's chief designer. Originally employed as a welder in the factory, Platz had shown a great intuitive flair for structures and aerodynamics, and had been made chief designer. Perhaps more important than these other qualifications for the job, Platz was a reticent man who would allow Fokker himself to claim credit for the designs. The hallmarks of Platz's designs were simplicity and strength: welded steel tube fuselages allied to wings of wooden construction but great depth, allowing massive box structures to be used for strength, at a time when other designers preferred very thin sections that required masses of internal and external bracing by struts and wires. Platz's designs had the elegance of simplicity, and his three most celebrated designs, the Dr I triplane, the D VII biplane and the D VIII parasol monoplane which entered service only at the end of the war, were all excellent flying machines. The D VII, in particular, was feared by Allied pilots, and was the only aeroplane to be singled out by name to be surrendered in the armistice agreement of 1918. With an excellent BMW engine, the D VII had outstanding high-altitude qualities, including the ability to hang on its propeller and fire upwards where Allied types would have stalled and spun. Luckily for the Allies, the Germans were unable to rush these new types of

the Balkans and the various Middle Eastern areas in which the British and Turks faced each other. On all these fronts, with the possible exception of the Italian one, air operations followed the pattern set over the Western Front, using aircraft 'handed down' after reaching obsolescence in the West. But although the nature of air operations in other theatres followed the lead of the Western Front, each made its own demands on men and machines, principally for geographic reasons. Thus, while such operations may have lacked the intensity of air fighting over France, for those involved they were just as strenuous and dangerous. On the Eastern Front, for example, the Russians, Germans and Austro-Hungarians had to contend with blazing summers and bitter winters, as well as having to cover vast areas. In the Balkans airmen had to operate over very inhospitable and mountainous country from primitive airfields in climatic conditions similar to those of the Eastern Front. In the Middle East, where yet again it was the Germans who proved the Allies most formidable adversaries, problems of dust, extreme heat and lack of water had to be overcome.

Of the subsidiary theatres, only the Italian Front found a pattern of its own. Both the Italian and Austria-Hungarian air industries were ill prepared for war when their conflict started in 1915, but both were soon swept up into a small-scale version of the Western Front. But although numbers were fewer, the intensity of operations was not, and soon the Italians and AustroHungarians were locked in a technical and tactical battle for superiority, with the Germans taking a hand later in the war. The greatest innovation on the Italian Front, however, was the early development and use of 'strategic' bombers by the Italians. Here they foreshadowed what was to happen in the air war between Germany and the United Kingdom. And in one other aspect, operations from water, the Italians and Austrians introduced new ideas: faced with a relative paucity of sites for airfields, both sides made considerable use of the natural airfields' provided by lakes and by the Adriatic for operations by flying-boat fighter and

fighter into service in sufficient numbers to prevent the British, French, American and Belgian fighter forces from exercizing almost total command of the air from the spring of 1918 onwards, allowing the other elements of the Allied air forces to get on with their work almost unhampered.

The Americans and Belgians during this period used in their front-line squadrons only aircraft of British and French design. The Americans in particular had failed to keep up with the rapid strides in aviation technology in the years between 1914 and 1917. They did, however, produce the 400-hp Packard Liberty engine which saw some service in 1918 despite persistent teething problems, and this engine would have played a great part in the fortunes of the Allies had the war gone on into 1919.

The Western Front was not, of course, the only theatre of war to see air operations in World War I. Yet the activities and types of aircraft used over the Western Front set the style for other theatres including the Eastern Front, Italy,

reconnaissance machines.

Unglamorous and unglamourized, it was in fact the work of machines other than the fighters which was of primary importance in World War I. Artillery spotters and photo-reconnaissance aircraft shared all the dangers of the fighters, indeed more than most, yet received little popular acclaim, the civilians at home preferring to read of the actions of dashing 'scout' pilots. Yet the fighters were only there to protect their own two-seaters and bombers, and to prevent the enemy's machines from acting freely.

Because they had to carry at least two men, armament and their specialized equipment, artillery spotter and reconnaissance aircraft were usually heavy and fairly clumsy. And because they needed to be able to fly steadily for lengthy periods, a fair measure of inherent stability was called for. This had been too much in evidence in the B.E.2 series, but about the right measure was found in the too often reviled R.E.8. These machines had to operate in all

The Roland C II proved itself a good if not outstanding reconnaissance and artillery spotting type. The hooped arrangement over the upper wing was designed to protect the pilot should the aeroplane turn over on landing.

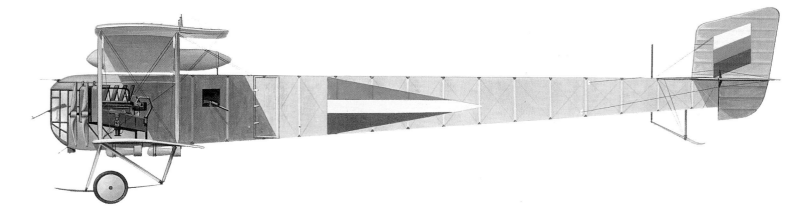

The Sikorsky Ilya Muromets was the world's first four-engined bomber, and was built in a number of differently engined variants for service with the Imperial Russian air service.

Seen here on the beach of a naval air station in the Mediterranean, the FBA Type H was one of the best flying boats available to the Allies, and served in the coastal patrol and anti-submarine roles.

weathers, within reach of anti-aircraft fire and enemy fighters, so anything which detracted from their manoeuvrability was a hindrance to survival. For all these reasons, the problems of designing a front-line two-seater were formidable, and it is remarkable how many good designs emerged in the second half of the war, usually as a result of making the aircraft as small as possible to ensure agility, and giving the observer a good field of fire for his flexible machine-gun. The Germans produced the Albatros C X and XII, Deutsche Flugzeugwerke (DFW) C IV and V, Halberstadt C V, Luft-Verkehrs Gesellschaft (LVG) C V and VI, and Rumpler C IV and VII. The French had the first-class Salmson 2, Powered by an odd water-cooled, rather than air-cooled, 260-hp radial. The Italians produced the sleek Ansaldo SVA 10, and the Austro-Hungarians the useful Ufag C I. It is difficult to underestimate the heroic proportions of the work done with these unsung aircraft.

A less important role than that of spotter and reconnaissance machines was played by bomber and ground-attack aircraft, but it was a role which consistently grew in importance as the war progressed. The idea that one could drop a bomb on what could be seen from the air was as old or possibly older than flight itself. The first primitive efforts from aircraft had been made by the Italians in their war against the Turks in Libya during 1911 and 1912. So ineffective were early bombs, especially in the absence of any form of bombsight other than the dropper's eyes, and so small was the load that could be carried by early aircraft that bombing was at first next to useless. The successes of a few men in raiding German Zeppelin sheds, however, and the success m terms of propaganda and morale attending the German bombing of Paris at the end of August 1914 made

it clear that time and ingenuity would eventually lead to the development of bombing as a useful weapon of war. Surprisingly, it was the Russians who led the way, despite the fact that the French had started an ad hoc bombing service in the autumn of 1914 with Voisin biplanes. The Russians realized that large aircraft would be needed to carry a significant quantity of bombs, and they already had such aircraft in the form of two four-engined machines, the Russkii Vitiaz and the Le Grand, both designed by Igor Sikorsky and built in 1913 by the Russian Baltic Railway Car Factory in St Petersburg. These were the world's first four-engined aircraft. Early in 1914 the Russian technical bureau ordered 10 examples of an improved and enlarged version, the Ilya Muromets, for the Imperial Russian Air Service. Eventually some 80 of the type were built, but lack of suitable engines seriously hampered operational efforts. Nonetheless, over 400 sorties were flown with bombloads of about 1,100 lb (500 kg). In reality, however, bombers of the size of the Ilya Muromets were inefficient even by the standards of the day.

Despite the efforts of the Royal Naval Air Service and the fledgling French bombing force, the Germans beat them to the first serious investigations of the possibilities of bombing. Here they had a head start, as a fair amount of preliminary work had been undertaken before the war during investigations into the use of Zeppelins as bombing craft. First into the field, during the summer of 1915, was the Allgemeine Electrizitts Gesellschaft (AEG) G II, a large twin-engined biplane capable of delivering a 200-kg (441-lb) bombload. This was joined in the autumn by the same company's G III, capable of lifting some 300 kg (661 lb) of bombs. A year later three other bombers had joined the German air service: the AEG G IV with a 400-kg (882-lb) bombload, the Friedrichshafen G II with a 450-kg (992-lb) bombload and the Gotha G III with a 450-kg (992-lb) bombload. These aircraft served a useful purpose in paving the way for later types, but were not m themselves very successful. With the arrival of the Gotha G IV early in 1917, however, the Germans had at last found a useful long-range bomber. Zeppelins had been launching sporadic attacks on targets in the southern half of the British Isles, principally London, since May 1915, but by 1917 the British defences had been so strengthened, albeit by the removal of squadrons from France, that Zeppelin losses were no longer tolerable. The Germans therefore

decided to use the Gotha G IV and V over England, and the first Gotha raids were launched in June 1917 to the total consternation of public and government alike. Although the Zeppelin raids were the first 'strategic bombing' ever attempted and had caused a great public shock, the aircraft raids proved a greater threat to life and property. There was an immediate outcry for the government to do something to curb the German daylight raids. The raids continued into 1918, causing a steady stream of casualties and damage, despite the removal of further squadrons from France. Only with the deployment of aircraft such as the S.E.5a, which could climb fast enough to intercept the Gothas before they flew out of range, was the threat curtailed. The immediate result of these Germans raids, at first carried out with almost complete impunity, was the total reorganization of the British air services. The most important reform was the unification, on 1 April 1918, of the hitherto separate RFC and RNAS to become the Royal Air Force, the world's first independent air force. In 1918 the Gothas were joined by a few Zeppelin (Staaken) R Vl bombers, huge machines that could carry 2000 kg (4,409 lb) of bombs over short ranges. The Germans had a penchant for Riesenflugzeug (giant aircraft), and devoted great effort to the production of a number of types.

The importance of the German strategic bombing campaign in terms of other factors far outweighs its military success, which was minimal. For the first time the British people, who had imagined themselves immune from war in the personal sense, found themselves embroiled in the 'front line', an evil they had previously thought to be wholly European. With the realization that everyone, not just the fighting men or the unfortunate civilians living in the combat area, could from now on be involved in the actual 'fighting', the era of total war may be said to have appeared.

The British decided to use heavy bombers, at first under the impulsion of the Admiralty, whose Air Department head, Commodore Murray Sueter called for a 'bloody paralyser' of an aeroplane early in 1915. This took the form of the Handley Page O/100, which entered service in September 1916 and proved an immediate success, being capable of carrying some 2,000 lb (907 kg) of bombs. A more powerful version was designated O/400, and entered service in 1918. This basic type was selected as the standard equipment of the world's first true strategic bomber force, the RAF 's Independent Force, and 40 aircraft of the type took part in the largest 'strategic' raid of the war in September 1918, when the Saar area was bombed from bases near Nancy. Only three of Britain's first four-engined bomber, the Handley Page V/1500, had been built before the Armistice.

Although 'heavy' bombers pointed the way to the future, their military effect in World War I was minimal, and it was light bombers that played an important part in land operations during the closing stages of the war. Considering their importance, it is surprising that the Allies used only two basic types: the Airco (de Havilland) 4 and its two derivatives, the D.H.9 and 9a, and the French Breguet 14.

The D.H.4 was in every respect one of the most remarkable aircraft of World War I. As well as being very agile and well armed it had a speed of 143 mph (230 km/h) when most fighters were only capable of speeds in the region of 130 mph (209 km/h), and was capable of carrying a bombload of 460 lb (209 kg). The D.H.4 entered service in 1917, and was joined in squadron use during 1918 by the supposedly improved D.H.9, which had the pilot's and observer's cockpits close together to obviate the D.H.4's main tactical failing, the near impossibility of the pilot and observer speaking to each other as they were separated by the bomb-bay. But reduced engine power meant that performance suffered badly, a factor only partially rectified by the development of the D.H.9a. The French equivalent

of these de Havilland bombers was the Breguet 14, which began to enter service in September 1917. Sturdy and fairly fast, this bomber played an important part in harrying the retreating Germans in the second half of 1918, and also proved a more than adequate reconnaissance aircraft.

While the Allies concentrated on light bombers, the Germans placed more faith in ground-attack machines to support their land forces in basically the same way as that pioneered by the British in the Battle of the Somme in 1916. These types were at first modified reconnaissance aircraft used by Schlachtzstaffeln (protection squadrons) and Fliegerabteilungen-Infanterie (infantry contact units) pending the arrival of more suitable, heavier, armoured designs such as the all-metal Junkers J l, designed by Dr Hugo Junkers, one of the pioneers of metal construction. In the autumn of 1917, however, the need for a lighter type which could fulfil both the ground attack and reconnaissance roles became evident. This new type was to be operated by Schlachtstaffeln (battle squadrons), and the first of the new models, the Halberstadt CL II and Hannover CL II and III, were ready for the new squadrons to use with considerable success in the last-gasp German offensives in the spring and early summer of 1918.

Aircraft had entered World War I as unknown quantities: their role was seen basically as reconnaissance and very light bombing, with aircraft of distinctly limited performance and reliability. Yet by 1916 aircraft had altered out of all recognition and become durable, efficient fighting machines, capable of exerting some influence on the outcome of the decisive land operations. Two years later, towards the end of the war, aircraft had again advanced m overall performance, and were now to a certain extent the arbiters of the land battle.

Operations, certainly on the Western Front, also had profound psychological effects. Trenchard's determination from the middle of 1916 onwards that the aircraft under his command should play an offensive role at all times had in the end made the United Kingdom the dominant nation of the war in the air. But the cost had been very heavy, and this increasingly grim aspect began to turn the public's attention away from the 'romance' of air war to-wards a truer understanding of its tragic implications. And with the German development of strategic bombing, people became all too aware of the long-term possibilities of aviation in a military sense. Thus the intensity, and consequently the unrelenting rise in losses, forced on by Trenchard combined with public fears of strategic bombing to produce in the 1920s and 1930s a fear that bombing could herald the end of civilization. These feelings grew during the Abyssinian War and the Spanish Civil War, and it was not until the survival of London in the Blitz of 1940 and 1941 that the limitations of strategic bombing were seen.

Although overshadowed by the superlative Fokker D VII with its biplane wing cellule and higher-powered engine, the Fokker D VIII was also an excellent fighter based on Reinhold Platz's typical combination of a fabric-covered welded steel tube fuselage and a plywood-covered wooden wing of thick section. Based on a rotary piston engine of only modest power, the D VIII offered good performance as a result of its low weight and drag, which resulted from the use of a parasol wing that also provided the pilot with first-class fields of vision.

Sad Years of Retrenchment

If World War I had made aviation, the peace that followed almost broke the new industry. For the terrible cost of the war, both emotional and financial, put aviation back where it started in the last few years before 1914, at least from the constructors' and pilots' point of view. In those halcyon days there had been only a few hundred aircraft in the world (of perhaps 150 different types), with about three times that number of pilots. The war had brought vast and rapid growth: by the time of the Armistice in November 1918, France had built 68,000 aircraft, the United Kingdom 55,000, Germany 47,600, Italy 20,000, the United States 15,000 and Austria-Hungary 5,400. The scale of expansion may also be gauged by the number of pilots lost during the war, which was a relatively small proportion of the number actually trained: on the German side, for example, 5,853 had been killed, 7,302 wounded and 2,751 taken prisoner or listed as missing; on the British side 6,166 had been killed, 7,245 wounded and 3,212 taken prisoner or listed as missing.

With the war finally over, it was time to take stock of the consequences. Europe and the United States were dazed by the horrors of the war and the enormity of their losses; the people were all too ready to believe that World War I (or the Great War as it was then) had been the war to end all wars. After years of slaughter it was a natural reaction to turn away from all military machinery, including aviation; and the war's financial cost had an equally devastating impact on the industry. Europe was almost bankrupt. France, the United Kingdom and Italy had spent all, or almost all, of their resources on the war and had then gone deep into debt with the United States to pay for the period 1917-18.

Germany and Austro-Hungary were exhausted. There was no money in Europe for anything but essentials, and military spending was clearly not essential after the end of 'the war to end all wars'. With the run-down of the world's major air forces, there was no work for the aircraft industries that supplied them.

The drastic nature of the cutback was exemplified by the decline of the Royal Air Force in the immediate postwar period. At the time of the Armistice the RAF had 188 operational squadrons, with 291,000 men and women to fly, service and otherwise keep them in the air; by the end of 1919, less than 14 months later, the force had dropped to 12 operational squadrons, with manpower down to 31,500. Although the government soon realized that so small an air force was hardly worth having, expansion was limited to 25 squadrons by March 1920 and 43 squadrons by October 1924.

More significant for aviation in general was the fact that a new generation of aircraft was just entering service at the time of the Armistice, and it was immediately decided that these would be sufficient for peacetime. Thus the RAF's equipment in the first years after the war consisted of the

Designed in 1913 and used right through World War I, the Avro Type 504 was one of the great aircraft of all time, and remained in gainful service as a trainer right into the early 1930s.

Bristol F.2B Fighter, the Sopwith Snipe, the de Havilland D.H.9a and Vickers Vimy machines. The first new bomber, the Fairey Fawn, did not enter service until 1923, and the first new fighters, in the forms of the Gloster Grebe and Armstrong Whitworth Siskin, came a year later. Although severe, the British government's cuts were matched throughout most of Europe as well as in the United States.

Aircraft builders found themselves in an extremely difficult position. No new orders could be expected for some time, and production capacity was being gradually run down as existing orders, heavily cut back at the Armistice, were filled. Without military interest other work had to be found, but this was difficult while the market was glutted with ex-government machines being sold off at ludicrously low sums. The majority of aircraft firms were unable to cope and went out of business. Those that survived, by forethought and careful planning, had to contract enormously. The companies that had sensibly bought their wartime premises were now able to sell them, using the capital so realized to keep themselves above water until business started to pick up again in the early 1920s.

The people who suffered most from this retrenchment

his diminutive dirigibles and lightplanes, believing that most middle-class families would soon see aircraft as their natural means of transport, far superior in speed and convenience to anything on land or sea. Now in semi-retirement in Brazil, Santos-Dumont would have been delighted with the aircraft companies' aspirations.

Yet what is a lightplane, as opposed to normal light aviation? The best answer would seem to be an aeroplane intended purely for personal sporting use. Such a machine, capable of lifting only one person, and having no facility for a worthwhile payload, would be small, cheap to build and cheap to run. Performance would not be a vital asset, so a low-powered engine would be sufficient. In short, it was to be the 1920s equivalent to the sports car, intended for enjoyment rather than utilitarian purposes.

Early in the field were

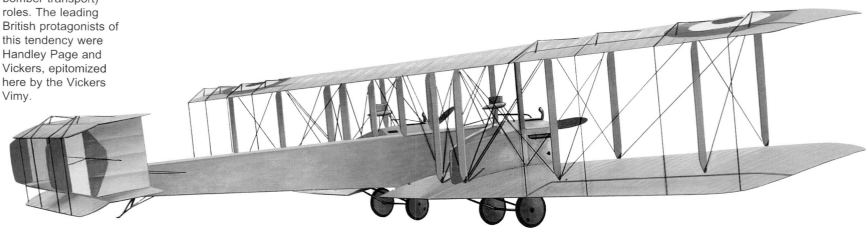

Above: Designed in the losing stages of World War I but appearing too late for service in that war, the Vickers Vimy was a standard bomber of the Royal Air Force in the early 1920s. The type seen here is a Vimy Mk II.

in aviation were the workers, who were laid off in great numbers, but the loss of many experienced and talented design staff was even more damaging to the industry. Before the war a single man could easily design an adequate aeroplane; by 1918 design had become the province of a team. Admittedly one man usually had overall control, but he needed the services of structural engineers, stress calculation and aerodynamics experts, production engineers, engine specialists and others from a host of allied fields. Many of these men were now lost to the world of aviation, mostly turning to civil engineering and the growing car industry.

Those left were faced with deciding what type of aircraft they should build. With no military demand, the only possibility was civil aviation. But what sort of aeroplane would sell? With money in short supply, the new aircraft would have to be not only cheap to buy and to run, but also cheap to produce, for none of the companies could afford much experimental and development work. They had only one real hope: the civilian lightplane, meant for what was confidently expected to turn into a mass market within the next few years.

This type of machine had been pioneered before World War I by Santos-Dumont with his Demoiselle. Santos-Dumont had tried to revolutionize personal transport with

machines such as the Blackburn Sidecar and the Avro Baby, but with masses of wartime aircraft still on the market at very low prices their success was limited. Towards the middle of the 1920s, however, the British government decided to encourage these developments by sponsoring both lightplane competitions (and therefore designs) and flying clubs, where the public might keep any machines they decided to buy.

The first light aeroplane competition was organized by the Royal Aero Club, for which the Air Ministry provided some £3,000 in prizes. Among the entries were the Hawker Cygnet (the first design for the company by Sydney Camm, one of the greatest designers ever), the Shackleton ANEC, the English Electric Wren and the de Havilland D.H.53. The competition was a success but the public, wanting high performance and a good level of manoeuvrability, expected too much of the lightplanes. With one notable exception, lightplanes were a commercial failure.

The exception was the Pou-du-Ciel (normally translated as flying flea although the French really means

Below: The financial restrictions of the 1920s meant that most air forces had to sacrifice not only numbers of aircraft, but also dedicated single-role optimization in most types. This dictated that the same basic design was used for aircraft intended for the bomber and transport (or even bomber-transport) roles. The leading British protagonists of this tendency were Handley Page and Vickers, epitomized here by the Vickers Vimy.

sky louse), designed by Henri Mignet and built in 1933. This remarkable little aeroplane enjoyed immense popularity in the middle 1930s, and at one time there were over 100 in use, with a variety of engines, within the United Kingdom alone.

Mignet's idea was for a relatively fast machine of small dimensions and good small field take-off and landing performance, which amateur constructors could build at home from easily available materials. The Pou was also interesting aerodynamically: the normal wing/tailplane relationship was abandoned in favour of two 13-ft (3.96-m) wings mounted in tandem. With the forward wing slightly above the rear wing, this gave a slotted effect with consequent improvements in lift and control. Inherently stable laterally, the Pou was controlled in yaw by a large rudder and in pitch by the alteration in incidence of the wings. Unfortunately, the Pou was so stable in certain attitudes that the pilot could not right the machine, and after a number of crashes in a short period the Pou lost favour. With World War II approaching, the lightplane concept was shelved yet again until the 1950s.

One man, however, had seen the implications of the lightplane's failure: Geoffrey de Havilland, the designer of the Moth. This beautiful little single-bay biplane combined reasonable performance and manoeuvrability with a fair amount of economy; powered by a 60-hp de Havilland Cirrus engine, it carried two people in tandem. The D.H.60 Moth was an immediate success and became the standard aeroplane found in the flying clubs springing up first all over the United Kingdom, and then in the more advanced parts of the British Empire. Directly descended from the Moth itself came a line of aircraft culminating in the D.H.82 Tiger Moth, one of the most famous and best loved machines ever built. The success of the first Moth, moreover, persuaded other aircraft designers that this was the type of machine wanted by most would-be buyers; among several to follow in the Moth's footsteps were the Avro Avian, the Westland Widgeon and the Avro Bluebird.

The United States, by contrast, showed little or no inclination towards private flying during the 1920s and no light aircraft worthy of note were produced. Commercial flying consisted mainly of aerial circuses, in which both men and women took part. The war had shown the public what aircraft could do, and the latter-day 'barnstormers' were called upon to undertake the most hazardous of aerial exploits, including aerobatics, wing-walking, stepping from one aircraft in flight to another, and parachuting. Needless to say, accidents were frequent, but public demand had to be met if the circuses were to stay in business. The men who operated and flew in the circuses were normally ex-service pilots who could not settle down to a humdrum existence after the war. As the number of these pilots declined in the late 1920s and early 1930s and as the growth of civil aviation began to attract governmental supervision and regulation, the flying circuses gradually died out.

In Europe air displays remained much the same as they had been before 1914 as regards events, although the aircraft were different and the flying was far more professional. Flight had lost its novelty, however, and the displays attracted a far more critical public. As regular air force appearances became the norm, with superb demonstrations of aerobatics by both single aircraft and formations, the displays gradually became less exciting, and more of an opportunity for the public to assess their expenditure on the air forces. Nonetheless, they still exercised a considerable fascination; and the smaller, travelling displays did much to take aviation to people who would otherwise never have come into close contact with the fascinating world of flight. By taking the mystique out of flying, and especially by taking large numbers up for

Air-mindedness was promoted during the 1920s by racing, record breaking and aerial stunts such as that depicted here.

short joy-rides, they showed the public at large that flight was nothing special and that everyone could take part if they wished.

Competitive aviation provided another outlet for the 'flying bug' among wartime pilots, and this made a more dramatic appeal to the public. There were two types of competition: racing against other pilots over a particular course, and flying to establish records, particularly for absolute speed, altitude and distance. It was the latter that caught the public's attention in the first years after the war.

In 1914 the Daily Mail, a great sponsor of aviation, had offered a prize of £10,000 for the first nonstop flight over the Atlantic. Several aircraft were being prepared or built for the event in the summer of 1914, but perhaps fortunately for their crews the outbreak of World War I put an end to these almost hopeless efforts. By 1919, however, aviation had advanced so far that a trans-Atlantic flight was a distinct possibility.

Sopwith had already decided as early as July 1918 that one of his aircraft would try to win the Daily Mail's prize as soon as hostilities were over. A Sopwith B.1 bomber was quickly converted and shipped over to Newfoundland for the attempt. Like all such early attempts on the Atlantic it was to be a flight from west to east to take advantage of the prevailing winds. On 18 May 1919 the celebrated pilot Harry Hawker set off with K. K. Mackenzie-Grieve as his navigator. At first all went well, but then the cooling system developed trouble. After several anxious moments Hawker decided to abandon the effort and head south towards the shipping lanes. Spotting a suitable ship, he ditched the Sopwith in the Atlantic and both the aeroplane and its crew were rescued. The steamer had no radio and could not communicate the news until she arrived off the United Kingdom on 25 May, just after the distraught Mrs Hawker had attended a memorial service for the two men.

The first successful crossing of the Atlantic came just six days later, though it was not nonstop. Three Curtiss NC flying-boats of the US Navy had set off from Rockaway, New York on 1 May 1919, a fortnight before Hawker's departure. Stopping several times before reaching Newfoundland, the three boats then set off for the Azores. Two came down before their objective, one sinking after its crew had been rescued, the other taxiing the last 200 miles (320 km) across the water. From the Azores the remaining boat flew to Lisbon and finally to Ferrol in Spain, where it arrived on 31 May after travelling almost 4,000 miles (6440 km). This considerable

Left: The Boeing Model 40 marked the beginning of a new era in commercial aviation, with much reduced payload/range cost derived from careful design and a fuel-economical radial piston engine.

achievement by the pilot, Commander A. C. Read, was proof that the Atlantic could be beaten.

Of even greater importance, however, was the first nonstop crossing of the Atlantic. In a modified Vickers Vimy twin-engined bomber, Captain John Alcock and Lieutenant Arthur Whitten Brown set off from St John's, Newfoundland, on 14 June 1919. Just under 16 hours later, on the 16th, they crash-landed in a bog near Clifden in County Galway, Ireland, after a flight of some 1,890 miles (3050 km). The flight has become legendary, not only for the men's achievement, but also for their courage. The two men encountered appalling weather conditions, and six times Brown had to climb out on to the wings to attend to the engines. After receiving a welcome as heroes in London, the two men were knighted.

Far Left: Aircraft controls were developed steadily during the 1920s, larger commercial aircraft acquiring a control wheel on the control column and gaining more sophisticated instrumentation.

Graham Wallace, one of aviation's greatest chroniclers, has left the world an admirable, if slightly fulsome, account of the trials during the crossing in his book The Flight of Alcock and Brown. He tells us that at first the flight was uneventful. After gaining height over Newfoundland, the Vimy was set on course for Ireland over St John's, where the coast was crossed at 16.28 Greenwich time. The weather was excellent, and the Vimy slowly gained height. Despite the pain of his crippled right leg, Brown took frequent sun sights and drift measurements, which involved a lot of movement. No sooner had the Vimy entered a thick bank of fog, than the radio transmitter went out of service because the propeller of the wind-driven generator had sheared off. At about 18.00 the starboard engine suddenly began to sound sick. To quote Wallace: 'A section of the inner exhaust pipe was splitting away from the engine casing and vibrating in the wind. Slowly it turned red, and then white-hot and incandescent until finally it melted away, leaving the six inner cylinders exhausting into the slipstream. Flames were belching out and were blown backwards in a long fiery streamer by the wind . . , The noise was sufficient to prevent any talk from this time on.'

Because the electrical power to their heated flying suits had failed, cold became an acute problem for both men, especially after night had fallen. Shortly after 03.00 on the 15th the Vimy flew into a storm, Alcock lost control, and the aeroplane plummeted down to within a few feet of the sea before he was able to regain control and start climbing again.

Now the engine air intakes began to get clogged up with snow and ice. Brown, realizing that only he could remedy the situation, clambered out onto the port wing: 'The snow sheathed his body in a shroud of ice as he clung grimly on to the strut and fumbled in his pockets for a jackknife. He had to cling on with all his strength, the wind tore at his face and hands, forcing him backwards, his feet were slipping on the icy surface of the wing.' With great care Brown chipped away at the ice until the engine was running smoothly again, and then painfully clambered over to the starboard wing to repeat the exercise. Five more times Brown had to climb out on to the wings to clear ice from the air intakes and engine dials, mounted on the inside of the nacelles. Meanwhile ice was also making enormous difficulties for Alcock, the pilot. The ailerons now iced up and refused to move, making lateral control impossible, and the other controls, too, became very heavy.

It is impossible to imagine the exhilaration of the two men when the coast of Ireland came into view. The Vimy made history by crossing the shore at 08.25 on the morning of the 16th.

While individual airmen were performing these heroic feats, commercial flight was still in its infancy. German airships had flown passengers between major German cities even before World War I but airships did not prove entirely satisfactory as civilian vehicles, especially from the point of view of safety. Here the heavier-than-air craft, which had also been used commercially before the war, came into its own. On 4 July 1911, for example, Horatio Barber had flown a consignment of Osram light bulbs across Sussex in England, from Shoreham to Hove, for the considerable fee of £100. Air mail had been carried for the first time on 18 February 1911, when Henri Pequet flew some 6,500 letters across the River Jumna from Allahabad to Naini Junction for the Indian Government. Less celebrated, but just as important, was the establishment by the Benoist company of the first aircraft passenger service with regular schedules, in January 1914. This airline, using a flying-boat designed by Benoist himself, operated between Tampa and St Petersburg in Florida.

There was every reason to hope, therefore, that regular air services would become the norm, especially with the development of larger, faster and more reliable aircraft during the war. So confident was George Holt Thomas, in fact, that in October 1916 he registered the Aircraft Transport and Travel Ltd in London. In 1919 he began operating a mail service with D.H.9s between London and Paris, principally for those involved in the negotiations leading up to the Treaty of Versailles. Even before this there were at least two regular mail services.

From March 1918 Hansa-Brandenburg C I biplanes had carried mail between Vienna and Kiev for the Austro-Hungarian armies in the region, and the United States Post Office Department had inaugurated a service between New York and Washington in August 1918. The United States, in fact, made the greatest early use of air mail, where the service was particularly desirable because of the size of the country.

The first passenger services after the war were started in Germany by the Deutsche Luft-Reederei, which in February 1919 established a commercial link between Berlin and Weimar, respective seats of the old imperial and new republican government. Other nations were quick to follow, with ex-service pilots flying hasty conversions of wartime bombers. Legal restraints were minimal, and the skies of northern Europe were soon full of converted bomber types such as the D.H.4, carrying up to four passengers. Larger machines such as the Vickers Vimy and Handley Page O/400 and V/1500 operated in the United Kingdom, and Breguet 14s and Farman Goliaths in France. The most popular route was between London and Paris, which could be covered in about two and a half hours. At first the service was temperamental and exploratory, but by August 1919 Aircraft Transport and Travel was operating a regular service over this prime route. Accurate figures are not available, but it seems that some 5,000 passengers were carried in 1919, and that 'airliners', as the new form of transport was soon labelled, flew about a million miles.

At first the airline companies could carry any passenger who would take the risk in virtually any aeroplane, but during the 1920s regulations were introduced which increased safety requirements and otherwise put matters on a more formal basis. Many of the little companies which had started up in the aftermath of the war closed down or were bought up by larger concerns; in time these became the national companies that form so great a feature of modern European aviation. Imperial Airways, for example, was formed in 1924 by the amalgamation of Daimler Hire, Handley Page Air Transport, British Marine Air Navigation and Instone Air Line, and this eventually became British Overseas Airways Corporation and finally British Airways. First of these national airlines to be formed was the Dutch KLM, which was created in 1919.

Money for experimental and development purposes was hard to come by, but a certain amount of fundamental research was being carried out in various parts of the world. Governments were unwilling to let other nations secure any advantage in aerodynamic theory or other aeronautical disciplines that might be useful in military terms. This research was marked by a sense of purpose and direction that had been sadly lacking from aircraft development before 1914. World War I had demonstrated the problems involved in getting ever more complicated aircraft ready for service, whether military or civilian. Development work was no longer concerned with the primary problem of flight itself, but with performance, aerodynamics and cost.

Thus although there was a considerable retrenchment in the aircraft industry immediately after World War I, with the loss of many jobs in both production and design, the aviation world in general was able to absorb the lessons of World War I into the slow process of developing more advanced aircraft. With the growth of competitive flying, still more information became available about the performance of aircraft under stress. Unlike in wartime, this information could be gathered in an ordered and scientific manner, particularly from the speed tests and time trials that were beginning to gain popularity.

Many de Havilland (ex-Airco) D.H.9 series warplanes were converted after World War I for civil use as light transports with enclosed accommodation.

Emergence of New Technologies

The 15 years following the end of World War I saw enormous advances in the theory and practice of flight. Speed, range and altitude increased at an astonishing rate, and a host of other factors were improved. Yet perhaps the most significant advances were made in the field of aerodynamics, where the Germans, British and Americans led the field. Previously, designers had been content with a somewhat rudimentary appreciation of the effects of air pressure in flight, and this had hampered the development of fast aircraft. Now considerable work was done both theoretically and in wind tunnels on the precise natures of lift and drag.

Reinhold Platz was typical of the early designers, especially with regard to the wing sections he used. Platz's favourite aerofoil was very thick, particularly at the leading edge. Such a section had obvious advantages from the structural point of view, and seemed attractive aerodynamic ally. If lift was caused by the pressure differentials between air flowing over and under the wings, then an aerofoil with a heavily cambered upper surface should give more lift by increasing those differentials. For Platz, such considerations outweighed the disadvantages of increased drag caused by the thick section.

This concept of aerodynamic lift, while broadly correct, raised many questions not subject to empirical test until the early 1920s. Yet the problems had in many cases been foreseen and their solutions postulated as early as the 1890s, by a remarkable pioneer in the field of aerodynamics.

F. W. Lanchester, today best remembered for the line of cars that bore his name, is an important figure in aviation history, but he was almost disregarded in his own time. His interest in aerodynamics went so far beyond current theories that he encountered problems and concepts for which no words or mathematical expressions existed, and he was forced to make up his own. Every effort Lanchester made to have his work considered seriously met with ridicule, for no one else could understand what he was writing about, or even had the inclination to try.

It was in 1892 that Lanchester was bitten by the aviation 'bug' and began experimenting with models. These little gliders were based on his observation of bird flight, a method Lanchester had in common with a great number of other pioneers. In 1894 he read to a learned society in Birmingham a paper entitled The Soaring of Birds and the Possibilities of Mechanical Flight. No copy of this paper has survived, but in the next two years Lanchester developed his ideas. In 1897 he had the galling experience of having his latest paper turned down by the Physical Society on the ground that it was almost totally unintelligible.

Yet this paper was the first mathematically formulated

The Fairey Flycatcher was a British carrierborne fighter that remained in service despite its conceptual obsolescence, and was much loved by its pilots for its viceless handling characteristics and superlative agility.

Right: The Vickers Virginia was the RAF's standard heavy bomber between 1924 and 1937, by which time this large, lumbering and extremely noisy biplane was completely obsolete. After retirement as a bomber, the Virginia was used as a parachute trainer with jump-off platforms installed behind the two wing-mounted engines.

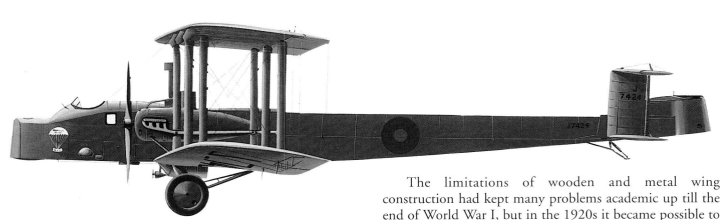

exposition of the true nature of lift. Lanchester had discovered that lift is caused by the envelope of air circulating round the wing, producing kinetic energy in the form of a 'downwash' field. It is this energy that provides the lift, and all aerofoils should because of this be designed to produce the greatest possible downwash field with the minimum amount of drag.

Lanchester continued to work on the mathematics of flight over the next 10 years, producing his definitive *Aerodynamics* in 1908 and *Aerodonetics* a year later. Like his earlier papers, these two books were extremely difficult to understand, and their effect at the time was minimal. It was not until 1915, when Lanchester recast his theories in a more intelligible form, that aircraft designers began to find practical uses for his work.

Consequently, the accolade of theoretical and practical father of aerodynamics must go to a German physicist, Ludwig Prandtl. Working independently of Lanchester at much the same time, Prandtl also evolved the theory of circulatory lift. Unlike Lanchester, Prandtl was able to turn his ideas into intelligible form, both verbally and mathematically. And while Lanchester's work ended when he lost interest in aerodynamics, Prandtl continued to exert a strong influence both with his own work and through the school of aerodynamics he set up at Göttingen. For 30 years after World War I his school was a leading centre of aerodynamic thought, developing the theories on which wing sections were and often are still designed.

Two key figures of this era, whose work bore much of its fruit in the 1920s and 1930s, were the German mathematician Wilhelm Kutta and the Russian Nikolai Jukowski. These men laid the practical foundations for the ideas which began to lead to high-lift, low-drag aerofoils in the later 1920s. Their work was seized upon and expanded by another great aerodynamicist, the Hungarian-born Theodore von Karman, who lived and worked in the United States. Karman was prominent in the growing American school of theoretical and practical aerodynamicists working for private industry and the National Advisory Committee for Aeronautics (NACA).

The limitations of wooden and metal wing construction had kept many problems academic up till the end of World War I, but in the 1920s it became possible to build long-span cantilever wings out of light alloys. Aspect ratio, which is the ratio of wing span to wing width (chord), became a critical factor. Designers had previously worked on a rule-of-thumb basis, but now the theorists were able to show that a high aspect ratio, that is great span combined with small chord, had major advantages over a low aspect ratio. The downwash field was increased by the greater span while the small chord of the wing meant a reduction in drag.

As the necessary materials became available, therefore, designers began to give their wings the highest aspect ratio commensurate with the kind of performance required of the planes. For long-distance aircraft, high aspect ratio wings proved an excellent choice; for military aircraft, on the other hand, they hampered manoeuvrability especially in the rolling plane. The general tendency towards high aspect ratios was most notable in aircraft making the fullest use of refined aerodynamic factors, such as high-altitude and long-distance aircraft. It is particularly noticeable in modern gliders.

During the 1920s the problems of drag also received considerable attention. The early pioneers had experienced great difficulties with drag, but no serious consideration was given to the problem until just before World War I. The development of types such as the Deperdussin Monocoque racers, with their careful stream-lining, marked a complete change of emphasis from the various 'box-kite' types, in which structure demands had made drag-reduction a very low design priority. Yet the nature of drag remained imperfectly understood right up to the mid 1920s.

The second half of the decade saw great advances, however, culminating in The Streamline Aeroplane (1929) written by a British theorist, Professor B. Melville Jones. From this time onwards, the various components of drag and their relationship to each other began to receive detailed attention from designers, and aircraft performances improved out of all proportion to the extra power of the latest aero engines. (Increases in performance, especially in speed, had previously been seen as functions of more power,

Below: British fighter development followed two paths in the period leading to the advent of the monoplane fighter. The earlier stream was based on the comparatively bluff biplane with an air-cooled radial piston engine as exemplified by the Bristol Bulldog Mk II (right), while the later stream paid greater attention to streamlining and used a liquid-cooled Vee piston engine as exemplified by the Hawker Fury Mk II (left). It was the latter stream that paved the way for first-generation monoplane fighters such as the Hawker Hurricane and Supermarine Spitfire.

yet speed increases only as the cube root of extra power.)

There are four basic types of drag: profile drag (composed of form drag and skin friction), induced drag, parasite drag, and interference drag. Drag is a very complex matter, and it was only when wind tunnels became a standard piece of equipment in the 1920s that designers could see and appreciate all the drag forces acting upon their designs. In carefully controlled conditions the exact nature of the various types of drag acting upon a model could be seen with the aid of telltales, or by introducing coloured smoke into the air flow. Most important of all was the discovery that drag was developed not only by the mass of the aeroplane itself, but by the very air moved aside in the passage of the aeroplane. Exact measurements of form and parasite drag were complemented by an understanding of induced drag and interference drag, allowing the designer to produce cleaner designs with much reduced drag coefficients.

Developments along these aerodynamic lines continued into the 1930s, when the name of another great German theorist and practical designer, Dr Alexander Lippisch, began to make itself felt. Lippisch was convinced that the traditional use of a long fuselage was hopelessly inefficient, and that as the wings were the only essential component for lift, they should be made to hold the payload, engines and fuel. Shortening the fuselage and sweeping the wings back would allow the control surfaces for the pitch and yaw axes to be mounted behind the centre of gravity. And why not fill in the area behind the 'trailing edges' to make the wing shape a delta? This would provide extra volume for load or fuel, as well as aerodynamic advantages.

The idea of delta-winged aircraft had been current for several years but it was Lippisch who finally made it a possibility. Unfortunately, he was ahead of his time, and the greatest benefits of such a wing planform only became apparent with the introduction of the reaction-type engine, when aircraft speeds approached that of sound. Yet in the late 1920s and early 1930s Lippisch built a number of small experimental machines that performed quite well within the limits of their size and power.

In the United Kingdom, Dr Geoffrey Hill was also interested in aircraft with heavily swept wings, which avoided the need for a large fuselage with its attendant drag and weight. Hill's first practical machine, named Pterodactyl because of its peculiar shape, was built in 1926, the first of a long series. Interest was shown by a number of bodies, including the RAF, but the Hill type of aeroplane failed to find any practical use. Nonetheless, much important aerodynamic information was obtained, especially on the design and use of elevons as dual-purpose control surfaces on heavily swept wings, and on the problems of stability in tailless aircraft.

While these men were pushing forward the theoretical limits of aerodynamics, a multitude of others, mostly within the aircraft industry itself, were working on the practical applications of the new knowledge. The two main fields in which they worked were aerodynamics and structures, and their concern was to improve performance and safety. The most remarkable development from the latter point of view was the 'slotted' wing, a solution to low-speed handling problems.

One of the major vices of aircraft

before and during World War I had been the stall, especially at low altitudes. When a pilot was landing his aeroplane, he would approach the airfield slowly with his engine throttled back; to keep as much lift as possible, the standard practice was to hold up the aeroplane's nose. Though this helped maintain lift at slow speeds, the extra area presented to the airflow had the effect of slowing the aeroplane further. The pilot might then raise the nose still higher, and at an angle of about 15° or slightly more disaster struck in the form of the stall.

Aerodynamically, the stall is easily explained. As the wing's angle of incidence gets higher, the pressure beneath it increases rapidly while that above it decreases. At first this helps to produce more lift, but then the airflow over the wing becomes increasingly turbulent and develops less lift. At the critical angle, the airflow breaks away from the upper surface entirely and all lift is lost. The result is that the aeroplane falls freely and gathers speed; lift is then developed once again and the pilot can usually resume his normal angle of flight.

The stall is only a problem at low altitudes: an aeroplane about to land will probably crash before it has

Top: Designed by Huff Daland (later Keystone), the radial engined bombers beginning with the LB6 were the most important light bombers available to the U.S. Army Air Corp in the late 1920's and early 1930's.

Above: Air transport seemed to offer great potential in the 1920s, but it was difficult to begin any real fulfilment of this potential given the limited size and load-carrying capabilities of current transports such as this Farman F.60 seen with a light car attached under its fuselage.

Dating from the late 1920s, the Curtiss B-2 Condor was a workmanlike but unexceptional heavy bomber bought in small numbers by the USA.

regained flying speed. If the aeroplane is slightly higher, there is a better chance of recovery, but early machines often went into a spin after stalling, and pilots were not always able to pull out in time.

Many methods of mitigating the effects of stalls had been tried even before World War I. Leader of the designers working on stall characteristics was Frederick Handley Page, a pioneer British designer, pilot and builder of aircraft. His pre-war aircraft were notable for a variety of anti-stall devices, but during the course of the war he came up with an enduring solution. The object had been to control the circulation of air around the wing. Handley Page reasoned that if air could be bled from the high-pressure area under the wing to the low-pressure area above the wing, the differential would be reduced and the stall would be delayed. The method he devised, the slotted wing, seems absurdly simple today yet is still used and is one of the most important safety devices ever invented for aircraft.

Handley Page patented his idea on 19 February 1918, but it was not widely used until the late 1920s, when Dr

Gustav Lachmann moved from the Gˆttingen laboratories to join Handley Page and work on the development of slotted wings. Quite independently, Lachmann had been working along the same lines and had come to the same conclusions, but realized that a large company such as Handley Page would offer him the best chance of seeing practical results for his work. Whoever invented the slotted wing first, Handley Page brought it to practical use.

The slot runs along the length of the wing just behind the leading edge, connecting the lower and upper surfaces of the wing; it is angled backwards toward the trailing edge on the upper wing side. As the aeroplane approaches the situation in which its wing will stall, the pressure differential is kept down by high-pressure air forcing its way through the slot to the low-pressure area on the upper surface of the wing. Since the slot is angled backwards, the air arriving on the upper surface helps smooth out the airflow, reducing the turbulence. The slotted wing thus allows a greater angle of incidence and lower speeds than was previously possible, making take-off and landing much safer.

This simple type of slot found favour almost immediately and Hugo Junkers adopted it on many of his aircraft. The main disadvantage is that the slot is permanently

open, which saves the pilot a job but also produces drag. So Handley Page and Lachmann went one stage further and developed 'automatic slots', which placed no extra burden on the pilot but still reduced the drag.

Knowing that the airflow does not separate right at the front of the wing but just before it, and is therefore not turbulent, Handley Page set slats into the upper part of the leading edge. These were free to move forwards and upwards, creating a slot between the leading edge and the slats themselves. In normal flight the slats formed part of the leading edge, and so produced no significant drag; as the aeroplane approached the stall, however, a combination of pressure differential and their own aerofoil shape lifted the slats to balance the pressures above and below the wing and smooth the airflow round the leading edge.

Demonstrations in the 1920s proved the efficiency of the Handley Page slotted wing, and in 1928 it became standard on all RAF aircraft. Many types of light aircraft had already been fitted with the device, and in the 1930s it was a feature of most machines around the world. The worst characteristics of the stall, namely its suddenness and unpredictability, were removed, and with them much of its dangerous reputation.

At the same time, other pioneers were helping to solve airflow problems at the trailing edge of the wing. Their work was also aimed at minimizing the dangers of take-off and landing, by developing the wing's lift capacity and controlling drag. What was needed was some means of increasing lift at low speed for take-off, and of increasing both lift and drag at low speed for landing. The solution

The F4B was typical of the series of Boeing fighters evolved for the US Navy with an exceptionally sturdy structure and a powerful air-cooled radial piston engine for good performance.

aspect ratio 'winglets', which drop down and back from the wing when operated, thus increasing its area are increasing its lift. Properly designed Fowler flaps can double the lift of a wing, with great advantages at the lower end of the aeroplane's speed range. Finally there is the slotted flap, working on the same principle as the Handley Page leading-edge slot. At the trailing edge, slots are usually combined with the Fowler type of area-extending flaps to provide a smooth airflow over these high-lift devices.

The availability of high-lift devices both at the leading and the trailing edge offer the designers great scope in wing design. But all these mechanisms had to be installed as neatly as possible, to ensure that they produced minimal drag when not in operation, and that their weight was not excessive. This second factor was of particular importance, for the value of high lift devices was quickly diminished if their weight raised the wing loading too much. The interaction of the various devices also repaid careful study. Leading-edge slots, for example, could produce the smooth airflow that would allow Fowler and slotted flaps to operate with maximum efficiency. The wing had to be tested in a wind tunnel to test the positioning of the devices, and to find the exact aspect ratio that would produce the best results.

All these developments took place within a few years, and it was some time before designers took full advantage of slots and flaps. But the Americans, with the great resurgence of aviators in the late 1920s and early 1930s, were soon using both devices, particularly for their airliners. Here the public was especially sensitive to questions of safety, and flaps and slots found favour quickly. The airlines also liked them, for profits were improved by the efficiency of the new aircraft.

The flaps served a dual purpose: at take-off they were depressed only moderately (about 12∞) and served as high-lift devices only, but for landing they were depressed quite severely (about 20∞) in the final-approach stage and served both as high-lift devices and as airbrakes. But the fact that both slots and flaps enhanced the safety of aircraft almost entirely escaped many British pundits of the early 1930s. The greatly influential Charles Grey, editor of The Aeroplane, condemned the Douglas DC-2 entered by KLM

was found in trailing-edge flaps, which appeared in a bewildering variety of types, and were used singly or in combination with each other.

There are four basic types of trailing-edge flap, all of which made their appearance in the 1920s, and such flaps were adopted universally in the 1930s. First there is the plain flap: this consists of a long, relatively narrow portion of the rear of the wing, hinged so that the pilot can lower it a few degrees and so deflect the airflow downwards. Plain flaps affect the basic airflow over the upper surface of the wing very severely when in use, however, and the split flap was designed to avoid this: instead of the whole rear section of the wing hingeing down, in the split flap only a portion of the under surface does so, thus deflecting the airflow under the wing but leaving the airflow over the upper surface intact. A variant on this split flap is the oddly-named 'Zap' flap, in which the hinge moves to the trailing edge before the flap drops.

The Fowler flap is far superior to the plain or split flap which both increase lift solely by deflecting the airflow downwards. The Fowler flap consists of one or more high

Below: The Mignet Pou-de-Ciel was a fascinating attempt to produce a wholly safe lightplane design, but suffered from one intractable flight-control problem. This is a homebuilt example in the USA.

Right: Japan began to develop its aero industry with designs and concepts from the Western nations, and then began to base its first indigenous designs on the lessons of this experience. This tendency is readily identifiable in the Nakajima A2N carrierborne fighter, which was an extensive development of the Type 3, the Japanese version of a British fighter, the Gloster Gambet.

Below: Much of the pioneering work into high-speed flight was undertaken by American designers seeking to produce effective racing aircraft. The Travelair Model R of 1931, for example, had a fuselage nicely contoured to the diameter of the type's radial piston engine, and other low-drag features were the spatted landing gear units and the low-set wing wire-braced to the fuselage and landing gear for additional strength.

in the 1934 'MacRobertson' race from the United Kingdom to Australia for its apparently high wing loading and consequent high landing speed. Yet the DC-2 had a landing speed lower than many of the old-fashioned, large-winged types favoured by critics such as Grey.

Such criticism should have been silenced long before, by the exceptional performance of aircraft like the Handley Page Gugnunc, built in 1929 for the Guggenheim safe aircraft competition held in the United States. Admittedly the Gugnunc was entirely uncommercial, but it was capable of a top speed of 112 mph (180 km/h) on only 130 hp and had a stalling speed in the vicinity of only 30 mph (48 km/h). This extraordinary speed range, the mark of a safe aeroplane, was achieved with the full use of flaps and slots. The Gugnunc had a very short take-off and landing run, and could climb very sharply immediately after take-off. In the air, it seemed capable almost of hovering and flying into the wind it could descend vertically when it was under full control.

Flaps and slots were used on a large number of European and American light aircraft at this time. The most remarkable example of this type of aircraft, known today as STOL (Short Take-Off and Landing), was the Fieseler Fi-156 Storch, adopted by the German air force for communications and liaison. This excellent little machine could operate from almost any little field and proved its worth countless times in World War II: indeed, the Allies were only too pleased when they managed to capture such aircraft and put them to their own use.

Other advances were also contributing to the safety of flight. Before World War I the problem of blind flying, when the pilot cannot see the horizon or an other fixed point of reference, had not caused much concern: the pilot had a natural sense of balance, it was reasoned, and this would be his internal 'point of reference'. But things did not turn out that way, as the large number of blind-flying accidents showed. The balance canals of the inner ear soon become disorientated without external checks: so a pilot flying in cloud may imagine that he is flying straight and level, and then discover that he is in fact diving steeply and side-slipping as well. Until the advent of adequate blind-flying instruments pilots avoided clouds and starless nights whenever possible, and if they did have to venture out, did so only for short periods.

Blind-flying problems of this sort were solved mainly by the efforts of an American, Elmer Sperry, using the peculiar characteristics of the gyroscope. He started work in 1912 on an automatic pilot, and spent much of the next 18 years perfecting this and other instruments. Sperry had the valuable help of an excellent analytical pilot in James Doolittle and an instrument maker of genius in Paul Kollsman; he was also greatly aided by money from the Guggenheim Fund for the Promotion of Aeronautics.

In 1928 Sperry finally perfected his artificial horizon (allowing the pilot to fly in cloud by giving him as external reference a gyroscopically stabilized artificial horizon on his instrument panel) and gyro compass. A year later, on 24 September 1929, Doolittle took off in thick fog, with his cockpit hooded over, in a modified Consolidated NY-2 trainer and landed safely 15 minutes later, having used his instruments and specially arranged radio beams for direction. Swift progress was made in the early 1930s and blind flying began to lose its terrors. The rapid development of rate of climb and descent indicators, quickly reacting altimeters, good turn-and-bank indicators, and efficient radios, allowed safe and accurate flying in all but the very worst weather.

Meanwhile, important advances were being made in the aerodynamics of aircraft controls. These had become all but standardized by the middle of World War I: a fin-mounted rear rudder for control in yaw, tailplane-mounted rear elevators for control in pitch, and wing-mounted ailerons for control in roll. The control surfaces themselves had been improved, for while plain surfaces hinged to the rear spar of the wings or the trailing edge of the fixed fill and tailplane had been perfectly adequate for small planes, the arrival of large, fast aircraft during World War I began to pose problems. Size and speed had the effect of increasing control forces very considerably, sometimes to the point where even a strong man found it difficult to control his machine properly. Naturally enough, the problem was more acute still in combat, where aerobatic manoeuvres were required.

During the war, a solution was found in the balancing of controls: the hinge line was moved from the junction point of the control surface and its main surface to a point about one-third of the way into the control surface. This meant that one-third of the control area was located forward of the hinge, and so helped to balance the rest of the area: in an elevator, for example, the front third of the surface rose while the remaining portion went down, reducing the control forces necessary for the pilot but in no way altering the overall effect of the elevator.

Developments with aerodynamic balancing continued into the 1920s, with excellent results. At much the same time work on the mass balancing of control surfaces was at last paying off. This relieved the 'flutter' caused by turbulence and high speeds, when the ailerons in particular would shake violently, placing great strain on the pilot and airframe, and sometimes resulting in structural failure. The nub of the problem was that the weight of the control surfaces was often balanced badly about the hinges: the solution was to balance the surfaces with metal weights, usually cantilevered out in front of the leading edges in the form of horn-mounted metal bullets. This kept down the weight of metal needed, while damping any incipient flutter before it became dangerous.

The question of balancing the aeroplane around its longitudinal centre of gravity also received much attention in the closing stages of World War I and the years immediately following. All aircraft are sensitive to the position of the centre of gravity relative to the centre of lift, and this was very noticeable in the small and relatively light aircraft of the early period, where the weight of the pilot

Above: Introduced to limited service in 1938, the Grumman F3F carrierborne fighter was a fascinating blend of old and new. The most obsolescent feature was the retention of the biplane wing cellule, while modern features included the well cowled radial piston engine, the enclosed cockpit and the retractable main landing gear units.

Below: Despite its obsolescence, the Bristol Bulldog remained in service throughout the 1930s, being retired from British service in 1937 but remaining operational with the Finnish air force to 1940.

Above: The Dornier Wal long-range flying boat was typical of Dornier's design thinking, and was a successful type that incorporated fuselage-mounted stabilizing sponsons and a parasol wing with a tandem push/pull pair of engines installed in its centre section.

Below: As one of the leaders in the development of four-engined heavy bombers, the USSR had a number of advanced designs under design or test in the mid-1930s. Typical of these was the Bolkhovitinov DB-A that was first flown in March 1936 and revealed outstanding performance. The type had no open gun positions, and the main landing gear units retracted into the 'trouser legs' extending down from the inboard engines. This arrangement reduced drag but avoided the higher weight that would have resulted from the use of main units that retracted into the underside of the inner nacelles. The type was not ordered into production as the Tupolev ANT-42 was superior and entered service as the Petlyakov Pe-8.

might comprise some 10 per cent or more of the machine's flying weight. While it was possible to locate the heaviest items, such as the engine, fuel and armament, on either side of the centre of gravity so that they balanced each other, this was not always the case with the crew: there just was not enough space near the centre of gravity to allow every major item of weight to be located in the optimum position.

Designers were faced with the problems of crew changes: one day the gunner, normally located half way between the centre of gravity and the tail, might be a man weighing 150 lb (68 kg) but on the next day a man turning the scales at 200 lb (91 kg). The trim problems were acute, but all the designer could do in working out the dispositions of the aircraft was work on the average weight of a gunner. If, for example, the aeroplane had a heavy gunner it would become tail heavy, which was not necessarily dangerous but meant that the pilot had to fly with a constant amount of down elevator to hold the aeroplane in the right flying attitude. This was tiring for the pilot, and reduced the speed of the aeroplane slightly because of the slight drag of the elevator.

The problem became acute with larger machines, but Herbert Smith of the Sopwith firm came up with the solution: a tailplane of variable incidence, first used in 1916 on the remarkable Sopwith 1½ Strutter escort, bombing and reconnaissance machine. Operated by a worm gear controlled via cables by the pilot, the incidence of the whole tailplane could be changed from 0° to a slight positive angle if the gunner were heavier than average, and to a slight negative angle if he were lighter than average. There was a price to be paid in slightly increased drag, but at least the strain on the pilot was removed. And the adjustable tailplane offered numerous further advantages over the fixed tailplane

once the problems of weight distribution were eased.

In the 1920s the same idea was extended to other controls, in the form of trim tabs, either attached to, or constructed as part of, the main control surfaces. So, for example, if the pilot discovers that his machine is loaded slightly eccentrically with a tendency for the port wing to fly marginally lower than the starboard one, he can set the trim tabs on the port aileron a few degrees up. This depresses the aileron and brings up the port wing, at the same time lowering the starboard wing. In the 1930s such trim tabs became common features on all three main control surfaces, greatly assisting the pilot.

Perhaps the most important application of the idea is the trim tab on the rudder of multi-engined aircraft. If an engine fails on one side of the aeroplane, the rudder must be used to counter the asymmetric thrust of the remaining engines and make the aeroplane fly straight. This puts great strain on the pilot's legs, which operate the rudder control. A rudder trim tab copes neatly with the problem.

As the increasing size and weight of aircraft made control difficult once again, balanced controls were no longer sufficient, and the solution favoured by the British in particular, on bombers and transports, was servo control. This uses the aerodynamic forces at the pilot's disposal to operate the main control surfaces. On a large rudder, for example, an auxiliary control some two to three times larger than the trim tab might be set into the trailing edge, or fitted on short booms just behind the trailing edge. When the pilot wants to turn left, by moving the rudder's trailing edge in that direction, he operates the controls in the normal way. These now turn the servo flap to the right, and little force is needed since the area of this surface is relatively small. But since the servo flap is mounted some way behind the hinge line of the rudder's main control surface, its leverage is increased and the effect is to turn the main rudder to the left. The turn required by the pilot has therefore been achieved, with the main work done by the servo flap.

Boulton Paul used this idea extensively in its bombers, but the increased drag and other technical factors prevented the servo flap from really catching on. A better solution was found in the 1930s, when power-assisted controls came into use on larger aircraft. Here the control surfaces were adjusted by powered mechanisms within the wing when the pilot moved his controls. Combined with balanced surfaces to reduce the power needed, this last solution is still used today, although in a greatly developed form. With feedback circuits to give the pilot 'feel', the pilot can get the best out of the whole system without over stressing the aeroplane's structure.

In the 1920s, therefore, aerodynamicists and other technical innovators had produced the information and means of producing safer, larger aircraft capable of highly improved performance. Yet their achievements could never have been properly exploited without the efforts of the structural engineers. The designers and theorists may dream up ever more advanced aircraft, but it is engineers who give those dreams concrete expression, and their work was never more important than in the period between the two world wars.

With a few exceptions such as the Junkers and Dornier aircraft in Germany and the advanced but impractical Antoinette Latham (Monobloc) of 1911, aircraft structures up to the end of World War I had followed the tried and tested formula of wooden construction with canvas covering. Wood had great advantages as the main structural material: it was light, cheap, easily worked and had a good strength-to-weight ratio. Large quantities of well-seasoned wood were available: light but strong spruce for fuselage longerons and spars; plywood for fuselage formers and wing ribs; and ash or hickory for the landing gear, where great strength was needed regardless of weight. Metal was restricted (in the airframe) to fittings and bracing wires.

Yet from the earliest days of heavier-than-air flight designers and engineers realized that wood had its drawbacks, especially as the size of aircraft began to increase. Large aircraft could indeed be built of wood, but their structures were prohibitively heavy and complex. Here metal offered distinct advantages, particularly when light alloys such as Duralumin arrived on the scene during World War I. But it was not only on grounds of weight and complexity that wood had its limitations. The trouble with the conventional wooden structure was that it allowed little aerodynamic refinement.

The fuselage, for example, consisted of four wooden longerons running the length of the structure and giving it its basic form. These were held apart and given rigidity as a structure by a series of transverse formers or spacers, braced three-dimensionally by wires in most aircraft. The whole structure thus resembled a long, often tapering, box. Where no aerodynamic refinement was required in the way of streamlining, the structure could merely be covered with canvas, which was then doped to tighten and windproof it.

If the designer wished to give his creation a streamlined appearance to improve its performance, the basic box was fitted with a number of external formers complete with longitudinal stringers, which could then be covered with canvas. Yet this canvas was still rough in finish and was laced onto the structure with string, the whole looking superficially streamlined but offering great resistance to the air. The wings, built up in a similar fashion, also produced considerable drag, as did the interplane struts and the flying and landing wires which braced the whole biplane structure into a rigid box.

There were thus three basic parts to the structure of early aircraft a basic frame, shape-giving struts and a canvas covering.

Forward-looking pioneers soon turned their attention to ways of simplifying this confusion, and producing stronger and better streamlined shapes. The problem was that wood made it difficult to design aircraft in which the three basic elements could be combined into one, or at most two. Progress was made just before the war by Louis Bechereau, Deperdussin's chief designer and the man responsible for the Deperdussin Monocoque racer. Monocoque, an improvised word whose two components translate as 'single' and 'shell', is the term that had come to be used for the type of fuselage which combines the three

components of earlier structures. In these pre-war types, the fuselage was a hollow shell of plywood, sometimes stiffened with internal formers and stringers, which bore the load and also provided the right streamlined shape. The advantages were obvious: good shape, rigid structure and relative simplicity. Bechereau, developing the ideas of a Swedish engineer, had set aircraft construction on the road towards the modern fuselage.

Unfortunately, the same sort of construction cannot be used for the wings. Junkers got half way to a solution to this problem during World War I, with his cantilevered monoplane wings of metal construction, before Dr Adolph Rohrbach devised his concept of wings with 'stressed skins', later worked up and improved by H. A. Wagner in the United States. In Rohrbach's stressed-skin structure, the wings were covered in metal, which could itself bear a considerable part of the loads acting on the wing structure. Inside the stressed skin were spars bearing the main part of the loads, and ribs to give the skin its shape. This concept differed radically from that of Hugo Junkers, whose corrugated skinning bore little of the load, but depended on a wing structure of conventional design. Rohrbach's structure featured a smooth covering that could support a considerable load, allowing the inside structure to be lightened, while at the same time producing a reduced

Above: one of the greatest of all biplane flying trainers, the Boeing (Stearman) PT-13 Kaydet was built in very large numbers during World War II, and is still a popular type with enthusiasts and, until very recently, crop-spraying pilots.

The Loening OA-1 was an amphibian flying boat originally intended for the observation role. It was an interesting type that maintained considerable utility into its technical obsolescence.

amount of drag because of the very much improved streamlining. Rohrbach's ideas had been paralleled in Germany during World War I by Claude Dornier, one of the Zeppelin company's chief designers. In 1917 he designed the CL I experimental fighter, which had conventional wings, but a metal monocoque fuselage.

The first full expression of the ideal combination of stressed-skin flying surfaces and a metal monocoque fuselage was in the Short Silver Streak (first called the Swallow), built in 1920 and exhibited at the Olympia Aero Show of the same year. All agreed that the type was very interesting, but the principle of stressed-skin and monocoque construction seemed no more than an oddity.

In the United Kingdom the idea passed almost immediately into a temporary limbo. Traditional structures still seemed to offer sufficient scope to the designer, although metal came to be used increasingly in place of wood for the main structural components. There were two reasons for this. First, the increased availability of light alloys offered the designer and engineer the chance to built conventional aircraft out of modern materials that would last well and were easy to make. Second, the British Air Ministry was disturbed at the way in which good-

quality timber for airframe construction had become difficult to procure during World War I. In 1924 it was decided that the main structure of all military aircraft should henceforth be of metal; and this had its effect on other types of aircraft.

The tendency to ignore the new techniques was world-wide in fact: Junkers aircraft, for example, were designed on World War I principles and merely translated into metal, and the same applied in the United States. Yet these were steps, however tentative and slow, in the right direction; and the economic situation of the 1920s would have made it hard for companies to go over to stressed-skin construction even had they wanted to. The use of metal in place of wood for old-fashioned structures was quite cheap, for the same type of jigs could be used, and no expensive machine tools were required. All that was needed were trained welders and basic welding equipment.

Yet experience in the use of metal was slowly gained, so that when the advantages of stressed-skin construction became apparent to all during the 1930s, the conversion was relatively painless. Once the Americans had shown the way forward, the rest of the aeronautical world followed swiftly.

Right: The 1920s and 1930s saw limited but far-sighted interest in the concept of tailless aircraft as a means of reducing drag and thereby boosting performance with an engine of given power. The leading British protagonist of such aircraft was Dr (later Professor) Geoffrey Hill, whose Pterodactyl series was built by Westland. This is the Pterodactyl V.

The widespread introduction of metal was especially noticeable in the design of the landing gear. During World War I this part of the aircraft had comprised a pair of steel-tube or wood 'vees' attached to the lower two longerons of the fuselage and splayed outward at their lower ends, where the axle ran through the angle of the vees, to which it was bound down with 'bungee' or rubber shock cord to provide a measure of springing. Together with the wheels, the whole structure created a massive amount of drag.

The increasing weight and size of aircraft towards the end of the war and in the years immediately afterwards made matters worse, and the landing gear of civil transports became a tangle of steel tubes attached to the wings, fuselage and engines. The only important developments in landing gear design was a gradual widening of the track, to provide more stability on the ground. Bungee gradually disappeared, to be replaced by vertically coiled springs, but there had been little advance even by the late 1920s.

Suddenly, however, designers saw the need to do something radical to the landing gear. There were two alternatives: either to 'clean up' the fixed landing gear and so reduce its drag, or to make it retract into the wings or fuselage and so remove the drag entirely. The first solution was favoured by many designers, for advances in metallurgy and the development of oleo-pneumatic suspension made it possible to design neat cantilevered single legs, usually well faired and with the wheel incorporated in low-drag spats. This helped to improve performance, and avoided the weight and complexity of a retractable system. Smaller aircraft, especially fighters, profited greatly from such installations during the early 1930s.

Larger machines tended towards retractable landing gear. The first such units had been developed as early as 1908 by an American, M. B. Sellers, but he had worked in almost total isolation and had had no effect on subsequent developments. Experiments with semi- and fully-retractable landing gear continued in desultory fashion up to the end of World War I; then the idea was used on a variety of racing aircraft. The weight of such units was too great for conventional aircraft, however, until the new breed of American transport aircraft appeared in the late 1920s and early 1930s.

During this period there was rapid progress, with the Americans and Europeans producing a bewildering variety of landing gear arrangements, retracting into the wings, engine nacelles and fuselage; backwards, forwards, inwards, and outwards; manually, electrically and hydraulically operated. The power of the engines that began to appear in the decade after World War I gradually made the weight penalty of such landing gears acceptable, and did much to make the new era of high-speed flight a possibility.

The two most important types of engine used in World War I had been the inline and the rotary, with the latter slowly declining in importance as it approached its theoretical limits and problems with the torque of the rotating crankcase and cylinders became acute. The inline continued to develop more and more power, but this type of engine was water-cooled and the weight of the water, radiators, pumps and all the associated 'plumbing' seriously affected performance.

In the closing stages of the war there began to appear a number of engines based on the radial layout, in which the cylinders are arranged radially round the crankshaft. Such an engine, its devotees claimed, had the great advantage that all it cylinders could easily be exposed to the slipstream as the aeroplane passed through the air and could be cooled by this rather than water.

Few such engines had been fully developed before the end of World War I, and much more work was done during

the 1920s, particularly by Bristol and Armstrong Siddeley in the United Kingdom, Wright and Pratt & Whitney in the United States, BMW in Germany, Gnome-Rhône in France, and Alfa-Romeo in Italy. By 1929 the average military radial engine was developing about 600 hp, compared with some 250 hp at the end of World War I. Improvements in fuels, metallurgy and design led to rapid advances in the early 1930s, moreover, and the Americans were soon building radials developing1,200 hp or more, with most contemporary European engines rated at about 1,000 hp.

As its advocates claimed, the radial was considerably lighter than an inline of comparable power. The only disadvantage was that the radial was also considerably larger in frontal area, and so tended to produce a lot of drag, especially when the cylinder heads protruded beyond the lines of the fuselage, which they commonly did in the 1920s. This mattered little in commercial aircraft, where power, reliability and fuel economy were more important than performance, but it was a serious disadvantage for military aircraft.

The problem was eased by careful cowling of the cylinder heads, with fairings in front and behind each one, but this was only an interim solution that still developed a lot of drag. The two best solutions were in the Townend ring and NACA cowlings. Both worked on the same principle as the slotted wing. The Townend ring, as its name implies, was a ring fitting closely round the nose of the fuselage, just over the cylinder heads. It was of aerofoil section, with the 'lifting' side innermost: this smoothed out the airflow past the heads, and also aided cooling. The NACA cowling went a step further, and gave the Townend type of cowling much wider chord as wind tunnel tests had shown that this improved the airflow still more.

The Americans, who had the fuel and metallurgy skills to make the most out of radials, soon became dominant in the field and most American civil and military aircraft of the last 15 years before World War II were radial-engined. The Europeans, with the exception of the Italians, tended to favour inline engines for military aircraft. The small frontal area of the inline allowed aircraft to be well streamlined, and offered enemy gunners a smaller target than radial-engined aircraft. But, like the Americans, the Europeans found radial engines best for medium-speed, high-payload operations, so most airliners and military transports were powered by radial engines.

Left: Another means of reducing drag that witnessed considerable experimentation in the 1920s and early 1930s was retractable landing gear. One of the first such machines was the Bristol Racer of 1922, a British machine with a portly but low-drag fuselage, cantilever wings, and main landing gear units that were retractable into the undersides of the wings by a chain-and-sprocket system manually operated by the pilot.

Below: Notable for its utter reliability, the Junkers W 34 was one of the classic light transport aircraft of the period, and was of Junkers' standard metal construction with corrugated skinning. The type could be operated on wheel, float or ski landing gear.

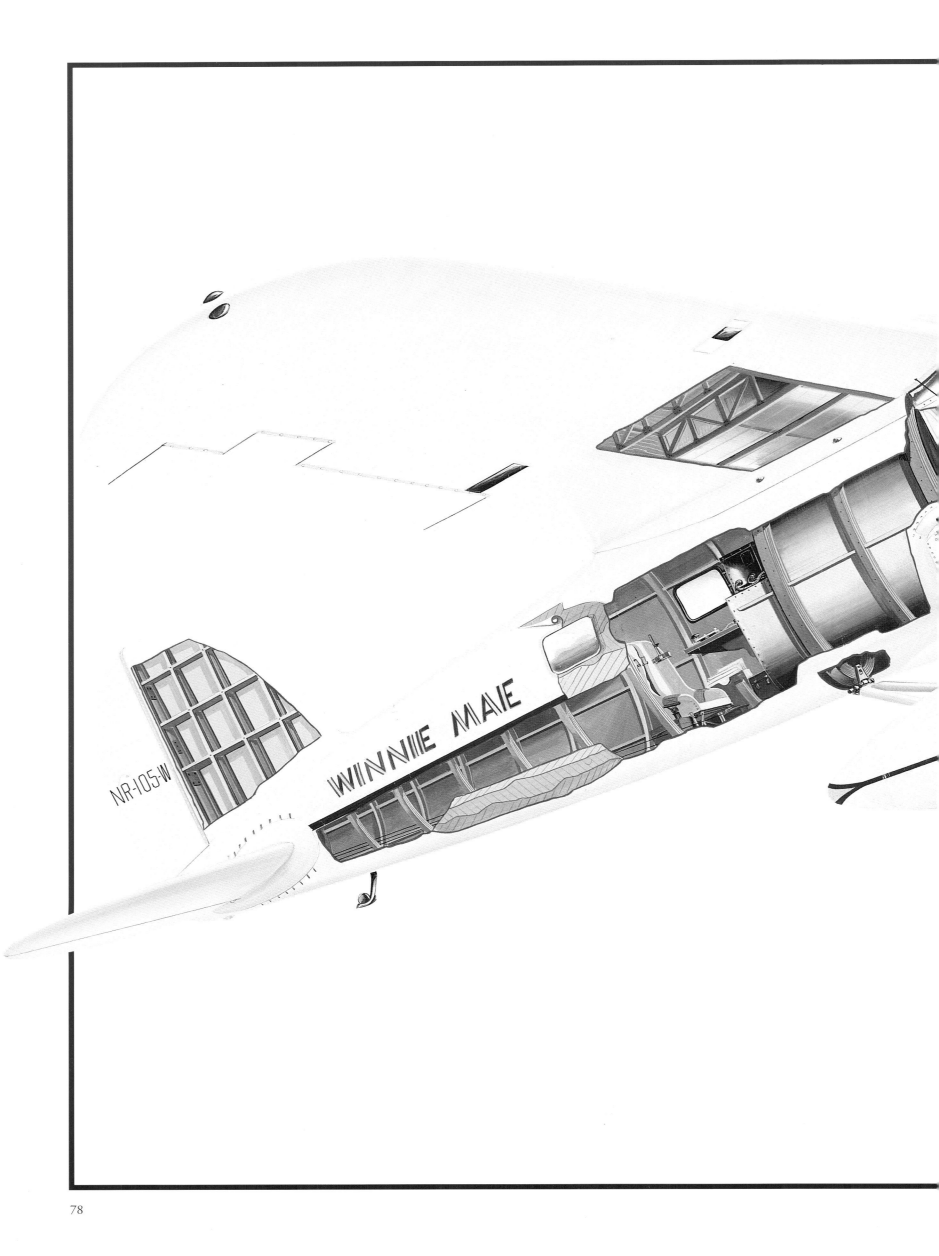

The Distance Flights

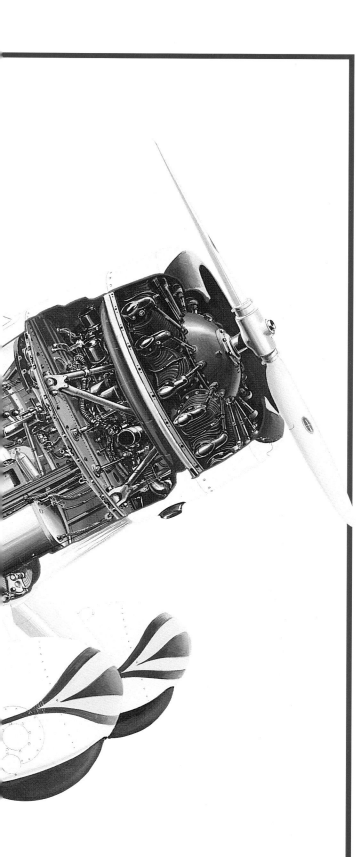

The Winnie Mae of Oklahoma was a Lockheed Vega high-wing monoplane and, as the aeroplane in which Wiley Post flew around the world, remains one of the most celebrated record-breakers of all time. The type also secured useful sales as an executive transport and air taxi, thereby providing ample proof of its reliability as well as its excellent performance.

Racing series like the Schneider Trophy competitions produced the ultimate aircraft of the period, when measured in terms of performance at any cost. Yet the same period in the late 1920s and early 1930s saw another type of competitive flying: record-breaking flights over increasingly long distances. While the purely speed contests required advanced technology and received government sponsorship, long-distance flying was generally the domain of private pilots.

The technical requirements for speed racing and for distance flying were, inevitably, completely different. Where the speed racers could exploit technical advances to the maximum, in airframes, engines and fuels, aircraft designed for long-distance flying placed far greater emphasis on reliability. Thus they generally pushed forward the boundaries of existing technology rather than broke aerodynamic and metallurgical boundaries.

The engines of speed racers, for example, needed to deliver very high power for only a few hours before wearing out; the engines of long-distance aircraft, on the other hand, were required to run for a long period at a steady if unspectacular output. Failure to do so could easily force the distance flyer down into the vastness of some ocean or desert, or indeed in any of the world's other inhospitable regions. Furthermore, long-distance aircraft had to provide at least a modicum of comfort to mitigate the onset of pilot fatigue, and for the same reason needed basically sound flying characteristics.

In practical terms, the most immediate beneficiaries of such long-distance flying were the burgeoning number of civil airlines, especially those that were starting to provide regular services. Bombers also derived benefits from the experience of long-distance flying and aircraft: as a direct result, navigational skills increased and machines capable of carrying a significant payload began to appear on the designers' drawing boards.

There had been a number of pioneering long-distance flights immediately after World War I, the most notable being the first crossing of the Atlantic by American Curtiss seaplanes, and the first nonstop Atlantic crossing by Alcock and Brown, both in 1919. The aircraft used in these flights were basically World War I types modified for the specific demands of these epoch-making flights, but from the early 1920s long-distance flights were made in an increasing number of new aircraft.

In 1924, four Douglas 'World Cruisers' of the US Army departed on the first flight round the world. Departing from Seattle, Washington, on 6 April, the four aircraft flew via the Aleutian Islands, Japan and India, through Europe to Scotland, Iceland and Greenland, and so back to Seattle. Two of the aircraft arrived back at their departure point on 28 September after a remarkable journey which had lasted 175 days. Although the average speed of the aircraft was slow, the achievement was an extraordinary one in every other respect. The mere fact that two of the four aircraft, operating from wheeled or float landing gear as required, had even managed to fly around the world was in itself a great feat, especially considering the inhospitality of some of the areas through which they passed. The next round-the-world flight was not made until five years later, when the Graf Zeppelin, an airship, achieved the feat in 21 days, 7 hours and 34 minutes. It was a further two years before another heavier-than-air craft flew round the world again.

The Atlantic remained the chief lure for long-distance fliers, however, and in 1924 while the American 'World Cruisers' were still on their great flight, the Italian pioneer Locatelli attempted a trans-Atlantic flight in a Dornier Wal flying boat. Forced down into the sea, the flying boat stayed afloat for some time and three days later Locatelli and his crew were rescued by a passing ship

In 1926 the same type of flying boat had been used by Major Franco and his crew of three in a successful crossing of the South Atlantic from Spain to Rio de Janeiro in Brazil via the Canary Islands, the Cape Verde Islands and Pernambuco. The Wal was a relatively ungainly machine, but proved a very popular model for long-distance flights because it had good range in its basic form and also because it had well-proved qualities on the water. The latter was a factor offering considerable comfort to long-distance crews who could well be forced down onto the sea and then have to await rescue by a ship.

Not all failures in the Atlantic had as fortunate an outcome as Locatelli's. On 8 May 1927 the great French ace of World War I, Captain Charles Nungesser, set off with Captain FranÁois Coli to fly from Paris to Newfoundland in a Levasseur PL 8 named Oiseau Blanc (white bird). Flying against the prevailing winds, Nungesser and Coli failed to arrive in Newfoundland at the time expected. France buzzed with rumours that the intrepid pair had met with all manner of unlikely fates, but no trace of the two pilots and their aeroplane was ever located. It seems most likely that they ran out of fuel or suffered engine failure, came down in the Atlantic and were drowned.

While the loss of Nungesser and Coli was still fresh in people's minds, the greatest of all the early long-distance flights took place. On 20/21 May 1927 Captain Charles A. Lindbergh flew across the North Atlantic from Long Island, New York, to Paris. The world was astounded by the achievement and heroism of this unknown American pilot.

Lindbergh's flight was a landmark in every respect. It was the first solo nonstop transatlantic flight and, unlike earlier pioneers, Lindbergh had flown in effect from one major city to another. Alcock and Brown, for example, had set off from Newfoundland, the most easterly point ill the Americas, and landed near Clifden in County Galway, on Ireland's western coast, thus making their crossing by the

shortest possible route. Lindbergh had taken off just outside New York and landed just outside Paris, so winning the $25,000 prize offered by Raymond Orteig for the first New York-Paris or Paris-New York flight.

Desperately short of money to commission and buy an aeroplane for the attempt, Lindbergh had received great assistance from a group of businessmen in St Louis, Missouri. Designed to his own specifications by the Ryan company of San Diego, California, the NYP Spirit of St Louis was an advanced and attractive design powered by a Wright air-cooled radial, which was a type of engine currently gaining great favour in the United States for its lightness and reliability.

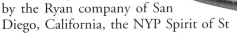

The Spirit of St Louis had one very odd and potentially dangerous feature, namely the lack of direct forward vision from the cockpit. This was unavoidable because the large quantity of fuel needed for the flight weighed a great deal and had to be located near or on the aeroplane's centre of gravity. In a machine of the NYP's relatively small size, the only place was immediately behind the engine in the space normally occupied by the pilot's cockpit. Ryan and Lindbergh were forced to relocate the cockpit farther toward the tail, behind the fuel tank, with conventional side windows and a periscope so that the pilot could see forward.

Lindbergh was a very competent pilot, having learned to fly with the US Army before becoming a barnstormer, exhibition pilot and mailplane flier. He needed all his skill right from the start, for the tricky take-off from Long Island with his great load of fuel. The difficulties of flying and navigating across the Atlantic, and just keeping awake, were equally taxing and then there were the problems of landing outside Paris, where a large crowd had gathered to greet him. Sad to relate, the American press had mocked Lindbergh's preparations as those of a fool. After the event, however, they joined with the European press and people all over the world in lionizing the first man to fly solo across the Atlantic.

The fame resulting from his triumph proved a mixed blessing for Lindbergh. At first it brought him wealth and an enviable position in the United States, but it also made him a target for the criminals who kidnapped and murdered his child. After visiting the Germany of the Third Reich, Lindbergh was so impressed by its apparent invincibility that he attempted to revive traditional feelings of isolationism in the United States and so fell into disfavour with the American public during World War II.

Below: Though conceived as a long-range bomber, the Vickers Wellesley was a great example of the range performance attainable in the mid-1930s through the combination of a sturdy airframe, a large and lightly loaded wing, and a reliable radial piston engine. Such a combination was readily transferable to civil transports, and in aircraft such as the Boeing Model 247 and Douglas DC-2 proved that civil transport was feasible in terms of despatch reliability, passenger safety and commercial profitability.

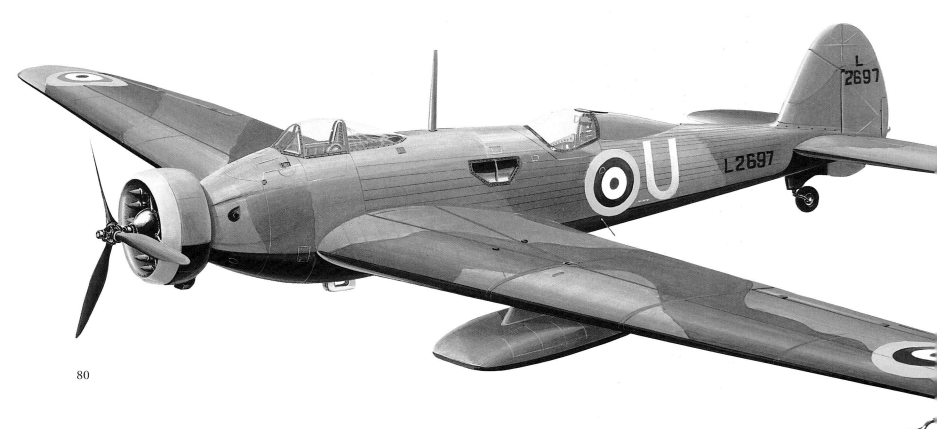

Nevertheless, Lindbergh's place in aviation history rests on the remarkable achievement of his flight between New York and Paris, the preparations for which were almost entirely his own work. His success also served to stimulate other aviators keen to make their mark on history. Shortly after Lindbergh's flight, Clarence Chamberlin, with C. A. Levine as his passenger, attempted a nonstop flight from just outside New York to Berlin. Chamberlin took off in his Wright-Bellanca W.B.2 Columbia monoplane on 4 June 1927, but came down in Eisleben, well short of Berlin, two days later after a flight of 3,911 miles (6394 km).

Flights across the Atlantic still beckoned the adventurous, but there now followed a series of disastrous failures. F. F. Minchin, L. Hamilton and the Princess Loewenstein-Wertheim were lost over the North Atlantic during an attempt to fly from the United Kingdom to Canada; and the great British pioneer airline pilot, Captain W. G. R. 'Bert' Hinchcliffe, together with the Hon. Elsie Mackay, also died in the ocean.

Finally, a successful east-to-west crossing was made. Captain Hermann Kohl, Colonel James Fitzmaurice and G‚nther, Graf von H‚nefeld left Baldonnel, Ireland, in a Junkers F13 named Bremen, and landed on Greenly Island off Labrador one day later on 13 April 1928. The Atlantic had now been conquered in both directions and the great feats in long-distance flying moved elsewhere.

Yet the Atlantic still exerted a strong pull on would-be record breakers, and many who would win fame for other flights served their apprenticeship crossing the North and South Atlantic. The high-wing monoplane Fokkers were now at their peak: in 1928 Amelia Earhart, an American pilot destined for a mysterious end, crossed from west to east as passenger in a Fokker, while Charles Kingsford-Smith made an east-west crossing, also in a Fokker.

Pilots were now attempting increasingly lengthy routes: for example, on 15/16 July 1931 the Hungarians Gyorgy Endres and Alexander Magyar flew from Newfoundland to Budapest in their Lockheed Model 8 Sirius, and on 28/30 July 1931 Russell Boardman and John Polando flew a Bellanca from New York to Istanbul. By 10 August 1934 the North Atlantic had been flown 45 times, in all cases but four by heavier-than-air machines. By the end of September 1934 the South Atlantic had also been flown many times: 31 crossings, all by heavier-than-air craft.

Other long-distance flights, often as difficult but generally less well known, were also being tried. In 1920, for example, a small fleet of Italian aircraft comprising four

Capronis and seven SVAs set off from Rome to fly to Tokyo in a journey that was more fraught with difficulties than can easily be imagined. The aircraft had to cross some of the most desolate and backward areas in the world. Of the 11 aircraft only two SVAs reached Tokyo, one flown by Masiero and the other by Ferrarin, who later made a great name for himself both in the Schneider Trophy races and with several record-breaking flights over long distance. It had taken the two Italians almost three months to make the trip.

Other great flights to the Far East were those of Pelletier d'Oisy and Bésin, who took a little less than seven weeks to fly a Breguet 19GR from Paris to Tokyo in 1924, and de Pinedo and Campanelli who in 1925 flew from Lake Maggiore to Tokyo and back in a Savoia-Marchetti flying boat. The outward leg of this 34,000-mile (54720-km) journey included a flight round Australia. In the same year, Pelletier d'Oisy flew from Paris to Peking in the remarkably short time of one week.

Yet it was not only Europeans who were making these great flights to the Orient. In 1925, for example, the Japanese Abe and Kawashi flew their Breguet 19 from Tokyo to Paris. This type was the most celebrated French long-distance aeroplane of the time and made many great flights, including two crossings of the Atlantic. The most famous Breguet 19 was the one named Point d'Interrogation (question mark), flown from Paris to New York by Costes and Bellonte of France on 1/2 September 1930. Unusually for the period, the Breguet 19 was a military aeroplane, specially adapted with extra fuel tankage, at a time when most other long-distance machines were built specifically for this task or alternatively adapted from civil machines that had already proved their range capabilities.

The first flights over the Arctic region were made between 21 May and 17 June 1925 in a pair of Dornier Wal flying boats crewed by the great Norwegian explorer Roald Amundsen with Lincoln Ellsworth and by the four Norwegians Dietriebsen, Feucht, Omdel and Ruser-Larsen. The base for these flights was the island of Spitzbergen. The greatest feat in Arctic flying, however, is credited to two Americans, Commander Richard Byrd and Floyd Bennett. Leaving Spitzbergen in a Fokker F VII monoplane on 9 May 1926, the Americans claimed to have flown over the North Pole. This claim, accepted without hesitation at the time, has more recently been disputed, but there is no definite proof either way.

The first flight over the Antarctic was made by an Australian, Captain Sir Hubert Wilkins. With Lieutenant Carl Eielson as his pilot, Wilkins flew from Deception Island south over Grahamland and then back to Deception Island on 20 December 1928 in a Lockheed Model 1 Vega high-wing monoplane. Earlier in the same year, on 20/22 April, Wilkins and Eielson had made another remarkable flight in the same type of aeroplane, covering 2,200 miles

(3540 km) over the Arctic from Point Barrow in Alaska to Green Harbour in Spitzbergen via the area north of Grantland and Greenland. It was for this exploit that Wilkins had been knighted.

As with the North Pole, however, the United States is credited with the first flight over the South Pole: starting from Little America, a US base in Antarctica, Byrd flew in a Ford 4-AT-15 Trimotor monoplane, piloted by Berndt Balchen, south to the pole and thence back to Little America on 28/29 November 1929. Other members of the crew were the Americans June and McKinley. Byrd, by then a rear-admiral, made one more flight over Antarctic regions in December 1933, in a Curtiss-Wright Condor, flying as far south as latitude 70∞ from a base in the Ross Sea area.

Although not particularly impressive as regards distance, these

The Fokker type of high-wing monoplane had particularly good range, and was doing well in both civil and military service.

On 28/29 June 1931, Harold Gatty and Wiley Post flew the North Pacific from Solomon Beach, Alaska, to Khabarovsk in Siberia in their Lockheed Model 5 Vega, as one of the stages in their epic flight round the world. An even greater landmark was the first nonstop flight across the North Pacific on 4/5 October 1931. In one of the popular Bellancas, named Miss Veedol, Hugh Herndon and Clyde Pangborn flew from Tokyo to Wenatchee, Washington, on their way around the world.

Flying a Lockheed Model 8 Altair, Kingsford-Smith, now knighted and with Captain Taylor as his crew, made the first crossing of the Pacific in a single-engined aeroplane between 22 October

Above: The newly created Soviet state made great strides in the development of aviation and its supporting aero industry in the 1920s, and among its most impressive products was the Tupolev ANT-25 long-distance aeroplane.

pioneering flights over the poles did emphasize the growing confidence pilots had in their machines to carry them over regions in which any forced landing would almost certainly have proved fatal: indeed, a landing in the Arctic or Antarctic was certain death, for there was no chance of being picked up, and the weather and lack of food would quickly have ended any efforts to walk out. The polar flights also helped pave the way for the type of polar exploration that became common in the 1940s and 1950s, with aircraft an accepted vehicle for transport and supply.

After the conquest of the North and South Atlantic the great challenge of long-distance flight was the mighty Pacific Ocean. The first crossing had been made during the US Army's round-the-world flight in 1924, when the four Douglas 'World Cruisers' had flown from the Aleutian Islands to Japan. A gap of almost three years followed before the next attempt: on 1 June 1927, Lieutenants Lester Maitland and Albert Hegenberger flew a Fokker C-2 Bird of Paradise transport over the 2,400 miles (3850 km) from Oakland, California to Honolulu in the Hawaiian Islands in a fraction under 26 hours.

So great are the distances involved that it was quite out of the question for aircraft of the 1920s and early 1930s to fly nonstop across the full breadth of the Pacific Ocean. The main routes between land masses therefore became the important factors. The first man to make the significant crossing from the United States to Australia was Squadron-Leader Charles Kingsford-Smith, with fellow Australian Flight-Lieutenant Charles Ulm and Americans Harry Lyons and J. W. Warner as crew.

In the now famous Fokker F VII/3m Southern Cross, Kingsford-Smith and his crew set off from Oakland on 31 May 1928. Flying via Honolulu and Fiji, a remarkable feat of navigation, Kingsford-Smith and his crew arrived in Brisbane, Queensland on 10 June after a nine-day flight.

and 4 November 1934. His route was the reverse of the one he had taken in 1928. This great flight provides striking evidence that confidence in the reliability of aircraft and their engines had increased still further.

Women played their own part in the conquest of the Pacific: on 11/12 January 1935 Amelia Earhart became the first woman to fly across the ocean when she took a Lockheed Model 5 Vega from Oakland to Honolulu. On 21/22 May 1932, as Mrs Putman, she had also made the first solo west-to-east crossing of the North Atlantic by a woman, flying from Harbour Grace, Newfoundland, to Londonderry in Northern Ireland.

One of the greatest women pilots ever, Amelia Earhart was finally lost on the trans-Pacific leg of an attempted round-the-world flight in 1937. To this day, stories are told of her being shot down by the Japanese and executed as a spy. It is possible that she was indeed involved in reconnaissance of Japanese military developments on their Pacific islands, but it was always more probable that she suffered an engine failure, or hit a major storm, crashed in the Pacific and was drowned. In the early 1990s, however, the probable remains of her aeroplane were located on a remote Pacific island and it has become almost certain that she suffered a navigation failure, landed on this island and subsequently perished from lack of water.

While pilots of all nations, together with American civilian aviators, were concentrating their efforts on record-breaking flights across the major oceans, pilots of the US Army made a number of remarkable flights within their own large country. In September 1922, for example, Lieutenant James Doolittle, later a celebrated Schneider Trophy pilot and leader of the famous 'Doolittle Raid' on Tokyo in 1942, made a great flight across the United States from Jacksonville, Florida to San Diego. He completed the journey in just over 21 hours, with only one refuelling stop, in an Airco D.H.4 built in the USA as a de Havilland DH-4 Liberty Plane. Eight months later, Lieutenants John Macready and Oakley Kelley flew a single-engined Fokker T-2 over a nonstop distance of 2,500 miles (4025 km) from New York in just under 27 hours. The two men had only just established a world duration record of just over 36 hours in the same machine.

June 1924 saw yet another triumph for the US Army when Lieutenant Russell Maughan 'raced the sun' across the United States in a Curtiss PW-8 fighter from New York to San Francisco, a distance of 2,670 miles (4300 km).

A further advance in long-distance flying was made during the first week of January 1929, when a Fokker C-2A was kept in the air for 150 hours with the aid of air-to-air refuelling. The aeroplane, named Question Mark, was crewed by Major Carl Spaatz, Captain Ira Eaker, Lieutenants Harry Halverson and Elwood Quesada, and Sergeant Roy Hoe: all four officers were to rise to high command in World War II.

In the course of the flight the C-2A was refuelled no less than 37 times from a Douglas O-2C, which also supplied oil and other necessary items. The technique was rudimentary, to say the least, requiring someone in the C-2A to grasp the hose as it was lowered from the O-2C and then lower the nozzle into the opened filler of the fuel tank before reversing the process at the end of the refuelling. Nevertheless the experiment was successful and paved the way for the air-to-air refuelling techniques now vital for any modern air force.

Although denied the international enthusiasm reserved for the record-breaking trans-oceanic flights, these US Army achievements received much favourable attention within the United States. They helped keep the Air Corps in the limelight and also paid handsome dividends for the US Army's theory and practice of long-range flight and navigation. This interest gradually bore fruit in the mid-1930s, with the development of the first American four-engined heavy bombers.

Other air forces began to acquire an real interest in long-distance flight during the 1920s. Inspired by a desire to publicize the attainments of the first fascist state, General Italo Balbo, Mussolini's air minister, seized upon the idea of mass flights over record-breaking distances. Perhaps excited by the nonstop flight from Italy to Brazil, successfully undertaken on 3/5 July 1928 by Ferrarin and del Prete in a Savoia S.64, Balbo decided that mass flights by Italian aircraft over impressively long stages would suitably enhance Italy's prestige.

For his first effort Balbo led a formation of 10 Savoia S.55 flying boats from Portuguese Guinea to Natal in Brazil on 6 January 1931. Encouraged by the success of this first effort, Balbo then planned a formation flight by no fewer than 24 S.55X twin-hulled flying boats from Italy to the World's Fair, held in Chicago during July 1933. The flying boats took off from Orbetello in Italy on 1 July and arrived in Chicago, after flying via Iceland, on 15 July.

The aerial armada began its journey home 10 days later, but the return was marred by the loss of one flying boat in the Azores, and the death of a crew member in the accident. The remaining 23 S.55Xs arrived home on 12 August to a heroes' welcome. It later became fashionable to regard the whole exercise as comic opera undertaking typical of the grandiose aspirations of the fascist state, but the fact remains that Balbo had achieved a unique feat in aviation, one whose success not many other countries could have emulated.

Meanwhile, the private individuals who had dominated the 'sport' so far were setting their sights on greater objectives. Perhaps the most adventurous of these men were Wiley Post and Harold Gatty. Like Hinchliffe and Coli, who had both disappeared over the Atlantic, Post was blind in one eye, and habitually wore a black patch. Flying possibly the best long-range type of the period, a Lockheed Model 5 Vega named Winnie Mae of Oklahoma, Post and Gatty set off from New York early on 23 June 1931. Stopping to refuel at Harbour Grace in Newfoundland, Chester in England, Berlin, Moscow, Novosibirsk, Blagoveshchensk, Khabarovsk, Fairbanks in Alaska and Edmonton in Canada, Wiley and Post returned to New York on 1 July after a heroic flight of eight days.

The next round-the-world flight was made by Herndon and Pangborn in a Bellanca, and took 81 days. Then followed the first circumnavigation by a flying boat, a Dornier Wal flown by Wolfgang von Gronau, Gerd von Roth, Fritz Albrecht and Franz Hack, in 111 days between 21 July and 9 November 1932.

The greatest long-distance flight of the period, however, took place when Wiley Post flew solo round the world in the remarkable time of 7 days, 18 hours and 49 minutes, between 15 and 22 July 1933. Post's arrival back in New York, to a tumultuous welcome, stole much of the thunder from the departure of Balbo's air armada two days later, much to the displeasure of the Italian air supremo.

To have kept the Winnie Mae of Oklahoma flying at optimum speed and optimum altitude, as well as checking constantly that he was on the right course, was an extraordinary flying accomplishment, especially considering the physical demands of solo flight. But the achievements of men such as Post and Gatty did much to show the public how small the world was, when even single-engined aircraft could circle it in just over seven days.

In many ways Post was typical of the aviators of the period. He had led an adventurous life for some time, having been an exhibition parachutist and worked on an oil-rig. It was while working on the oil-rig that Post lost his left eye, when part of a bolt flew off and hit him.

Opposite Top: The aeroplane that helped to spark a revolution in air-mindedness and thus pave the way for the emergence of civil air transport as a major social and economic force was the Ryan NYP. Named Spirit of St Louis, this was the machine in which Charles Lindbergh made the first solo, nonstop crossing of the North Atlantic between New York and Paris.

Fortunately for the aviation world, Post and Gatty collaborated on a written account of their circumnavigation, and Around the World in Eight Days makes splendid reading. Take, for example, Post's account of their departure from Edmonton, the last stop before New York:

'As we warmed up the engine, the rain stopped. I had told Harold to stay away from that propeller and let the mechanics at the field do all the work. The ship was towed out to the sidewalk and a pair of "mounties" dashed up and down the street in an automobile, clearing away all the traffic.

'At 3.30 am by the local time and 6.30 by the New York daylight (the time on my watch which I had for the past 8 days so that I could time our entrance into Roosevelt Field), I taxied out to the unused streetcar tracks and faced the nose towards the hotel, 2 miles away, at which we had stayed.

'People crowded uncomfortably close to the ship, and I am afraid we seemed impolite to them. Dirt, mud, and spray flew all around while I "revved" the motor up one last time before letting go the brakes. We were to bobble off headed straight for the centre of town, and I didn't want to take any chances of being let down among the corners of the buildings.

8.45 am and I let the Wasp have her head. Curbstones and electric-light poles clipped by the wing tips so fast that I was just a little scared myself. The wind was slightly across our path, and if one wing ever dropped, it would have been just too bad.

'I'm sure neither Harold nor I ever want to or ever will go down a street so fast again. I got a new idea of the ground speed of the Winnie Mae. Loafing along an airport runway, with nothing upright nearer the plane than 100 yards or so, reduces the sensation of high speeds, but now I know what 75 miles an hour feels like!

'Within 15 seconds the outlying houses of town had dropped under the nose. By the time we had reached the first turn in the street, we had a good 500 feet and as I came over the Hotel MacDonald, where our late maÓtre d'hÙtel was on the roof with his whole army of bellhops in array to salute us going by, the ground dropped away fast, and we turned over the high bluff which the hotel tops.'

Post's becoming modesty is apparent throughout the book, not least at the end where he says: 'In our flight around the world, I had satisfied my life's ambition. But it

Below: Another type featuring Bellanca's lifting struts, the Wright-Bellanca WB-2 Columbia was typical of American light transports of the late 1920s and early 1930s in its use of a high-wing layout and a radial piston engine with its cylinder heads exposed to the airflow for the best possible cooling.

was Harold who was the guiding hand of the Winnie Mae. All I did was to follow his instructions in steering, and to keep the ship from spinning out of the thick "pea soup", of which we encountered so much in our trip around the world in eight days.'

The comparison with Balbo's My Air Armada is illuminating. Here, for example is Balbo's version of his reception by Mussolini:

'The first person to greet me as I stepped ashore was the Duce. Neither of us spoke for quite a long while, but the look in his eyes and the warmth of his handclasp were eloquent of tense emotion. Then in a tone of camaraderie he congratulated me and my men on the successful conclusion of our task in a few simple and sincere words, which rang in my ears like anthems of victory. He added that he had arranged the details of a triumph for us such as greeted the return of the Roman legions in the ancient days. The route of the procession would be under the arch of Constantine and along the Imperial Way. Afterwards we were to go to the Palatine. "It is a tribute that your country owes you, Balbo," he concluded with a kindly smile. ...

'When the whole squadron was drawn upon the wharf, I called out in a loud tone: "Attention!" There was a sharp click of heels as they stood at the salute. "God save the Duce! "I shouted. "God save the Duce!" they repeated with one voice, fixing their eyes proudly on their chief. Their words had hardly died away when the crowd redoubled their thunderous applause and clapped their hands in a frenzy of enthusiasm, while the last rays of the sun were reflected in the waters, and the shadows of our first night in Italy began to descend.'

The simplicity of Post's words compares very favourably with the sanctimonious effusiveness of Balbo's, written only two years later. Flying has yet to produce many writers whose works grip the reader, but Post may fairly be ranked with Cecil Lewis and V. M. Yeats of World War I, Antoine de St Exupéry of the years between the wars and into World War II, and Richard Hillary of World War II.

Most of the famous long-distance flights, especially those made by Americans and Italians, were undertaken in monoplanes. In the middle 1920s the United States and Italy had taken a distinct lead over the rest of the world in the development of such long-range monoplanes. The British, on the other hand, were concentrating on developing the last ounce of benefit from the tried and tested biplane formula which had proved so successful during World War I, for the legacy of the War Office's short and misjudged ban on monoplanes as being potentially dangerous was still with the country.

Some interesting monoplane designs had reached prototype form, but these had for the most part been either very large, such as the Rohrbach-Beardmore Inflexible bomber and the Fairey Long-Range Monoplane, or very small lightplanes such as the Blackburn Sidecar (dating from 1918), the Short-Gnosspelius Gull, and a variety of other Short machines. In both these categories, monoplane design was the only practical possibility, for biplane construction was too heavy and clumsy for large aircraft, and produced too much drag for very small aircraft.

Yet no sooner had World War I ended than British aviators were off on a variety of flights to what were to prove their most successful stamping grounds: Africa, India and Australia. First off the mark were Squadron-Leader A. C. S. MacLaren, Lieutenant R. Halley and Brigadier-General N. D. K. McEwen, who between December 1918 and January 1919 flew a Handley Page V/1500 bomber from Martlesham Heath in Suffolk to Delhi in India.

On 12 November 1919 a Vickers Vimy set off from Heston, just outside London, for Australia. Four weeks and two days later the Vimy arrived at Port Darwin in northern Australia after an extremely hazardous flight. The crew of four were Captain Ross Smith, Lieutenant Keith Smith and Sergeants W. H. Shiers and J. M. Bennett. The Smith brothers were knighted for their great efforts in planning and carrying through this difficult flight across areas where there was little chance of finding the right sort of fuel, let alone spares of any kind for the engines. A month after the Smith brothers had arrived in Australia, Lieutenants Parer and McIntosh set off from Hounslow on 8 January 1920, also bent on flying to Australia. Parer and McIntosh were beset by such great difficulties, however, that they did not reach Port Darwin until 2 August 1920, almost seven months after they had set out.

Cape Town was another objective for ambitious pilots, and on 4 February 1920 the first flight to South Africa started from London, the aviators being Colonel Pierre Van Ryneveld and Captain Quintin Brand. The trip started in a Vickers Vimy, but Ryneveld and Brand finished their journey at Cape Town on 20 March, having flown some 8,500 miles (13680 km) in an air time of 4 days 13 hours 30 minutes, in an Airco D.H.9.

Below: The Dornier Do X was an attempt to create a heavy-lift flying boat capable of operating over long-range routes, but was drastically underpowered and therefore a commercial failure.

After the first heady flights from the mother country to each of the three major, and relatively accessible, parts of the British Empire, pilots planning long-distance flights paused for a couple of years to take stock and prepare for the next objectives, which would be to cover the same routes more quickly and economically, and so pave the way for regular air communications with these three important areas. Although Canada was just within reach of aircraft, as proved by Alcock and Brown in 1919, the absence of land en route made any idea of regular communications impossible for the time being.

First in this next wave of venturers were Captain Norman MacMillan, later a celebrated aviation author and journalist, and Major Wilfred Blake in a D.H.9. These two men set off for Calcutta from Croydon in May 1922, and arrived there in August. It was some time before another long-distance proving flight was undertaken.

Alan Cobham and A. B. Elliott, with Sir Sefton Brancker, the Director of Civil Aviation, as their passenger, set off from London for Rangoon in a de Havilland D.H.50 on 20 November 1924 and returned on 17 March 1925. This was the first long-distance flight to be made with the overt intention of surveying the air route to India for the purposes of commercial air traffic. Cobham and Brancker were both key men in Britain's pioneer days of air transport.

Born in 1877, Sir Sefton Brancker had joined the Royal Artillery and in 1910, while serving in India, had seen his first aeroplane and was immediately convinced of the aeroplane's long-term importance as a means of transport. Brancker secured his pilot's licence during 1913, and during World War I was initially the Deputy Director of Military Aeronautics, and then in due course the Director of Air Organization and commander of the Royal Flying Corps in the Middle East, before taking up the post of Controller General of Equipment and Master of Personnel.

After the war Brancker left the Royal Air Force, as the RFC had meanwhile become, and after a brief spell in the aviation industry threw all his considerable talents and enthusiasm into the development of civil aviation. With his appointment as Director of Civil Aviation in 1924, Brancker was able to help the United Kingdom's air transport industry get off the ground both literally and metaphorically. The nation lost a valuable servant with his death in the R-101 airship crash on 5 October 1930.

While Brancker was an organizational genius with a flair for the dramatic and the ability to convey his ideas to the sceptical, Cobham was the complete practical aviator but also had the personality and dynamism to infect others with his ideas. Born in 1894, Cobham served in the RFC and RAF during World War I, and joined the new de Havilland company when this was created after the war to succeed Airco. Like Brancker, Cobham was a true enthusiast of civil aviation, and his proving flights did much to pave the way for the development of civil air routes. His personality and writings were equally influential, and were largely responsible for the development of civil air-mindedness in the United Kingdom.

On 16 November 1925 Cobham set off in his D.H.50 to fly to Cape Town and back, a distance of some 16,000 miles (25750 km) which he flew in four months. Knighted after this flight, Cobham now set his sights on the route to Australia. Again in the D.H.50, Cobham took off with his mechanic from Rochester in Kent on 30 June 1926, arriving in Melbourne five weeks later, on 5 August. The

86

next month Cobham left for England again, arriving in London on 1 October after a flight of 27 days.

The significance of Cobham's flights lay not in their speed, but in their consistency and planning, for Cobham was interested primarily in proving that the distance could be flown safely in a number of legs, and in validating the concept that if airfields with fuel and maintenance facilities were located at strategic intervals along the route, this would make it not just feasible but fully practical to inaugurate passenger transport to the farther reaches of the empire.

During the same period, while he was making his great proving flights, Cobham also entered several air races, and started a campaign to persuade the British that each major town should have its own airfield. He toured Africa in a flying boat, the Short Singapore, during 1927 and 1928, and made other important flights before starting his 'National Aviation Day Campaign' in 1932. This took the form of a travelling air display and very many Britons must have made their first flight in one of Cobham's aircraft when the display arrived at their home town.

By this time a new type of aircraft, the touring biplane pioneered by de Havilland, had entered the lists and intrepid amateurs were setting off for all points in the empire. Powered usually by the very reliable 60-hp Cirrus four-cylinder air-cooled engine, two-seater planes of the 'Moth' type were usually flown solo on these flights, the second cockpit being converted into accommodation for extra fuel tankage to increase the aeroplane's basic range.

The first of these notable flights was to Karachi in India, by a pair of D.H.60 Moths flown by Neville Stack and B.S. Leete between 15 November 1926 and 8 January 1927. Soon the skies seemed full of British light aircraft heading for the corners of the globe. Between 1 and 28 September 1927 Flight-Lieutenant R. R. Bentley made the first solo and light aeroplane flight to Cape Town in his Moth, covering some 8,300 miles (13350 km) in just four weeks. Then, on 14 October 1927, Captain W. N. Lancaster left Croydon for Australia with Mrs Keith Miller as his passenger. The two arrived in Port Darwin in their Avro Avian on 19 March 1928 the first light aviation flight to Australia. The three main objectives of British pilots had now all been conquered by light aircraft.

Perhaps the most remarkable feat on the Australia route was C. A. Butler's time of only 9 days 2 hours to fly from Lympne in Kent to Port Darwin, where Butler arrived in his tiny Comper Swift on 9 November 1931. The route to Cape Town also produced some interesting flights. Miss Peggy Salaman and A. Gordon Store covered a route 7,000 miles (11250 km) long flying a de Havilland D.H.80 Puss Moth in 5 days and 40 minutes during October and November 193 1. Two years later, on 9/13 March 1933, Victor Smith covered 5,830 miles (9380 km) from Lympne to Vanrhynsdorp, 130 miles (210 km) short of Cape Town in just 3 days 21 hours in a Comper Swift.

The period also saw some remarkable flights by the Fairey Longe-Range Monoplane on the Africa and India routes. On 24/26 April 1929 an RAF crew consisting of Squadron-Leader A. G. Jones Williams and Flight-Lieutenant N. H. Jenkins flew the Fairey nonstop from Cranwell in Lincolnshire to Karachi in 50 hours 48 minutes, the first ever such flight to India. Then, on 6/8 February 1933, Squadron-Leader O. R. Gayford and Flight-Lieutenant G. E. Nicholetts flew from Cranwell to Walvis Bay in South-West Africa, a distance of 5,309 miles (8544 km) in 57 hours 30 minutes.

In the late 1920s and early 1930s the tasks of lightplane pilots were made easier, though they were still not easy, by the fact that proper air routes to the main destinations bad been surveyed, and facilities were beginning to appear along the route. Nevertheless, long flights over developed parts of the world were still very dangerous.

The growing social as well as political emancipation of women in the aftermath of World War I was strikingly apparent from the relatively large number of women taking part in these pioneer long-distance flights. Amelia Earhart and Jacqueline Cochran were two of the American heroines, while Amy Johnson was perhaps the most remarkable of all the many British women pilots. While working as a shorthand typist, Miss Johnson got the flying 'bug' after seeing the 1928 film production Wings, depicting life in a World War I air squadron. She took out all her savings and learned to fly. Although she showed no more than an average ability at first, Miss Johnson gradually became a good, if cautious, pilot. Determined that nothing should stand in her way, she made a number of excellent long-distance flights, the first of which, to Australia, swept her into the hearts of the nation.

Miss Johnson's popularity was further enhanced when she met and married another extraordinary pilot, James Mollison. Together the two made a number of great flights across the Atlantic as well as on the empire routes. Ironically, James Mollison was the antithesis of Amy Johnson as a pilot, being noted for extremely risky enterprises. While they were married the couple did a great deal to popularize flying.

So far these British distance flights had been conducted only against the clock or to prove that the flight could be made. In 1934, however, the classic MacPherson Robertson (generally abbreviated to 'MacRobertson') air race from London to Melbourne took place. This marked the beginning of a new age in aviation. The race attracted an odd assortment of aircraft, ranging from the sleek and beautiful de Havilland D.H.88 Comets, designed specially for the race, via a number of comparatively advanced airliners, to a de Havilland D.H.89 Dragon Rapide biplane air transport.

The results of the race, in which a Comet won but was closely followed by a fully laden but unmodified Douglas DC-2 entered by the Dutch national airline, KLM, did a great deal to persuade European designers to turn their attention to the design features of the new breed of American airliner: all-metal construction, a low-mounted cantilever monoplane wing, and well-cowled radial engines.

Below: The Short Maia/Mercury composite was a fascinating British attempt of 1935 to maximize payload in the lucrative air mail business. The Maia flying boat was designed to lift the very heavily laden Mercury floatplane into the air and release it at a useful cruising altitude, where all its fuel could be used for very long range. In 1938 the Mercury set a world seaplane distance record of 5,997.5 miles (9651.8 km), and this record remains unbroken.

Commercial Aviation: a Hesitant Start

Racing series like the Schneider Trophy competitions produced the ultimate aircraft of the period, when measured in terms of performance at any cost. Yet the same period in the late 1920s and early 1930s saw another type of competitive flying: record-breaking Commercial transport in heavier-than-air craft had started in the months immediately after the end of World War I, but initial success was no guarantee of long-term viability. Neither the machines nor the routes were satisfactory at first. The aircraft were World War I bombers adapted for the role of passenger-carrying. This meant that the interior of the wooden-framed and fabric-covered fuselage was converted to accommodate a limited number of passengers, while the rest of the airframe was left unaltered. Conditions for the passengers were spartan, for the cabin was both cold and draughty.

The routes, meanwhile, served short-term political interests rather than long-term economic ones. Linking the capitals of the victorious nations, principally France and the United Kingdom, they allowed diplomats, civil servants and politicians to untangle the complex political and financial legacy of the war with the greatest possible speed. These fledgling routes were open to the general public but private passengers needed to be wealthy and interested as much in the novelty of air transport as in getting to their destinations quickly. A market of this type, depending on a small and short-lived passenger base, could not allow the evolution of a sound airline business.

Gradually the number and extent of airline routes began to grow, however, as airlines realized that 'joyriding' passengers could, and in the long-term must, be supplemented by businessmen and other travellers who had a vested financial reason for rapid transport.

As the airlines that had survived the first heady months of peace started to rationalize their routes in the early 1920s, the generation of converted wartime machines was being phased out in favour of newer types designed specifically for the air transport role. Age was beginning to catch up with the initial conversions, and the new breed of passenger was not prepared to put up with the discomfort of such machines.

First progress was made in Germany, where there were several excellent and farsighted designers. By the terms of the Treaty of Versailles Germany was not allowed to design, build or possess any military aircraft, so German designers was perforce limited to civil types. This concentration of effort greatly aided the production of the world's first proper airliner, discounting the Sikorsky Le Grand of 1913. This was the Junkers J13, later redesignated F13, which appeared in 1919 and entered service with Deutsche

The Boeing model 314 was arguably the finest commercial flying boat ever built, and offered super accommodation combined with great reliability and range.

Above: With its enclosed accommodation and all-metal structure, the Junkers F 13 was a remarkably prescient transport aeroplane that appeared in the year following the end of World War I.

Below: Bearing strong structural and aerodynamic similarities to the Fokker fighters that appeared late in World War I, the Fokker F VII transport was one of the seminal air transports to appear in the 1920s, and reached its apogee with the introduction of the F VII-3m as the three-engined definitive version.

Luft Hansa shortly afterwards. (The airline's name was altered to Deutsche Lufthansa later in the 1920s.)

The J13 bore a clear family relationship to the low-wing cantilever metal fighters and ground-attack aircraft that Junkers had produced towards the end of the war, and was so different in overall concept that it met with considerable resistance at first. The low wing position, it was claimed, would make the centre of gravity too high, and the metal structure was also considered suspect. But the J13 was years ahead of its time, as later events were to prove: apart from the clumsiness of the engine installation and the standard fixed landing gear with a spreader bar, the J13 had lines that were sleek by the standards of the day and carried its pilot and four passengers in the relative comfort of an enclosed cockpit and cabin respectively.

Hugo Junkers went on to produce other very successful airliners, most of them featuring the type of corrugated Duralumin skinning Junkers had taken up in the war when steel skinning proved too heavy. There were two disadvantages with corrugated skinning, however, and these became apparent to Junkers only in the 1930s, when other airline manufacturers began to produce much more advanced types. Firstly, the strength of the skinning along the streamwise corrugations was not matched by strength at right-angles to the corrugations: as the skinning was strong in one direction but not in the other, no really significant economies in structure weight could be made and, furthermore, the corrugation ruled out any possibility of stressed skin construction with all its attendant advantages. Secondly, although the corrugations lay parallel to most of the airflow, a number of them lay at an angle to eddies or parts of the flow diverted by the airframe. This was not noticed at first but when other designers started to use sleeker lines, the disadvantages of the Junkers type of construction became apparent. The extra drag of the

corrugations meant that on a given power and fuel capacity the Junkers transports were slower and shorter-ranged than their commercial adversaries, or that more power and more fuel were necessary for the attainment of the same performance.

By the standards of the early 1920s, however, the Junkers airliners were very advanced machines. British and French transports of the period were clumsy and old-fashioned in appearance, having the biplane configuration with its attendant mass of rigging and bracing wires. The only other manufacturer to match the Junkers advances was Anthony Fokker, who had spent the war years in Germany, where his company produced a number of important training and fighter designs for the Imperial German Air Service.

An astute businessman, Fokker had realized in 1918 that Germany was about to lose the war, and prepared for flight accordingly. Dutch by birth, he had managed to cross over into the neutral Netherlands at the end of the war with a train carrying large numbers of dismantled aircraft, engines, tools, machines, and plans. Using money salted away in easier times, Fokker was able to set up in business again in his native country. He found a ready market for his World War I designs in the Netherlands and Sweden, and then set about developing new military and civil aircraft.

Although his fighting machines were to achieve some success in the next few years, it was civil aircraft that really made Fokker's reputation the 1920s and 1930s. As chief designer he still had the untrained, intuitive and retiring Reinhold Platz, one of the ablest designers to emerge from World War I, as shown by his great Dr I, D VII and D VIII fighters of 1917 and 1918. Platz saw no reason to abandon the constructional features that had contributed so much to the success of the three fighters, and set about producing civil airliners with the same clean lines, simplicity and strength.

The first such airliner to enter service was the F II, which appeared in 1920. This was a typical Platz design: a welded steel-tube fuselage of rectangular section covered with canvas except for the engine cowling, which was covered with metal sheeting; sturdy but simple landing gear; and a massive cantilever wing covered with plywood. Platz favoured thick wings for two main reasons: they made possible the use of box spars (spars with a hollow rectangular cross-section) of great depth and strength, and also produced a fair amount of lift, for which Platz was prepared to pay the price in drag. As usual with his designs, Platz located the wing on top of the fuselage. This left the fuselage entirely clear for the passengers; allowed the construction of a single-piece wing that was very strong; and also gave a measure of pendulum stability to the whole aeroplane.

The contrast in wing location between Junkers and Fokker aircraft provoked much discussion at the time. Platz could scarcely be faulted by the standards of the day, before retractable landing gear came into use; Junkers, on the other hand, could incorporate retractable landing gear into his basic design far more easily once the need became pressing. But the lower wing position was originally chosen by Junkers to give the pilot of a military aircraft the best possible view, and the passengers of a civil aircraft the best possible chance of survival in a crash. Junkers correctly reasoned that a low-mounted wing would be the first thing to come into contact with the ground in a crash and therefore absorb much of the impact, giving the passengers and crew slightly more chance of getting out alive.

Like the J13, the Fokker F II carried a crew of one and up to four passengers, but was considerably slower than the Junkers machine despite being powered by the same type of

185-hp BMW engine. Yet the F II proved the forerunner of a great line of Fokker airliners that would dominate European and American airline operations until the early 1930s. After the F II came the F III, capable of carrying five passengers; the F IV 10-passenger transport that failed to attract airline orders; the F V which was built only in prototype form, and intended as an eight-seat airliner; the F VI produced as an experimental fighter; and then the great F VII, first of the most famous Fokker series of the period.

The F VII family (comprising the original single-engined F VII, aerodynamically cleaned-up F VIIA , F VIIA/3m tri-motor and long-range F VIIB/3m tri-motor versions) was possibly the most successful airliner and long-distance record breaker of its day, and contributed beyond measure to the acceptance of long-distance flying as a normal part of airline operations.

The Fokker company had paved the way for large-scale air transport, and in the 1920s and 1930s very few European airlines had not used some of their aircraft. Yet, because of its associations with the Germans in World War I, the American authorities felt that the name of Fokker would not be popular with the American people. When Fokker started to build aircraft for the US Army and US Navy, and to supply these services with technical assistance about the manufacture and maintenance of steel-tube airframes, it was decided to call the new factory in New York the Atlantic Aircraft Corporation rather than Fokker.

Fokker was not even on Atlantic's board of directors. The 'Flying Dutchman' did eventually become known to the American public as a result of the efforts of Harry Bruno, one of aviation's greatest publicists, who insisted on introducing Fokker to the public at an air display in St Louis, Missouri. Thereafter the name Fokker began to achieve its true position of prominence in the United States. In any case, it would have been hard to disguise the phenomenal success of various Fokker types, in both civilian and service hands, after the introduction of the F VIIA/3m in 1925.

The influence of Fokker airliners on other designers was nowhere more apparent than in the best American airliner of the 1920s, the Ford Tri-Motor. This appeared in June 1926 and combined what the designer, William Stout, thought to be the best features of both the Fokker and Junkers type of aircraft: the Tri-Motor resembled the Fokker F VIIA/3m in appearance, but was built with the Junkers type of corrugated skinning. Eloquent testimony to the ruggedness and basic strength of the Tri-Motor is provided by the fact that a few were still in service in South America 50 years after their introduction, and also by the fact that a few of these legendary aircraft are still used for tourist flights over the Grand Canyon, Colorado, during the mid-1990s.

Junkers had not been standing idle all this time: the company had produced a series of typical Junkers aircraft, culminating in the G31 of 1926. This was a tri-motor transport powered by three 450-hp radials, and could carry

Above: Bearing a strong conceptual similarity to the Fokker F VII, the Ford Tri-Motor was an exceptionally durable tri-motor transport that differed from the Dutch aeroplane in using an all-metal structure.

Below: One of the many light transports evolved by the burgeoning US aircraft industry in the late 1920s was the Stinson Detroiter, here epitomized by a ski-equipped aeroplane for service in Alaska.

16 passengers at 160 km/h (100 mph). Like the F VII, it had a wide-track split landing gear, and in turn proved the starting point for further Junkers aircraft, which culminated in the single-engined Ju 52 of 1930 and its three-engined derivative, the Ju 52/3m which became the most famous and prolific German transport of the 1930s and World War II.

Like the Tri-Motor, the Ju 52/3 in remained in service for many years, and its ruggedness and wide-track landing gear proved invaluable for operations on and off mediocre if not poor airfields. Ironically, the lives of these aircraft have been considerably longer than might have been expected, largely as a result of ignorance. Modern airliners are built to an exact specification which details, among other things, the fatigue life of the main structural components: the closer the manufacturer can come to meeting the buyer's specification, the lighter he can make the aeroplane, and the lowest possible structure weight helps the airline by increasing payload or range, or by reducing fuel consumption. The exact gauging of structural weights, to meet both the buyer's specifications and the certificating government body's safety regulations, is today a vital part of airliner design. Most important, manufacturers now have a wealth of metallurgical knowledge to guide them.

This was certainly not the case in the 1920s. Little or nothing was known of the fatigue lives of the various alloys coming into increasingly common use, and so regulations concerned themselves only with the strength of structural components. The result was that the Ju 52/3m and Tri-Motor designs were built with unnecessarily long fatigue lives. It is almost inconceivable that new aircraft will ever notch up the number of airframe hours achieved by some of the earlier types up to and including the legendary Douglas DC-3, which was and still is possibly the greatest transport aircraft of all time.

Trouble with fatigue principally as a result of vibration in very high-powered piston engines, began to manifest itself as a major problem only in World War II. The first civil type to suffer from acute problems of metal fatigue was the world's first jet airliner, the de Havilland D.H.106 Comet, where vibration, cold and air pressure all had an effect. Naturally enough, these factors had little or no importance in aircraft that flew only at low altitudes and had, for operational reasons, an average life of perhaps only 1,000 hours in the air.

By the middle of the 1920s, most European nations had established their own national airlines. Companies such as Fokker sold its transports to the airlines of most technically advanced nations, but the general tendency was for the national flag-carrying airline to operate machines built in the same country. Imperial Airways, the British airline, operated a variety of types, the most important early machine being the de Havilland D.H.66 Hercules.

This machine was typical of the design practices used in British transport aircraft in the mid-1920s: it was a large machine with wide-track landing gear, a slab-sided fuselage mounted over the lower unit of the biplane wing cellule, and a tail unit carrying triple fins and rudders of classic de Havilland shape mounted above the monoplane tailplane and elevator. The spacious 14-passenger cabin was located over the lower wing, and the three engines were mounted in

Opposite page, top: One of the first aircraft to enter service as a transport after World War I was the de Havilland D.H.9 conversion of the Airco D.H.9 light bomber.

Opposite page, top centre: The Farman F.60 Goliath was one of the most important airliners evolved in France during the 1920s, and was also developed in bomber form.

Opposite page, bottom centre: The most important transport developed in Europe during the period leading up to World War II was the Junkers Ju 52/3M tri-motor development of the original Ju 52 single-engined transport.

Opposite page, bottom: Operating in a technical limbo as a result of its peculiar requirements for imperial air transport, the United Kingdom produced some classic but innately obsolescent biplane transports including the half-brother Handley Page H.P.42 and H.P.45.

the nose of the fuselage and above the main landing gear wheels, one in each lower wing. With a cruising speed was just under 100 mph (160 km/h), the Hercules was employed mainly on the 'intercontinental' flights operated by Imperial Airways, first to Egypt, then in 1927 to Basra in southern Iraq, at the convergence of the Euphrates and Tigris rivers, and finally to Karachi in north-western India during 1929. The British transport used most frequently on European routes was the Armstrong Whitworth Argosy, another cumbersome biplane of tri-motor and triple-finned design.

So poor was the payload/range performance of these and comparable airliners into the early 1930s that passengers undertaking longer journeys were faced with the need to change aircraft several times, and on some routes to complete part of their travel by railway in sectors where airfields had yet to be completed. Although it might be possible to fly to the French Riviera or Italy's Adriatic coast, for instance, it was more common for the long-range passenger to travel that far by train. Once arrived on the edge of the Mediterranean, the passenger would then embark in a flying boat for the sector to Alexandria in Egypt. From here, depending on whether he was going south towards the Cape of Good Hope or east towards India, he would travel by a variety of aircraft and trains to his final destination.

By the standards of the day, however, this was quick travel, and could be undertaken in some degree of comfort. The cabins of the airliners were fitted out as saloons, with tables and wicker chairs, and the food and drink were of a higher standard than one would normally get on a commercial airliner today. Overnight stops were made, and the passengers put up in hotels.

Imperial Airways' chief concern was the maintenance of services on colonial routes, to the outlying parts of the Empire, and the demands of European travel were virtually ignored. As the only airline flying passengers and mail over long-haul routes, Imperial Airways could afford not to concern itself with mundane matters such as speed, but to concentrate instead on moving a relatively small number of passenger steadily and in comfort. In many respects Imperial Airways was operating in splendid isolation at a time when virtually every other airline in the world was beginning to consider a switch to monoplane transports

with their considerably higher performance.

Imperial Airways ordered two versions of one basic biplane type for its European and intercontinental routes: these four-engined Handley Page aircraft were the H.P.45 Heracles carrying 38 passengers on European routes, and the H.P.42 Hannibal carrying 24 passengers over long distances. In their way these were great aircraft, for in their years of service not one passenger suffered an injury. Both variants had the triple fins and rudders that were almost the trademark of British airliners in this period.

France was also behind the times, and only acquired a national airline, Air France, in 1933. As in the United Kingdom, various airlines had concentrated their primary commercial efforts on services to the farther-flung parts of the French Empire. Unlike the British, however, the French had relatively few stepping stones to the Far East, and so placed great reliance on a series of old-fashioned Lioré-et-Olivier (LeO) and Breguet flying boats, the best means of air travel to the remoter parts of the world as they required no airfields of the type that were and still are the single most expensive item in the infrastructure required to support airline operations.

Italy, on the other hand, used the excellent tri-motor monoplanes (most of them produced by Caproni and Savoia) as well as a miscellany of smaller types for its airlines' routes within Europe and across the Mediterranean to Libya and thence to Italian Somaliland.

In common with countries such as Germany, Italy made great efforts to produce transport aircraft that were highly cost-effective as they could be used as airliners in times of peace they could serve as airliners, and as troop transports or even primitive bomber in times of war. Another attraction of this operational philosophy for the Germans and Italians, moreover, was the fact that the relevant production lines could quickly be adapted to produce a dedicated warplane modelled on the basic transport's combination of airframe and powerplant. This had obvious advantages in the rapid production of military aircraft, and also opened the possibility of reduced development and production costs, which was a factor of considerable importance to a country such as Italy, which was relatively underdeveloped so far as its industrial base

Left: The accolade for introducing the 'modern' airliner must go to Boeing, whose Model 247 introduced all-metal construction of the stressed-skin type, a cantilever low-set wing, retractable main landing gear units, and a powerplant of two supercharged air-cooled radial piston engines mounted on the leading edges of the wings in low-drag nacelles. Illustrated is the definitive Model 247D with a rearward-rather than forward-sloped windscreen and variable-pitch propellers in place of the original Model 247's fixed-pitch propellers.

was concerned. For Germany, the policy had a most sinister rationale as the country was prohibited by the Treaty of Versailles from developing and/or producing any military aircraft: dual-role aircraft could thus be passed off as civil transports rather than bombers.

This aspect of German aircraft development and production was not particularly significant in the late 1920s and early 1930s, but it became of paramount importance between the time that the Nazis had come to power in 1933 and Hitler's rejection of the treaty structures in 1935.

Even if its aircraft did not have an overt military aspect, Lufthansa had considerably greater numbers of flying personnel than other airlines in relation to the number of aircraft it operated. This was because the Germans had discovered early in the 1920s that by training an excess of pilots and navigators they could produce the aircrew that would be essential to the effective rearmament of Germany once this was set in hand. Supported by the clandestine air ministry, Lufthansa kept a large number of training aircraft on which those aircrew not engaged on active airline operations could develop their skills.

Germany was also the first European state to realize the economic advantages of an air route network that was both extensive and well organized. By the early 1930s Lufthansa had the most comprehensive network in Europe, linking Germany's centres of industrial production with the most important financial and trading hubs on the rest of the continent.

On the other side of the Atlantic, the American airline industry was almost non-existent during the 1920s. The main regions of population were linked by an extremely efficient network of roads and railways, and mass production was already making the car part of every home. Long air flights involved noise, a considerable amount of dirt and refuelling stops every couple of hundred miles: by comparison, trains and buses provided a higher level of comfort, little noise, fewer refuelling stops and lower cost.

With the exception of those to Canada, Mexico and the closer islands in the Caribbean, there were no external routes for the Americans to launch, for the distances involved in intercontinental routes were far beyond the technology of the time. The only possible routes with an economic future were those to the main cities of Canada, but these were mostly close to the border and already well linked with the United States by road and rail.

There were several small private operators, however, and these operated limited services in heavily populated areas and places where road and rail transport was difficult, as well as services to the holiday centres of the Caribbean. Moreover, the Americans did develop a remarkable and forward-looking route network for the carriage of mail. Organized by the US Post Office, the airmail service started in May 1918 with a service between New York and Washington DC, but was soon expanded right across the continent to San Francisco in California. The inauguration and subsequent development of the network was beset by a number of technical and operational problems, but by 1925 a crude yet increasingly serviceable navigation system was available across the centre of the continent: this consisted of great blazes about 25 miles (40 km) along each route, with all the airfields revealed and illuminated by searchlights.

Then, in one of those extraordinary reversals that seem to characterize the period, the government took over all these private-enterprise airfields, and in return put the mail flights themselves out to commercial tender. The change was ultimately to the benefit of US commercial aviation since the government was in a position to improve airfields and navigational aids such as radio; it also ensured adequate maintenance for all the mailplanes. The mail had to be delivered in all weathers to meet the terms of the contract, which paid by the ton of mail collected and delivered, and this had a great effect in spurring the development of fast all-weather aircraft capable of carrying a reasonable payload.

The development of such aircraft, even in the limited

Below: Often known as the 'Staggerwing' for the reverse stagger of its biplane wing cellule, the Beech Model 17 proved an excellent and very popular light transport whose low landing speed was combined with a moderately high cruising speed as a result of the use of a mechanism to retract the main landing gear units.

numbers required or the servicing of the nation's airmail network, laid the foundations on which American civil aviation began to grow into the towering giant it is today: the manufacturers produced the required technological developments; the routes opened up the best courses between the main cities; nocturnal and, more importantly, all-weather flying improved piloting and navigational skills, and also proved the need for blind-flying instruments; and the whole operation showed the American people some of the benefits that could result from fast and reliable air services.

In 1927 Boeing, soon to emerge as a giant of the aeronautical world, made an extremely low tender for the Chicago to San Francisco route, and to the amazement of the pundits actually made a profit on the contract. The plane used was the Boeing Model 40A, for its time a remarkably efficient and economical aeroplane, though not at all radical in its aerodynamic qualities. The Model 40A had been designed as a very clean machine whose basically low drag was enhanced by the considerable attention that was paid to factors such as carefully considered detail design and features to reduce structural weight: the result was a transport aeroplane which could maintain a high average speed over long stages. With the emergence of this machine, the age of World War I aircraft and their derivatives was finally on its way out.

In 1930 Boeing produced the Model 200 Monomail as most advanced mailplane yet built. Here, for the first time in an American aeroplane, was the latest design philosophy: a circular-section fuselage of metal monocoque construction, a neatly cowled radial engine offering good power and reliability with low fuel consumption, a cantilever low-set wing of metal stressed-skin construction, and retractable landing gear. The Monomail was a revelation, for its full use of the latest stressed-skin metal construction endured that this thoroughly practical machine was as clean as any aeroplane of its period.

The combination of stressed-skin construction for the wings and a monocoque structure for the fuselage offers many advantages: fully cantilevered structures of reasonable thinness (and hence minimal drag) are possible, as are rounded fuselages of maximum volume but minimum area (and hence again minimal drag) and also a good streamlined shape. All these factors are readily apparent in the Monomail.

A year later Boeing produced another aeroplane based on the same core design formula but scaled up to twin-engined size and intended as a bomber. This was the B-9, the immediate predecessor of the first truly modern airliner, the Model 247, in 1932. The Model 247, which reached its most refined form as the Model 247D in 1934, was a remarkable aeroplane, and perhaps deserved to enjoy greater commercial success than it did. Nevertheless, with this type the day of the biplane, together with wooden structures and canvas coverings was over, even though it took some considerable time more for the more reactionary aviation specialists and designers to face the fact.

Powered by a pair of 550-hp Pratt & Whitney Wasp radials well faired into the wings as smooth nacelles, the Model 247 was an all metal stressed-skin and monocoque construction, with an oval fuselage, fully enclosed cockpit and a main landing gear units that retracted into the undersides of the engine nacelles. To improve the safety factor at high altitude, rubber de-icing 'boots' were fitted to the wings and tail surfaces, and this was the first time such a system had been used on a commercial aeroplane. These boots worked quite simply: when not in use, they lay flush along the leading edges of the wings and tail surfaces; when ice started to form, the boots were inflated with compressed air and so expanded, breaking the ice away from the leading edges and allowing the slipstream to get under it and prize it away from the wing and tail surfaces.

To bring the Model 247 right up to date, the Model 247D also had variable-pitch propellers, which allowed the engines' power to be used more economically. The one trouble with the aeroplane was that it was just slightly too small, its passenger capacity being a mere 10 persons at a time when the airlines were just beginning to look for

Above: The Armstrong Whitworth A.W.XV Atalanta was something of a hybrid as it was a cantilever monoplane that retained something of the United Kingdom's innate aeronautical conservatism in its fixed though nicely spatted main landing gear units.

something larger. However, the Model 247 did enter service with United Air Lines, formed in 1934 from Boeing Air Transport and two other companies, and did much to make this new giant airline a major force in American air transport.

Other major American airlines already in existence were Pan-American Airlines, founded in 1927, and Transcontinental and Western Air otherwise known as TWA (today the letters stand for Trans World Airlines), founded in 1930 through an amalgamation of four smaller airlines. Not to be outdone by United Airlines' Model 247 fleet, TWA asked Douglas to produce a similar but superior machine. The man chosen by the Douglas company, Arthur Raymond, went about his task in a slightly unusual way: he took a flight across the United States in TWA's most important current transport, the Tri-Motor, to see the standards of comfort and performance he was being asked to better.

The long journey had a profound effect on him, convincing him principally that although he had to design an aeroplane that was efficient in structural and aerodynamic terms so that it could carry the required payload over stages of the right length at the specified speed, though Raymond also appreciated that the comfort of the passengers was just as important. Raymond's experiences in the Tri-Motor were a telling commentary on the standards of air transport in the United States as late as 1930, contrasting strongly with Britain's Imperial Airways, which put the comfort of its passengers before all other considerations.

The result of Raymond's efforts was the Douglas DC-1 (Douglas Commercial 1), the only example of which flew for the first time in July 1933. The performance of this 12-passenger machine was so encouraging that Douglas immediately decided that the basic design could be 'stretched' without any difficulty to produce a 14-seater. The DC-2, as this upgraded derivative was called, went into straight into production, and the first aeroplane emerged in May 1934. The DC-2 could carry its full passenger payload at almost 170 mph (274 km/h) by comparison with the Model 247's ability to carry 10 passengers at 155 mph (250 km/h). Just as important for airline operations, the DC-2 had a considerably greater stage length than its rival. The aeroplane also introduced features to improve passenger comfort, including a previously unknown degree of soundproofing and other amenities.

The success of the DC-2 was immediate. By the

middle of 1934 Donald Douglas had orders for 75 of his new transport, clear proof that it met the needs of the world's airlines. Orders arrived from operators in several parts of the globe and even KLM, previously a staunch purchaser of Fokker aircraft, was among the first to contract for the new airliner. It was one of these DC-2s that KLM entered in the great 'MacRobertson' race from England to Australia in 1934, winning the event on handicap.

The United Kingdom was the only major aeronautical nation to voice any appreciable degree of scepticism about the new transport. The critics argued that since the DC-2 was a monoplane and offered high performance in level flight, its landing speed must be correspondingly high - and it was during take-off and landing that most crashes occurred. But these critics ignored the fact that the DC-2 was fitted with split flaps along the rear portions of its inboard wing sections. These flaps were lowered for take-off and landing, and fulfilled the dual function of slowing the aeroplane while at the same time providing a considerable amount of lift. Thus the minimum flying speed of the DC-2 was slightly under 60 mph (100 km/h), as slow if not slower than most transports of the late 1920s. The aeroplane's fine performance soon silenced even the most determined of British critics.

Realizing the scale of its achievement, the Douglas design team decided to capitalize on the basic layout of the DC-2 in the evolution of a larger machine offering better performance and payload. The result was the crucially important DC-3 that made its maiden flight during December 1935 and won immediate approval from the airlines. Essentially a scaled-up DC-2, the DC-3 was offered in its production form with a powerplant comprising a pair of 1,000-hp Wright Cyclone or 1,200-hp Pratt & Whitney Twin Wasp radials in place of the DC-2's 710-hp Wright Cyclones. The DC-3 carried 21 passengers at about the same speed as the DC-2 but over the longer stage length of 500 miles (805 km).

The DC-3 rapidly supplanted the DC-2 on the Douglas production line to meet airlines' rapidly growing volume of orders for the improved type, and by 1938 the DC-3 dominated American airline operations. By the time production ceased In 1946, about 13,000 DC-3 civil airliners and military C-47 Skytrain/R4D military transports had been built, making this the most prolific transport plane ever put into production. Even now, nearly 50 years after the type was taken out of production, there

The D.H.84 Dragon was an early machine in the stream of increasingly elegant two- and four-engined biplane light transports designed by de Havilland.

are
several hundreds of
the basic type still in regular service.
The design was advanced for its time in 1935,
and its combination of ruggedness and
uncomplicated handling characteristics
made it popular in the remotest areas,
which are the regions where this evergreen
transport is still to be found in the largest numbers.

The DC-3 did much to popularize air travel
within the United States as a feature of everyday life.
The car and the train could compete on favourable terms
with the airliners of the late 1920s for these aircraft were
uncomfortable and not particularly fast, but the situation
changed dramatically in favour of the Aeroplane with the
arrival onto the scene of the DC-2 and DC-3. The new
aircraft were almost as comfortable as trains, and improved
stage lengths meant that only four or five stops had to be
made to get right across the continent in a far shorter time
than was possible by train.

While Douglas was securing the upper end of the
market for airliners in the late 1930s with its DC-2 and
DC-3, Lockheed was enjoying success in the middle of the
airliner spectrum with its high-performance transports of
lower passenger capacity. From the mid-1920s onward,
Lockheed had concentrated its efforts on small, very fast
aircraft of considerable range for mailplane and other long-
distance operations: the classic example was the cantilever
high-wing Vega with its all-wood construction, monocoque
fuselage and radial piston engine, and this was produced in
four-passenger Model 1, 2 and 5 variants. With the growth
of civil air transport in the late 1920s, Lockheed had
produced another startling design, the Model 9 Orion. This
was a very advanced machine with sleek lines, mixed metal
and wood construction, a cantilever low-set monoplane
wing, a nicely cowled radial piston engine and retractable
landing gear. A relatively small firm, Lockheed then decided
to risk all they had on an advanced twin-engined airliner
somewhat smaller than the Boeing and Douglas transports
as it was aimed at a different market. The new machine
emerged in February 1934 as the Model 10 Electra, a trim
low-wing monoplane of all-metal construction,
accommodation for eight passengers and a powerplant of
two 450-hp Pratt & Whitney Wasp Junior radials. The
aeroplane was a success, so Lockheed pressed on with the
slightly smaller but faster Model 12 Electra Junior and later
the definitive light transport of the period, the Model 14
Super Electra.

A low-wing monoplane with fully retractable landing
gear and all-metal construction of the stressed-skin and
monocoque type, the Super Electra was a delightful little
aeroplane capable of maintaining an average speed of 190
mph (306 km/h). Its most distinctive features were the tail
unit with its twin ovoid fin-and-rudder assemblies, the
Lockheed trademark from the Electra onward, and the odd-
looking extensions poking out from the trailing edges of the

wings. These were part of the Super Electra's secret: to make
the aeroplane as fast as possible, the designers had
concentrated on keeping drag down to a minimum by
reducing the wing area; this meant that the landing speed
would be unacceptably high unless some special device
could be found, and such a device was in fact available in
the form of Fowler flaps. Thus the Super Electra was the
first aeroplane to use such flaps.

Douglas had opted for the straightforward split flap on
their machines, but Lockheed found the Fowler flaps had
distinct advantages. Sliding backward on tracks protruding
from the trailing edges, they increased wing area at take-off
for additional lift and safety at low speed; the flaps were
extended farther backward and downward during landings,
and thereby slowed the aeroplane while still offering lift.

Appearing in 1937, the Super Electra was in
aerodynamic terms the most advanced civil aeroplane to
appear before World War II. It was also the first airliner to
use two-speed superchargers for its engines, and the first
civil aeroplane with constant-speed propellers, which
helped save fuel by constantly adjusting the pitch of the
propeller blades to the air speed and power output of the
engine; this feature was later to become standard on all but
the smallest and lightest piston-engined aircraft.

With the Douglas and Lockheed series of airliners, the
United States had suddenly emerged from the aeronautical
wilderness and taken a commanding lead in the field of
civil aviation. Important factors in this sudden flowering
were the absorption of the stressed-skin theories of
Rohrbach, the fact that there was no mass of older aircraft
and traditions to hold back the development of the new
types, and the ready availability of reliable radial piston
engines in a number of power brackets from several well
established manufacturers.

This last factor was principally the result of the
commercially healthy rivalry that had grown up when some
of the Wright company's ablest designers, unhappy with the
company's complacency, resigned in 1925 and secured the
considerable financial backing to create a rival company in
the form of Pratt & Whitney.

The American pattern of civil transport development
had been followed, albeit more slowly, by the European
manufacturers, but these had to struggle against the inertia
of an established pattern of air transport that had evolved
after World War I. Junkers, for example, introduced his

One of many types
designed with
interchangeable wheel
and float landing gear
for maximum
operational versatility
was the Curtiss-Wright
T-32 Condor II that saw
service as a
bomber/transport with
air forces as well as an
airliner with civil
operators.

carrying 17 passengers, the Ju 52/3m was technically inferior to the DC-3 and this was reflected in its lower speed and poorer payload/range performance. This qualitative shortfall was primarily responsible for Junkers' belated appreciation that its corrugated skinning had become outdated and so turned its attention to smooth skins. The result was sleek aircraft with good performance.

The Ju 60 of 1933 and the Ju 86 of 1936 were two examples of this technical advance in Junkers aircraft. The Ju 60 was designed to compete with the Model 9 Orion, but proved too old-fashioned, and the Heinkel He 70 Blitz (lightning) was instead chosen as Lufthansa's counter to the American aeroplane. The Ju 86 was a larger transport designed to compete with the DC-2, as was the Heinkel He 111. Both German types enjoyed mixed fortunes. The Junkers design was used fairly extensively by Lufthansa, but the Heinkel aeroplane was apparently more suitable for carrying bombs than passengers, and so became one of the Luftwaffe's principal medium bombers throughout World War II. The Ju 86 was also used as a bomber, and with wing-tip extensions as a high-altitude reconnaissance aeroplane. Even the Ju 52/3m was used as a bomber in the Luftwaffe's early days, and later became its chief transport, paratrooping and glider-towing aeroplane.

In the United Kingdom, designers also sought to match the Americans and in the mid-1930s developed some interesting transport aircraft. In the same class as the Lockheed light airliners was the Bristol Type 142, designed in 1933 and rolled out in 1935. With a top speed above 300 mph (483 km/h), the Type 142 was faster than any fighter in current first-line service with the Royal Air Force, and this became an important factor in its later development as intended by Lord Rothermere, the air-minded newspaper magnate who had sponsored the Type 142's design as a high-speed executive transport. The Type 142 was generally unsuccessful as a light transport as it carried only six passengers, but its performance at last brought home to the British people and the RAF the extent to which their front-line combat aircraft were being rendered obsolete by the pace of aerodynamic advance. It was rapidly appreciated that the majority of RAF combat aircraft were now of negligible value. Rothermere presented the Type 142 to the nation as an example. This had profound political repercussions, and led to the development of the basic airframe into the Type 143 Blenheim light bomber.

Although this episode had provided the right type of shock, it was large or vigorous enough to push the British airline business out of the comfortable non-competitive habit to which it was accustomed. To all intents and purposes, Imperial Airways had abandoned the European routes on which its constituent companies had cut their teeth in the early 1920s, in favour of the long-haul imperial routes that brought it revenue and a secure place in the official scheme of things. Fully supported by the

Above: The Fokker F XI Universal was a braced high-wing monoplane of typical construction for Fokker aircraft of the late 1920s, but was not a great commercial success.

G38 in 1929. This monster, which started flying Lufthansa's route between London and Berlin in 1931, was an odd mixture of old and new. The horizontal tail was a biplane structure in which the two horizontal surfaces were separated by triple fin-and-rudder assemblies, and the landing gear was a cumbersome example of the obsolete fixed type. The monoplane wing, on the other hand, was a cantilever unit of metal construction and thick section with the four engines neatly buried in its leading edges. Since the seven members of the crew and the 34 passengers were accommodated in the centre section of the wing, the fuselage was simply a boom connecting the wings and tail surfaces. Technically an interesting machine, the G38 cruised at only 185 km/h (115 mph).

Contemporary with the G38 was a British airliner, the Short Scylla. This was a four-engined biplane capable of carrying some 40 passengers at 100 mph (160 km/h). Slightly later, in 1932, came the more advanced Armstrong Whitworth Atalanta, which was a four-engined monoplane of the Fokker type. The Atalanta presented a neat and fairly clean appearance marred by the fixed landing gear and the propellers, which were dwarfed by the thickness of the high-set wing. Used mainly on Imperial Airways' long-haul routes, the Atalanta carried 20 passengers at a steady speed of 125 mph (201 km/h).

Comparison of these and other contemporary European airliners, including the Fokker F XVIII of 1932 with its payload of 14 passengers carried at 250 km/h (155 mph), with the American designs on the drawing boards or under prototype construction, reveals clearly how swiftly the European aircraft industry was starting to lag in the technological race that had not even been declared. Yet American advances were so comprehensive in concept and scale that US transports had virtually cornered the market for civil transports in the mid- and late 1930s.

This is not to deny, however, that the Europeans could and did indeed develop and produce some good aircraft in the 1930s. The Junkers Ju 52/3m three-engined evolution of the single-engined Ju 52 became Europe's equivalent to the DC-3 in terms of its numbers and widespread adoption. About 4,300 were built, most of them for military use, and several remained in service until the mid-1980s. Capable of

Below: Like many of the civil transports of its period, the Fokker F VII-3m could be operated on wheel, ski or float landing gear for maximum versatility in any and all operating environments.

government and lacking any real competition, Imperial Airways demanded and received small numbers of a variety of airliners which were sufficient for the tasks required of them but expensive to build: in short, the transports resulting from the requirements of Imperial Airways were of innately conservative design and lacked all but the most limited export potential.

There were a few successful British airliners in this period, but these resulted wholly from private enterprise. The three most important of these successful transports were the Airspeed AS.6 Envoy, a pretty little twin-engined monoplane with retractable main landing gear and accommodation for six or eight passengers, and two de Havilland twin-engined biplanes, the D.H.84 Dragon and D.H.89 Dragon Rapide with fixed landing gear and accommodation for six and eight passengers respectively. All three of these transports were built in quite large numbers for British and foreign operators.

The French aviation industry had slowly fallen into decline during the 1920s. There were too many small companies, few of them with adequate capital to finance major new projects and set up the necessary production tooling and jigs. A succession of short-lived French governments had seen the problem but lacked the time in office to devise and effect any solution, so by 1936 the

flow off the drawing-boards and then out of the experimental shops. By the late 1930s Air France was extending its routes all over the world with a number of first-class aircraft, mostly, of Dewoitine, Farman and Potez design. It is worth noting, however, that the very excellence of these new designs and prototypes was something of a problem, for the French authorities could not decide which types to produce and which to cancel, and this led to the production of several types in small numbers rather than the wholehearted concentration on a single type in each class with all the advantages that would have accrued from larger production runs.

In the United States, meanwhile, the manufacturers were forging ahead to extend the world lead they had now established in commercial aircraft. With a new generation of very high-powered engines not yet available, the designers saw that the next step in performance would be with four-engined aircraft. These, it was hoped, would be able to carry more passengers at higher speeds over longer stages. Boeing already had a head start, having designed two four-engined bombers by 1935. These were the Model 294 built in prototype form as the XB-15, and the Model 299 later built in large numbers as the B-17 Flying Fortress.

Up to the mid-1930s, civil aircraft had operated at relatively low altitudes, in the region of 10,000 ft (3050 m)

French were in the humiliating position of trailing behind the United States, United Kingdom, Germany and even Italy after having led the aviation world in 1918.

In 1936 the French government realized that with Germany rearming rapidly and evincing distinct aggressive ambitions, the time was well past for inaction. The nettle was seized, and the French aviation industry was nationalized and subjected to a thoroughgoing reorganization: as a result, the most important companies in each region were grouped together to make one large company. The effect was immediate, and the French genius for designing elegant high-performance aircraft re-emerged. There were continued problems in co-ordinating research, development and production efforts, but an increasing number of excellent military and civilian aircraft started to

or lower. For their new airliners, the designers wanted high-altitude operation, where the use of supercharged engines would allow the transports to reach a higher maximum speed for minimum power. The problem here was comfort for the passengers for, at the altitudes of 20,000 ft (6095 m) and upward where such transports would be cruising, the air is both thin and cold.

The planned new generation of civil transports would therefore have to be pressurized with warm air, and this presented designers with a whole set of entirely new problems. Provision of air at the right temperature and at the correct pressure was relatively straightforward, for the air could be tapped from the supercharger and warmed by the heat emitted from the engines. The main problem lay with the construction of the fuselage itself, which would

Above: The Douglas DC-2 was a larger transport than the Boeing Model 247 and, being sized to the requirements of many airlines, was a great commercial success that also paved the way for the immortal DC-3.

have to be made airtight in order to maintain a positive pressure differential between the cabin and the outside air.

In theory it is comparatively straightforward to make a monocoque fuselage airtight, but in practice during the mid-1930s there were considerable difficulties with the riveted construction that was standard in the period. Both the British and the French had worked on such cabins in the 1920s and early 1930s, but it was not until the Lockheed XC-35 (a much modified Model 10 Electra) flew in 1937 that the problems appeared to have been overcome. Swifter progress might have been made had the military been interested in these developments, but the air forces of the time were happy to let their crews wear thick clothes and breathe from oxygenated face masks, thus avoiding the additional weight, complexity and cost of pressurization. Such solutions were unthinkable for civil airliners, so high-altitude flight was out of the question for several years.

Douglas had decided to enter the four-engined race, but its DC-4E, which flew for the first time in June 1938, was a failure as it was too far ahead of the aeronautical state of the art in a number of its advanced systems. (This was the first large aeroplane to use a tricycle landing gear.) Boeing, with the experience of two other large four-engined aircraft to help it, developed the Model 307 from the Model 299. Using the same wing and tail unit as the bomber, the Model 307 introduced a new circular-section fuselage. Entering service in a developed form as the Model 307B Stratoliner in 1940, this transport could carry 33 passengers over long distances in the comfort of a fully pressurized cabin. Five such machines were delivered to TWA before the United States entered World War II, and these were subsequently used by the US Army Air Forces as VIP transports.

The Europeans had already placed four-engined transports in service, but realized that a new generation of considerably more capable machines was needed for the late 1930s. They decided that high-altitude operations were an unnecessary and indeed unaffordable luxury, and therefore concentrated their efforts on highly streamlined aircraft that would have excellent range at lower altitudes. The highest an airliner could operate without some form of pressurization was about 8,000 ft (2440 m), and the Germans and British each produced two interesting designs.

The German aircraft were the Focke-Wulf Fw 200 Condor designed by Kurt Tank, and the Junkers Ju 90. The Ju 90 saw little commercial use before the war, but the Condor, which first flew in 1937, made an excellent flight from Berlin to New York in 1938 and paved the way for nonstop flights between major cities on opposite sides of the Atlantic. The war intervened before the Condor had been able to make its mark as a civil transport, and later production switched to maritime patrol and reconnaissance bomber derivatives of the baseline transport. Surviving pre-war aircraft were also used as the personal transports of the Nazi leaders.

The two British four-engined airliners were the de Havilland D.H.91 Albatross of 1937 and the Armstrong Whitworth A.W.27 Ensign of 1938. The Albatross was a very beautiful aeroplane with excellent performance, and was constructed using the type of wooden construction pioneered by the D.H.88 Comet and eventually brought to fruition by the superb Mosquito multi-role aircraft of World War II. The Albatross could carry some 35 passengers over moderately long routes, but airlines were deterred from large-scale orders by the type's wooden

Above: After cutting its air transport teeth on the biplane Model 17, Beech moved to a more advanced technical level with the monoplane Model 18 that was introduced before World War II, was built in very large numbers during that war, and remained in production after it, latterly with tricycle rather than tailwheel landing gear.

construction. The Ensign was a high-wing type of more workaday conception and could carry 40 passengers, but the outbreak of war put paid to any civilian chances it may have had.

The period's other major aeronautical powers were Japan and the USSR. Japan's aviation industry and airlines grew steadily during the late 1920s and 1930s as the country extended its empire on the Asian mainland. Starting virtually from scratch as an aeronautical power in the period immediately after World War I, Japan was at first happy to purchase the latest Western types for examination and production under licence. Impressed by some of these aircraft, the Japanese also built extensively developed versions, and this Japanese tendency persuaded the Americans and British in particular that Japan had little real expertise in the fields of aircraft design and construction.

This was far from being the case. The Japanese concentrated their main design strength on military aircraft but, even though they were less important to Japan's imperialist ambitions, Japanese civil aircraft were very well made and in general somewhat lighter than the Western types from which they had been derived: the redesign process placed great emphasis on the elimination of excess weight as a means of securing the best possible speed and range on a given power.

The Soviet aviation industry was a virtually total enigma to the countries of what later became the Western world, although it was known that Soviet factories had produced vast numbers of aircraft, of which the great majority were for military use. Comparatively few Soviet aircraft were seen in the West before the Spanish Civil War, which broke out in 1936, but these appeared t be poorly made. The Western authorities failed to notice that many of these aircraft, even if poorly made and finished, were of advanced design and incorporated several novel ideas. In fact, Soviet technicians had devoted considerable attention to the problems of flight in the late 1920s, once the new Soviet regime had reorganized and then expanded the rather haphazard aviation industry in had inherited from the Tsarist empire.

With little need for international air transport and only marginally more for internal air services, Soviet civil aviation had not flourished. There had been a considerable expansion in the numbers and activities of flying clubs, so a number of sporting types and trainers had been produced, but for the moment the Soviet authorities were content to let air transport develop slowly. Meanwhile, a major part of the country's aeronautical resources were concentrated on record breaking and experimental aircraft, both of which would help keep aeronautical science up to date. Soviet designers seemed to excel in the development of long-range aircraft, the most notable of which was the Tupolev ANT-25, a graceful single-engined monoplane which its three-man crew (Gromov, Yumashev and Danelin) flew nonstop from Moscow to San Jacinto in California on 12/13 July 1937, a distance of 10239 km (6,362 miles).

The USSR's more significant designer of large aircraft, and virtually the only designer of civil aircraft, during this period was Andrei Tupolev. He produced a variety of machines of which the most successful were a number of giant monoplanes, including the strange ANT-20 of 1934. This was powered by eight 900-hp inline engines, six mounted in the leading edges of the wings and the other two in a nacelle (one engine driving a tractor propeller and the other a pusher) strut-mounted above the wing centre-section; the ANT-20's wing span was an enormous 63.0 m (206 ft 8 in), which made the aeroplane the largest of the period.

The ANT-20 carried a crew of 20 and up to 80 passengers, although it was used mostly as a mobile propaganda office, complete with a cinema in the rear fuselage, a printing press in the port wing, a photographic studio in the starboard wing, radio, and a telephone exchange. It even had generators for loudspeakers and lights on the under-surfaces of the wings so that the aeroplane could put out messages as it flew sedately over its audience. Aeroflot in 1932 as the national airline, but on the whole Soviet civil aviation before World War II was well behind that of the Western powers, both in size and technical development.

Land-based air transport was destined to dominate civil aviation in the long term, but during the 1920s and 1930s many people hoped and expected that most of the future's long-distance airliners would be water-based for maximum exploitation of advantages such as no need for expensive airfields, elimination of landing gear (always a weak section of early aircraft) in favour of a sturdy pair of floats or a boat-shaped hull, great load-carrying capacity for the payload and/or fuel within the large hull/ fuselage, and ability to float if the machine was forced down by engine failure over water.

The first of the classic airliner flying boats was the Short Calcutta, built in 1928 to the specifications of Imperial Airways for its routes to Africa and India, on which the three-engined Calcutta carried 15 passengers at a cruising speed of 90 mph (145 km/h). With its metal hull, the Calcutta proved an admirable machine and such flying boats gave excellent service until well into the 1930s, setting the example of punctuality and comfort that characterized flying-boat operations. In 1931 there appeared the Short Kent, powered by four radials, which could carry 16 passengers.

The pre-war British flying boats reached their peak with the Short 'Empire' class. These were four-engined machines of the classic monoplane flying boat layout. The wing accommodated the engines in leading-edge nacelles and was mounted on top of a deep, sturdy hull so that the propellers would clear the water and the engines would not be drenched with spray during take-off and landing. To ensure waterborne stability, small auxiliary floats were strut-mounted under the outer wing panels.

Below: Despite its somewhat unlovely appearance, fixed landing gear and open pilot's cockpit, the Northrop Alpha of 1929 was a true precursor of the 'modern' airliner in is low-drag design and all-metal construction, the latter including the multi-spar cantilever wing of exceptional fatigue life. The forward fuselage could be configured for up to six passengers in a windowed compartment though a more typical arrangement was three passengers and 465 lb (211 kg) of mail, or a larger load of mail or freight.

So impressive did the design look that Imperial Airways ordered no fewer than 28 such flying boats 'off the drawing board' for use on all the mail routes of the Empire Air Mail scheme. From 1937 onwards, the 'Empire' class flying boats were a regular and well-loved sight on all of Imperial Airways' more important routes.

One of the oddest experiments undertaken at the time was the Short-Mayo composite. For all their efficiency, the 'Empire' class boats could not deliver mail across the Atlantic as quickly as was desired. So in 1938 a composite was tested: an 'Empire' class flying boat with a Short-Mayo Mercury four-engined floatplane mounted on its back. The idea, which worked well in practice but was never put into general service, was for the Mercury to be loaded with as much mail and fuel as possible and then to be lifted into the air by the 'Empire' class flying boat (the Mercury being a high-speed aeroplane with small wings which could not rise from the water when fully laden). Once the composite was airborne and in full flight toward the United States, the Mercury would lift off from the back of the 'Empire' class flying boat's back and make a high-speed dash to New York with the mail.

In Germany, too, there was an early interest in flying boats, and the great successes of a number of Dornier Wal boats did much to impress on the world that the German aviation industry had not faded away in the 1920s. But Dornier had greater things in mind, and in 1929 unveiled the monstrous Dornier Do X, a huge flying boat spanning 48.0 m (157 ft 6 in) and powered by no less than 12 inline piston engines. Driving six tractor and six pusher propellers, these engines were mounted in pairs in nacelles above the wing. Instead of stabilizing floats, Dornier used his favourite stubby wing-like sponsons, which extended laterally from the hull below the wing to provide waterborne stability. The Do X was too big and heavy for its engines, however, and the flying boat was not a success. Nonetheless its size alone was enough to earn the crew a great reception on the single occasion it reached New York.

Like the British, the Germans were interested in swift mail delivery and hit on an ingenious scheme : fast liners would cross the ocean towards the mail's destination, and when within range would catapult off a large floatplane loaded with the mail. The type selected for this exercise was the Blohm und Voss Ha 139, an attractive four-engined twin-float machine with cranked wings and twin endplate fin-and-rudder assemblies. The scheme went into operation during 1938, but was abandoned a year later when the Dornier Do 26 entered service.

The Do 26 was one of the most beautiful flying boats ever built. The hull was very streamlined and the four engines (two tractor and two pusher units) were installed in the angle of the gulled wings. To reduce airborne drag and thereby improve speed and range, the stabilizing floats were designed to retract into the under-surfaces of the wings once the Do 26 had taken to the air. The Do 26 had a speed of almost 320 km/h (200 mph) and a range of 8000 km (4,970 miles). Had not war broken out, the Do 26 would surely have become a successful mailplane on the prestigious North Atlantic route.

The United States, prevented by the United Kingdom from operating a trans-Atlantic flying boat service, concentrated on routes in the Caribbean, South America and the Far East, where American flying boats had been operating with increasing success since the middle 1920s. Three classic American flying boats made their appearance in the 1930s and operated services that were to become legends in their own time. These were the Sikorsky S-42 and Martin M-130 of 1934, and the Boeing Model 314 of 1938.

The Sikorsky flying boat had a hull of very fine proportions, and this carried both the wing and the tail unit above it on strut-braced pylons. Twin fin-and-rudder assemblies were mounted above the tailplane, and the four engines were located in the wing leading edges. The S-42's maximum speed was almost 190 mph (300 km/h), and the passengers were seated in great comfort in a number of small lounges. The M-130, also known as the Martin Ocean Transport, was another attractive flying boat with a high-set wing, Dornier-like sponsons and a single vertical tail surface with the horizontal surface located half way up it. The Model 314 was similar to the M-130 in basic concept, but somewhat larger, slightly bluffer in its contours and without the wing bracing struts. Additional vertical tail surfaces were mounted towards the outboard ends of the tailplane.

Between them these three types of American flying boat established a reputation for luxury travel, especially across the Pacific, rivalled only by the British 'Empire' class flying boats. Various routes crossed the Pacific to Australia, New Zealand, the Philippines and China, via the islands of the Pacific.

France also placed strong emphasis on flying boats to link it with its imperial possessions in the Far East and equatorial Africa, and also for routes across the South Atlantic. Flying boats of CAMS, Breguet, and Lioré-et-Olivier design were notably advanced for the late 1920s, and still held several flying boat records in the early 1930s before the gradual decline of the French aviation industry took its toll. No new machines were forthcoming to replace the older boats, which were still doing an adequate job. There were signs of improvement after the nationalization of the industry, but the outbreak of World War II put an end to many promising projects.

By the late 1930s civil aviation had advanced considerably. The first tentative commercial flights had in general been extemporized affairs, planned only in the sketchiest of terms and very much dependent on the vagaries of the weather and of the aircraft itself. The reliability of aircraft improved gradually but steadily, however, and with the beginnings of comfortable air flight the airline market started to grow considerably. The airliners of the late 1920s were still austere in their accommodation, which was noisy, constantly shaken by vibration and somewhat draughty, but their seating was comfortable and not too closely spaced.

In the 1930s transport aircraft underwent a substantial change for the better. In the new breed of all-metal airliners developed in the United States the combination of more powerful, smoother running engines and improved structures reduced the level of vibration that had to be endured by the passengers, and large amounts of sound proofing material built into the fuselage went a long way towards reducing noise levels. The larger, more rounded fuselages of the new airliners also made it possible to carry greater numbers of passengers without seriously reducing the space allowed for each fare-paying person. Commercial passenger flight continued to grow in the 1930s.

As the safety of airline operations was proved insurance rates for airline passengers gradually fell: in March 1933 insurance rates for travel on Imperial Airways, which had just completed 10 million miles (16.1 million km) of operations, were reduced from 12 shillings (60 pence) to 1 shilling (5 pence) per £1,000.

The outbreak of World War II halted European expansion just at the time that American airlines were really getting into their swing, but the 1930s had seen a rapid expansion of commercial flying. In 1929, for example, the world's airlines flew 96.3 million passenger miles, of which the European and North American airlines contributed 48.9 and 44.2 respectively. By 1934 the figures had grown to a grand total of 421.9 million passenger miles, represented by 151.7 million in Europe and 231.6 million in North America. The Americans and Canadians (even

though the latter contributed only 6.3 million passenger miles) had overtaken the Europeans by a very considerable margin. By 1939 the figures had again increased enormously: total passenger miles flown were 1,395.5 million, with the Europeans responsible for 434.5 million and the North Americans 771.3 million. Within five years, therefore, the Europeans had boosted their passenger flying by 280% and the North Americans by 333%. The effect of the outbreak of World War II in Europe was immediately apparent, however, and by 1941 European passenger miles had fallen to 292,600 passenger miles, while the North Americans had again increased their total to 1,602.7 million passenger miles.

Such figures are impressive, but cannot tell the whole story. Clearly the Americans had taken a lead with the introduction of airliners such as the Model 247 and DC series in the first half of the 1930s, and had thereafter moved from strength to strength. But the sheer growth of passenger miles perhaps disguises that commercial flight was still in its adolescence. Despite the fact that they were a very considerable technical advance over their immediate predecessors, the all-metal airliners of the 1930s were nonetheless distinctly limited: lack of cabin pressurization meant that they had to operate at the medium altitudes where their operations were seriously affected by air turbulence and other weather factors. The comparatively small size of the first-generation metal airliners meant that payload and range were still small. Only with the arrival of the Model 307 Stratoliner, with its pressurized fuselage and four engines, at the end of the decade could the first truly efficient long-haul modern airliner be said to have

appeared. Air travel across the Atlantic, which has no stopping points, became practical only at a late date, but the Pacific posed fewer problems, despite its greater width, because of the many islands at which flying boats could put down for refuelling. The first scheduled crossing of the Pacific was an airmail flight by a M-130 of Pan American Airways on 22 November 1935: the flying boat departed from San Francisco and arrived at Manila in the Philippines by way of staging points in the Hawaiian Islands, Midway Island, Wake Island and Guam in the Marianas group. The first commercial survey flight across the North Atlantic was not made until 3/5 July 1937, when both Pan American and Imperial Airways launched flights, the former an S-42 Clipper III from west to east and the latter the Short 'C' class flying boat Caledonia from east to west. Scheduled passenger operations did not begin until 1939, when Pan American started a service from New York to Southampton via Bermuda and Lisbon with Model 314 flying boats.

Within the United States the first passenger transcontinental flight, using a number of staging points, had taken place on 15 June 1929. Operated the Universal Air Lines System, the whole crossing had taken some 60 hours from New York to Los Angeles and had involved several stages by rail. Even by the end of the 1930s airline flights across America were little faster than train trips.

Despite the great strides that had been taken in the development of commercial aviation especially in the United States, pre-war air transport was mainly limited to short haul operations with passengers paying high fares. It was to be only after the end of World War II that commercial aviation really became a major industry.

Seen here in the markings of American Airlines, the Douglas DC-3 was the airliner that fully capitalized on the pioneering efforts of the Boeing Model 247 and Douglas DC-2, and therefore emerged as the first transport aeroplane with all the features that came to be regarded as essential in any 'modern' airliner.

Build-up for War

The world's air forces passed through a lean and hungry period during the late 1920s and early 1930s. Against a background of financial retrenchment and a combination of public and political antipathy toward 'militarism', it was inevitable that there should be a tightening of the purse strings where the military was concerned. Air forces suffered more than armies and navies as the value of the latter two services had been evident for centuries, but air forces had yet to prove their full worth. Air forces therefore fell well below armies and navies in proportion of their slice of the financial cake allocated toward national defence.

This factor was particularly noticeable in terms of matériel. A ship is very expensive to build, but it remains serviceable for years with little chance of loss. The same applies to army equipment: pieces of artillery, machine-guns and rifles, all enjoy long service lives. Aircraft, on the other hand, have a comparatively high cost but are essentially flimsy and, by the standards of the 1920s and early 1930s, might not survive for long enough for the investment in them to be recouped. This presented air staffs with a difficult problem: with governments unwilling to spend lavishly on machines that might have only a short life, the numbers of aircraft provided was almost invariably too little for what the staffs considered to be the minimum for the tasks allocated by the political leadership that fixed these tasks! The sole solution that the air staffs could find was a quantum improvement in the reliability and cost-effectiveness of military aircraft.

The effect of such a policy were readily apparent in the United Kingdom between the two world wars. The Royal Air Force received small numbers of specialized fighters and bombers, but the majority of service aircraft were general-purpose machines. By their ability to undertake two or more operational roles, such aircraft were more cost-effective to a considerable degree than any single-role aeroplane, and this was an important factor in the plans of Sir Hugh Trenchard, Chief of the Air Staff throughout most of the 1920s.

As service chief of the world's first independent air force, Trenchard had to combat constant attempts by the army and navy to take over the RAF, and decided to counter by highlighting the RAF's general cost-effectiveness compared with the other two services. The United Kingdom's predominant military concern during this period was the nature and cost of policing its imperial possessions, particularly those in the Middle East and in East Africa, so Trenchard saw these areas as ideal for the role of proving the RAF's cost-effectiveness. The great advantage of aircraft, Trenchard surmised, was their combination of strategic, operational and tactical mobility and their almost total immunity to effective countermeasures from the ground by opponents of low technical sophistication. A number of successes quickly proved Trenchard's point.

Unrest in remote areas could be dealt with by the army, but that generally required a lengthy march through hostile

The Hawker Hurricane was the first modern monoplane fighter adopted by the British, and was an epoch-making machine despite its retention of a fabric-covered airframe of metal construction.

Above: From the 1930s until a point well toward the end of World War II, most advanced navies relied on catapult-launched floatplanes for long-range reconnaissance and to spot for the guns of their larger warships.

numbers of well equipped troops to spots in which air demonstrations and bombings were either inappropriate or inadequate. This resulted in a number of odd looking but useful aircraft, such as three Vickers aircraft, namely the Vernon and Victoria of the early 1920s, and then the Valentia of the early 1930s.

A notable 'first' gained by the Victoria was the first major airlift in history. Between December 1928 and February 1929 the Victorias of No.70 Squadron evacuated 586 civilians and their luggage from Kabul in Afghanistan to Peshawar in India, to escape the insurrection led by the 'Mad Mullah'. Like their general-purpose contemporaries, however, these troop transports were built for range, reliability and capacity rather than outright performance, making them unsuitable for operations in any but secondary theatres of war.

France was the only other nation to make considerable use of aircraft in a similar role. In the early 1920s, the Rif rebellion in French and Spanish North Africa caused severe problems, and aircraft were used to support the regular ground forces. In other areas Breguet 14s and Salmson 2s played an important independent role very similar to that of the British policing aircraft.

The number of advanced military aircraft built in the 1920s was further reduced by a general acceptance of what the British termed the ' 10-year rule'. This postulated that an impending European war would be apparent at least 10 years before its eventual outbreak, providing more than ample opportunity to build advanced military aircraft in quantity. So there was a feeling in the 1920s and early 1930s that only a few first-class specialized fighters and bombers need be built, mainly to maintain design and production facilities and to provide experience of high-performance flight and aircraft.

Combined with financial restrictions and a certain reluctance to take the risks involved in developing advanced machines, this meant that military aircraft gradually began to lag behind civilian machines in terms of outright performance. The gradual emergence of a financially and technically powerful commercial market, especially in the United States, led to the development of structural and aerodynamic features which increased both the profitability of airliners and the performance of record breaking and racing aircraft. So while contemporary military aircraft improved only step by step, usually as a result of increased engine power, civilian machines advanced in capability by leaps and bounds.

It has often been noted that in the early 1930s the air forces of the United Kingdom, the United States, Italy and France were admirably prepared to fight the air battles of World War I again. Their first-line aircraft were still basically the same as those which had proved their capabilities during 1918: fighters and bombers had limited armament (both offensive and defensive) and were biplanes with fixed landing gear. Yet if no single country had secured a clear advantage, neither had any of them fallen behind. And the more important air forces equipped themselves with thoroughly modern aircraft very quickly once the need became apparent in the mid-1930s.

territory and its constant dangers of ambush or other disasters. RAF aircraft, on the other hand, could fly without delay to the location of the trouble and demonstrate the futility of resistance to British rule by bombing a native village. If there was an uprising, aircraft could usually disperse ill-trained and poorly armed tribesmen with light bombs and machine-gun fire. The speed and flexibility of an aerial response to incipient were thus factors that offered the RAF the opportunity to eliminate trouble before it had become truly serious, and this was a virtual impossibility for the army.

The RAF's success in such operations finally secured the service's continuance as an independent arm of the British military forces, but had unfortunate consequences in other respects. The type of aircraft needed for such work had excellent reliability, good range and could carry a fairly small but varied bomb load and other armament: in other words, the aircraft were general-purpose types. This accorded nicely with the British government's demand for aircraft with long service lives and the cost-effective capability to undertake a variety of roles. The result was a number of good general purpose aircraft, from the Bristol F.2Bs and de Havilland (Airco) D.H.9s left over from World War I to the Westland Wapitis and Hawker Audaxes of the early 1930s.

Such aircraft were ideally suited to policing the British empire, where there was little or no serious opposition, but were wholly inadequate for the type of aerial combat that would be encountered over a European battlefield, where even good general-purpose machines could not compare with machines optimized for a single role.

These aircraft nonetheless exercized some beneficial effects on aviation. Operating mostly in inhospitable parts of the world, they had to be comfortable to fly and reliable to operate under adverse climatic and geographical conditions. It was soon realized, moreover, that though such general-purpose aircraft were vitally important for the imperial policing role, there was also a need for troop transports that could be used to fly in small

Right: The biplane lasted longer in first-line military service than in civil transport service, and much experimental development of operational techniques and tactics was accomplished on aircraft such as this, a Curtiss O-1 Falcon of the US Army Air Corps that became the US Army Air Forces in June 1941.

While they had been unwilling to provide their front-line squadrons with the most advanced aircraft that could have been built, they had followed the latest developments in structures and aerodynamics with very small numbers of experimental and record breaking aircraft.

Oddly enough, the gradually increasing technical inferiority of military aircraft relative to their civilian counterparts during in the 1920s was balanced by major advances in the theory of air warfare. This resulted largely from the efforts of three men. Building on the concepts first proposed during World War I by an Italian, General Giulio Douhet, Trenchard and two Americans, Brigadier General 'Billy' Mitchell and Rear Admiral William Moffett, averred that the bomber would be the decisive factor in any future war. These three officers and their supporters forecast that bombers, flying in mass formation so that each aeroplane was covered by the defensive cannon and machine-guns of several of its brethren, would fight their way through to targets deep in enemy territory. Such bombers forces could or, according to the bomber enthusiasts, would destroy the both the ability and the will of the enemy to wage war: this the bombers would achieve by smashing war industries, transportation systems and power production, and by demoralizing the civilians with devastating raids on residential areas.

This concept of strategic air power was seized upon and expanded considerably by both service and civilian theorists. The threat of massed bomber attack became one of the most clichéd yet believed ideas of the period leading up to World War II. With little or no practical experience of strategic bombing to guide them or, perhaps more practically, to temper their ideas the adherents of strategic bombing were believed almost without reservation, and the dread of massed bombing found powerful expression on films such as Things to Come. The effect of the strictly limited quantities of bombs that could be dropped by

current bombers was greatly exaggerated and the strength of civilian resistance was minimized or indeed ignored, and strategic bombing came to be seen as a distinct threat to the survival of civilization.

As the primary British advocate of strategic bombing, Trenchard was ideally placed to impose the idea on the RAF, which came to rely heavily on bombers in the 1920s. The Americans rejected the idea at first. Mitchell was nothing if not forceful and persistent, and he was finally court martialled and dismissed from the US Army for his constant attacks on established army and navy dogma. He is best remembered today as the first man to demonstrate the obsolescence of the battleship as the arbiter of sea power.

In 1921, to the amazement of most of the US Navy, aircraft under his command succeeded in sinking the surrendered German battleship Ostfriesland, widely believed to be unsinkable. The feat was achieved under perfect test conditions by bombs exploding in the water alongside the ship: sceptics pointed out that the Ostfriesland had been stationary and had offered no defensive fire, ignoring the fact that practice and improved techniques would surely enable aircraft to achieve similar results in future against a manoeuvring warship throwing up a wall of defensive anti-aircraft fire.

While Mitchell was in disgrace, Admiral Moffett

worked with greater discretion in the background and as a result was instrumental in the gradual emergence of the US Navy as a major offensive air arm. By the late 1920s the American military establishment was well on the way to accepting the concept of strategic air power, and had subscribed fully to it by the mid-1930s.

For the bombing theorists the most important factor to consider was invariably the weight of bombs that could be dropped on the target. Aircraft speed at first played only a small part in their thinking: there was a firm conviction that 'the bomber will always get through'. British bombers such as the Vickers Virginia, Boulton Paul Sidestrand and Handley Page Heyford were all slow biplanes, while the American Witteman-Lewis NBL-1 was a triplane. Only in the early 1930s, therefore, did the need to combine a heavy bomb-carrying capability with high performance gain proper recognition. This led to the appearance of the first real heavy bombers in the United States: the Boeing B-9 and Martin B-10 were both advanced monoplanes of metal construction with performance equal or superior to that of contemporary biplane fighters.

Despite the currently disorganized nature of its air force and aircraft industry, France also adopted the concept of heavy bombing and produced a number of such aircraft in the late 1920s. Almost all were notable for a singular lack of streamlining and a slab-sided appearance of great ungainliness. The twin-engined Amiot 143 and Bloch M.B.200 bombers, together with the four-engined Farman F.221 bomber, were the most notable examples of this aerodynamically unrefined tendency and entered service in the early 1930s. Yet even these French machines seem modern by comparison with a British contemporary, the Handley Page Heyford that was a large biplane with the fuselage attached to the underside of the upper wing and the bomb load stowed in the thick centre section of the lower wing.

Meanwhile, fighters remained little more advanced in concept than World War I types. The first such machines to

Above: A patrol flying boat that served the US Navy long and faithfully was the Naval Aircraft Factory PN evolved from the Curtiss F-5L flying boat of World War I. This is a PN-9, and the series was later evolved into the Hall PH with an aluminium rather than plywood-covered wooden hull.

Left: A wholly obsolete type that survived into World War II was the Farman F.222, a slab-sized and angular monstrosity of a heavy bomber with four engines in tandem push/pull pairs strut-mounted under the wings in nacelles that also accommodated the retractable main units of the landing gear.

Above: With its clean lines and carefully cowled Vee piston engine, the Hawker Fury Mk I was the first British fighter with a maximum speed in excess of 200 mph (322 km/h).

enter service with the RAF after World War I were the Armstrong Whitworth Siskin and the Gloster Grebe, both of which made their service debuts during 1924. Several companies produced experimental monoplane fighters during the decade, but the RAF adhered rigidly to the well proved biplane formula, usually with a radial engine, for a period of some 15 years after World War I. Later types such as the Bristol Bulldog, Gloster Gauntlet and Gloster Gladiator continued this tradition, and the only notable exception was the Hawker Fury. Powered by a Rolls-Royce Kestrel inline piston engine, this was the first British fighter to exceed 200 mph (320 km/h) in level flight.

Keynotes of the design philosophy that created these fighters were the strong yet light biplane layout, the excellent manoeuvrability, and the armament of two rifle-calibre machine-gun located with their breeches within reach of the pilot, who could thus clear the all-too-common jammed rounds. British light bombers followed the same basic formula, but carried a gunner behind the pilot and a small bomb load under the lower wings. Classic examples were the Fairey Fox, Hawker Hart and Hawker Hind. The key difference between all these aircraft and their counterparts in World War I was the widespread use of metal in the structures of the later machines. This was Air Ministry policy after 1924, to avoid the problems encountered in World War I through shortage of suitably seasoned timber for airframes. Metal gradually became more common in other parts of British military aircraft, but as the basic design philosophy remained unaltered the aircraft were essentially wooden types rendered in metal.

Though often condemned for being behind the times in the 1920s and 1930s, the French were well up with the leaders in the field of fighters. Several advanced monoplane designs were evolved during the 1920s with heavily braced parasol or gull wings. These offered strength, relatively low drag and a good field of vision for the pilot. Unlike the British, many of whose aircraft companies had disappeared in the troubled times after the war, the French could rely on long established firms such as Morane-Saulnier, Nieuport and SPAD, as well as more recent companies such as Dewoitine, Loiré and Wibault. The 1920s, therefore, saw a large number of interesting fighters, and a smaller number of reconnaissance and light bomber

Below: France was one of the first countries to adopt a monoplane fighter in the form of the Dewoitine D.500 series with a stressed-skin monocoque fuselage and a cantilever wing. This is an example of the definitive D.510, whose careful streamlining was partially offset by the retention of an open cockpit and massive fixed main landing gear units.

machines, which were being offered both for the home market and also for export sale.

At the end of the decade the French air force was equipped with the parasol-winged Nieuport-Delage NiD.62 series, Loiré/Gourdou-Leseurre 32 and Wibault 72, all capable of a maximum speed in the order of 260 km/h (160 mph). In 1930, however, the French air staff realized that all its fighters were approaching obsolescence, and so issued specifications for a new standard fighter. The best response came from the Dewoitine company, which had tried its hand in the 1920s with a number of sturdy parasol types and had won a good export record. For its D.500 series Dewoitine adopted a new layout: it was thus a cantilever low-wing monoplane powered by a closely cowled Hispano-Suiza 12Y inline piston engine (soon to become the most important French aero engine of the decade) and supported on the ground by wide-track fixed landing gear. The new fighter had a top speed of 360 km/h (225 mph), which was far higher than the maximum speeds of current first-line French fighters.

It was at this time, however, that the organizational and financial weaknesses of the French aviation industry first became readily apparent. There were too many small companies, and as the cost of prototype construction began to rise rapidly none of them had sufficient capital to finance the rapid development of the new types that the country was now beginning to need as a matter of increasing urgency. Rationalization was clearly was urgently needed, but although the problem was seen and understood, the political turmoil in which France found itself prevented the prompt, enforced action that was needed. With government succeeding government at intervals of just a few months, what appeared to be a relatively minor problem did not receive the attention it deserved until too late, and the French aircraft industry entered a temporary decline.

The United States, on the other hand, was at last beginning to emerge from the aeronautical limbo into which it had fallen during the middle of the decade. The gradual development of the fledgling commercial airlines was partially responsible for this renaissance, but equally significant was the amalgamation of a number of small builders into a few large and increasingly well organized concerns, each operating in a large custom-built and therefore modern factory accommodating design staff, experimental workshops and production lines. Wright and Pratt & Whitney had become the two highly most important and competitive major aero engine manufacturers, and these two major companies were producing reliable air-cooled radials such as the Pratt & Whitney Wasp and its derivatives, and the Wright Whirlwind and Cyclone and their derivatives. Finally, the American long-term research programme was now producing valuable dividends in the field of structures and aerodynamics.

The American revival became fully evident with the advent of a number of new and formidable aircraft produced in the late 1920s and early 1930s. The Boeing B-9 and Martin B-10 bombers mentioned above were two clear examples of advanced aerodynamic theory allied to advanced military concepts, but the fighter equipment of the two American air forces also revealed that the American aeronautical machine now possessed strength in depth. The US Army and the US Navy each had its own air force, with the US Marine Corps operating further air formations flying basically the same types of aircraft as the US Navy.

Although the perpetuation of two major air forces had some drawbacks, leading to a certain unnecessary duplication of effort, the keen competition between them was a useful spur to the development of superior combat aircraft. By 1927, the US Navy had received its first two large aircraft-carriers, the Saratoga and Lexington, sisterships which could each accommodate and operate a large number of high-performance aircraft. The two ships were the first practical results of Admiral Moffett's steady pressure for a naval air arm which would show itself capable of confronting land-based air power on perfectly equal terms.

Authorities in most countries with aspirations toward naval air power, principally the United Kingdom, felt that the complex requirements of carrierborne operations meant that naval aircraft had to embody a compromise between several design factors, and therefore could not be a match for land-based aircraft. The US Navy, on the other hand, realized that its carriers would play a dominant part in any future war, principally because of the geographical isolation of the United States between the Pacific and Atlantic oceans. It was therefore crucial that the aircraft-carrier arm's aircraft be capable of combating land-based aircraft. The early realization of this fact proved highly significant in America's struggle with Japan from 1941 onwards.

The most important carrierborne fighters of the US Navy were the Curtiss Hawk and Boeing F2B, each possessing a maximum speed of 155 mph (250 km/h), later supplanted by the Boeing F4B, which was capable of 190 mph (305 km/h). The US Army Air Corps' fighters of the period were the Boeing PW-9 and Curtiss P-6 capable of 155 and 108 mph (250 and 318 km/h) respectively, later joined by the Boeing P-12 (the land plane equivalent of the F4B) and in 1933 by the Boeing P-26 'Peashooter', the first American monoplane fighter, which was capable of 235 mph (380 km/h). Of these only the P-26 represented an extraordinary advance on its predecessors, but they were all workmanlike aircraft notable for their sturdy construction, high manoeuvrability and generally good performance: though they had no long pedigree, therefore, they were in most respects the equals of contemporary British and French fighters.

The development of aircraft had not yet become prohibitively expensive, so it was normal for all but the very poorest countries to try their hand at the design and production of fighters and other small aircraft. Most notable of these products was the Polish PZL P-7 fighter of 1932. An inverted gull-wing monoplane clearly inspired by French design thinking, the P-7 was powered by a licence-built Bristol Jupiter radial and capable of 320 km/h (200 mph). Further development led to the P-11 and P-24, both of which performed well in the hands of Polish and Greek pilots against the Luftwaffe in 1939 and 1941.

Yugoslavia and Czechoslovakia were also building fighters in this period, and some mention must also be made of Italy. Although not a poor country, Italy had gone into an aeronautical slump in the late 1920s, despite her excellent seaplanes and heroic efforts in the Schneider Trophy races. Not until 1933, with the development of the Fiat CR.32, did all Italian combat aircraft reach world standards. Designed by the illustrious Celestino Rosatelli, the CR.32 was very strong and manoeuvrable, and it was fast for its time, with a top speed of 370 km/h (230 mph). The very capabilities of the CR.32 led to unfortunate consequences for the Italians, however: so good was the CR.32 that little notice was taken of the rapidly advancing theory of air warfare and accordingly no priority was given to the development of an advanced successor.

By 1933, therefore, the design philosophies of World War I had been completely revised. There were still believers in the biplane formula, including the Italians, but this design concept's practical limits had been reached by fighters such as the Gloster Gladiator from the UK, Fiat CR.42 from Italy and Polikarpov I-153 from the USSR.

Even before this, however, the nature and shape of the biplane's inevitable successor had been demonstrated by the Boeing and Martin bombers, the French monoplane fighters, and the racing aircraft developed by the United Kingdom, Italy and the United States. The high-drag biplane with fixed landing gear was to be supplanted by the low-drag monoplane with retractable landing gear. This change had already begun when the process was boosted by the reappearance of Germany on the military scene.

With the connivance of Sweden and the USSR, Germany had circumvented the clauses of the Treaty of Versailles prohibiting its development of advanced offensive weapons. In both these countries German designers had been free to plan and build military aircraft and tanks, and in Germany itself fighters and bombers had appeared in the guise of sporting planes and airliners. A clandestine air force had been prepared under cover of the air ministry, the national airline and various flying clubs that had sprung up all over Germany.

The Allied nations of World War I detected elements of this process, but seemed content to let matters rest until Germany made some overt military preparation. When Adolf Hitler came to power in January 1933, he was able to order an immediate expansion and acceleration of German rearmament. In 1935, he renounced the military terms of the Treaty of Versailles and a fully fledged Luftwaffe was unveiled overnight. This force possessed a large number of aircraft and also enjoyed the backing of a powerful aircraft industry together with a large number of well planned and staffed military airfields all over the Third Reich.

At first the Luftwaffe was not equipped with particularly advanced aircraft, the standard fighter and bomber being the Heinkel He 51 biplane and Junkers Ju 52/3m monoplane respectively.

Left: The Polish aero industry developed some interesting and far-sighted aircraft in the 1930s. Typical of this trend was the PZL 4, which was an all-metal tri-motor transport that did not progress past the prototype stage.

Above: The Arado Ar 68 was the second biplane fighter adopted by the German air force whose existence was revealed by Adolf Hitler in the mid-1930s. The type was superior to its Heinkel He 51 predecessor, but was nonetheless obsolescent even as it entered service and saw only limited first-line service. A few such aircraft survived into the first months of World War II as emergency night fighters.

Below: The Aero A 304 was a bomber and reconnaissance derivative of the A 204 transport, and a few aircraft were built for service with the Czech air force.

Knowing
that military
operations were still probably
some way in the future, the Luftwaffe high
command was satisfied with these aircraft as 'operational'
trainers that, in the period before the advent of more
advanced aircraft, could suffice as 'front-line' machines.
Newer types were already being designed or placed in
production, and it was these aircraft that would provide for
the establishment of the Luftwaffe as an extraordinarily
potent exponent of tactical air power in the first campaigns
of World War II.

The Luftwaffe was in some respects the world's first
truly modern air force: it was the first to equip its front-line
units with cantilever monoplane aircraft, most of which
had retractable landing gear. Lacking numbers of expensive
and still serviceable obsolescent aircraft to be replaced by
advanced monoplane types, the service had a head start in
the introduction of modern machines. The new Luftwaffe
was a highly efficient force, but this should not be allowed
to disguise the fact that it also possessed failings. There
were important gaps in its inventory, especially in
categories such as heavy bombers, ground-attack aircraft
and advanced trainers. And while the high command
should have been investigating the possibility of second-
and third-generation advanced combat aircraft as early as
1936, it believed that any future war would be of short
duration and therefore remained loyal to its first-
generation aircraft until 1940. By then it was too late to
accelerate the development programme in time to make a
significant difference to the air war that raged over Europe
into the early summer of 1945.

Exaggerated claims for the Luftwaffe have helped to
obscure the great advances made by the USSR in the late
1920s and early 1930s. After experimenting with strategic
heavy bombing on the basis of aircraft such as the Tupolev
ANT-6, and causing a number of aeronautical eyebrows to
be raised as a result of its long-distance record breaking
aircraft, the USSR decided that the most important role for
air power was tactical support of the ground forces that were
believed to be the most important element of the Soviet
armed forces. A new generation of tactical
aircraft was developed, based on
the latest advances

in aeronautical
techniques. The
Soviets also
b u i l t
competitive
a i r c r a f t
pressing the limits
of current experimental
concepts so that the widest
spectrum of aeronautical and structural
notions could be tested in hardware form.

One of the earliest and most important results of this
Soviet programme was the 1934 appearance of the
Polikarpov I-16, which has the distinction of being
the world's first cantilever low-wing monoplane
fighter with retractable landing gear. The first
examples of this epoch-making type also possessed another
advanced feature in the form of an enclosed cockpit, but
pilots did not like this enclosure and it was eliminated from
later variants. The 700-hp radial engine was mounted in a
very bluff, high-drag nose, but this notwithstanding the I-
16 could attain 450 km/h (280 mph), comparing very
favourably with the maximum speed of 223 mph (359
km/h) attained by the Gloster Gauntlet which appeared in
the following year. The Soviets then seemed to rest on their
laurels, and the German invasion six years later found the
Soviet fighter arm still equipped for the most part with later
models of the I-16, and even large numbers of the I-15 bis
and I-153 biplane fighters.

The country which then took the practical lead in
introducing advanced combat aircraft was Germany. After
lengthy evaluation, the Messerschmitt Bf 109 was selected
as the Luftwaffe's primary fighter, the Dornier Do 17 and
Heinkel He 111 as its standard medium bombers, and the
Junkers Ju 87 Stuka (abbreviated from Sturzkampfflugzeug,
or dive-bomber) as its basic tactical support aeroplane.

The Stuka, destined to achieve great notoriety in the
opening campaigns of World War II, was basically
American in concept. Ernst Udet, who with 62 victories in
World War I had ranked second only to Manfred von
Richthofen in the list of German air aces, was head of the
technical branch of the new Luftwaffe when he toured the
United States in 1933. Here he witnessed a hair-raising
display of dive-bombing by the new Curtiss F11C Hawk
biplane. Highly impressed, Udet bought two examples of
the aeroplane for examination in Germany, where the dive-
bomber concept was already under consideration there as a
means of securing highly accurate bombing accuracy in
missions flown to support the ground forces. Udet's
revelations of the practical tests he had witnessed in the
United States convinced the high command.

The last of the Luftwaffe's mainstay aircraft to appear
before World War II was the Junkers Ju 88 medium bomber,
which entered service in 1939. A classic aeroplane of great if
not unrivalled operational versatility, the Ju 88 was originally
intended as a fast medium bomber with limited dive-
bombing capability, but served with
great distinction in a great variety of
roles throughout World War II. In terms
of versatility, the Ju 88 was rivalled only by the
remarkable British de Havilland D.H.98 Mosquito.

The Germans tested the standard European concept of
air power during the Spanish Civil War, which started in
1936. German aircraft were involved from the beginning,
when Ju 52/3m transports were used to ferry General
Francisco Franco's Nationalist troops from Spanish
Morocco into southern Spain. As a bombers, however,
the Ju 52/3m proved a failure, as did the Heinkel He 51
fighter when opposed by the formidable Soviet I-15 and I-
16 fighters.

As the latest German combat aircraft emerged from their production lines they were sent to Spain in small numbers for operational evaluation. It was here that most of Germany's early World War II aircraft first saw combat and pilots learned how to get the best out of their aircraft. The problems with German aircraft in combat were seen and cured, and as a result the Luftwaffe was a confident and experienced air force by the start of World War II in 1939.

The Germans entered into the Spanish Civil War with a firm belief in using their aircraft in a strategic role, but soon discovered the vulnerability of their bombers when these were forced to operate without long-range fighter escort. After the death in a 1936 flying accident of Lieutenant General Walther Wever, the Luftwaffe's first chief-of-staff and Germany's primary protagonist of strategic air power, the Germans effectively turned their backs on the concept of strategic bombing and devoted virtually their full attention to the development of tactical air power to be used as 'flying artillery' in support of the German army's new fast-moving, hard-hitting armoured divisions. Thus the Luftwaffe became a tactical air force in terms of its equipment, practical experience, training and operational philosophy.

The initial successes enjoyed by the Axis powers (Germany, Italy and Japan) were partially due to the fact that all three nations had gained before the outbreak of World War II. Italy had not only supported the Nationalists in Spain, but had also been able to test her forces in the conquest of Abyssinia, which began in 1935. The Italian bombers, principally the Savoia-Marchetti S.M.79 tri-motor monoplane, distinguished themselves in Spain, but the CR.32 and CR.42 fighters seemed better than they were because their phenomenal agility enabled them to keep out of trouble.

The Regia Aeronautica therefore emerged from these two campaigns overestimating the operational utility of its first-line fighters. Three very promising designs for monoplane fighters, the Fiat G.50 Freccia, Macchi MC.200 Saetta and Reggiane Re.2000 Sagittario, were developed just before World War II, but the Italians had failed to keep up with the development of high-powered inline engines.

All three of these potentially good fighters were therefore fitted with low-powered radials: furthermore, speed and rate of climb were also sacrificed to the pilots' expressed preference for manoeuvrability. Armament was poor, especially compared with the standards set in German fighters, which had 20-mm cannon firing explosive shells.

Like Germany, Japan came late to modern aviation, and developed a good air force almost right from the beginning. Although the army and navy had each possessed their own air arms since 1911, Japan only began to develop her aircraft industries and air forces in the 1930s. Content at first to build Western types under licence, and so absorb the latest production and design techniques, Japan began a major expansion of her air forces, in the mid-1930s, using her own designs.

The Western nations were only too glad to condemn these Japanese aircraft as inferior copies and adaptations of Western designs. In fact they were skilfully designed to take advantage of Japan's capacity for producing lightweight structures with heavy armament, superior agility and good performance especially in speed, climb rate and range.

Some inkling of Japan's success could have been gained from reports coming from China, where the Japanese had started a full scale war in 1937, but Western intelligence staffs were amused rather than impressed by high assessments of Japanese aircraft. Yet the Mitsubishi A5M and Nakajima Ki-27 low wing monoplane fighters had very good performance despite their retention of fixed landing gear arrangements, and the next generation of fighters was even better. The Mitsubishi A6M Reisen (zero fighter), later known as the 'Zeke', received a glowing assessment from Americans flying against them in China, as did the Mitsubishi G3M 'Nell' and G4M 'Betty' bombers. All such warnings were disregarded, and this was to cost the Allies dearly in 1941 and 1942.

By 1936 the United Kingdom and France had become thoroughly alarmed by the nature and rate of German military expansion and decided to institute major rearmament programmes in which aircraft had a high priority. France had at last divorced the air force from the

Below: The French air force of the early and mid-1930s revealed an almost astonishing predilection for bombers and transports of monumental ugliness with features that looked as though they had been incorporated merely to increase drag. Two good examples of this tendency were the Potez 65 transport (below) and Amiot 143M bomber (bottom).

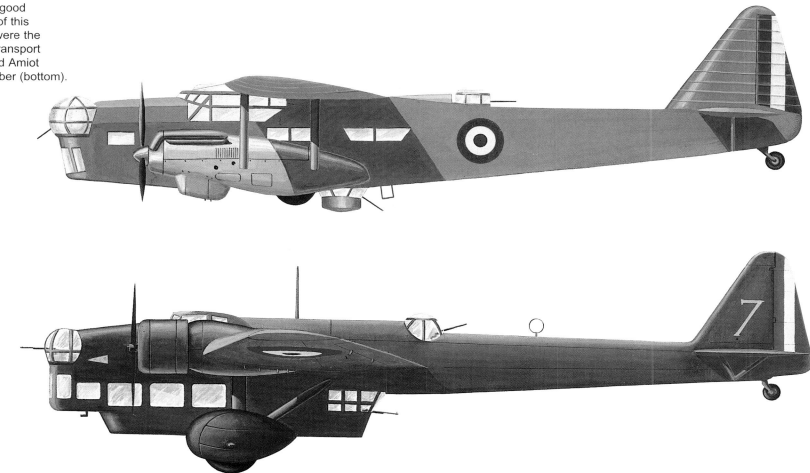

army by creating an independent Armèe de l'Air in 1933, but the new air force was still tragically short of modern aircraft. In 1936 the French government finally got round to nationalizing most of the aircraft industry, forming major groups in the north, centre, west, south-west and south-east of the country, and leaving only a few successful firms in private hands.

The nationalized groups had produced some excellent designs by the beginning of the war, but these were not ready for the French campaign of 1940. The main burden fell instead on aircraft designed by the few successful private firms: Dewoitine's beautiful little D.520 fighter, Morane-Saulnier's angular M.S.406 fighter, Bloch's stubby but powerful M.B.151 fighter, Breguet's promising Br.690 twin-engined fighter and Potez's useful Type 63 twin-engined fighter-bomber. Other excellent machines that could have played an important role had more of them been delivered in time were the Bloch M.B.175 light bomber, the elegant Lioré-et-Olivier LeO 451 medium bomber and the useful Amiot 350 series bomber.

Large-scale reorganization of the French air force and aircraft industry had been needed for some time, and even after the necessary organizational changes had been effected a sensible policy of producing large quantities of a few good types was not actively pursued. Time and invaluable resources were therefore wasted on building and testing a multitude of promising prototypes, which led to production orders and deliveries far too late for effective use in the impending war.

The British almost managed to land themselves in the same position. Only a providential blend of official demands and private enterprise supplied just enough of the right aircraft for survival in 1940. The same combination had also seen the development of several intermediate types in the early 1930s, including the technically fascinating Vickers Wellesley bomber with the geodetic structure invented by Dr Barnes Wallis.

By the middle of the decade the British aircraft industry was well on the way to producing important new fighters: the RAF abandoned the biplane formula after the Gloster Gladiator and now turned to the low-wing monoplane. The two that became best known were the Hawker Hurricane and the Supermarine Spitfire, each powered by the magnificent Rolls-Royce Merlin, a descendant of the 'R' racing engine, and each armed with eight rifle-calibre machine-guns. Both these interceptors had top speeds in the order of 350 mph (565 km/h), about 100 mph (160 km/h) faster than the Gladiator. With their retractable landing gear, trailing-edge flaps and enclosed cockpits, the aircraft caused problems at first in operational units, but as soon as pilots had mastered the necessary techniques the Hurricane and Spitfire won great popularity.

The British bomber force was also given completely new equipment in the shape of the Armstrong Whitworth Whitley, Handley Page Hampden and Vickers Wellington, each of these being a cantilever low-wing monoplane bombers with twin engines and retractable landing gear. There was also the Fairey Battle single-engined light bomber, which was to prove almost worthless in combat, and the twin-engined Bristol Blenheim light bomber, an advanced and speedy aeroplane for its time though somewhat flimsy and under-armed.

While most of the other leading aeronautical powers had switched to heavy machine-guns and cannon for fighter armament, the British still believed in rifle-calibre weapons. To deliver the necessary weight of fire, however, British fighters had to be fitted with at least eight guns. It is still debatable as to which system of armament was the more efficient.

RAF pilots were excellently trained and prepared by 1939, and the number of aircrew available was rising rapidly. By comparison with the Luftwaffe it remained a small force, however, and for the defence of British air space great reliance was placed upon r, a new and still unproved invention, to get British fighters to the right place at the right time.

The Americans were producing some very advanced aircraft, including the first Boeing B-17 Flying Fortress four-engined heavy bomber in 1935, but were still behind the Europeans in the theory and practice of air warfare. American aircraft had good performance, and allowed the pilot to perform his tasks in some comfort, but they lacked the 'edge' of their European counterparts. Nonetheless, American production was considerable, and the European powers were happy to order large quantities of such aircraft as the Curtiss P-36 and P-40 fighters, the Douglas DB-7 and Martin Maryland bombers and a number of other types. Meanwhile the Americans were hard at work on a new generation of aircraft that would make great and enduring reputations for themselves in World War II.

During this period, British and German scientists had been working on a new type of powerplant that would revolutionize aircraft design and operation. This was the turbojet engine, which was intended to thrust the aeroplane forward by the reaction of a stream of gases flowing backwards. Frank Whittle's early prototype ran for the first time in April 1937, and Hans von Ohain's model a month later. These British and German pioneers were working entirely independently of each other and evolved radically different types of engine.

In fact, the Germans soon overtook the British, and scored a considerable success when in August 1939, less than one week before the outbreak of World War II, the Heinkel He 178 became the world's first jet-powered aeroplane to fly. Yet the authorities in both Germany and the United Kingdom were slow to see the possibilities of such engines, and operational jet aircraft did not appear until late in World War II, when they outclassed their opponents completely.

Left: A truly impressive machine for its time, the eight-engined Tupolev ANT-20 was designed to provide the Soviet authorities with a flying propaganda installation complete with film development and projection capabilities, a 'voice from the sky' loudspeaker system, pharmacy, printing press and leaflet dispenser.

Below: The Avro Anson was designed as a coastal reconnaissance aeroplane for the Royal Air Force, and after short but worthy service in this role was more extensively operated as a light transport and as a multi-role trainer.

Right: The Junkers Ju 88 was conceived as a high-speed bomber, and entered service as the excellent Ju 88A illustrated here. The type was then developed as an exceptional multi-role type whose versatility was rivalled in World War II only by the de Havilland Mosquito.

Below: Further development of the basic design concept embodied in the Ju 88 resulted in a number of improved variants that were not built in very large numbers. Illustrated here is a Ju 388K high-altitude bomber.

right at the start of hostilities: undertaken on a large scale by the medium bombers, such raids were truly devastating and generally caused such destruction that airfields were rendered inoperative by the comparatively few combat aircraft likely to have survived the bombers' attentions. While the bombers roamed deep into the enemy's rear areas to destroy airfields and then turn their attentions to targets such as transport chokepoints and communications centres, the German fighters attacked their counterparts in the air during the first few days of the campaign. The success of this operational method is attested by the fact that in their first campaigns, the Germans encountered virtually no significant air opposition after the first few hours or days of any campaign, and this allowed the bulk of their tactical air strength to be allocated to the direct support of the ground forces.

The Ju 87 was central to the German concept of tactical support. A very sturdy aeroplane with wide-track fixed landing gear, the Stuka could operate from rough airstrips close behind the front line, allowing it to make frequent sorties and to respond rapidly to calls for close support. The aeroplane's performance was adequate and its offensive load quite good by the standards of the day, making it an effective combat type.

Yet a large part of the Stuka's success was due to its psychological effect. The angular Ju 87 had a belligerent and aggressive aspect, most impressive as it dived under full control thanks to the powerful and effective dive-brakes under its wings, and this aspect was enhanced by the screaming of the pair of 'Jericho trumpets' installed as single units in each landing gear fairing. These emitted a banshee howl of increasing pitch as the Stuka swooped down to release its bombs only a few hundred feet above the target. The combination of the Stuka's appearance and sound, and later its reputation, did much to demoralize opposing ground forces during 1939 and 1940.

The Polish campaign which opened World War II began on 1 September 1939, and the Luftwaffe soon proved its worth. Using combat aircraft such as the single-engined P-11 gull-winged fighter, single-engined P-23 Kar·s light bomber and twin-engined P-37 LU's medium bomber all produced by

PZL, the state aircraft company, the Polish air force fought back gallantly and in the initial stages of the fighting inflicted some severe losses on the attackers. But the weight and experience of the Luftwaffe was bound to tell in the end. After a few days the Poles could offer no large-scale aerial resistance, and the main weight of the Luftwaffe was switched to tactical support of the Panzer divisions, whose pincer movements were biting deep into Poland. German aircraft losses to ground fire were moderately heavy, but Luftwaffe aircraft continued to support the advancing Panzer formations.

The fate of Poland was hastened, perhaps, by the devastation of Warsaw on 25 September: high explosive and incendiary bombs rained down on the city, which suffered very heavily destroyed.

The campaign for Poland had been short but costly, and it taught the Germans still more about the practical aspects of air/ground co-operation. The Blitzkrieg had been born, increasing Allied apprehensions about the ruthless efficiency of Germany's war machine. The advance had been rapid, and for the first time in modern conflict the war had involved an entire population. Warsaw had been a target of minor significance in military terms, and its destruction showed to what lengths the Germans were prepared, and indeed able, to go to crush a country. At the same time, German losses had been heavy and Luftwaffe

Far Right: In the last few years before World War II, Poland produced some comparatively advanced warplanes including the PZL P.37 Los medium bomber of which only a handful had been delivered before Poland was overrun in September 1939.

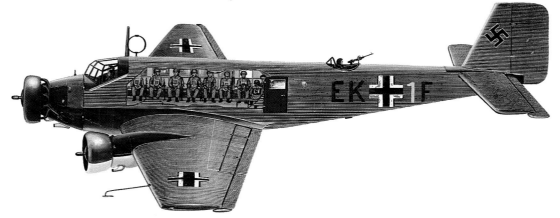

Above: The Junkers Ju 52/3m was Germany's most important transport of World War II, and was also used in the airborne forces role as a paratroop transport and glider tug.

Below: The Morane-Saulnier MS.406 was available in larger numbers than any other French fighter of 1939, but was an obsolescent type that was unable to check the hordes of German warplanes covering the German invasion of May 1940. These are aircraft from a squadron manned by Polish pilots who managed to escape from their country's defeat in September 1939.

operations were correspondingly weaker in the last few days of the campaign. The lesson to be learned, even though the Germans themselves did not fully appreciate its ramifications, was that Germany's great military expansion had not provided sufficient matériel reserves for a sustained campaign. This was particularly true of the most modem combat aircraft.

If any doubts remained about the efficiency of the German armed forces, they were soon dispelled by the capture of Denmark and the most important strategic points in Norway by airborne and seaborne landings on 9 April 1940. The subsequent Luftwaffe operations in Norway followed the pattern set for them in Poland. The Norwegian air force was negligible, and the only major air support sent by the Allies was a number of British aircraft, most of them obsolete compared with the German opposition. It is interesting to note, however, that the Gloster Gladiator biplane fighter did achieve some success against the German bombers, although they stood no chance of altering the course of the campaign, and this success is a useful reflection of the British pilots' high level of training and the relatively small qualitative superiority of first-generation monoplane bombers over last-generation biplane fighters.

While the Germans were clearing up the last Allied pockets in central and northern Norway, momentous events were taking place in western Europe. On 10 May 1940, Hitler unleashed a huge offensive against the Netherlands, Belgium and France, which were defended by their own forces as well as elements of the British services. The German attacks followed the Polish pattern, and were therefore centred on breakthrough and deep exploitation by the Panzer formations. These struck through the 'impassable' Ardennes to reach the Channel coast, splitting the Allied armies in two. The Germans then concentrated on eliminating the two halves in detail. With the Dutch, Belgians and French defeated to the north of the 'Panzer corridor', and the British and a number of their allies escaping from Dunkirk, the Germans turned their full weight on the remnants of the French army holding that portion of France south of the corridor, and the last elements of the French army surrendered towards the end of June.

Again it had been the Blitzkrieg combination of Panzer formations and aircraft that had proved decisive. But losses in this campaign had been proportionally even heavier than in the Polish campaign. In the north, against the Netherlands and Belgium, Germany had used its airborne forces on a major scale for the first time, and losses had been severe. The most important effect on the Germans was that the Junkers Ju 52/3m transports now had to be used both for training the Luftwaffe bomber forces and as operational aircraft. This affected the whole aircrew training programme, with a consequent lowering of standards. In the shorter term this was relatively unimportant, but it set in progress the chain of longer-term events that led to the appearance from 1944 of aircrews that were totally inadequate in numbers and quality to replace the highly skilled men who had succeeded so often in the period up to 1942.

The northern sector of the Allied defeat also suffered the kind of raid that had destroyed Warsaw. This time the victim was Rotterdam, whose old quarter was razed in the attack of 14 May. The Germans had threatened this raid as a means of forcing a capitulation in the area, and the Dutch had in fact surrendered. But a communications failure prevented the local German commander from calling off the attack, and Kampfgeschwader 54 burned out the mainly wooden quarter of the historic city for no military purpose whatsoever, and the action was seized upon by Allied propagandists as another example of Nazi ruthlessness.

The Belgian air force's few Hawker Hurricanes and the Dutch air force's Fokker D XXIs put up a spirited defence against the Germans, but courage and determination were not enough to halt the Luftwaffe, which enjoyed considerable numerical as well as qualitative superiority. The Belgians and Dutch performed well, but their aircraft were soon swept aside.

The air war over France followed a similar but altogether more extensive course. Here the Germans were faced by the Armée de l'Air and elements of the Royal Air Force as well as a handful of Czech units formed of refugees and some Polish squadrons, whose personnel had escaped to the west via Romania. Both the Czechs and the Poles flew under French colours and in French aircraft.

It was in this campaign that the French and British first encountered the full nature of German air capability, and the shock to the two Allied powers was considerable. Yet despite their greater operational experience and the general superiority of their aircraft and tactics, the Germans did not have matters entirely their own way in the air war over France. On 10 May, for example, the Luftwaffe lost 304 aircraft destroyed and 51 damaged, although a few of these were in Norway, where fighting still continued.

Despite the mixed assortment of good and mediocre aircraft they had to fly, the French fought the Germans with determination and certainly shared the honours in the first few days of fighting. But the French effort could not be sustained in definitely: the altogether too recent reorganization of the French aircraft industry meant that deliveries of new aircraft were too slow. Although the front-line squadrons had a fair proportion of modern aircraft, spares were in short supply and replacements were almost non-existent. As the campaign went on, the quality of available French equipment gradually deteriorated, giving even the more seasoned and able pilots the constant and dispiriting feeling that there was little hope of victory.

On the ground, moreover, the Panzer formations were enjoying their customary success, forcing the French into

withdrawal followed by further withdrawal. As they fell back in increasing disarray, French airfields, depots and factories fell into German hands, further weakening the Armée de l'Air. When France finally capitulated, most of the French pilots flew their aircraft to the unoccupied zone in the south of France or even to the French territories in North Africa. Eventually they became part of the Vichy French air force, which later operated against the British in Syria and the Lebanon. Some pilots escaped to the United Kingdom and joined the Free French forces under General Charles de Gaulle, and these men now fought under British colours.

The United Kingdom's part in the French air campaign was relatively small. Serving with the British Expeditionary Force were a number of fighter and light bomber squadrons of the Advanced Air Striking Force, sup ported from England by the main part of Fighter Command and the medium and heavy bomber squadrons of Bomber Command. Uncertain about the probable course of events in France, the Air Ministry had given the AASF only 'semi-expendable' types such as the Hurricane fighter, considered slightly inferior to the Spitfire, and the Fairey Battle light bomber. Moreover, home-based units had priority in the supply of new machines and the retrofit of modern features such as armour plating, self-sealing fuel tanks, bulletproof windscreens and constant-speed propellers.

The AASF nevertheless played a useful if forlorn part in the defence of France, and suffered very heavily in the process. The Hurricane did well, but the Battle proved a disastrous failure, frequently suffering virtually total losses when committed against vital targets which the German protected with a screen of fighters and a mass of anti-aircraft guns. The British bomber force in France was virtually wiped out in the first few days of the campaign, attempting to destroy the bridges the Germans were using to cross the canals and rivers of Belgium and northern France. The British fighters continued to harry the German bombers, but were far too few in number to check let alone halt them.

Here, too, the German experience in Spain proved valuable: their tactics employed naturally by their fighter pilots were far superior to those ingrained in their British and French opposite numbers. The Allies believed in mass attacks by at least six, and usually 12, aircraft in the belief that all the fighters could thus make a firing pass at the target, almost guaranteeing its destruction, before selecting a new objective. While excellent in theory, such attacks were clumsy in practice: it took far too long for the fighters to change from their patrol formation (a series of 'vees') into their attack formation (line ahead or line abreast) preparatory to the firing pass and then ready themselves for the next attack.

Such manoeuvrings were ponderous, and thus ideally suited to decisive defeat by the new German tactics, which were based on units of two aircraft: a leader and his wingman. Small and easy to handle, these German tactical formations carved their way through those of the Allies. Once exposed, individual Allied pilots were at a distinct tactical disadvantage to the German two-aircraft Rotte (element) comprising the lead pilot and his wingman as the offensive and defensive components respectively. Two Rotten constituted a Schwarm or Kette (flight) of four aircraft, and from there upwards the Luftwaffe fighters were grouped in Staffeln (squadrons) , Gruppen (wings) and Geschwadern (groups), the last having a nominal strength of 106 aircraft.

Operational flexibility was the keynote of the German tactics, and it was only toward the end of the Battle of France that the Allies realized the error of their ways and started to copy the Germans. By 1941 the British had developed their own loose patrol formation, the 'finger four', in which the four aircraft of a section flew in positions related to each other as the nails on the four fingers of the hand. This gave the pilot of the formation good fields of vision, and allowed the formation to split instantly into the ideal combat teams each comprising two aircraft.

When the French appreciated the full strength of the German onslaught, they asked the British to send more aircraft. Although the request gained the support of the British government and the Air Ministry, Air Chief Marshal Sir Hugh Dowding, commanding Fighter Command, threatened to resign if any more of his fighters were wasted by despatch to France. He also categorically refused to allow Spitfires to be based outside the United Kingdom. Virtually alone among senior British commanders, Dowding had realized that the total defeat of France was inevitable and that the United Kingdom should cut its losses there, regardless of the political repercussions. Dowding was adamant that the United Kingdom should prepare for the next German move, most probably a seaborne invasion of England preceded by a major air offensive and then airborne landings. Dowding managed to

convince Winston Churchill, who had succeeded Neville Chamberlain as prime minister on 10 May, that this strategic appreciation was essentially correct. From the end of May, therefore, the home-based British fighter squadrons were limited, so far as France was concerned, to covering the evacuation of the BEF and other Allied forces from Dunkirk. By the end of June the United Kingdom stood alone against Germany, which had been joined by Italy on 10 June. The Luftwaffe now held an excellent strategic position with its combat aircraft on captured airfields facing the United Kingdom's eastern and southern coasts from north-eastern Scotland to south-western England.

As these events were unfolding the western Europe, one of the strangest campaigns of the war had been fought to the east of the Baltic. Having swallowed the eastern part of Poland by agreement with Germany, the USSR decided to seize parts of Finland, particularly in the Karelian Isthmus and at the western end of the Gulf of Finland. When his ultimatum demanding these areas was refused, the Soviet dictator Josef Stalin launched a massive campaign against the Finns, who at first fought back with great success. The campaign lasted from November 1939 to the spring of 1940, and the communist forces eventually triumphed only by the sheer weight of numbers, losing more than 600,000 men to Finland's 68,000.

Above: The Vickers Wellington Mk I was the best medium bomber available to the Royal Air Force in the first months of World War II, but after disastrous losses in a number of unescorted daylight raids was switched to the night attacks that became a feature of the British bombing effort during the rest of the war.

Top: The finest heavy bombers operated by the Royal Air Force in World War II were two four-engined types, namely the Avro Lancaster (top) and the Handley Page Halifax (above). Interestingly enough, both bombers had twin-engined origins, the Lancaster in the Manchester that saw limited but unsuccessful service, and the Halifax in the H.P.56 design that was not built.

Below: The Junkers Ju 86 saw its early service as an interim bomber type characterized by a ventrally mounted retractable 'dustbin' turret, but was more important in its later variants optimized for the high-altitude reconnaissance role.

conquest of the United Kingdom, to be accomplished by an invasion codenamed Seel^we (sealion). The German navy had suffered crippling losses in the Norwegian campaign, and plans for the landings progressed only spasmodically. But G^ring, promoted to the unique rank of Reichsmarschall for his part in the Luftwaffe's triumph over France, now declared that his air forces could render invasion unnecessary by the aerial destruction of the United Kingdom's ability and will to resist. This boastful, and indeed highly rash, claim led to the Battle of Britain, which was the world's first strategic all-air battle.

The Battle of Britain fell into three main phases: firstly, the attacks on convoys and coastal installations; secondly, the assault on Fighter Command's bases and fighter production centres; and thirdly, the campaign against urban areas. The coastal shipping phase began as France fell, and was typified by raids, usually by a few bombers and a heavy fighter escort, against British coastal convoys and the ports and naval installations on the English south and east coasts. The Germans had a threefold objective: to avoid bombing British towns or other civilian areas, to cause damage to shipping and port facilities and, most importantly, to engage the RAF's fighters on tactical terms favouring the German fighters. British fighter strength could thus be worn down, making the next stages easier.

With the aid of radar, the RAF was able to meet the Germans on equal terms and inflicted fairly heavy losses. Since this coastal phase proved relatively inefficient, the Luftwaffe high command decided at the beginning of August to attack British fighter bases and radar stations. The bombers would be used to lure the British fighters aloft, and could also cause considerable damage to industrial areas and air bases, but again it was the fighters that were expected to inflict the main damage as the British fighters clawed for altitude on their bomber-interception mission.

This second phase of the battle exposed the existence of major flaws in the German air machine. The coastal phase had already proved the Stuka to be useless wherever the enemy had just parity, let alone air superiority: the Ju 87 was hopelessly vulnerable at the bottom of its dive, where it was virtually stationary and lacked the energy for any type of effective defensive manoeuvring. The fighter phase now revealed that the Bf 110, much favoured by the German propaganda machine and the Luftwaffe high command, was comparatively easy prey for the faster ad nimbler British fighters. Losses were severe on both sides, but with the slower Hurricanes taking on the bombers and Bf 110s, and the Spitfires holding off the Bf 109s, the RAF slowly but inexorably gained the ascendancy over the Luftwaffe, especially Luftflotten 2 and 3 along the Channel coast.

By the beginning of the last week in August, Luftwaffe attacks were extended to inland fighter bases and centres of fighter production. Fighter Command's most serious problem was now pilot fatigue rather than shortage of fighters, but Air Vice Marshal Keith Park, commanding No.11 Group in south-east England, showed tactical genius in handling his front-line squadrons and Dowding constantly replaced exhausted squadrons with unit that had been rotated to less threatened areas for rest as they undertook the defence of these secondary areas. Fighter

Nowhere was Finland's epic struggle more successful than in the air. Despite using the excellent Polikarpov I-16 fighter, Tupolev SB-2 and Ilyushin DB-3 twin-engined bombers and other fairly modern aircraft, the Soviet pilots were very severely handled by the excellently trained and highly dedicated pilots of the small Finnish air force, which had at its disposal only a limited and motley collection of obsolescent fighters of which the D XXI and Gladiator, most of the latter flown by Swedish volunteers, were notably successful. Soviet air operations were undertaken in an extremely doctrinaire fashion, and the Finnish pilots exacted an enormously heavy price from the Soviet bomber formations. Only in February 1940, the last month of this 'Winter War', did the Soviet effort improve in quality.

As Dowding had predicted, Germany's next move was to attack the United Kingdom. Hitler had been amazed by the British declaration of war after the German invasion of Poland, and now urged the United Kingdom to make an honourable peace on the basis of the status quo. When this offer was refused, Hitler had no option but to plan the

Command was nonetheless very close to its limits of endurance by the end of the month, and losses continued to rise. On 15 September, now remembered as Battle of Britain Day, Fighter Command had no reserves left.

Salvation for Fighter Command was at hand, however, courtesy of the Germans. On 7 September, the Germans switched the focus of their offensive from Fighter Command to the great conurbation of London and the other great industrial cities of the United Kingdom. This change was demanded by Hitler, who was furious that Bomber Command had made air raids (as a result of navigational error) on Berlin.

The Germans compounded this strategic error with a tactical change that was wholly ill-conceived. The fighters were now ordered to abandon their roving (and therefore fuel-economical and tactically advantageous) loose escort of the bombers and instead concentrate on close escort of the bombers: this denied the fighters advantageous use of their speed and agility, and also forced them into a flight regime that was distinctly wasteful of their already strained range capabilities. This meant that the fighters had sufficient fuel for only about 10 minutes of combat over London, after which the bombers had perforce to be left largely unprotected and therefore easier meat for the British fighters, which began to inflict increasing losses.

This whole episode revealed the major failing of German pre-war planning: in bombing London and other industrial centres, the Germans were attempting a strategic task with an air force that had been schemed and developed solely as a tactical air arm. With no heavy bombers available to it, the Luftwaffe was doomed to failure in this task.

By the end of September daylight raids on London had proved to be prohibitively expensive in the face of a defence that the Luftwaffe's intelligence staff claimed could no longer exist, and were discontinued. The daylight effort was replaced by a fighter-bomber campaign of low-level sneak raids designed to give the British no respite while the night-bombing Blitz was prepared for November. But the British had already won the Battle of Britain. Between 10 July and 31 October the Luftwaffe lost no fewer than 1,733 aircraft while Fighter Command suffered the loss of 1,379 aircraft, almost all of them single-engined fighters. Most of the German losses had involved multi-seat aircraft, more expensive to replace, together with their highly-trained crews. But as early as July 1940, Hitler had decided to invade the USSR, and thus the continued prosecution of the war against the United Kingdom became a secondary task entrusted to an air strength that was steadily reduced as Luftwaffe units were gradually shifted east in preparation for the war against the USSR.

The Battle of Britain had shown the weaknesses of the aircraft on both sides, particularly in performance and armament. When caught in adverse tactical situations, German aircraft had frequently been able to escape by

making the type of sharp dive which the British fighters could not copy as their engines had float carburettors instead of the fuel injection system that allowed the German aircraft to perform a negative-g bunt without their engines cutting out as a result of fuel starvation. The British had also been hampered by their lack of cannon, but basically the aircraft in service since August and September 1939 were already showing their age and in the spring of 1941 both sides made strenuous efforts to update existing designs and rush forward new combat aircraft. Cannon appeared in British fighters, and new models of both the Bf 109 and the Spitfire were fitted with more powerful engines and better superchargers, raising maximum speeds from some 350 mph (565 km/h) to 400 mph (645 km/h).

The Luftwaffe kept up its night attacks on British cities until the end of spring 1941, and RAF Bomber Command also began a campaign of nocturnal raids on German cities. While the German bombers found its relatively easy to find London and other major British cities from their bases in northern France and the Low Countries, however, British bombers found it far more difficult to find German cities. An operational research report at the end of 1940 showed that only a very small percentage of British bombs was falling anywhere near any intended target. Yet this night bombing campaign was the only means available to the United Kingdom for direct attack on Germany, and the effort was therefore continued, gradually increasing in strength if not initially in accuracy.

The Blitz came to an eventual end in May 1941 for two reasons. Firstly, the twin-engined Bristol Beaufighter night-fighter, fitted with the new AI (airborne interception) radar, was taking an increasingly heavy toll of the raiders; and secondly, German air formations were being transferred east for the invasion of the USSR. By June 1941 the United Kingdom was faced by only two fighter Geschwadern, but these managed to check British offensive operations over north-west Europe with the aid of the latest German fighter, the Focke-Wulf Fw 190. Powered by a closely cowled radial piston engine, this structurally sturdy fighter was highly manoeuvrable, carried very heavy armament, and enjoyed the advantage of performance generally superior to that of any British fighter.

The German plans for the conquest of the USSR were postponed for a short, but fatal, time by Hitler's decision to invade Yugoslavia and Greece in April. Belgrade was subjected to the now customary 'terror' bombing on 6 April 1941, the day on which

Above: In the last years before its embroilment in World War II, France suddenly began to switch away from its fascination with monumentally ugly bombers to the design and production of extremely elegant bombers. A classic example of the latter was the LiorÈ-et-Olivier LeO 451 offering excellent performance, a useful bomb load and a potent defensive armament.

Below: Experience in World War II soon revealed to the German air force that one of its primary failings was lack of a heavy transport. Initial thoughts turned to heavy-lift gliders such as the Messerschmitt Me 321 that could be towed by converted twin-engined bombers, and from this was then developed the Me 323 Gigant powered version with six radial piston engines and increasingly heavy defensive armament tat never succeeded in providing adequate protection against Allied fighters.

Below: The US Army Air Force's two most important medium bombers of World War II were the North American B-25 Mitchell and Martin B-26 Marauder, both of which were developed into potent types that were really attack bombers with a heavy battery of fixed forward-firing guns in or round the nose and forward fuselage. This cutaway reveals the salient internal details of a B-26 in 'D-Day stripe' marking for the invasion of North-West Europe in June 1944.

the Germans crossed the borders. Despite the presence of British ground and air forces, the Germans swept all before them in the air and on the ground, although the Greeks and British managed to inflict relatively severe losses on the Luftwaffe. The Blitzkrieg combination of armoured and aerial power prevailed, and by the end of April both Greece and Yugoslavia were in German hands.

In May the Germans launched an invasion of Crete using their high-quality airborne arm supplemented by mountain troops. The island was finally secured after some extremely heavy fighting that marked both the high point and finale of the German airborne forces in that role, but the Luftwaffe suffered very heavy losses, especially to their dual-purpose Ju 52/3m fleet. Yet again, the German aircrew training programme was suffered.

By mid-June 1941 most of Germany's offensive strength gathered along the Soviet frontier. Hitler planned to destroy the USSR as a political entity within four months, and as usual a major tactical role was allocated to the Luftwaffe in the Germans' overall plan for the operation codenamed 'Barbarossa'. The invasion started on 22 June, and from the first hours of the campaign the Germans secured total air superiority all along the front.

Tactical surprise was complete and most of the forward-based Soviet aircraft were destroyed on the ground, in the process constituting the majority of the thousands of Soviet aircraft knocked out or captured in the fighting's first few days.

For the Germans this was an amazing success that was, by the type of paradox typical of war, of enormous benefit to the Soviets in the longer term. Standards had declined radically during Stalin's purges of the Soviet armed forces during 1937 and 1938, and the Red air force was only just emerging from the shock of its mauling by the tiny Finnish air force in the 'Winter War'. Worse still, at the time of the start of hostilities with Germany the Red air force was saddled with vast numbers of obsolete aircraft that the government was unwilling to scrap. The Luftwaffe did the job for the Soviets, and in the process forced the communist leadership to accelerate the design, development and production of new aircraft.

The Soviets were already producing one of the war's finest ground-attack types, the single-engined Ilyushin Il-2 Shturmovik, and this was soon joined by the excellent twin-engined Petlyakov Pe-2 tactical medium bomber and the improving series of single-engined fighters designed by Lavochkin and Yakovlev. With just these four series as the core of their operational inventory, the Soviets were able to produce vast numbers of aircraft that were, by Western standards, austerely equipped but which were nonetheless ideally suited to the USSR's climatic extremes and simple military tactics. Other types that were used in significant but nonetheless smaller numbers were the Mikoyan-Gurevich fighters and the Ilyushin Il-4 bomber, but the main strength of the Red air force from 1942 to 1945 depended on the four types listed above.

The Soviets' tactical doctrine was straightforward and simple, and derived from the basic operational premise that the war would be fought and won by the overwhelming power of the Red army. Thus the role of the Red air force was to support the army at the operational and, more importantly, tactical levels. The Petlyakov Pe-8, the one Soviet heavy bomber in production, was kept for nuisance raids on Germany, supply missions to partisans operating behind the German forces (in co-operation with older heavy bombers now turned into transports) and for transport of Soviet VIPs. Aircraft with good performance at high altitude (above 5000 m/16,405 ft by Soviet standards) were required only for strategic reconnaissance work. Thus most of the Red air force's aircraft had engines rated for optimum performance at medium down to low altitude.

Thus the Red air force was content to operate at lower altitudes, leaving the Germans in command at the higher altitudes which were considered relatively unimportant. This meant that while the maximum speed of the Lavochkin La-5 was lower than that of the Bf 109G-2 at the latter's optimum altitude, its performance at 3000 m (9,845 ft) was higher as evidenced by a superiority of 35 km/h (22 mph) in speed.

There were other respects in which Soviet aircraft were 'inferior' to their Western counterparts but better suited to their tasks. Sophisticated structural techniques were seldom used, for these increased building costs and time. Wooden covering over tubular steel or alloy frames, or even wooden structures, offered a better compromise between strength, well proved Soviet mass production techniques, and the right aerodynamic lines. Sophisticated instruments were virtually unknown, and engines were ruggedly serviceable units admirably suited to the extremes of the Russian climate and the indifferent attentions of Soviet groundcrew.

Thus the very sophistication of their machines sometimes worked against the Germans. The story is told of a Soviet pilot, taken prisoner after his aircraft had been shot down, who saw German groundcrew, or 'blackmen' as they were called because of their black coveralls, trying to start a frozen engine in mid-winter. The Soviet technique in such an eventuality, he told his captors, was to fill a drip tray with petrol, place this under the engine after the cowling had been removed, and light the petrol. In the bitter cold of Russian winters this was just enough to melt the engine lubricants and allow the engine to be started, but not enough to burn the insulation off the engine's electrical components. Tests revealed that the Soviet prisoner had been telling the truth.

Soviet tactical techniques matched the crudeness of the aircraft, but were again well suited to the tasks in hand.

These tactics placed great reliance on numbers and weight of fire, heavy losses being considered acceptable. Gradually, however, the poor flying so often described by German aircrew in the first year of the war was replaced by a higher level of basic piloting skills as the worse pilots were killed and the better men survived to increase their own capabilities (and chances of further survival) and to pass their skills down the training syllabus to tyro pilots.

By absolute standards, Soviet tactics were on the whole no more than adequate, although the Il-2 units were unrivalled in the particularly exacting task of low-level ground attack. With superb timing and excellent concealment, even with large formations of aircraft, they frequently caught German units entirely unawares and kept such ground forces under constant attack until they had been effectively destroyed.

The Germans enjoyed general air superiority over the Soviet front from the beginning of the war until the Battle of Kursk in July 1943. But from that time on, the Red air force gradually won superiority at the low and medium altitudes that was important to it. Right to the end of the war the Luftwaffe could generally regain temporary command of the air in a particular area, but the huge size of the Soviet general offensives between July 1943 and May 1945 meant that such limited setbacks were no more than pinpricks to the Red army, and stood no chance of halting its advance.

Realizing the importance of tactical aircraft in the Soviet campaign, the Germans deployed two special types, the Henschel Hs 129 tank-buster and the Focke-Wulf Fw 189 tactical reconnaissance aeroplane, in this theatre. The Hs 129 was potentially an excellent machine, but a completely suitable powerplant was never found for the aeroplane. Even so, the Hs 129 was a potent anti-tank weapon, and in one form was fitted with a powerful 75-mm anti-tank gun under the fuselage: a single round from this could halt any Soviet tank. The Hs 129 performed very creditably in the Battle of Kursk, as did late-model Ju 87Gs fitted with a pair of underwing 37-mm anti-tank cannon, but as soon as the Soviets discovered the poor performance of the Stukas, their fighters kept a constant watch for them. The Fw 189 was not an offensive machine, but did well In

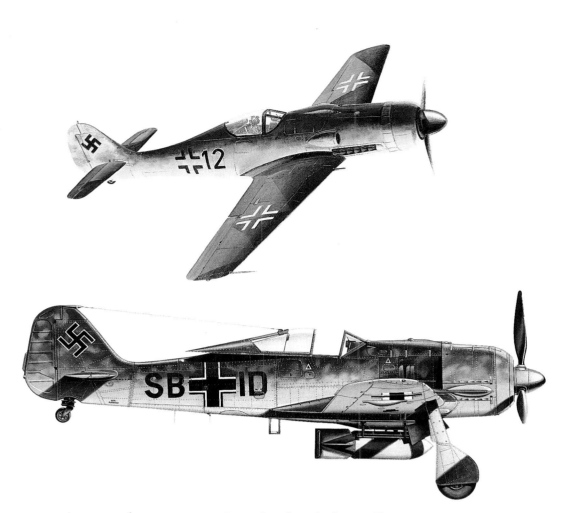

reconnaissance and army co-operation roles, for which its extensively glazed central nacelle proved ideal.

Although the Germans tried a number of weapons in their efforts to find the ideal anti-tank type, they found in the end that heavy cannon provided the best solution. The Soviets, on the other hand, found high-velocity cannon in 20- and 23-mm calibres were usually effective, and that rockets, although unguided, were also very useful. The Soviets had undertaken much experimental work with rockets in the years before the war, and most of their fighters could carry a number of 82- or 132-mm (3.2- or 5.2-in) rockets.

During the war with the USSR, the Germans came to appreciate how remiss they had been in not persevering with the development of the heavy bomber as effective weapon. As the Germans drove into the European portion of the western USSR in 1941, Stalin had realized that heavy industrial plant was one of the few keys to the USSR's long-

Though the Messerschmitt Bf 109 remained in development and production right to the end of World War II, and retained the admiration of its pilots and foes up to that time, it is arguable that from mid-1941 it was overtaken as Germany premier fighter by the great Focke-Wulf Fw 190 that was also a more capable fighter-bomber. The first production variant was the Fw 190A (above and left) with the BMW 801 radial piston engine, but the definitive fighter was the 'long-nose' Fw 190D (top) with a Junkers Jumo 213 Vee piston engine in a cowling that retained its radial-engined appearance as result of its annular radiator.

Above: The Heinkel He 177 Greif was a belated attempt to provide the German air force with a genuine heavy bomber, and was plagued by the unusual powerplant in which paired engines were geared to a single fire-liable transmission so that two propellers were driven by four engines.

Above: The Focke-Wulf Fw 189 was a tactical reconnaissance aeroplane based on a heavily glazed central nacelle to provide the best possible fields of vision.

Below: The United Kingdom's first four-engined heavy bomber was the Short Stirling. This was compromised in performance by its small wing, which resulted from official demands that the aeroplane should fit into existing hangars.

term military survival and had ordered that whatever the cost in manpower, all such plant was to be removed and moved to locations east of the Ural Mountains, where the Germans could not attack them. The task would have been incredibly difficult if undertaken in peace and with the benefit of complete planning, but was a success of monumental proportions when the plant was uprooted and moved under all the pressures of the fast-approaching German advance, the shortage of rail transport and the sheer bulk of equipment to be moved.

This tremendous achievement deprived the Germans of nearly all the industrial prizes they had anticipated. Without a long-range heavy bomber they now found themselves in the position of being unable to attack the main centres of Soviet armament production. The old ideas of strategic bombing were revived and a 'Ural bomber' project was pushed ahead, but

it was now too late to get so advanced an effective heavy bomber into widespread production.

The most ambitious of the heavy bombers designed at the time was the four-engined Heinkel He 177 Greif (griffon). This had the unusual feature of a pair of engines buried in each wing and geared to drive a single propeller. The idea offered interesting possibilities, but development of the coupled engines and their associated gearbox proved intractable. The He 177 was therefore plagued with engine fires, making it very unpopular with aircrews. As had been the case during their attack on the United Kingdom, the Germans lacked an essential element of their aerial

inventory at the crucial moment.

Although Germany's main interests from June 1941 lay in the east, the departure of most German air units did not lead to a halt of air operations in the west. Throughout 1941 fighter-bombers kept up a constant series of nuisance raids on targets in southern England, but on the whole the year was notable for the gradual emergence of the RAF as an offensive force, and for the increasing importance of air power in the Mediterranean theatre.

The most fascinating aircraft to enter widespread service in the RAF during the year was the de Havilland Mosquito which, with the possible exception of the Ju 88, may be judged the war's most versatile aeroplane. It was almost certainly the most effective combat aeroplane of the war in terms of successes and achievements against losses. Conceived as a private venture, the Mosquito was planned as a high-speed bomber using the same type of wooden sandwich-material structure pioneered in the pre-war Albatross airliner, and among the features desired by the design team was a maximum speed so high that the Mosquito would need no defensive armament. The Air Ministry was initially sceptical, but when the prototype appeared in November 1940 its exquisite lines, extraordinary high speed and viceless handling characteristics revealed immediately that the basic design was right.

Further flight tests proved that the aeroplane's appearance was not deceptive. Performance was phenomenal on the powerplant of two Rolls-Royce Merlin engines, the handling characteristics were delightful, and the Mosquito could outpace any German fighter then in service. The combination of performance and agility convinced all who saw the Mosquito prototypes that the type was ideal for a variety of tasks. By the end of the war it had appeared in a virtually nonstop stream of variants optimized for tasks as diverse and important as bombing, fighter-bombing, night-fighting, photo-reconnaissance, maritime attack, meteorology, high-speed transport, training and target-towing.

For almost the rest of the war the Mosquito bombers roamed unmolested over Germany, delivering their 2,000-lb (907-kg) and later 4,000-lb (1814-kg) bomb loads with unprecedented accuracy. Impressive as its everyday war-winning work was, however, the factors that made the Mosquito immortal were its unique construction, supremely appearance and magnificent performance. The Mosquito was also employed for daring raids such as those on Amiens gaol to breach the walls and allow many French prisoners to escape, and on Gestapo headquarters in Oslo and Copenhagen to destroy their records.

Although the United Kingdom had accepted the philosophy of strategic bombing for some considerable time, the RAF had entered World War II with no true heavy bomber. The Armstrong Whitworth Whitley had a useful maximum bomb load of 7,000 lb (3175 kg) but possessed a range of only 470 miles (756 km) with this load; the Handley Page Hampden could carry 4,000 lb (1814 kg) of bombs for 1,200 miles (1931 km); and the Vickers Wellington Mk III had a range of 1,540 miles (2478 km) with 4,500 lb (2041 kg) of bombs. These were all twin-engine machines, and the RAF had already accepted the fact that the combination of significant bomb load and useful range required the power and fuel capacity that could be offered only by four-engined aircraft.

By the autumn of 1941 no fewer than three such four-engined heavy bombers had entered service with Bomber Command: the Short Stirling could carry 14,000 lb (6350 kg) of bombs for 590 miles (949 km), while the corresponding figures for the Handley Page Halifax were 5,800 lb (2631 kg) carried over 1,860 miles (2993 km). Undoubtedly the finest of the trio, however, was the celebrated Avro Lancaster that could carry 14,000 lb (6350 kg) of bombs over a range of 1,660 miles (2671 km) and also possessed a bomb bay large enough to carry considerably heavier special weapons over shorter ranges for specific missions such as dam-busting, bridge destruction and the penetration of reinforced concrete U-boat pens. With the Halifax and Lancaster as its primary weapons, Bomber Command could finally begin to take the air war to Germany in an increasingly effective fashion.

Throughout 1941 Bomber Command was learning the lessons of area bombing by night, and building up its strength and skills for the heavy bombing campaign. Unlike the Americans, who were confident that their heavily armed daylight bombers could fight their way through the German defences and use their advanced Norden bomb sights to succeed in pinpoint attacks on small targets of strategic importance, Bomber Command was convinced that night bombing was the only solution to anti-aircraft guns and fighter defences. The targets would have to be large industrial areas, in which bombing would damage industry and demoralize the civilian population, while keeping to a minimum the number of bomber lost to the German night-fighters.

Now under the command of Air Chief Marshal Sir Arthur Harris, Bomber Command attacked K^ln on the night of 30 May 1942, in the world's first 1,000-bomber raid. The city was not devastated, for as usual the bombers crossed the target in a long straggling stream, dropping their loads haphazardly in the target area. Despite its failure to secure any notable military success, the raid was a considerable boost for British morale at a time when little other success had been achieved. The authorities were careful not to reveal that they had scraped the barrel to raise the number of aircraft to the magical 1,000 mark: training and obsolescent aircraft had been called in, and considerable disruption was caused to the flying training of new bomber crews, but the effort over K^ln was considered worthwhile.

The problems of accurate navigation, and hence of accurate bombing, were acute and could be solved only in part by conventional techniques. Yet great financial and manpower resources would be wasted unless accuracy could be improved by a very considerable degree. Two clear advances came with the introduction of radar aids and 'pathfinder' forces. The first truly successful radar aid was H2S, a special downward-looking radar, with its antenna in a teardrop radome under the rear fuselage. (The Americans built their own H2X version of H2S.) The radar presented a moving map of the land or water directly under the aeroplane, allowing a navigator sufficiently experienced in the vagaries of the rather obscure 'map' to check his position with some accuracy.

A valuable navigation as well as bombing aid, H2S was not replaced in British bombers during World War II. There were two earlier, but less successful, bombing aids called Oboe and Gee. With the Oboe system the pilot flew along an arc running through the target, the origin of whose radius was a transmitting station in the United Kingdom which ranged the aeroplane very accurately with radar. The pilot followed a steady note marking the centre of the arc, receipt of dot or dash signals telling him if he had flown to

one side or the other. A second transmitting station broadcast another signal for the aeroplane's navigator, telling him when the bomber was over the target. Great accuracy was possible with the Oboe system, the only major drawback being that the pair of transmitting stations could handle only one aeroplane at a time. The Gee system allowed the navigator to find his position very accurately by referring to specially prepared maps marked with grids and using signals from three transmitters in the United Kingdom. Gee, the first real radio navigation aid, was easy to jam, however, and was quickly supplanted by Oboe.

These three British navigation aids finally allowed Bomber Command to attack German cities accurately, especially after the crews of the Pathfinder Force had been trained in their operation. At first there had been considerable antipathy within Bomber Command toward the establishment of such an élite force as, it was felt, the best crews would be drawn from average squadrons, lowering the overall standard of Bomber Command and damaging morale. These fears were soon dispelled by the increased effectiveness of Bomber Command.

The concept was for Pathfinder crews to use Oboe and therefore mark the target accurately with special pyrotechnic bombs, and for the rest of the bomber force then to arrive and bomb these flares. This demanded that great trust be placed in the accuracy of the Pathfinders. The markers used were red, and burned for only eight minutes, so other Pathfinder aircraft flew with the main force and dropped green markers, at intervals of less than eight minutes. The bomber stream was broken into a series of waves, with further Pathfinders slipping in between waves to re-mark the target with red markers. Inevitably there were problems with the system, which had many variations to take account of weather and geographical conditions, enemy jamming efforts and decoy flares. But it proved its worth finally with the destruction of large areas of Essen on 5 March 1943 by only 400 Bomber Command aircraft.

The steadily improving capability of Bomber Command spurred a comparable development in the size and capability of the German night-fighter arm. Ground radar was developed to vector the Ju 88 and Bf 110 fighters into the right area, and airborne interception sets installed in these night-fighters

Above: The original short-nosed Bristol Blenheim Mk I light bomber was being supplanted in the early part of World War II by the long-nose Blenheim Mk IV with more powerful engines, but neither type was adequate for daylight operations against determined fighter defence.

Left: The Y1B-17 designation was applied to 13 pre-production example of the Boeing Model 299 long-range bomber that eventually matured as the great B-17 Flying Fortress.

Below: The Boeing
plant at Seattle in
Washington state
produced very large
numbers of B-17 Flying
Fortress heavy
bombers within a
programme that
involved Douglas and
Lockheed (Vega) for a
grand total of 12,731 B-
17s.

losses began to climb alarmingly during the early summer, but a counter was soon found in the form of 'Window'. This comprised specially sized strips of metal foil, which were dropped in their millions to reflect the German radar beams and so cause a totally confused picture of the situation on German screens.

The device was used with great success in 'Gomorrah', an operation that involved four Bomber Command raids in late July and early August 1943. 'Gomorrah' almost completely destroyed the great port of Hamburg. Thereafter Bomber Command's growing fleet of heavy bombers turned its attention to the Battle of Berlin: this was

a series of 16 great raids launched against the Germany capital in the winter of 1943 and spring of 1944. At long last the bomber offensive was beginning to achieve results.

During the summer of 1943, the heavy bombers of the US 8th Army Air Force began to complement the effort of Bomber Command in ever-increasing strength. Catapulted into World War II by the Japanese attack on Pearl Harbor on 7 December 1941, the United States had agreed with the United Kingdom that Germany was the prime enemy and

should be destroyed first, and that only after this had been achieved would the full weight of the Allies be turned on the Japanese.

Most of 1942 was spent building up the US air forces in the United Kingdom, but from the summer onwards Boeing B-17 Flying Fortresses and Consolidated B-24 Liberator heavy bombers started to undertake daylight probes into northern Europe. Convinced that the quickest and surest way to defeat Germany was to destroy its factories and other point targets in its war-making capabilities, the Americans flew in great three-dimensional 'box' formations. Their bombers could thus cover each other with their many trainable heavy machine-guns, and so ensure that enough bombers got through to destroy small but vital targets with accurate bombing using optical bomb sights.

At first the US forces enjoyed some successes. Then, in August 1943, the 8th Army Air Force launched its first raid deep into Germany. Warned by radar of the American build-up over the Channel, German fighters scrambled to attack the bomber formations, which were cruising at high altitude and leaving highly visible vapour trails leading straight to the bombers that the Germans wished to destroy. The German fighters picked up the American bombers while still well short of the latters' target, and there followed a running battle to and from the target of Schweinfurt. The American bombers suffered crippling losses to the massed fighter attacks. A second attempt in October proved even more disastrous and deep penetration raids were temporarily halted.

The problem was that the fire of the bombers' defensive machine-guns lacked the weight and concentration to defeat the Germans' cannon-armed fighters. The bombers needed long-range escort fighters to protect them, and these were not available until the end of the year. At the time, the 8th Army Air Force's fighter squadrons were equipped only with the single-engined Republic P-47 Thunderbolt that was later to gain an enviable reputation as heavy attack fighter, and with the twin-engined, twin-boom Lockheed P-38 Lightning that was too large and heavy to dogfight with the German single-engined machines. There was also an increasing number of North American P-51 Mustang fighters, but these were of the early American-engined variants that offered their best performance at low altitude and were therefore unsuited to the high-altitude escort role. None of the American fighters had sufficient range to escort the heavy bombers deep into Europe, so they were confined to escort duty for the Martin B-26 Marauder and North American B-25 Mitchell medium bombers, creating havoc over the north of the continent.

The British Spitfires and new Hawker Typhoons also did escort duty across the Channel, but none of the Allied fighters had the range to penetrate into the area where the main German fighter defences operated. Since the beginning of the combined bomber offensive which had been put on a highly organized co-operative basis by the 'Pointblank' directive issued by Prime Minister Winston Churchill and President Franklin D. Roosevelt in January 1943, the Germans had built up their fighter forces in Western Europe, and these had taken a heavy toll of the Allied bombers.

The Mustang suffered an inauspicious entry into service, but was the fighter that ultimately provided the ideal answer to the Americans' escort problem. Designed to a British specification and produced in prototype form over a period of just 117 days, the Mustang was a departure from contemporary American practice in being powered by an inline rather than a radial piston engine. This was an Allison at first, and gave the new fighter excellent performance at low and medium altitudes. Then the decision was taken to

Right: The Lockheed P-38 Lightning was highly unusual in being a single-seat fighter with two engines and a twin-boom configuration, and excelled in the long-range fighter-bomber and reconnaissance roles.

change to a British engine, the Rolls-Royce Merlin, and the Mustang became perhaps the best fighter of the war. Armed with six 0.5-in (12.7-mm) heavy machine guns and able to use drop tanks (externally carried light external fuel tanks which could be dropped once their fuel had been exhausted, or on entering combat) the Mustang had excellent range and, once the drop tanks had been released, superb performance and the type of agility that allowed it to dogfight on equal terms with the best of the opposing German fighters. The Americans now had a fighter that could escort bombers as far as Berlin and back, and from December 1943 the 8th Army Air Force ranged deep into Europe with ever increasing success. This success could be measured not only in the number of targets attacked and destroyed by the bombers, but also in the swelling total of German fighters despatched to oblivion by the escort fighters.

Joined from the beginning of 1944 by the 15th Army Air Force based in Italy, the combined bomber offensive went from strength to strength, the Americans raiding by day and the British by night. German industrial potential was seriously affected, and the Luftwaffe's daylight losses were now being compounded by the increasing number of more expensive twin-engined and radar-equipped night-fighters destroyed by British night-fighters operating in the bomber streams. The heavy losses suffered on the Eastern Front in the last year were now combining with the falling standard of pilot training to reduce the efficiency of the German fighter arm, steadily easing the task of the Allied fighters.

In May and June 1944 the Allied heavy bombers turned their attention to isolating France from the rest of German-held territory in preparation for the Allied invasion of Normandy. Canals were broken open, bridges had spans removed, railway lines and marshalling yards were turned into giant scrapyards, and all types of transport were harried unmercifully right across north-western Europe. The German ground forces were virtually paralysed, and so heavy were the attacks on airfields that the remnants of the German air units in France were pulled back to Germany or southern France.

When the strategic bomber campaign resumed in July 1944, the British and Americans devoted their full attention to the German transport system and all types of power production, from electricity-generating stations to synthetic oil plants. All of Germany was virtually paralysed by the end of the year, and her armed forces were desperately short of fuel. Virtually all Luftwaffe training was halted, and even combat units were seriously restricted by lack of fuel.

By the spring of 1945 the bombing campaign had brought Germany to the verge of collapse, and there were few worthwhile strategic targets left. Consequently most of the heavy bomber force was switched to the tactical role, leaving strategic bombing to reach its horrific conclusion with the destruction of Dresden on 13/14 February 1945. Almost the entire city was destroyed in firestorms whose extremely high temperatures created soaring plumes of hot gases caused a great mass of oxygen-rich air to flow into the base of the fire as a high-speed inrushing wind that carried with it more material, and so fed the firestorm. Perhaps 100,000 people were killed, and the total may well have been higher since the city's normal population was swollen by a large number of refugees fleeing the Red army's advance from the east.

Meanwhile the Allies had evolved a tactical air power in most respects superior to anything the Germans had deployed between 1939 and 1941. The forcing ground for this Allied development had been North Africa, where a see-saw war had swayed across the continent from Egypt to

Tunisia for some 30 months. The British had gradually evolved an effective and very flexible technique of close air support based on the use of RAF controllers alongside the forward army troops to call in fighter-bombers and medium bombers as required from the 'cab-ranks' of such aircraft orbiting above the battlefield. By the end of 1942 the Allies had gained almost total air superiority over North Africa, and tactical air power played a decisive part in the final defeat of Axis forces on the ground by May 1943.

Although the tactical use of the fighter-bomber had been pioneered by the Germans over southern England, the real impetus for the development of tactically decisive fighter-bombers came from the British in the desert campaign. At first, obsolescent types such as early Hurricane fighters were fitted with makeshift bomb racks to use when the opportunity arose. Soon there was a demand for aircraft that could carry bombs or unguided high-explosive rockets under the wings to use against ground targets, after which the aircraft could revert to its straight fighter role with cannon and machine-guns. A special Hurricane with twin 40-mm anti-tank cannon was developed and proved a useful if limited weapon in the desert.

Most Allied fighters were eventually adapted for bombs and/or unguided rockets, with the Hawker Typhoon and later the Hawker Tempest particularly effective in this capacity. Curtiss P-40 Tomahawk and Kittyhawk fighter conversions were important in North Africa and Italy, where the ground-support tactics in difficult terrain placed particular emphasis on flexibility and swift response. When the Allies invaded Italy in September 1943, the ground troops were often locked closely together, so the British and American fighter-bombers had to develop great accuracy in the delivery of their weapons. Although there were accidents, the overall standard of accuracy achieved by

Bottom Right The North American B-25 Mitchell partnered the Martin B-26 Marauder to provide the US Army Air Forces with a pair of phenomenally capable medium bombers.

Opposite Bottom: Seen in company are Boeing's two types of heavy bomber in World War II: in the foreground is a B-29 Superfortress of the type used so devastatingly against Japan and in the background a B-17 Flying Fortress that carried the brunt of the offensive against Germany.

Below: The Martin B-26 Marauder had difficult take-off and landing performance because of its high wing loading.

Far Right: The most important seaplane operated by the US Navy in World War II was the Consolidated PBY that was produced in flying boat and amphibian forms as a long-range patrol and anti-submarine type. The PBY was also delivered to the United Kingdom and its allies as the Catalina, this being a Catalina Mk VI.

Germany was the first country in the world to introduce a turbojet-powered bomber in the form of the twin-engined Arado Ar 234 Blitz. The type was also developed in four-engined form as the Ar 234C with a four-engined powerplant for the reconnaissance and ground-attack roles, but very few were delivered.

Allied fighter-bomber pilots was extremely high; and the system would be brought to its fullest development in the Normandy invasions the following year in 1944.

These tactics were also used in maritime attack operations. From 1942 onward, British torpedo bombers had been attacking German ships in European coastal waters, and from 1943 rockets and cannon, as well as bombs, were used on an ever-growing scale by Beaufighters and Mosquitoes, severely restricting the movement of German coastal shipping and of Axis supply convoys operating between Italy and North Africa.

The main threat to the Allies at sea was the German U-boat fleet, and aircraft eventually helped suppress this threat. In the first part of the war anti-submarine operations were mainly undertaken by two aircraft: one was an obsolescent British machine, the Avro Anson, and the other and excellent American type, the Lockheed Hudson. But Hudsons were in short supply, and they lacked the range for long ocean patrols. Operations were therefore confined at first to coastal and offshore waters.

The need for four-engined aircraft offering the range

for oceanic anti-submarine operations was seen at an early date. Bomber Command refused to relinquish sufficient numbers of land-based aircraft for conversion to this role, so Coastal Command's mainstay remained the reliable Short Sunderland flying boat. Gradually, however, Coastal Command acquired small numbers of Consolidated B-24s and Handley Page Halifaxes, which were soon operational far over the Atlantic, where the U-boats had previously been out of range of air attack. With the new aircraft coming into service, as well as weapons effective against underwater targets, the 'Atlantic gap' between the limits of land-based aircraft based in the United Kingdom and the United States was slowly narrowed. It was finally closed by naval aircraft operating from escort carriers, while another American flying boat, the Consolidated PBY Catalina, was also used extensively. Gradually the Allied war against the U-boat became one of techniques with radar and weapons, and by 1944 aircraft and escort craft had combined to bring the U-boat threat down to manageable proportions.

Germany's main maritime aeroplane was the Focke-Wulf Fw 200 Condor, a conversion of the pre-war airliner, which was used as a patrol bomber and a reconnaissance type. The Condor was adequate as a bomber, sinking large tonnages at times, but poor serviceability and structural weakness prevented it from becoming a major threat. The Condor made a first-class reconnaissance aeroplane, however, and had the Luftwaffe and navy co-operated fully to exploit the type of information that could have been provided by the small Condor force, the U-boat successes would have been far higher, at least in 1941 and 1942. Other German aircraft that saw extensive use in the maritime role were two landplanes, the Heinkel He 111 and Junkers Ju 88 for torpedo and other attack modes, and flying boats of Blohm und Voss and Dornier manufacture were also used extensively.

By the end of World War II a brand new type of aeroplane had appeared. A considerable amount of work

Right: The Douglas SBD Dauntless, seen here in the form of an SBD-3, was the US Navy's most important carrierborne dive-bomber until the advent of the Curtiss SB2C Helldiver late in World War II.

had been devoted to the jet engine in the early years of the war with the object of improving its power and reliability, and by 1943 both the British and Germans had experimental combat aircraft flying. Not only were they fast, but they allowed the designer to do away with the large, vibrating piston engine in the nose of fighters, giving the pilot a much better field of vision and simplifying the task of installing in the nose a heavy battery of forward-firing cannon. Germany had pressed ahead more rapidly than the United Kingdom, but official vacillation and Hitler's later insistence that jet aircraft be used as bombers had then delayed the service debut of the world's first true jet-powered combat aircraft. Nonetheless, by 1944

Above: The Royal Air force's most important torpedo bomber of the mid-war years was the Bristol Beaufort, which was a capable type forming part of the family that also included the Blenheim light bomber and Beaufighter heavy fighter.

Right: The Curtiss Hawk 75 was the export variant of the US Army Air Corps' P-36 fighter, and large numbers were ordered by France but ultimately delivered mostly to the United Kingdom where they received the name Mohawk.

Germany had the Messerschmitt Me 262 twin-jet fighter and Arado Ar 234 twin-jet bomber in service.

These were both greatly superior to Allied aircraft, but tactical misuse, shortages of fuel and of top-class pilots, and a variety of teething problems meant that the few German jets produced could do little more than show their manifest superiority and give the Allies a disagreeable surprise before the end of the war. The only Allied jet fighter to see service was the Gloster Meteor, which was rushed into service in time to help defeat the V-1 flying bomb menace and enter the fray over north-west Europe. The Germans produced a fair number of experimental jet aircraft, along with the extraordinary Messerschmitt Me 163 Komet (comet) rocket-powered interceptor, and some of these types might have made a significant impact had the war continued longer. It was clear that German jet aircraft were aerodynamically superior to their Allied counterparts, and after the Allied victory there was a race

between the Soviets, Americans and British to secure as much German research material as possible.

Before the jet engine reached a fully practical stage, however, several superb piston-engined fighters were developed as the last generation of such aircraft. These aircraft all possessed a maximum speed in the order of 475 mph (765 km/h): among the British offerings were the Supermarine Spiteful, Hawker Fury and de Havilland Hornet; American competitors included the Republic XP-47J Thunderbolt and North American P-82 Twin Mustang; and the primary German contender was the Focke-Wulf Ta 152. Though none of these aircraft saw full-scale service in the war, some of them served as interim types pending the arrival of fully developed jet aircraft in the late 1940s.

The war against Japan also produced large-scale air warfare. Although the tactics used in the Pacific theatre were similar to those evolved in the European war, a number of differences were forced upon the combatants by the geographical circumstances of the campaign. The limitations of the aircraft, too, played an important part in both tactical and strategic developments. General Douglas MacArthur's reconquest of New Guinea, for example, took the particular form it did so that his land forces could enjoy all the benefits of superior air power, and the advances to the Marianas and Iwo Jima were largely dictated by the need for the former as heavy bomber bases and for the latter both as a base for escort fighters and as an emergency landing ground for bombers crippled over Japan.

At an individual level, Japanese aircraft proved so much more manoeuvrable than their Allied counterparts, especially in the first year of the war, that Japanese pilots

Right: The North American AT-6 was the Allies most important advanced trainer of the World War II period, and was known to the British forces as the Harvard. These are Harvard Mk IIs of a Canadian flying school.

Above: The torpedo-bomber counterpart of the Douglas SBD Dauntless dive-bomber was the Grumman Avenger, which was built by the parent company as the TBF and by the Eastern Aircraft Division of General Motors as the TBM.

Above right: In US Navy service the North American AT-6 was known as the SNJ, and this cutaway illustration reveals the type's fighter-type basic layout. In combination with a high power/weight ratio for good performance, this made the AT-6/SNJ/Harvard family an ideal lead-in type for pilots destined to fly high-performance warplanes.

Below right: The Mitsubishi Ki-21 was one of the Imperial Japanese army air force's most important bombers, and received the Allied reporting name 'Sally'. This is a Ki-21 I of the original production series, which possessed good performance but in combat with Allied fighters was soon discovered to be too lightly built and lacking in such defensive essentials as armour plate and self-sealing fuel tanks.

especially in the first year of the war, that Japanese pilots could almost fly circles round their opponents. Although a number of Japanese fighters had only machine-guns for armament, the redoubtable Mitsubishi A6M Reisen (zero fighter, dubbed 'Zeke' by the Allies) also had cannon, and this enabled it to decimate the clumsier Allied fighters such as the US Navy's Brewster F2A Buffalo and Grumman F4F Wildcat as well as the US Army's Bell P-30 Airacobra and Curtiss P-40, whose only defence lay in breaking off combat as quickly as possible by means of a dive in which their greater weight gave them higher acceleration than the Japanese types.

Gradually the Allies introduced better fighters that got the measure of the Japanese, and tactics were evolved to exploit the higher performance, superior firepower and better protection of these improved fighters to counter the superior agility of the Japanese machines. With the ever-growing number of American aircraft-carriers providing numerous and mobile 'airfields' all over the Pacific, the Americans were gradually able to dominate Japanese air power, and by the time the Japanese realized the need for more advanced aircraft it was too late. Right to the end of the war, however, American fighter pilots found it unwise to dogfight with the more agile Japanese fighters.

Although they prized agility and range (the latter an essential factor for operations across the Pacific) above outright performance, Japanese aircraft were fast and well armed. Compared with Western aircraft, however, they lacked structural strength, self-sealing fuel tanks and pilot protection. At first the A6M fighter, twin-engined Mitsubishi G4M 'Betty' bomber, single-engined Aichi D3A 'Val' dive-bomber and single-engined Nakajima B5N 'Kate' torpedo-bomber dominated the Pacific and eastern Asia, supported over land by the single-engined Nakajima Ki-43

'Oscar' fighter, twin-engined Kawasaki Ki-48 'Lily' bomber and twin-engined Mitsubishi Ki-21 'Sally' bomber. Elderly and outmoded aircraft such as the F2A, P-36, P-39 and P-40 stood little or no chance against these machines.

By 1942, however, Spitfires and F4F Wildcat fighters, the latter used by the US Navy and US Marine Corps, had begun to shift the balance, and by 1943 the advent of several new Allied types was clearly showing the obsolescence of these first-generation Japanese 'modern' warplanes. The Japanese swiftly turned their hands to the develop of newer and conceptually more advanced aircraft incorporating features such as the crew protection proved essential by combat experience, but they lacked a suitably powerful radial engine, the inline having been neglected in the 1930s. The American heavy bombing campaign had begun to affect Japanese

Below: The Mitsubishi G3M 'Nell' may be regarded as the Imperial Japanese navy air force's counterpart to the Ki-21. The type was a highly effective long-range level and torpedo bomber, but was again too flimsy to survive against determined Allied fighter opposition. This is a G3M2 of the type that entered service in mid-1943 with additional defensive armament.

industry, and once the submarine fleet had destroyed most of Japan's tankers, there were no ships left to bring crude oil from the Indies in large enough quantities.

The single-engined Aichi B7A Ryusei 'Grace' attack, single-engined Kawanishi N1K Shiden 'George' fighter, twin-engined Kawasaki Ki-45 Toryu 'Nick' fighter and Mitsubishi J2M Raiden 'Jack' fighter aircraft all had great potential, but did not enter service early enough or in large enough numbers to affect the course of the war. The only Japanese inline-engined fighter to be built in quantity was the Kawasaki Ki-61 Hien 'Tony', and this was an excellent machine, but could not stem the American tide alone.

The 5th Army Air Force, commanded by General George Kenney, was the major striking element in the South-West Pacific Area. Aircraft and tactics similar to those in Europe were used to harry Japanese shipping and support ground troops in the Solomons, New Guinea and the Philippines. The Pacific itself was dominated by the aircraft of the US Navy's growing carrier force under the overall command of Admiral Chester W. Nimitz, and these aircraft provided the tactical support that played so important a part in the successful invasions of the island campaigns across the Pacific.

The two most important fighters were the Grumman F6F Hellcat and Vought F4U Corsair, both excellent machines capable of high performance and carrying large offensive loads. The main strike aircraft were the Grumman TBF/TBM Avenger torpedo-bomber and Douglas SBD Dauntless dive-bomber later supplanted by the Curtiss SB2C Helldiver, all of which performed with great distinction.

The campaign against the Japanese in China was the responsibility of the Nationalist Chinese with support from the US Army, and Boeing B-29 Superfortress strategic heavy bombers began the strategic campaign against Japan from airfields in south-east China. From late 1944 onwards they were joined by similar machines from bases on the islands of Saipan, Tinian and Guam in the recently

Above: With the Messerschmitt Me 262 the Germans opened the door to a new aeronautical age, for though this turbojet-powered fighter was roughly contemporary with the Royal Air Force's Gloster Meteor it was a far more advanced aeroplane in all technical respects.

The Age of Turbine Propulsion

During the closing stages of World War II, the major powers gained sufficient experience of turbojet propulsion to see its manifest advantages for military aircraft but also to discover some of its attendant problems. Even in its original primitive state, the turbojet was designed, developed and produced in two basic forms as the axial-flow turbojet and the centrifugal-flow turbojet. In the former the air drawn though the inlet at the front of the engine is compressed longitudinally as it moves through a series of axial compressors on its way to the combustion chamber; and in the latter the indrawn air is compressed radially by a centrifugal compressor before being turned through a second right angle on its way to the combustion chambers arranged round the back of the engine casing.

The axial-flow turbojet was pioneered by the Germans, and the centrifugal-flow turbojet was the particular enthusiasm of the British. At first the simple engine pioneered by Air Commodore Frank Whittle and built in prototype form by Power Turbojets was more than adequate in its core conceptual layout, and development of this core concept was entrusted to companies such as de Havilland, Metropolitan-Vickers, Rolls-Royce and Rover. From this process emerged the first two operational turbojets to power in British fighters, namely the de Havilland Goblin installed in the de Havilland Vampire, and the Rolls-Royce Welland used in the Gloster Meteor. Such centrifugal-flow turbojets were more than adequate for the performance limits imposed by the aerodynamic knowledge of the time, but late in the war the British began to appreciate some of the inherent disadvantages possessed by this engine layout, namely its considerable bulk (especially in diameter) and its need to turn the air flow through at least two right angles. Combined with thoughts of pushing forward toward high subsonic performance from the levels currently imposed by straight-wing aerodynamic theory, this was sufficient to persuade British industry into the process of designing and developing axial-flow turbojets.

Perhaps more urgent problem was that of fuel consumption. One of the turbojet's great advantages is that it will run on a fuel as simple as kerosene, but the early turbojet was so thirsty for fuel that the range of aircraft with such a powerplant was severely curtailed from that of piston-engined aircraft with the same fuel capacity. As a result considerable effort was devoted to research designed to find a solution to the turbojet's high specific fuel consumption (the quantity of fuel burned to produce a given power for a given period).

Nations and operators wishing to introduce turbojet-powered aircraft faced a considerable dilemma. The US

The Lockheed S-3 Viking and Lockheed P-3 Orion are the US Navy's two most important maritime patrol and attack aircraft. The Viking is a carrierborne anti-submarine aeroplane with a powerful anti-ship capability, while the Orion is a land-based patrol type with potent anti-ship and anti-submarine capabilities.

Navy, for example, had long worked on the principle that its aircraft-carriers should operate combat aircraft in no significant degree inferior to the land-based aircraft they would encounter, and decided in the middle of World War II to start funding the development of turbojet-powered aircraft for carrierborne employment. Yet aircraft-carriers frequently operate at long remove from their targets to give them freedom of manoeuvre and to reduce the chance of counter-attack by land-based aircraft, and this requires the embarkation of aircraft with very good range capability. This was clearly impossible with current turbojet engines, whose thirst for fuel was so high that adequate range would have demanded aircraft so large that their speed and agility would have been degraded to the point of decisive inferiority to land-based aircraft. In the short term, therefore, the US Navy resorted to the odd combination of a hybrid powerplant. This was first used in the Ryan FR Fireball, a carrierborne fighter produced in small numbers largely so that the US Navy's carrier air groups could gain experience with turbojet-powered flight. The hybrid powerplant comprised an economical radial piston engine in the nose for long-range cruising and a turbojet in the tail for the power boost needed for high performance in combat as well as for improved take-off capability.

this tremendous power, designers had to fit propellers with four or five blades, or even a pair of three-bladed co-axial propeller units, turning in opposite directions so that the torque reaction of each unit counteracted that of the other.

Aerodynamicists were also discovering, moreover, that at high speeds the air approaching and hitting the aeroplane's wings and fuselage was being compressed around the leading edges of the wings and other airflow

Similar ideas were tried over the next few years, culminating in the 1950s with the British Saunders-Roe SR.53 that combined a turbojet and a liquid-propellant rocket. By this time the turbojet's specific fuel consumption had improved markedly, but the rocket motor was added to provide a major boost in climb rate, ceiling and maximum combat speed. The fighter would now cruise on its turbojet, but use the extra power of the rocket engine for high performance in combat and at high altitudes. Such ideas were extensively tested in the 1950s and 1960s, but few such hybrid powerplant designs ever went into production. One notable exception, was the French Dassault Mirage III, whose early models could be fitted with a rocket booster pack under the rear fuselage.

Increased power was causing difficulties for designers even before the turbojet had been widely accepted. The last generation of piston engines, which included the Rolls-Royce Griffon inline and Pratt & Whitney R-4360 Wasp Major radial, could produce more than 2,500 hp. To absorb

entry areas as it could not move out of the way of the onrushing airframe's relevant areas quite in time. This compression resulted in considerable turbulence and drag, leading In turn to extreme buffeting that could cause structural failure. An early solution, applied in the North American P-51 Mustang and other piston-engined fighters, was the laminar-flow wing, which was much thinner in section than earlier types and was designed to smooth the flow of air round it and thus to reduce both turbulence and drag. But this could not cope with the main problem, which was the high-pressure shock wave streaming back and out from the nose, the first part of the aeroplane to meet the airflow.

Despite their failure to co-ordinate research, the Germans had discovered the answer: sweeping the wings back out of the line of the shock wave. With a top speed of 870 km/h (541 mph), the Messerschmitt Me 262 that entered service in 1944 twin-turbojet fighter had modestly swept wings. This planform was adopted for structural and

Below: The diminutive de Havilland Vampire was the United Kingdom's second turbojet-powered fighter, but was just too late for service in World War II. The type played a major part in the Royal Air Force's plans after the war, however, and was developed into fine fighter-bomber, night fighter and trainer variants. The basic design concept was then continued into the Venom and Sea Vixen multi-role fighters.

other aerodynamic reasons as much as for avoidance of the shock wave, but the success of this slight sweep combined with the data revealed in captured German aerodynamic research to give the Americans and Soviets an insight into the manner in which the effects of air compression could effectively be overcome.

The Germans had made great strides in the pure research side of high-speed flight for both manned aircraft and missiles, and the Soviets and Americans in particular gathered as much of their work as possible for themselves. The United Kingdom and France were laggardly in this respect, but the two new 'superpowers' made every effort to recruit German research workers and theorists after the war: the Soviets pressed captured Germans into forced labour, but the Americans generally used financial inducements as well as the offer of freedom from prosecution for past political crimes.

Even so, there was still much to be learned before aircraft would be capable of approaching let alone breaking the 'sound barrier'. Although there was an immediate reduction in the financial resources available for military hardware after the war, the lessons of the 1920s had been learned and a high level of research was encouraged so that new military hardware could be developed quickly should such a need materialize. The USSR and the United States took a quick lead in devoting a large proportion of their research effort to high-speed flight, and soon emerged with some formidable combat aircraft and impressive research types. Yet while they were absorbing German engine technology, most of the world's military powers used British turbojet engines, either imported or built under licence. The importance of the turbojet engine was well appreciated in the United Kingdom, and research and development continued with a high priority.

The Meteor had been the only Allied turbojet aircraft to serve operationally in World War II, though just three examples of the Lockheed P-80 Shooting Star had also reached Italy for operational trials. After the war the Meteor was quickly joined by the delightful little Vampire, perhaps the last first-class fighting aeroplane of an unsophisticated type to enter service with any of the major powers. Although turbojet-powered, the Vampire still had a wooden central nacelle for the pilot, and had excellent handling characteristics despite the fact that its controls were unpowered. Good aircraft for their time, Meteor and Vampire were thought more than adequate for their tasks by the government of a financially impoverished United Kingdom, so no priority was given to creating either a newer type or even the research data that would be required for the creation of such a type; the British government also opined that supersonic aircraft would not be needed at all.

As a result of this short-sighted failure, the United Kingdom was destined soon to slip down the aerodynamic ladder.

The United States' main turbojet fighter of World War

II had been the highly disappointing Bell P-59 Airacomet, which had seen no active service. Already on the drawing board, however, was the Lockheed P-80 (soon to be F-80) Shooting Star, which was to use a British-designed engine. Like the Meteor and Vampire, the Shooting Star did not feature a swept wing, but was clearly superior to the Meteor, which had established a world speed record of 975 km/h (606 mph) in 1946. So too was the chunky Republic F-84 Thunderjet, which also had a straight wing.

In 1947 North American, a firm that had been left behind in the race to build turbojet-powered fighters because of its commitment to the P-51 Mustang and P-82 Twin Mustang programmes, produced a classic fighter that succeeded largely because it incorporated the results of German research. This aeroplane was the F-86 Sabre, the West's first swept-wing fighter. The Sabre's lines looked just right and, despite its lack of a suitably powerful engine, it was transonic (on or about the speed of sound) in a shallow dive. A year later the type was in service with the US Air Force, as the US Army Air Forces had been renamed when the service was made fully independent of the US Army. Export orders had been received, and several countries were interested in the possibilities of licensed production and development with different engines (the Orenda in Canada and the Rolls-Royce Avon in Australia) and different gun armament (two 30-mm cannon in Australian aircraft replacing the standard American battery of six 0.5-in/12.7-mm machine-guns). Far more advanced than other Western type when introduced, the Sabre was eventually built to a total of some 10,000 aircraft.

Yet the Sabre had been preceded into the air by a Soviet type that would prove its greatest foe, the Mikoyan-Gurevich MiG-15, which first flew in July 1947, just three months before the Sabre. Although not as neat as the Sabre, the MiG-15 fully incorporated the results of German as well as Soviet research, and featured swept flying surfaces. Power was provided by a British-designed engine, for which the Labour government had granted export licences. Like most Soviet aircraft of the 1930s and 1940s, the MiG-15 was crude in finish and equipment, but was rugged, reliable and an excellent performer in the air.

Although the MiG-15 had entered widespread production and service use as early as 1948 and later received the NATO reporting name 'Fagot', the Soviets had been more than normally secretive about their new fighter's performance. Thus when they first encountered the MiG-15 after the outbreak of the Korean War in 1950, American pilots were completely startled. Indeed, it was the success of the MiG-15 against straight-winged American fighters that persuaded the US Air Force that the Sabre had to be deployed to this theatre. Even then, pilots soon discovered that the Sabre was marginally inferior in overall combat terms to the MiG-15, but the combination of the American pilots' superior training and the Sabre's incorporation of a radar-aided gunsight enabled the American pilots to turn the tables entirely on their Soviet opponents.

Another result of the Korean War was the eventual American realization that the standard battery of heavy machine-guns was now inadequate for high-speed fighter combat; the Americans also discovered the disadvantages of relying on highly advanced and therefore maintenance-intensive equipment under unsophisticated operating conditions.

Against the MiG-15, for example, many of the better American pilots discarded their radar gunsights, obviating a frequent cause of technical failure and also saving weight. Instead they relied on a blob of chewing gum attached to the windscreen to give the pilot his sighting line. Although the procurement services and aircraft manufacturers took some notice of the pilots' reactions, American combat aircraft still tended towards sophistication where none was needed. On the other hand, many successful pilots did keep their radar gunsights and used them to full advantage, so paving the way for the advanced computer-linked sights used in modern high-speed combat.

By the early 1950s, the development cost of new aircraft had risen so sharply that governments and manufacturers alike were determined to wring every last particle of development potential out of basic designs. To the Western powers this usually meant the minimum of alteration to the basic airframe and engine, but constant updating of the avionics (aviation electronics) which are largely responsible for combat efficiency.

The first Western aeroplane of this type was the F-86D Sabre, which featured an advanced avionics package that provided an all-weather capability, and also enabled the fighter to engage targets automatically after the pilot had selected his objective. Once locked on to the target, the F-86D's radar and computer instructed the pilot as to course and speed until the target was in range: the computer/radar complex then extended the retractable rocket pack under the nose, fired the requisite weapons at the target, and retracted the pack.

Although some later American fighters (especially those of the US Navy) were fitted with a multiple cannon battery, from the Korean War until the late 1960s the Americans in general and the US Air Force in particular preferred a primary armament of missiles. At first these were unguided rockets rather than true guided missiles, and were fired at the target in salvoes in the case of the 2.75-in (70-mm) calibre Folding-Fin Air Rocket series, or individually in the case of the MB-1 Genie with its command-detonated nuclear warhead. Developed from the early 1950s, however, guided missiles with heat-seeking IR (Infra-Red) or radar guidance were in common service by the late 1950s. The radar-guided missiles fell into two basic categories depending on the specific nature of their guidance package: active radar guidance system sends out its own search pulses and then homes on them, while the semi-active guidance system homes on the target radar-illuminated by the attacking fighter, the guidance system steering the missile toward the source of the electromagnetic echoes it receives from the illuminated target.

Another improvement introduced on the F-86D was the use of afterburning, or reheat as it is often called. In this system, extra fuel is injected into the exhaust gases of the engine, to mix and burn with the oxygen surviving in the exhaust gases and so produce more thrust for little extra weight and complexity but considerably increased fuel consumption. Such a system had commonplace on all high-performance military aircraft by the early 1960s.

Even with afterburning and a fully developed engine, the Sabre was limited by its aerodynamic layout to transonic speeds. North American had recognized this factor, however, and had designed a Sabre-derived fighter that would be fully supersonic in level flight. Wings of markedly increased sweep and reduced thickness/chord ratio were added to a beautifully streamlined fuselage to create the Sabre 45 (the figure of the wing's sweep angle), which was accepted for service as the F-100 Super Sabre. This was the first of the US Air Force's 'century' series of supersonic fighters, and entered service in 1954 at the start of a service career that lasted to the mid-1980s with some of the United States' allies.

Lockheed was also well aware of the limitations suffered by the current generation of fighters, for its F-80 Shooting Star and F-94 Starfire had received a rough handling from the MiG-15 in the Korean War, and now produced a thoroughly supersonic fighter. This was based on a design concept thoroughly different from that of the Super Sabre,

however. Rather than use a high angle of sweep to reduce the problems of air compression, the Lockheed design team opted for an extraordinary layout that made its fighter resemble a missile in that it was based on a large and basically cylindrical fuselage accommodating the pilot, electronics, very powerful afterburning turbojet and most of the fuel: to this were added a large T-tail and a tiny but unswept wing that was tapered on its leading and trailing edges: thus the aeroplane relied on high engine thrust and its extremely thin wing to cut through the compression barrier. This F-104 Starfighter first flew in 1954 and was ordered into production for the US Air Force, which ultimately ordered only a comparatively small number of Starfighters as its equipment policies shifted. The type was then saved by a large order from the new West German air force for the F-104G much developed multi-role fighter development that was also ordered by several other European nation as well as Canada, Japan and a number of other American allies.

At first the F-104G was not an operational success. Kept in hangars and used for short interception missions, the delicate F-104 was quite adequate; but kept outside most of the time and used for the rough and tumble of ground-support and attack work, the F-104G proved failure-prone and so many aircraft were lost that the type acquired the German nickname 'widow maker'. Matters started to improve once German groundcrew had become more skilled and increased hangarage became available, and this reduced the incidence of crashed aircraft, whose pilots also enjoyed an enhanced survival rate after the original downward-firing American ejector seat had been replaced by an upward-firing British seat. The F-104G remained one of the most valuable combat aircraft used by the European countries of the North American Treaty Organization until the mid-1980s, and is still in limited service with some American allies. It is also worth noting that Italy, in addition to participating on the European licensed production programme for the F-104G, developed its own variant as the Aeritalia (now Alenia) F-104S for service with the Italian and Turkish air force.

The USSR had an avionics capability considerably inferior to that of the United States or even the European nations during the 1950s, and therefore concentrated its efforts on the full exploitation of current types. Thus there was a marked similarity between the MiG-15 and the MiG-17 'Fresco', which first flew ill 1952. The structural problems and aerodynamic limitations which had caused the loss of many MiG-15s were overcome, and power was provided by a greatly uprated engine so that handling and performance were both improved considerably. Roughly contemporary with later models of the F-86, the MiG-17 had a higher performance than its rivals, but was not met in combat by its Western contemporaries. However, the MiG-17 was later passed to a number of Soviet allies and clients including North Vietnam and many Arab states. The North Vietnamese used the MiG-17 to good effect against the American 'century series' fighters in the early part of the Vietnam War during the mid- and late 1960s, capitalizing on the Soviet fighters' agility and heavy firepower to close with their American opponents and engage in the type of turning fight that best suited the MiG-17's capabilities. The Arabs also used the MiG-17 in combat against French- and American-built fighters, though in this instance flown by the Israeli air force. In the Middle Eastern theatre the MiG-17 did not fare as well as in the Far Eastern theatre, for the Arab pilots were poorly trained and suffered heavily at the hands of the very able Israeli pilots. Thereupon, the Arab air force relegated the MiG-17 largely to the ground-attack role.

Just one year after the appearance of the MiG-17,

however, the same design bureau produced its MiG-19 'Farmer'. This was the first Soviet fighter capable of supersonic performance in level flight, and in most respects it was a match for if not actually superior to the F-100. The MiG-19 had clear conceptual links with the MiG-17 and MiG-15, but was an altogether more refined design based on considerably improved aerodynamics and a much improved powerplant. This latter comprised two Soviet-designed turbojets of the axial-flow type in place of the earlier fighters' single British-type turbojet of the centrifugal-flow type. The greater power and compact dimensions of the side-by-side engine installation allowed the design team to refine the somewhat tubby lines of the earlier types for supersonic flight. The USSR had also begun to catch up with advanced avionics, and the MiG-19 appeared in a number of models with different avionics packages for a variety of roles including limited all-weather interception with radar and up to four primitive beam-riding air-to-air missiles.

Like the F-100, the MiG-19 enjoyed a long operational career, so it is right to say that both these Mach 1.3 fighters stood the test of prolonged service very well. The greatness of the MiG-19 can be measured in the fact that while the F-100 was soon switched from the pure fighter to the tactical fighter role, the Soviet fighter generally retained its pure fighter role. Even after it had been superseded in the USSR by more advanced fighters, the type remained a mainstay of the air forces of most Soviet allies, clients and satellites. By the mid-1960s the West generally regarded the MiG-19 as obsolescent if not obsolete by comparison with the latest Western fighters offering Mach 2+ performance. Events in the Vietnam War and the Arab Israeli Wars of 1967 and 1973 then revealed the error of this judgement: its heavy cannon armament and light wing loading made the MiG-19 an excellent air-combat fighter at high subsonic speeds. This factor is still important in the mid-1990s, and the MiG-19 (including its Chinese-built Shenyang J-6 variants) remains in comparatively widespread service.

The pace of turbojet development was quite dramatic during the 1950s, however, and the F-104, which appeared only a year after the MiG-19, was far superior in terms of legend performance with a maximum level speed in excess of Mach 2 and far superior climb rate together with service ceiling.

In the early 1950s Republic also produced a supersonic fighter, developing the F-84F Thunderstreak from the F-84 Thunderjet, the substitution of swept for straight flying surfaces on a fuselage that was otherwise little modified producing a useful increase in overall performance. This gave an improved fighter at minimal cost, but the Thunderstreak was only an interim type, despite a long and distinguished career as a fighter-bomber and reconnaissance aeroplane with the US Air Force and several allied nations.

To create a truly supersonic type, the Republic design team echoed the North American team in the adoption of highly swept flying surfaces, a sleek fuselage and a powerful turbojet with full afterburning. First flown in 1955, this Republic aeroplane was the F-105 Thunderchief, one of the classic US Air Force aircraft of the period after World War II. Although it was classified as a fighter, the Thunderchief was in reality a massive and hard-hitting strike and attack aeroplane characterized not

only by its high supersonic performance but also its incorporation of an internal weapon bay to supplement the hardpoints that had become standard for the carriage of external drop loads. Nicknamed 'Thud', the Thunderchief also featured an advanced avionics suite that created a number of maintenance problems but found a new lease of life in the 1960s during the Vietnam War. Even though many analysts had decided that the nuclear-capable F-105 was obsolescent, the type was revealed by operations to be versatile and capable of absorbing the levels of battle damage that would have downed most other types. Even when damaged on the way to the target, the F-105 could often deliver its weapons load (now generally carried on one under-fuselage and four under-wing hardpoints) with pinpoint accuracy and only then turn for home.

With their powerful engines and advanced aerodynamic features, multi-role fighters could, by the late 1950s, carry an offensive load far greater than could be stowed inside the airframe, even if it had been possible to locate a weapons bay among the masses of avionics equipment scattered through the fuselage. Pioneered during World War II, streamlined pylons under the wings and fuselage could accept a dazzling variety of under-wing stores. Not only bombs, but unguided rockets either singly if they were of large calibre or in multiple launcher pods if they were of small calibre, guided missiles of the air-to-air and/or air-to-surface varieties, napalm tanks, chemical tanks and other offensive stores could be carried, as well as drop tanks for extra fuel. The mass of wiring and plumbing needed to connect the stores and tanks to onboard computers and the aeroplane's main fuel system greatly increased the complexity of the problems faced by the now enormous design teams.

The Europeans were meanwhile advancing more slowly the Americans and Soviets. World War II had devastated Europe, and of the major aeronautical powers before World War II only the United Kingdom and France were in any position to design and construct advanced combat aircraft. Yet the British government could foresee no war before the late 1950s and, with finance in short supply, the development of new fighting aircraft received a low priority. In France the work of reconstruction after World War II was more urgent and, despite a number of interesting experiments, the combat aircraft brought into service were chosen for their serviceability rather than inspiration in their design or for high performance.

The limitations of the United Kingdom's Meteor and Vampire as front-line fighters were highlighted by the Korean War, but the lack of research and development in the previous years meant that the British aircraft industry was in no position to push forward the production of a new fighter. In 1952,

Below: The Republic XF-91 Thunderceptor was a fascinating supersonic interceptor that did not progress past the stage of two prototypes. The XF-91 had inversely tapered swept wings, a hybrid powerplant with one turbojet and one liquid-propellant rocket motor, and (in the second prototype illustrated here) a butterfly tail.

the United Kingdom was put in the humiliating position of having to accept 430 Sabres built by Canadair and paid for by the American and Canadian

Above: The most important turbojet-powered British fighter of the 1950s, and a classic type that remains in service with some smaller countries, was the Hawker Hunter. This was built in variants with the Rolls-Royce Avon and Armstrong Siddeley Sapphire turbojets, and in its later forms was produced as a fighter-bomber in variants such as this Hunter FGA.Mk 6 and as a trainer with side-by-side accommodation.

Right: The Dassault Super MystÊre B-2 was the first supersonic fighter to enter production and service in Europe, and was an evolutionary development from the straight-winged Ouragan and modestly swept MystÊre II and IV.

governments. Two years later, however, as several supersonic types were being introduced in the USSR and the United States, two swept-wing but only transonic British fighters entered service after prolonged development.

The first of these was the Supermarine Swift, whose production programme was curtailed as a result of the type's intransigent aerodynamic problems; the second was the classic Hawker Hunter, perhaps the best transonic fighter and ground-support aircraft of its kind. With clean lines, excellent handling characteristics and a good load-carrying capacity, the Hunter was built in greater numbers than any other postwar British aeroplane, and is still in first-line service with several smaller air forces during the mid-1990s.

French fighter aircraft have been supplied almost exclusively by the firm set up in 1945 by Marcel Bloch, whose aircraft manufacturing company had been nationalized in 1937 as part of the SNCASO group. Returning from Germany, where he had been incarcerated during the war, he changed his surname to Dassault (his codename in the wartime resistance), and built up the company bearing his new name into the biggest military aircraft manufacturer in France. The machines supplied by Dassault have been based on sound engineering and inspired design, with costs carefully kept down by repeating as many components and ideas as possible from design to design.

The first turbojet-powered Dassault fighter was the Ouragan (hurricane), which was built in moderate numbers for the French and Indian air forces before being replaced by the more advanced swept-wing MystÊre. The MystÊre was built in some numbers both for the home market and for export, and was the first French aircraft to exceed the speed of sound, although only in a shallow dive. Just as the F-100 had been evolved in concept terms from the F-86, so too the Super MystÊre, of which Dassault flew the first

prototype in 1955, was the truly supersonic development of the MystÊre. With its more streamlined fuselage, a Rolls-Royce Avon axial-flow afterburning turbojet and very thin wings, it proved a first-class fighter, and served the Israeli air force well in combat.

In the mid-1950s several NATO forces became interested in lightweight fighters. These were expected to be cheaper than the current generation of aircraft, to give high performance with smaller engines than those used in the heavyweight American type of aircraft, and to offer the tactical advantages of being able to use grass or semi-prepared airstrips. This last factor reflected the fear felt in NATO at this time about the vulnerability of its complex of fixed air bases with their concrete runways for heavyweight tactical aircraft. The availability of swarms of lightweight tactical aircraft would ensure a continued air capability, it was felt, and lightweight tactical aircraft were also thought to provide advantages for the support of ground forces as they could operate from extemporized airstrips right behind the front line of a mobile battle and thus provide speedy assistance whenever required. Several very interesting designs appeared, including the miniscule Gnat built by the Folland company in the United Kingdom, the Taon (horsefly) from the French Breguet company and, winning the design competition for a modest production run, the G91 from Fiat (later Aeritalia and now Alenia), an Italian manufacturer.

Dassault produced two designs, the conventional looking Etendard (battle standard) and the delta-winged Mirage. Both of these had started life as small, lightweight fighters with a pair of low-powered turbojets, but initial trials soon confirmed the feeling that Dassault had perceived some time earlier, namely that the designs would be capable of realizing their full potential only if they were scaled up and powered by a single large turbojet. The results were the Etendard IV transonic carrierborne attack fighter, and the Mirage III that was Europe's second Mach 2 fighter to enter service.

The first Mach 2 European fighter was the English Electric (later British Aircraft Corporation and finally British Aerospace) Lightning. This had entered service in 1960, after a design and development period of 13 years that had turned a supersonic research aeroplane into a phenomenally fast-climbing interceptor whose two main limitations were indifferent armament and poor range. The Mirage III, adopted in 1961, came six years after the first flight of the Mirage I lightweight prototype. The prolonged gestation periods of these fighters, comparing poorly with

the speed at which the Soviets and Americans were able to put new types into service, was a clear indication of weakness in the European aero industry and the strength of the superpowers.

The Mirage III has been the most successful European combat aeroplane designed since World War II, and has formed the basis of a large number of advanced and high-performance combat aircraft. Essentially a scaled-up Mirage III, the Mirage IV is a Mach 2 bomber for the delivery of France's atomic bombs; the Mirage 5 was designed to an Israeli requirement as a simplified clear-weather version of the all-weather Mirage III for use as a ground-attack fighter but since upgraded in most cases to Mirage III standards or higher as miniaturized electronics were developed; the Mirage F1 was designed as a multi-mission fighter and attack aeroplane based on the Mirage III's fuselage but with new swept wings and tailplane; the Mirage G was designed as a variable-geometry fighter again based on the well-tried Mirage III fuselage; and the Super Mirage was designed as a very advanced multi-role fighter. Israel was concerned that deliveries of its Mirage 5 force might be delayed by Arab political and economic pressure on France, and set in hand a programme of indigenous but wholly unlicensed production and further development of the Mirage III. This foresight paid handsome dividends when delivery of the Mirage 5 force later embargoed completely and not just delayed, and Israel Aircraft Industries was able to respond with its Nesher (eagle) version of the Mirage III as work continued on the much upgraded Kfir (lion cub) derivative with an American turbojet and an advanced suite of Israeli electronics. Israel used its Mirage IIIs to stunning effect in the 1967 'Six-Day War' and had introduced the Nesher in time for the 'Yom Kippur War' of 1973, when the Mirage III also played a useful role. Surplus Neshers were later exported to Argentina with the name Dagger, and were used against the British during the latters' successful campaign to wrest the Falkland Islands from Argentine occupation. In Israel, further development of the Kfir produced the Kfir-C2 with canard foreplanes to improve field performance and to enhance manoeuvrability in air combat, and Israel has continued to develop this useful type in variants with more refined aerodynamics, greater power from a 'tweaked' engine and, most importantly of all, much more sophisticated electronics in single- and two-seat variants. Many exported Mirage IIIs and Mirage 5s have been upgraded to a comparable standard, and South Africa undertook a comparable upgrade effort to produce the Atlas Cheetah by rebuilding French aircraft delivered before the imposition of a United Nations' embargo of arms supplies as a supposed counter to South Africa's policy of separate racial development. This embargo was lifted in 1994 after the swearing in of a new multi-racial South African government, and this has opened the possibility of South African exports or involvement in further Mirage III/5 upgrades.

The basic design of the remarkable Mirage III has thus proved enormously adaptable, and with different engines, flying surfaces, avionics and armament can undertake a variety of combat tasks ranging from short-range interception to medium-range operational-level nuclear strike bombing, through all-weather fighting, training, daylight ground attack and reconnaissance. The Mirage III and Mirage 5 are still operational in some numbers with European air forces although it is now rapidly declining in importance as more advanced types have assumed its primary roles, but is likely to remain one of the most valuable combat types of several South American and African countries for some time to come: indeed, Pakistan bought a large number of ex-Australian Mirage IIIs during the early 1990s with a view to supplementing its current fleet of Mirages with an upgraded variant.

A notable factor in fighter design since the early 1950s has been the wide range of tasks which operators expect their smaller combat aircraft to be able to undertake. Up to about the middle of World War II, it was possible to build a combat aeroplane for one specific role, but development costs have since been prohibitively high for such development to be considered by any country other than one of the two superpowers. The tendency has therefore been toward the creation of multi-role aircraft, and this tendency was discernible even during World War II in the evolution of supremely versatile types such as the de Havilland Mosquito and Junkers Ju 88.

Each role demands its own electronics package and specialized weapons, but this has actually eased the designers' task. As long as the electronics packages for the all-weather interception, reconnaissance and ground-attack roles can all fit into the same fuselage, the basic aeroplane can be used in a number of roles. Reduced to its simplest terms, the designer's task from the mid-1950s until very recent times has been to produce an aeroplane capable of high performance at all altitudes and in all conditions, but with the ability to carry a heavy offensive load on the exterior hardpoints and sufficient internal volume for accommodation of the relevant avionics. Although simple in concept, such design is vastly complex in practice, and has been made still more complicated by the realization that missiles have some disadvantages in combat. Internally mounted guns, with all their bulky ammunition and fire-control radars, must now be designed into the airframe.

Advanced combat aircraft are so expensive that the economies of the United Kingdom and

France were severely strained by the development and production of machines such as the Lightning and Mirage.

Other European countries, apart from Sweden, could not match this expenditure, and so bought aircraft from one of the main producers, or concentrated on less advanced types with limited capabilities. Italy, as noted above for example, produced the lightweight G91 close-support aircraft, and developed its two most important turbojet-

Right: Designed as a diminutive fighter that could be carried by the Convair B-36 long-range strategic heavy bomber for air launch and aerial recovery using a trapeze lowered from the mother aeroplane, the McDonnell XF-85 Goblin was an extraordinary difficult aeroplane to fly. The wings folded upward for internal accommodation in the mother aeroplane, there was no landing gear other than skids for emergency alightings, and the compact tail unit had multiple surfaces to minimize overall size without loss of adequate area. Needless to say, the type secured no production order.

powered trainers into useful but limited light attack types: the single-seat attack version of the MB-326 sold moderately well, but the comparable version of the MB-339 (an evolutionary development of the MB-326 with a revised forward fuselage offering vertically stepped accommodation) failed to attract any purchasers. This has been a growing trend since the mid-1960s, followed by countries such as the United Kingdom, France, Spain, Romania and Yugoslavia. Such machines have been and still are sold to Third World nations as primary combat aircraft, and provide a secondary attack capability for the home air forces. Virtually no trainer designed since 1970, even in the United States and the USSR, has lacked this secondary attack capability.

The US Air Force's inventory of modern combat aircraft designed between the late 1940s and late 1950s, ranging from the F-86 Sabre to the Convair F-102 Delta Dagger and F-106 Delta Dart interceptors, was impressive. Yet it was then matched by just one truly superlative type, the McDonnell (later McDonnell Douglas) F-4 Phantom II multi-role fighter developed for the US Navy but then adopted for the US Air Force. Design began in 1954, and by 1960 the type was recognized as the best all-round combat aeroplane developed in the United States since the end of World War II. With a lowering, aggressive appearance, the Phantom II was first conceived as a carrierborne attack aeroplane but built in prototype form as a two-seat carrierborne fleet defence fighter (the first

straight-winged Panther and swept-wing Cougar forms), the McDonnell F2H Banshee and F3H Demon fighters, and the Douglas F3D Skyknight all-weather fighter.

Later in the 1950s the Douglas A3D Skywarrior attack bomber and A4D Skyhawk light attack aeroplane appeared, and the US Navy moved into the supersonic age with the Vought F8U Crusader fighter whose configuration was later scaled-down to create the LTV A-7 Corsair II strike and attack aeroplane. The largest and heaviest carrierborne aeroplane yet to have entered service, the Mach 2 North

Above: The Vought Corsair II, seen here in the form of the definitive A-7E naval variant, was developed on the basis of the Vought F-8 Crusader fighter's aerodynamics to provide the US Navy with a medium attack warplane to complement the lightweight Douglas A-4 Skyhawk.

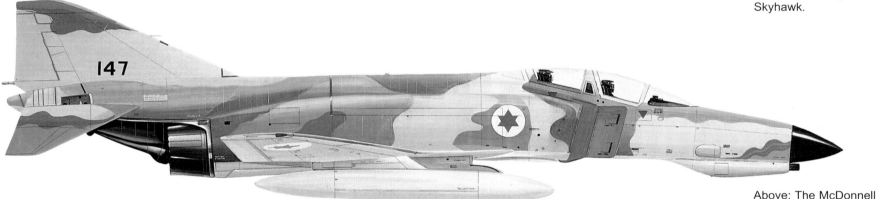

capable of undertaking the whole interception mission without support from surfaces ships) and then evolved into strike, attack, close support, electronic pathfinder, defence suppression and reconnaissance forms, and is still used by a number of Western air forces apart from those of the United States, where the type is due for retirement from US Air Force service in the second half of the 1990s.

The lessons of combat in Vietnam during the late 1960s and early 1970s led to the development of a new model with fixed gun armament in the form of the redoubtable 20-mm Vulcan six-barrelled rotary cannon capable of a rate of fire in the order of 6,000 rounds per minute This convinced the governments of most countries of the need for fighters with a fixed gun armament, and further evidence was provided by Israeli aircraft in the 'Six-Day War' of 1967, when cannon proved as useful as guided missiles, especially at the low speeds and short ranges at which air combat was joined.

Immediately after the end of World War II, the main strength of the US Navy's air arm lay with piston-engined types such as the Grumman F8F Bearcat fighter, the Vought F4U Corsair fighter and fighter-bomber, and the Douglas AD Skyraider attack bomber, which was still flying over Vietnam in the early 1970s. Interim turbojet-powered types were under development, however, and by the early 1950s the US Navy and US Marine Corps had accepted a number of new aircraft such as the Grumman F9F fighter (in its

American A3J Vigilante attack bomber entered service in 1960. All these aircraft operated in Vietnam, and constant updating of their engines and avionics kept them in the forefront of military technology until a time well into the 1970s. More than the aircraft of the US Air Force, perhaps, these US Navy types were resilient and versatile machines, disproving the theory that turbojet-powered aircraft and their avionics would be susceptible to battle damage. The only US Air Force aeroplane to match these US Navy types was the F-105, and this had serviceability problems that

Above: The McDonnell F-4 Phantom II was developed in the 1950s as a fleet defence fighter, but then matured as a truly great multi-role warplane for land-based as well as carrierborne operations.

Below: McDonnell F-4 Phantom IIs are seen on the production line.

would never have been permitted in a carrierborne combat aeroplane.

By the 1970s, the only other countries to develop carrierborne aircraft were France and the United Kingdom. Re-formed toward the end of World War II, the French naval air arm initially operated American naval aircraft, and in the mid-1990s still operates the Crusader, which was redesignated as the F-8 in 1962 as part of the rationalization of the US forces' previously separate tri-service designation systems into a single system. From the early 1960s, however, the Dassault Etendard IVM proved itself a more than adequate carrierborne attack aircraft, and the Breguet 1050 Alizé (tradewind) has also served well in the anti-submarine role.

The Fleet Air Arm of the Royal Navy possessed few high-performance aircraft during World War II apart from converted landplanes such as the Supermarine Seafire adaptation of the Spitfire. In the years after 1945, it soldiered on with piston-engined types such as the Hawker Sea Fury fighter, Fairey Firefly reconnaissance-fighter and Fairey Barracuda torpedo bomber, as well as a number of more advanced American aircraft such as the Grumman Avenger that was operated in the AEW (Airborne Early Warning) role. The FAA acquired its first turbine-powered types in the early 1950s: these were the Supermarine Attacker and Hawker Sea Hawk fighters, and the Fairey Gannet anti-submarine aeroplane. This last was powered by a turboprop engine, as was its French contemporary, the Alizé.

The turboprop is a combination of the turbojet engine's core with a propeller to provide tractive power. The turbine section in the exhaust area of the engine, which drives just the compressor section in the forward part of the standard turbojet, in a turboprop also powers a long axial shaft extending to the reducing gearbox that drives the large propeller at the very forward end of the engine. The exhaust gases are still powerful, moreover, and add a useful element of thrust to the tractive effort of the propeller. The turboprop is ideally suited for many intermediate-speed applications as its fuel consumption is relatively low and it incorporates the best features of the turbojet (small size and relative lack of vibration) with the best elements of the propeller (good power at low speeds).

By the late 1950s three swept-wing aircraft designs were under development for the FAA, and entered service late in the 1950s and early in the 1960s. These were the Supermarine Scimitar interceptor and strike fighter, the de Havilland (later Hawker Siddeley) Sea Vixen interceptor and the Blackburn (later Hawker Siddeley) Buccaneer strike aeroplane. The Buccaneer was a particularly good machine, with excellent performance 'on the deck' because of careful aerodynamic design, and first-class landing characteristics as a result of a 'super-circulation' boundary-layer control system. Despite its many virtues, the Buccaneer was long resisted by the Royal Air Force, which wanted the considerably more advanced BAC TSR-2 tactical strike and reconnaissance aeroplane. In the mid-1960s, however, the RAF reluctantly agreed to accept surviving ex-FAA aircraft when the Royal Navy's force of large aircraft-carriers was retired later in the decade. The TSR-2 project had been cancelled, and much to its surprise the RAF found the Buccaneer to be a truly great aeroplane that was then ordered in larger numbers whose last examples were retired only in 1994.

Transonic speeds are dangerous at very low altitudes, where buffeting might cause the aircraft to hit the ground before the pilot can correct. Design adjustments to prevent this buffeting are based on the American-developed notion of area ruling the fuselage to minimize drag and turbulent areas by reducing rapid changes in cross section along the

airframe. First introduced to service on the F-102 Delta Dart, area ruling has since been used on a number of aircraft and can usually be seen in the fuselage, which has a number of waisted and bulged sections to allow for the added cross-sectional area represented by the wing. In the Buccaneer, for example, there was a distinct bulge just aft of the rear end of the pipes for the engines, which were de Havilland Gyron Junior turbojets in the Buccaneer S.Mk 1 but altogether more powerful and fuel-economical Rolls-Royce Spey turbofans in the definitive Buccaneer S.Mk 2.

The USSR's air force moved into the Mach 2 era with the Mikoyan-Gurevich MiG-21 'Fishbed' fighter designed to supersede the highly successful MiG-19. Small and compact for a Mach 2 aircraft, the MiG-21 has a delta wing but conventional, highly-swept tail surfaces, and proved both popular and successful. Lacking the size, weight and versatility of the Phantom II, the MiG-21 was designed for the short-range interception mission in clear weather conditions and using GCI (Ground-Controlled Interception) techniques. Total production in the USSR, several Warsaw Pact countries and India totalled more than 6,500 aircraft, and an additional large but unspecified quantity has been built in China as the Chendu J-7 series,

Above: The finest advanced trainer produced in recent years has been the British Aerospace (originally Hawker Siddeley) Hawk, seen here in the form of the Hawk T.Mk 1 operated by the Royal Air Force. The type has secured considerable export sales, has been developed into the Hawk Mk 100 and Hawk Mk 200 warplane, and has also been adopted for the US Navy as the somewhat revised McDonnell Douglas T-45 Goshawk.

which has also spawned the export-oriented F-7M Airguard derivative with a large proportion of Western avionics.

Though conceived for the clear-weather interception role and first flown in 1955 with comparatively light armament, the MiG-21 was successfully evolved into a limited all-weather type capable of of the interception and ground-attack roles as a result of upgraded avionics and additional armament capability. The MiG-21 family also included several reconnaissance models and three tandem-seat operational conversion trainers, and such was its 'developability' that during its long production career the MiG-21 was built in many variants with three basic engine

Above: In its original form as the MiG-21F, the Mikoyan-Gurevich MiG-21 'Fishbed' was a clear-weather interceptor, but was then developed into a much more capable limited all-weather fighter with dual air-to-air and air-to-surface capabilities.

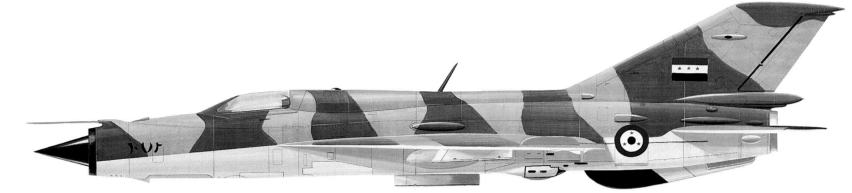

Above: The MiG-21MF is a good example of the Mikoyan-Gurevich MiG-21 'Fishbed' in its mid-period form as a dual-role fighter.

types, increasingly large dorsal spines allowing a major increase in internal fuel capacity and, in the last model, a completely re-engineered airframes. The MiG-21 series was built in larger numbers than any other Soviet warplane since World War II, and was used by virtually every Soviet ally, client and satellite. Although the type disappeared from Soviet first-line service in the late 1980s and early 1990s, the type survives in large numbers with the air forces of most other Soviet bloc countries, and the mid-1990s are witnessing a scrambled contest as the Russian parent organization competes with several Western countries for the lucrative upgrade of these obsolescent aircraft to a more modern standard. The update requested by most operators is concerned mainly with the MiG-21's avionics and weapons capabilities, and though India has opted for a Russian upgrade with Russian radar, it has also specified Western items for a large proportion of the other updated features. It is likely that most of the other upgrade customers will follow a similar course.

In its heyday the Soviet fighter could generally outfly contemporary American aircraft as a result of its small size and low wing loading, and with the MiG-19 helped to demonstrate that the art of dogfighting has not disappeared as a useful element of the fighter pilot's inventory of skills. Part of the MiG-21 's undoubted export popularity lay in its relative cheapness: in general this trim fighter cost between one-quarter and one-third of the price for a Phantom II.

The nearest Soviet equivalent to the mighty F-105 Thunderchief as an attack aeroplane was a series of sturdy swept-wing designs originating in the design bureau of Pavel Sukhoi. The Su-7 'Fitter' series equipped most of the air forces in the Soviet sphere of influence, but though it has much the same performance as the F-105, the Su-7 cannot carry the same offensive load and is also notably deficient in range even when carrying two drop tanks in place of disposable armament. In short, therefore, the Su-7 series may be regarded as a short-range close-support fighter whereas the F-105 was a long-range strike and attack fighter. In its milieu, however, the Su-7 was unrivalled until the late 1980s, for it was very fast at low level, monumentally strong, and a superb weapon platform because of its low gust response.

The origins of the Su-7 can be traced back to the operational planning that also led to the MiG-21. Both the Mikoyan-Gurevich and Sukhoi design bureaux were ordered to develop prototypes based on two basic layouts, namely the conventional configuration with flying surfaces swept at 60∞ or 62∞ and the tailed delta configuration with the flying surfaces swept at 57∞ or 60∞. The two Mikoyan-Gurevich prototype series were the swept-wing Ye-50 and Ye-2 and the tailed-delta Ye-4 and Ye-5. It was the last that formed the basis of the MiG-21. The comparable Sukhoi prototype series were the swept-wing S-1 and tailed-delta T-3, and of these it was the S-1 that paved the way for the Su-7, which was schemed as a pure fighter but then placed in production as a close-support fighter. Even though the Su-7 was a superb operational aeroplane in

its way, especially in its later variants with STOL (Short Take-Off and Landing) capability so that they could operate from semi-prepared airstrips immediately behind the front line, the Soviet air forces were unhappy with the type's very poor payload/range performance, and from 1960 the design bureau started work on a variable-geometry derivative offering improved payload/range performance. For a combination of technical and production reasons it was decided to pivot only the outer half of each wing, but this proved adequate to transform the basic close-support fighter's payload/range performance. The resulting aeroplane entered service in 1971 as the Su-17 'Fitter-C' that was also produced in differently engined Su-20 and Su-22 forms: with the outer wing sections in their minimum-sweep position, the Su-17 series aircraft had much improved field performance and greater tactical radius; and with the wings in the maximum-sweep position, speed was comparable with that of the Su-7. The net result was that the Su-17 series could carry 250% more payload over 30% greater tactical radius.

Unlike the other half of the Mikoyan-Gurevich prototype series, which did not lead to a production swept-wing aeroplane, the other half of the Sukhoi prototype series also resulted in a production aeroplane, in this instance of the tailed-delta layout. The first of these was the Su-9 'Fishpot' interceptor that was reserved for Soviet use from the time of its introduction in mid-1959. From 1966 the Su-9 was complemented by the improved Su-11 'Fishpot', and production of the two models totalled some 2,000 aircraft that were gradually supplanted from the early 1970s by the Su-15 'Flagon' probably designed also to replace the Yakovlev Yak-28P 'Firebar' Mach 1.9 interceptor. The Su-15 was an altogether more advanced interceptor offering Mach 2+ performance as a result of its more refined airframe with a large measure of area-ruling, and also its considerably more potent twin-engined powerplant aspirated via wing-root inlets rather than the earlier types' nose inlet. This latter allowed the incorporation of a much superior interception radar with its antenna in the large nose radome that was now possible. The last Su-15 interceptors were retired only in the late 1980s.

Also in service with the USSR's forces until the late 1980s was the Tupolev Tu-28P 'Fiddler', the largest interceptor fighter in service anywhere in the world and intended primarily for poor-weather operations in the USSR's northern regions. These areas were poorly equipped with air bases, but lay on the optimum transpolar route that would probably have been used by American strategic bombers attacking the USSR. The only way to provide effective patrol and interception capabilities in these regions was therefore the development of a moderately supersonic interceptor with an airframe large enough to carry considerable fuel, the two-man crew, an extremely powerful radar system, and four large long-range air-to-air missiles.

Not all the energy of the world's military aircraft designers went into the evolution of fighters, however. With the destruction of Hiroshima and Nagasaki, the strategic bomber had proved its value beyond all doubt. The invention of an enormously destructive device such as the A-bomb (fission or nuclear bomb) opened the possibility of true strategic air power in the form of just a few aircraft each crewed by less than a dozen men. The theories of such men as Douhet, Mitchell and Trenchard in the 1920s were finally proved by the destruction of Hiroshima and Nagasaki, and their concept of strategic bombing as the arbiter of war was made still more terrible by the development of the enormously more powerful H-bomb (fusion or thermonuclear bomb) shortly after the end of World War II.

It was inevitable that these weapons should come to dominate military thinking in the late 1940s. It was assumed that long-range guided missiles, based on the German V-2 of World War II, would eventually be developed as a delivery system for such weapons, but in the short term the only practical solution seemed to lie with the long-range manned bomber and then the long-range unmanned bomber, which was really a surface-to-surface missile of the type that would now have been classified as a cruise missile, albeit of considerably larger size than anything in service today. The manned bomber therefore became the single most important type of weapon in the arsenals of the United States, the USSR and the United Kingdom, the only three countries with nuclear weapons in the 1950s. And heavy bombers were always designed with the capacity to carry such weapons even if the specific type of bomb had not been fully developed at the time.

The only turbojet-powered bomber in operational service when the war ended was a German type, the Arado Ar 234 Blitz (lightning). The Germans had been experimenting with several other types of turbojet-powered bomber, most notably the Junkers Ju 287. This extraordinary aeroplane had a forward-swept wing, and the powerplant comprised four turbojets: these were installed as two under the wing and the other two on the sides of the forward fuselage. Fascinating experimental data on the use of forward-swept wings as a means of combating the worst effects of high-speed compression were obtained by the Americans and Soviets, but as yet no military aircraft with forward-swept wings has entered production.

By 1946 both the superpowers had instituted top-priority programmes to develop a strategic bomber capable of carrying nuclear bombs over very long ranges. At the same time the USSR was abandoning its virtually exclusive concentration on tactical air power for a more mixed approach. This reflected the fact that while the Soviet air force had shown itself to be the most powerful support arm in the world, aiding the Red Army in its massive pushes into Germany, the Soviet leaders had been greatly impressed by the devastation wrought on Germany and Japan by the combined Western bomber offensive.

Although the USSR had been a primary exponent of the strategic bombing doctrine in the late 1920s and early 1930s, it had, as noted in an earlier chapter, decided in the later 1930s to concentrate its efforts on the application of tactical air power for the support of the ground forces. As the Soviet forces pressed into eastern Germany, the Soviet high command and political leadership began to appreciate the extent of the strategic damage that heavy bomber fleets could cause. The Soviets were still digesting the implications of a shattered Germany when the American bombing of Hiroshima and Nagasaki convinced them, as it convinced others, that the strategic bomber was the final arbiter of warfare for the immediate future. So the Soviets started almost from scratch, since the Petlyakov Pe-8 used in the war years had been only a limited design. Nonetheless, they were hardly ignorant of the problems involved in constructing large machines. In the 1930s they had led the world in the production of very large aircraft, and the forced landings of three American Boeing B-29 Superfortress bombers in Siberia had given them good examples of the latest Western technology. Thus the Soviets started by building the Tupolev Tu-4 'Bull', a reverse-engineered derivative of the Superfortress, as their first strategic bomber type.

The United Kingdom's main heavy bombers at this time were the venerable Avro Lancaster, still a mighty load-carrier, and the new Avro Lincoln, a faster and more heavily armed derivative of the Lancaster with considerably more powerful engines. Worthy as the Lincoln was by the standards of World War II, the advent of new technologies (turbine propulsion and the advanced aerodynamic features of machines such as the B-29) had rendered it obsolescent by the time it entered production. The same was true of the Vickers Warwick, derived from the Wellington, and a number of other bombers in the light to medium category.

By the end of the decade, the United Kingdom's heavy bomber force, on which NATO placed considerable reliance, was completely obsolete and the United States lent the RAF's Bomber Command a number of B-29s in an attempt to remedy the situation. No modern British fighting aircraft could be sent to Korea, and by 1952 the country had received, quite free, modern fighters and bombers paid for by the taxpayers of the United States and Canada. More modern types were indeed under development, but progress was painfully slow, and this

technology gap left the country in a very weak military position up to the mid-1950s.

The United States had become convinced during World War II that it needed a completely new generation of bombers, and had therefore begun a large-scale research and development programme. Yet just after the war, before the new bombers could be placed in service, the most important aircraft in the Strategic Air Command was the Boeing B-50 development of the B-29, with more advanced systems, better armament and uprated engines. Even so, the very fact of the SAC's formation indicates the importance attached to the concept of nuclear strategic bombing in the United States.

The B-50 was essentially an interim type, pending the arrival of one of the oddest and most controversial aeroplane of all time, the Convair B-36. This had its origins in the American decision of 1943 to build a fleet of advanced bombers, but design and prototype construction

Below: Produced for the British, German and Italian air forces by an international consortium, the Panavia Tornado reflects the high cost of modern warplanes but provides its operators with exceptional capabilities for long-range interdiction at supersonic speed and very low altitude under any and all weather conditions by day or night. The Tornado has a variable-geometry wing planform for short take-off with the wings in the minimum-sweep position, good range with the wings in the intermediate-sweep

were delayed initially by the more immediate demands of production to meet the requirements of operations in World War II. When this important programme was again undertaken as a matter of high priority, it was soon discovered that the pace of technical development in this forcing period of history had been so fast that already the planned type was on the verge of obsolescence in all features but its phenomenally good payload/range performance, which ensured that a heavy bomb load could be delivered over intercontinental ranges. Thus development and procurement of the B-36 continued, and the type entered service in the late 1940s. With a wing spanning no less than 230 ft (70.1 m), the monstrous B-36 was powered by six 3,500-hp radial piston engines buried in the wings and driving pusher propellers located behind the wing trailing edges. At a time when advanced turbojet-powered fighters were opening the possibility of combat operations at high subsonic speeds, however, the B-36 was judged too slow for survivability in its basic piston-engined form. Thus the B-36D featured a boosted powerplant, with the original piston engines supplemented by four turbojet engines in pods, each accommodating two side-by-side engines, attached under the outer wing panels. This boosted the maximum speed to 435 mph (700 km/h), which was considerably below the figure attainable by current fighters but which was nonetheless deemed, in conjunction with the bomber's prodigious defensive armament of paired 20-mm cannon, to offer at least a measure of survivability. So large was the B-36, it is interesting to note, that crew members used a small rail-mounted cart to move between the major pressurized compartments in the long fuselage.

Among the notable experiments carried out to improve the B-36's combat survivability was the installation of a McDonnell F-85 Goblin fighter, which could be launched from the bomber in flight, deal with opposing fighters, and then be picked up by the parent bomber once more. The F-85, of which only two were built, was an extraordinarily compact and ugly little aeroplane that proved only marginally controllable in the air, and its development shows the extremes to which the Americans went in their efforts to capitalize on their possession of the A-bomb. The concept of using the B-36 as a parent aeroplane was repeated with the RF-84F Thunderstreak in an effort to give this reconnaissance aeroplane the range for deep penetration missions.

Although the B-36 had the prodigious range of 7,500 miles (12070 km) necessary for global missions, the US Air Force soon appreciated that the very size of the aeroplane was a hindrance to its survivability and therefore its likely success in combat: the B-36's radar signature was enormous, for example, and this made the type highly detectable even by the comparatively primitive ground-based radars then available to the Soviets.

The Americans reasoned that they should replace the B-36 with a smaller bomber that would be more survivable than the lumbering B-36 as it would be faster and less detectable. But a smaller airframe also entailed reduced fuel capacity and thus restricted range at a time when the SAC was being developed as the United States' primary method

Above: The Boeing B-47 Stratojet was the US Air Force's first 'modern' strategic bomber, and was designed for the medium role over transcontinental rather than intercontinental ranges. The type had its origins in design of World War II with straight wings and a turboprop powerplant, but was then evolved into its classic form as the Boeing designers digested the implications of German aeronautical research in World War II.

of strategic power projection. So new measures were needed to give any smaller and therefore more survivable bomber the range required for the SAC's worldwide strategic mission. The answer lay in aerial refuelling, which had been attempted as early as the 1920s. The British had undertaken a fair amount of experimental work with air-to-air refuelling before World War II, and had reached a similar conclusion about the need for this procedure for their new generation of bombers.

Despite the commonality of their operational objectives, the two nations arrived at markedly different solutions to the same technical problem. In the American system, an operator in the tanker aeroplane 'flies' a rigid but telescopic boom, with flight-control surfaces at its lower end, into the receptacle located on the upper surface of the receiving combat aeroplane and then opens the valve that releases fuel to flow into the receiver's fuel system. The British system, on the other hand, is based on a long flexible hose, with a drogue at its end, trailed from the tanker aeroplane: once this has been extended to its full length, the combat aeroplane then noses its refuelling probe into the drogue, completing a fuel-tight lock and initiating the flow of fuel, which is halted as the receiver aeroplane completes its refuelling and drops back, thereby breaking the connection. The British system is much simpler than the the type adopted by the US Air Force and is better suited to the demands of smaller combat aircraft. For this reason it was also adopted by the US Navy and other nations with their own tanker aircraft, notably the USSR. As air-to-air refuelling increased in importance, the US Air Force also began to appreciate the value of the hose-and-drogue system over the flying boom system for use with all but the largest aircraft, and many of its tankers now operate a dual system with a single flying boom under the rear fuselage and two hose-and-drogue units under the wings.

Tanker aircraft must have a large internal volume in which to carry the fuel, and civil transport aircraft have proved ideal for conversion to this exacting role. In the United States, the pioneering Boeing KC-97 tanker was derived from the Model 377 Stratocruiser, a civilian airliner in turn derived from the B-29 bomber. The KC-97 validated the concept of air-to-air refuelling, but the system really came into its own with the adoption of a turbojet-powered type possessing much the slow speed capability as the aircraft it was intended to support. The classic machine of this type has been the Boeing KC-135 Stratotanker. This had its origins in the Model 367-80, the Boeing-funded prototype that paved the way for the Model 707 airliner. Once it had completed its initial flight trials with this prototype, Boeing modified it with a flying boom for demonstration to the US Air Force. This led the way for a huge KC-135 order that started the successful production life of this important series of military and civil transports. As the value of air-to-air refuelling tankers became increasingly visible in the support of long-range deployments and operations by tactical aircraft, other nations started to buy such aircraft, generally in the form of surplus Model 707 transports converted to any of several tanker configurations.

The United Kingdom has used converted transports and latterly converted bombers, as has the USSR. It is hard to exaggerate the importance of these tankers, although they are not combat aircraft in their own right. Without them most of today's fighting aircraft would be incapable either of flying long missions into enemy territory or of covering cover the considerable distances between theatres required by modern combat efficiency. In combat operations the tanker has also proved invaluable in the rescue of tactical aircraft with damaged fuel systems: from the time of the

Vietnam War onward, many hundreds of aircraft have been able to return safely to base only because of tanker support.

The B-36 was an interim type in fact if not in theory, and was replaced from the early 1950s onwards by the remarkable Boeing B-47 Stratojet and Boeing B-52 Stratofortress turbojet-powered bombers operating in the medium and heavy strategic roles respectively. The B-47 was a developed version of one of five turbine-powered experimental bomber designs ordered by the US Army Air Forces in 1943. A superbly clean and sleek type whose swept-wing design was finalized only after the Americans had digested the implications of German research data captured at the end of World War II, the Stratojet revealed how the aerodynamics hitherto applied only to small fighters could be successfully used on a large aeroplane with its wings swept at 35∞. Although it was classified only as a medium bomber, its range of 4,000 miles (6437 km) and maximum speed of 600 mph (966 km) made the B-47 a combat aeroplane far more formidable than the larger and theoretically more devastating B-36.

The wings were very thin, but supported the six turbojet engines: there were located as two each in the pods under the inner wing panels, and one in each of the pods under the outer wing panels. So thin were the wings, in fact, that they could not accommodate the main landing gear units, which were therefore constructed as two pairs of wheels in an tandem (bicycle) arrangement under the fuselage fore and aft of the weapons bay for a maximum 22,000-lb (9979-kg) load of nuclear or conventional bombs; ground stability was provided by small outrigger units that retracted into the inner engine pods. The Stratojet's normal crew comprised only three men arranged in tandem on ejector seats under a fighter-type canopy, although three more were carried in the fuselage of the electronic reconnaissance version.

The United Kingdom at last entered the field of strategic nuclear bombing with turbojet-engined aircraft. The first of these, essentially an interim type, was the Vickers Valiant, a four-engined machine with pleasing lines, and this was the first of the United Kingdom's 'V-bombers' to enter service. The Valiant's performance was limited by its intermediate design, which resulted in a wing of only modest sweep, but the type was used for developing the tactics of British nuclear bombing, and also for testing the British fission and fusion weapons.

The Americans followed the Stratojet with the B-52 Stratofortress, which entered service with the SAC in 1955. The family likeness to the B-47 was immediately apparent, but the B-52 is an altogether larger and more powerful aeroplane with a maximum speed in the order of 660 mph (1062 km/h), a range of 10,000 miles (16093 km) and a normal bomb load of up to 27,000 lb (12247 kg) of nuclear weapons carried internally that can be increased in some models to a maximum of 75,000 lb (34020 kg) of conventional weapons carried internally and externally. Powered by eight engines in four twin-engined pods under the wings, and fitted with the same sort of landing gear arrangement as the B-47, the B-52 has proved an enormously versatile strategic bomber, and was also used to devastating effect for tactical bombing in the Vietnam War. In 1961 the B-52G variant entered service with the capability to carry and launch two North American AGM-28 Hound Dog nuclear-tipped air-to-surface missiles, and from 1981 the last two variants (the B-52G and turbofan-powered B-52H) were revised for carriage of the Boeing AGM-86 air-launched cruise missile. Although the B-52 was supplanted as the SAC's most important strategic bomber from 1986 by the Rockwell B-1 Lancer, the type is still in comparatively widespread service in the mid-1990s as a conventional bomber and sea-control aeroplane.

The United Kingdom's small fleet of Valiant bombers had to be grounded and scrapped in 1964 because of fatigue problems, but by this time the RAF had its two primary V-bombers in service. These were the Avro Vulcan, the first large delta-wing aeroplane to enter service anywhere in the world, and the more conventional Handley Page Victor whose 'crescent' flying surfaces featured a sweep angle that gradually reduced from root to tip. Both of these long-range heavy (by US standards medium) bombers resulted from a requirement drafted as early as 1946, but official vacillation meant that both types went into production, with a consequent increase in aircraft unit costs and a complete doubling of training, spares and other procedures in the RAF. The only redeeming feature of this duplication was that the Victor emerged as an excellent tanker, and the Vulcan as a low-level attack bomber. The last few Vulcans were rescued from retirement in 1982 to participate in the Falklands campaign, when very long multiply flight-refuelled missions were flown against the runway at Argentine-held Stanley airport from a forward base on Ascension Island in the South Atlantic. The last Victor tankers were retired only in the mid-1990s when their airframe hours were exhausted by intensive operations in the 1991 UN-led campaign to expel the Iraqi occupiers from Kuwait.

Following the German lead which saw the deployment of two operational weapons and the development of many other fascinating weapons for a host of applications, several nations started to develop guided missiles for strategic and tactical tasks in the later stages of World War II and the period immediately following it. By the mid-1950s the larger forms of guided missile seemed to be maturing as virtually unstoppable delivery systems for nuclear weapons, while the smaller forms had become high-speed and deadly anti-aircraft weapons launched either from the ground or from defending fighters. Many people were convinced that the day of the manned aeroplane was all but over for military applications.

The two leaders in the field, the USSR and the United States, thought that there was room, and indeed need, for both types of weapon system: the missile to attack very swiftly with devastating effect, and the manned aeroplane to make a slower but more flexible and, most importantly, recallable, limited response. In 1957, though, the British government decided that the era of manned military aircraft was over, and that its current aircraft would be sufficient to give the RAF an effective capability as long as the service lasted as an independent force. This decision had the immediate effect of halting all development work on advanced types, including supersonic bombers, and can be

Below: One of the two classic British strategic bombers of the 1950s and 1960s, the Avro Vulcan (seen here in the form of the definitive Vulcan B.Mk 2 with improved wings, greater power and enhanced defensive electronics) was for its time the world's largest delta-winged aeroplane.

said to mark the end of the industry as a viable and independent entity, condemning the United Kingdom to expensive imports once the error in the government's decision had become apparent.

Yet in the 1950s the missile threat to manned aircraft was very real, especially in strategic terms. Nuclear bombers, it was thought, stood only a moderate chance of success against surface-to-air missiles and the air-to-air missiles launched by the enemy's fighters. Even with ECM (Electronic Counter-Measures) to jam and distort the enemies' radar, some new attack system would have to be found. Stand-off-missiles, which could be launched from parent aircraft some distance from the target, were one possible solution as they allowed the bomber to release its weapon(s) and turn back before encountering the defences ringing important military and political installations.

Another possibility, initially employed by adapted high-level bombers, required the bomber to make the penetration phase of its attack at very low level, below the lower edge of the enemy's radar cover, thus leaving the enemy ignorant of attack until it was too late to undertake any effective interception.

This option demanded aircraft of great strength, for turbulence is acute at very low levels, and also required that the relevant aircraft be fitted with advanced avionics with forward- and downward-looking radar hooked into a computer which can fly any such aeroplane round or over obstacles in its path much more surely than a pilot. The Vulcan and Buccaneer had very sturdy structures and proved ideal for this task in the 1960s and 1970s.

Finally, it was thought possible to evade enemy interception by flying very high and very fast, and it was this option (combined with the launch of decoy missiles to distract the enemy) which the Americans at first saw as the best way forward: a major factor in the American thinking was the superior range capability conferred by high-altitude flight, and range was a key element in the US Air Force's ability to strike at targets deep in the USSR from bases in the continental USA. In the late 1950s there first flew the Convair B-58 Hustler supersonic bomber, which entered service in 1960. Powered by four podded turbojets, the delta-winged Hustler was capable of 1,385 mph (2229 km/h) and had a service ceiling of 60,000 ft (18290 m). To keep the Hustler's fuselage as clean as possible for minimum drag and thus maximum speed, the designers put both the fuel for the outward leg of the mission and the weapon load in a streamlined pod under the fuselage. This was designed

Above: The era of variable-geometry wing planforms for operational aircraft was ushered in by the General Dynamics F-111 long-range interdictor during the later 1960s. Though initially beset by a number of technical problems, this aeroplane soon proved itself a great warbird and is still in useful service.

to be jettisoned over the target, leaving the unencumbered bomber to fly home at maximum speed.

The Hustler was not entirely successful, however, and its task was taken over in the late 1960s by the General Dynamics F-111 series. The first major combat aeroplane to enter service with a variable-geometry wing planform, the F-111 was schemed for the US Air Force, but was then overtaken by a political decision that it could also be developed as a carrierborne fleet air-defence fighter for the US Navy, the use of a single airframe/powerplant combination being thought to offer every likelihood of reduced development, procurement and operating costs. Powered by a pair of advanced turbofan engines, the F-111 has a speed well in excess of Mach 2 and proved itself capable of undertaking the strike, attack and reconnaissance roles previously performed by a number of different types.

In many respects the F-111 lived up to expectations from the beginning of the programme, but rising costs, engine limitations and airframe weight all caused problems. Nonetheless the TFX, as the type was known before it first flew in 1964, has proved a versatile and hard-hitting aircraft, eventually meeting or exceeding most of its performance requirements in a highly successful service career slated to continue into the next century. It should be noted, however, that the F-111B naval version was cancelled at early stage of its development because of intractable weight problems. The real virtues of the machine were initially obscured by political controversy about its cost and worries about a basic design flaw after several early aircraft were lost in the Vietnam War for no apparent reason. A simply cured technical problem was then diagnosed, and the F-111 matured as an exceptional combat aeroplane with a number of very real virtues, not least of which was the pioneering introduction of variable-geometry wings.

The concept of variable geometry is essentially simple. At low speeds, for take-off or landing, the wings are moved forward into their minimum-sweep position to present as much area to the airflow as possible and so bring down the stalling speed. At medium speeds, when the aeroplane is cruising, the wings are moved to their intermediate-sweep position to secure the optimum combination of low drag with maximum wing area to ensure fuel economy. For combat or high-speed dashes the wings are moved to their fully swept position to minimize drag. The main problems for the designer of such a wing planform lie in the evolution of the pivot and wing-actuation mechanism and the design of the fairings to smooth out the airflow between the wing and fuselage at any angles of sweep. Yet the concept offers great advantages in fuel economy and aircraft performance, and became completely accepted in the 1970s.

Similar progress in the design of bombers in strategic roles was been achieved in the USSR. With her most likely opponent clearly the other great superpower, the USSR like the United States was faced with the problem of how to deliver a great weight of conventional bombs, or powerful nuclear weapons, over the long distance separating the two countries. The USSR also needed bombers for operational-level employment over shorter ranges, but the most important aircraft in the Soviet arsenal have been the strategic heavy bombers.

The Tupolev Tu-4, the Soviet copy of he B-29, was in service in 1947, less than two years after work on the project began. And if two years seems a long time merely to copy another aeroplane and put into mass production, it must be remembered that the Soviet designers started from scratch. They had to dismantle the American aircraft, produce working drawings of every component and supervise all the modifications that had to be effected to suit the type to Soviet production techniques and methods; metallurgists had to discover what alloys the Americans had used and instruct Soviet producers in the right way to achieve the same results; and the engineers and planners had to produce entirely new factories and techniques to build a type markedly different from any of their own. Yet the advantages were colossal: in the B-29 the Soviets found good examples of all the latest American systems, and these they could copy and modify without a long preliminary research phase.

This treasure trove was quickly exploited in the Tu-16 'Badger', the USSR's first turbojet-powered strategic bomber, which first appeared in 1954 and inherited much from the Tupolev's continued effort to evolve

which also came as a shock in the west, is capable of Mach 1.5 but was considered deficient in range by the Soviets.

These aircraft were kept in the forefront of Soviet bomber capability for as long as possible by updates of their electronics and improvements to their engines. The aircraft were adapted for carrying more advanced weapons, including stand-off missiles, but they grew in obsolescence during the mid-1960s, and many were converted for the maritime reconnaissance role in their economical cruising range was more important than outright speed or weapon-carrying capability. The Tu-95 and M-4 frequently took-off from the USSR to cruise north of the United Kingdom, then cross the Atlantic to land in Cuba where they refuelled.

bombers, transports and even airliners from the basic Tu-4. The wings of the Tu-16 are well swept, and the two Soviet-designed engines are neatly buried in the wing roots. The Tu-16 was a match for its Western contemporaries in every respect, and more than a match in defensive armament. The Soviet designers had eagerly accepted both the German research into swept wings and the British experience with turbojet engines. The Mikulin engine, which first ran in 1950, was capable of a thrust of 8750 kg (19,290 lb), compared with the 10,000 lb (4536 kg) of Pratt & Whitney's first American-designed turbojet, the J57 which appeared in 1952.

Tupolev sprang a further surprise on the aviation world in 1955, with his monstrous Tu-95 'Bear' bomber. Powered by four 14,795-hp Kuznetsov turboprop engines driving very large contra-rotating propeller units, the Tu-95 was very sleek and the wings were moderately swept. The type had an excellent range of 12000 km (7,457 miles) and a maximum speed in the order of 900 km/h (559 mph). The Tu-114 civil version of the Tu-95 appeared slightly later, and set a number of world range-with-payload records. Both the Tu-16 and Tu-95 remain in service with the Russian air force in the mid-1990s, the former generally being employed for roles such as maritime reconnaissance, missile launching and air-to-air tanking, and the latter in longer-range maritime reconnaissance, missile launching and strategic bombing. So successful was the Tu-95, moreover, that a modernized variant was evolved as the Tu-142 that is used for the long-range anti-submarine role.

The other important heavy bomber developed by the Soviets in the 1950s was the Myasishchyev M-4 'Bison', which entered service in 1958. Like the Boeing bombers, it perched on a tandem main landing gear arrangement with outrigger units for ground stability. Finally removed from service in the late 1980s, the M-4 was powered by four turbojets buried in the wing roots, but while it was nearly as large as the B-52, the M-4 could carry only a 10000-kg (22,046-lb) weapon load, and both its speed and range were inferior to those of its American counterpart. The Soviets judged early in the type's career that the M-4 was operationally inferior to the Tu-95 despite the latter's reliance on a turboprop powerplant, and the M-4 was switched to the shorter-range strategic role before being converted as an air-to-air refuelling tanker.

To match the B-58 supersonic bomber, the Soviets revealed the existence of the Tu-22 'Blinder' in 1961. This is another sleek aeroplane of aggressive but somewhat unusual appearance as its two engines are located above the tailplane, one on each side of the vertical tail surfaces. The Tu-22,

The USSR's next strategic bomber is a very formidable aircraft, the variable-geometry Tu-22M 'Backfire'. Capable of Mach 2.3 at high altitude, the 'Backfire' can carry the largest free-fall nuclear weapons or a pair of stand-off missiles.

The Americans did not continue with the concept of supersonic medium bombers after the B-58, but decided instead to design a supersonic heavy bomber for the penetration role. This aeroplane was the Rockwell B-1, which offered excellent capabilities in a role that was then deemed obsolete in the face of a steadily improved soviet surface-to-air missile capability. The B-1 was therefore cancelled in its high-supersonic B-1A form, only to be reinstated later as the more modestly supersonic B-1B Lancer optimized for the low-level role. As an alternative to the B-1A, the Americans decided to procure more ballistic missiles (both submarine- and land-launched) and large numbers of the new generation of cruise missiles. These small turbofan-powered aircraft carry a potent warhead and are guided by an INS (Inertial Navigation System) that is updated over major landmarks by radar comparison of the feature being overflown against an image derived from satellite reconnaissance and stored in the guidance's package's digital computer memory. Being light as well as small, these missiles can be carried in large

Above: Designed as the Soviet counterpart to the Boeing B-52 Stratofortress, the Myasishchyev M-4 'Bison' proved deficient in range and was built only in small numbers compared with its rival, the great Tupolev Tu-95 'Bear' that was ordered as a turboprop-powered backup type but showed itself to be an altogether superior warplane in everything but range.

Below: The Dassault/Dornier Alpha Jet was designed as the Franco-German equivalent of the BAe Hawk, but has not proved as successful as the British aeroplane in operational or commercial terms.

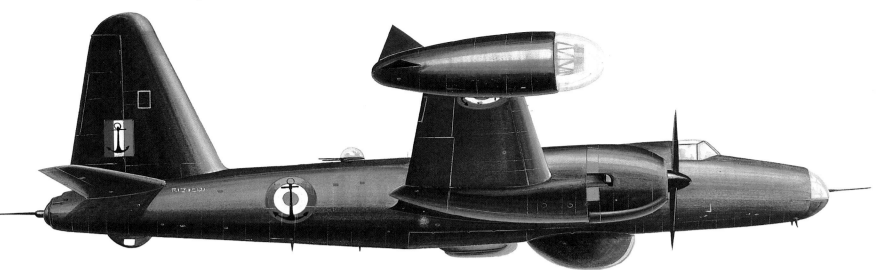

numbers by aircraft such as the B-52 and B-1B, and in addition to their ability to sneak through the enemy defences as a result of their 'stealthy' design (see last chapter), they can be programmed to fly a fast, jinking and very low trajectory.

Light bombers have been in decline since the end of World War II, principally because attack fighters can pack almost as great a punch and are considerably cheaper to build and operate. There have, however, been two classic examples: the British built the English Electric Canberra, and the Soviets produced the Ilyushin Il-28 'Beagle'. The Canberra was conceived in 1945, and the first prototype flew in 1949. Since then the aircraft has served with great distinction in many air forces, including that of the United States, and has still a limited future in smaller air forces. Extremely versatile and manoeuvrable, the Canberra could outfly most of the fighters current in its heyday, and

established a number of records. The Il-28 flew two years before the British bomber, and despite its obsolescence is still a popular aeroplane in the countries within the former Soviet sphere of influence.

The Americans have not relied on conversions of bombers for their maritime reconnaissance aircraft, but have produced such excellent machines as the Lockheed P2V Neptune, and the Lockheed P-3 Orion derived from the Electra airliner. After years of service from the Avro Shackleton derivative of the Lincoln, the RAF currently deploys the four-engined Hawker Siddeley Nimrod, based very loosely on the Comet airliner. This is possibly the best maritime reconnaissance aeroplane in the world, and combines long endurance on two engines with a high-speed dash capability when using all four. The Nimrod is the only such aeroplane in the world powered by turbojets rather than turboprops. Several other countries have also produced useful maritime reconnaissance aircraft, most notably the twin-engined Breguet Atlantic (later Dassault Atlantic 1 that is being superseded in the 1990s by the Dassault Atlantique 2) landplane from France, the four-engined Shin Meiwa PS-1 flying boat from Japan, and the four-engined Ilyushin Il-38 'May' landplane for the USSR.

The only other country to have produced advanced combat aircraft is Sweden, whose policy of strongly armed neutrality led to the development of the highly original and very interesting Saab 35 Draken (dragon) double-delta and Saab 37 Viggen (thunderbolt) canard multi-role aircraft, both capable of performance in the region of Mach 2. The success of these two Swedish aircraft should have been an object lesson for the West: the authorities decided what they needed, and then every effort was used to develop the right machine for the specification. Although costly, such a programme is nothing like as expensive as the competitive programmes which have been initiated in other countries.

The vast cost of advanced aircraft meant that the only aircraft produced by other nations have been of limited performance. Even the rich European countries reached the stage in the mid-1960s in which

Above: Designed in World War II as a land-based patrol type, the Lockheed P2V (later P-2) Neptune matured in service after that war as an exceptional anti-submarine type that was evolved with podded turbojets to boost performance from the level attainable with the original pair of powerful radial piston engines.

Left: The Douglas A3D (later A-3) Skywarrior was designed to provide the US Navy's aircraft-carriers with a bomber capable of delivering a nuclear bombload. The aircraft were later adapted to the conventional role and then evolved into variants for electronic warfare, reconnaissance and inflight refuelling. This is an EKA-3B Skywarrior that combines limited attack capability with ECM training and inflight refuelling tanker capabilities.

Opposite Bottom: The North American F-100 Super Sabre was the first Western fighters with genuinely supersonic performance.

collaborative projects became financially as well as politically attractive: only in this way could the cost be spread to sufficient numbers of taxpayers, and large, relatively economical production runs assured. Excellent examples of the trend were the SEPECAT strike, attack and reconnaissance fighter built by the United Kingdom and France, the Panavia Tornado variable-geometry multi-role combat aeroplane built by the United Kingdom, West Germany and Italy, and the Dassault/Dornier Alpha Jet light attack/trainer aeroplane built by France and West Germany. Such co-operation was both financially reasonable for the countries concerned and gave opportunities for the creation of exciting new aircraft.

The Hawker Siddeley (now British Aerospace) Harrier vertical take-off and landing aeroplane, with its radical arrangement of vectoring jetpipes to deflect the engine's thrust, was possibly the last major combat aircraft built by a single nation, with the exception of the United States, Russia, France, China and Sweden. This tendency is already evident, and in the early 1980s other collaborative ventures firmly under way were the Italo-Brazilian AMX International AMX light attack fighter developed by Aeritalia, Aermacchi and EMBRAER, and the Italo-British European Helicopter Industries EH.101 helicopter being developed by Westland and Agusta. During the first half of the 1980s the United Kingdom was actively seeking partners for the collaborative development of the Agile Combat Aircraft technology demonstrator to be built as a vital step towards the evolution of a new European combat aircraft based on the British Aerospace P.110 design with contributions from West German and French companies: this effort finally matured as the Eurofighter 2000 discussed in the last chapter. The other side of this same coin is perhaps demonstrated by the fact that further development of the Harrier concept crossed the Atlantic to the United States, where McDonnell Douglas was largely responsible for the much enhanced AV-8B Harrier II for the US Marine Corps and, in British-assembled form, Harrier GR.Mk 5 for the RAF.

In the field of combat aircraft capability, the features that were receiving the most avid development in the 1980s were not performance factors as such (though these were still considered desirable where they did not conflict with the following) but improved combat capability through aspects such as increased agility, weapons flexibility, accuracy of navigation and weapons delivery, and reliability in a number of concomitant operational roles. Advances were thus being made in the sphere of avionics (especially in the relation of external factors to the whole mission, using a

computer for data analysis and processing) and the controllability of aircraft in all flight regimes by the use of electronically signalled control movements ('fly-by-wire' control system), advanced aerodynamics and engines with considerably improved power/weight ratios. This led to a new generation of combat aircraft, epitomized by production machines such as the General Dynamics F-16 Fighting Falcon and McDonnell Douglas F/A-18 Hornet, and to planned developments such as the ACA, a rewinged version of the F-16 evaluated as the F-16XL, and the Saab JAS 39 Gripen (griffon) fighter. Much was also being achieved in the enhancement of the capabilities enjoyed by current aircraft, as indicated by the provision of canard foreplanes on the Dassault Mirage 4000 prototype and on the Israel Aircraft Industries Kfir-C2 production fighter, and by the increasing use of improved targeting aids carried as external pods.

Above: The Hawker Siddeley (originally de Havilland) Sea Vixen was a carrierborne multi-role fighter.

Below: The Mitsubishi T-2CCV was evolved as a Control-Configured Vehicle derivative of the T-2 supersonic trainer for research into the CCV technologies that could be applied to the FS-X Japanese development of the General Dynamics F-16 Fighting Falcon fighter.

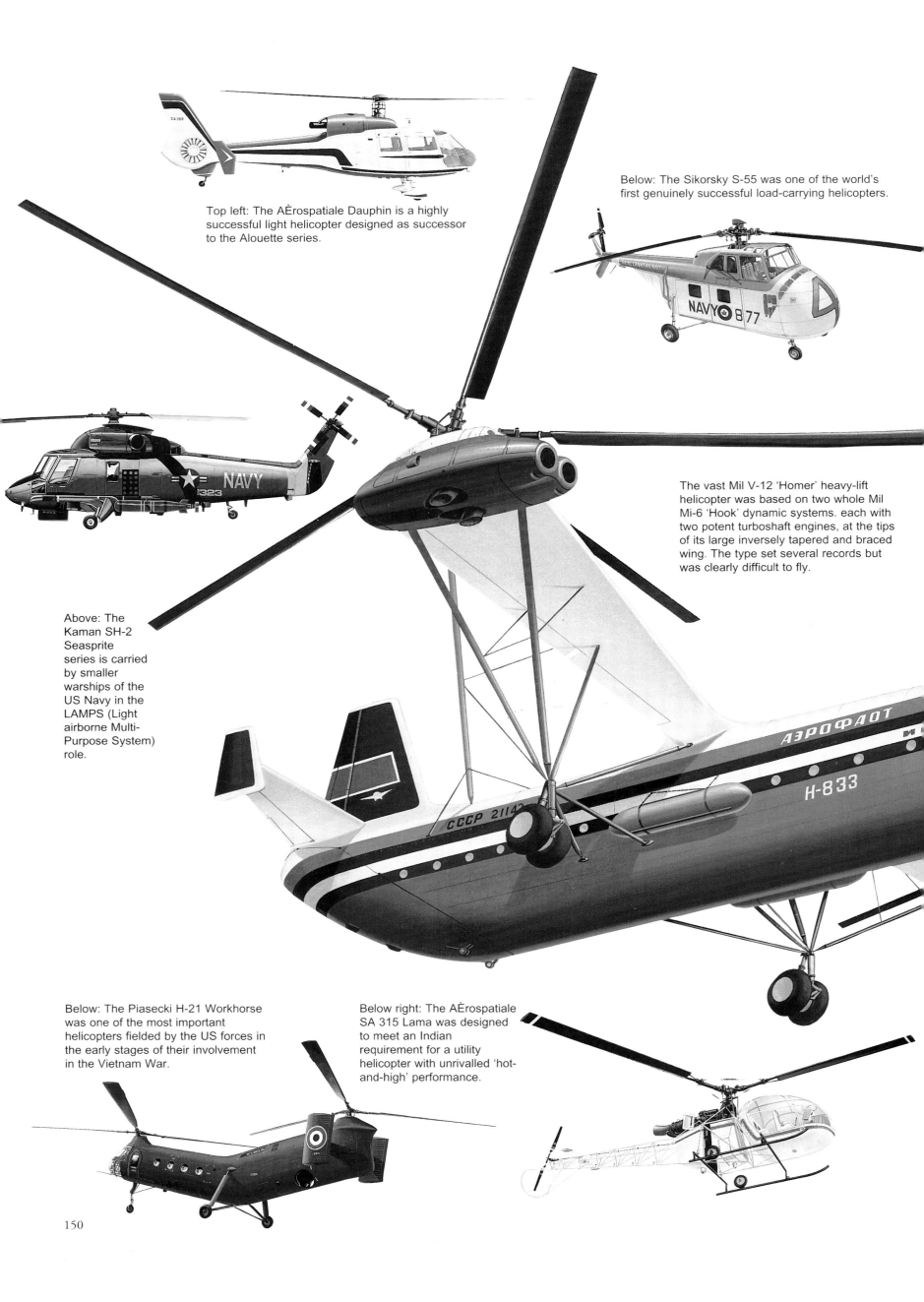

Top left: The AÈrospatiale Dauphin is a highly successful light helicopter designed as successor to the Alouette series.

Below: The Sikorsky S-55 was one of the world's first genuinely successful load-carrying helicopters.

The vast Mil V-12 'Homer' heavy-lift helicopter was based on two whole Mil Mi-6 'Hook' dynamic systems. each with two potent turboshaft engines, at the tips of its large inversely tapered and braced wing. The type set several records but was clearly difficult to fly.

Above: The Kaman SH-2 Seasprite series is carried by smaller warships of the US Navy in the LAMPS (Light airborne Multi-Purpose System) role.

Below: The Piasecki H-21 Workhorse was one of the most important helicopters fielded by the US forces in the early stages of their involvement in the Vietnam War.

Below right: The AÈrospatiale SA 315 Lama was designed to meet an Indian requirement for a utility helicopter with unrivalled 'hot-and-high' performance.

Rotary-Wing Flight and Vertical Take-Off

The earliest type of flying machine for which there is still definite evidence was a model helicopter. It resembled a small horizontal four-bladed windmill that lifted into the air when its spindle was rotated by a drawstring. The image of this model dates from about 1325, so it seems likely that the concept of what we now called the helicopter has fascinated aviation pioneers since a time before that date.

In about 1500 Leonardo da Vinci turned his fertile mind to the helicopter, although he had no concept of true aerodynamic lift. His drawing for a helicopter demonstrates its designer's natural genius and could possibly have risen into the air if built in model form, but it was very eccentric. Leonardo's design was basically an airscrew in the literal sense of the word: a helical wing which if rotated would have 'screwed' itself up into the air.

This and later designs might possibly have worked in model form but would have been completely impractical in full-size form because they ignored the problems of control, most especially over the effects of the rotor's torque. Like the aeroplane, the helicopter is based on the concept of aerodynamic lift. While a conventional aeroplane is propelled forward so that the circulation of air past the wings generates lift, the helicopter relies on the rotation of the rotor to create the flow of air past the rotor blades for the generation of lift.

By 1912 two French helicopters had left the ground, although neither could be said to have flown in the proper sense of the word since neither had cyclic pitch control or any other means of adopting a given course in the air. The first was built by the Breguet brothers. Powered by a 50-hp Antoinette engine, this Breguet-Richet Gyroplane I first rose into the air at Douai on 29 September 1907: four men, one at each corner of the machine, had to steady the craft with long poles. The honour of having built the manned free-flying helicopter must go to another French pioneer, Paul Cornu. Powered by a 25-hp Antoinette engine, his twin-rotor helicopter lifted (but only just lifted) its designer into the air on 13 November 1907.

The Breguet brothers were convinced that they were on the right lines and meanwhile persevered with their efforts: in 1908 they produced a developed form of their first machine as the Breguet-Richet Gyroplane II. On 22 July and 18 September the machine left the ground at Douai, and was then modified as the Gyroplane II-bis for exhibition in Paris at the end of the year. Test flights with the Gyroplane II-bis were made in April 1909, but the helicopter was destroyed in its hangar by a storm during the following month. The development of the helicopter then effectively ceased until after World War I.

Inventors and visionaries were hard at work again soon after 1918. Several experimental types managed to rise into the air, but none of them achieved anything more than that. It was 1924 before another French pioneer, Etienne Oehmichen, made the world's first closed-circuit helicopter flight of 1 km (0.62 miles) in his four-rotor No. 2 machine, at Arlonans on 4 May. This was an advance, but only a marginal advance, for the problems of control were still formidable.

Incidence and pitch control were at last brought to a practical level by the experiments of a Spanish pioneer, the Marquis Raoul Pateras de Pescara, who produced a series of helicopters in Spain and France between 1919 and 1925. Yet this far-sighted man, whose machines had clearly overcome the main problem of unequal lift, was denied fame by his failure in the matter of torque control. In other respects the Pescara helicopters were good machines, and showed what could be anticipated once full control had been achieved.

Other pioneers active in the early 1920s were the American Henry Berliner, who made a successful hovering flight in 1922 after having considered the problem since 1905, de Bothezat also in the United States, and Louis Brennan, superintendent of the United Kingdom's torpedo factory during World War I and later head of the rotorcraft department at the Royal Aircraft Establishment, Farnborough. Like Oehmichen, all these men saw their hopes founder on the problems of cyclic pitch control.

The key figure in the development of rotorcraft was now another Spaniard, Juan de la Cierva. The machine he invented (and patented as the Autogiro) was not a helicopter at all, however, but rather the gyroplane or, as it later became, the autogyro. In this type of machine, the lifting rotor is unpowered: lift is generated by the freely windmilling overhead rotor as an engine and conventional propeller drive the machine through the air: most early autogyros had a tractor engine/propeller combination at the front of the aeroplane-type fuselage, while most later autogyros have used a pusher engine/propeller combination at the rear of a fuselage nacelle that also supports the conventional tail unit by means of a boom extending rearward under the propeller. The autogyro depends on forward motion in the air, without which the rotor will stop revolving and the machine will fall.

Cierva's driving passion was the creation of heavier-than-air craft that could not be stalled, as had happened in the fatal crash of his first fixed-wing aeroplane. Cierva's first three autogyros, built and tested between 1920 and 1922, failed because of their use of inflexible rotor blades. In 1922, however, Cierva built a model with articulated hinges that permitted the blades to flap: as they rotated the blades were thus free to fall as they retreated at a lower relative speed and rise as they advanced at a higher relative speed, thereby

Below: The Focke-Wulf Fw 61 was the world's first successful helicopter, though the great overall width resulting from the side-by-side rotors was a distinct operational disadvantage.

NX 28996

Above: Though the Fw 61 was successful, the Vought-Sikorsky VS-300 must be deemed the precursor of the helicopter as a practical vehicle, for it was this machine that introduced the classic helicopter configuration with a single main rotor and effective cyclic-pitch control.

Right: The Cierva (Weir) W.9 was a British helicopter prototype that validated the concept of jet thrust to cancel the torque reaction of the main rotor. Engine cooling air, driven by a fan with multiple variable-pitch blades, was ducted to the rear of the boom and mixed with hot exhaust gases from the 200-hp de Havilland Gipsy Six inline piston engine and then ducted out of a variable-shutter outlet on the port side of the boom.

Right: The Flettner Fl 185 prototype that first flew in 1936 had a single main rotor driven by the Siemens-Halske (Bramo) Sh-14A radial piston engine. This was located in the central fuselage and also drove a nose-mounted cooling fan and two anti-torque propellers on lateral outriggers.

modifying the apparent angle of attack and equalizing the amount on lift generated on each side of the rotor. This system was applied to the C.4 Autogiro that made its first successful flight on 9 January 1923. Cierva had understood the full nature of the problem and found a practical solution to it. The real beauty of the system lay in its simplicity: the blades moved automatically until the whole rotating system was in equilibrium.

In 1925 Cierva decided to move to the United Kingdom, where he hoped there would be a better market for his Autogiro. The flapping mechanism became very sophisticated in later models, but remained essentially the same as in the C.4, operating entirely automatically and indeed simply under the influence of purely aerodynamic forces. Although its success gave helicopter designers a clear indication of what they should be looking for, the autogyro system could not be used as it stood: the application of power to the rotor prevented the system from operating automatically.

Cierva enjoyed a moderate success as his fully developed Autogiros became popular with both the public and the military. For this he was indebted to the exhibitions and test flights undertaken by his two most important assistants, Harold F. Pitcairn in the United States, and Captain Frank Courtney in the United Kingdom. The Autogiro's primary limitation, it should be noted, was its related inability to take-off vertically or to hover in the air.

The second aspect did not worry Cierva unduly, but he was determined to find some practical method for allowing vertical take-off, for this would increase the military utility of the Autogiro. Cierva had already introduced a system for spinning the rotor before take-off, thus shortening the ground run, and a pitch-changing mechanism was fitted to Autogiros in the

D-EFLT

late 1920s to supplement the flapping motion in equalizing lift. The final link, a clutch device, was demonstrated in July 1933. Power from the engine at the nose of the fuselage was now taken along a series of shafts back through the fuselage and up to the rotor. This was engaged to the drive and spun to flying speed before lift was allowed to develop, the clutch was released, and all the power was applied to the propeller that drove the machine through the air as soon as the spun-up rotor had lifted it into the air.

In this way the Autogiro could be made to jump start into the air, where the propeller provided the forward speed which made the rotor turn on its own. The key to rotor spin-up on the ground was the pitch-control mechanism, which kept the rotor blades at zero incidence, preventing them from generating asymmetric lift until the moment when the clutch was disengaged and the rotor resumed its natural performance. The whole machine 'jumped' some 20 ft (6 m) into the air before the propeller took over.

These Autogiros were a startling sight in operation and proved very successful, continuing in service well into World War II. After this they faded into obscurity until rescued in the 1960s by a wave of enthusiasm for miniature types intended only for sporting use. The main users of Autogiros in World War II were the British, who used the type's ability to stay almost in one spot to help calibrate radar equipment, a function that could not readily have been undertaken by conventional aircraft. The Germans developed an experimental unpowered autogyro, the Focke-Achgelis Fa 330,

for possible use as an observation platform for U-boats. It could be dismantled into small units for stowage, and ilot, which was a useful background for learning to handle a new type of aeroplane.

The prototype of the world's first successful helicopter flew on 26 June 1936 and soon proved its worth. Powered by a 160-hp Bramo (Siemens-Halske) Sh.14A radial piston engine, the Fw 61 was lifted and propelled by a pair of counter-rotating rotors mounted on the ends of two steel-tube outriggers set out from the fuselage based on that of the Focke-Wulf Fw 44 Stieglitz basic training aeroplane. As in the Breguet type, but rather more clumsily, the torque reaction of each rotor cancelled that of the other rotor and made the machine directionally stable. The Fw 61 set up some impressive world records for helicopters, including a distance of 230 km (143 miles), speed of 122 km/h (76 mpg), endurance of 1 hour 20 minutes 49 seconds, and altitude of 3427 m (11,243 ft).

The Fw 61 was fully controllable and thereby proved that helicopters were practical flying machines, but it was only a prototype and therefore lacked the power/weight ratio that permitted the carriage of any sort of payload. So the designers decided to refine and lighten their basic concept before producing a production model.

Four years passed before the Focke-Achgelis Fa 223 Drache (dragon) was ready for production in 1940, and even after the type was ordered for German military service, production was hampered by Allied air attacks and only nine production-standard Fa 223s were completed during the war; another three were built after the war from salvaged parts.

Sikorsky had considered the possibilities of helicopters and other rotorcraft (and indeed built two unsuccessful prototypes in 1909 and 1910) even before he left the U S S R , but did not start definitive work on such types until the 1930s. In 1938 he produced his Vought-Sikorsky VS-300. Although it appeared crude in finish, with its uncovered metal-tube fuselage, the VS-300 must be regarded as the true ancestor of the modern helicopters. Fitted with cyclic pitch control and powered by a 7 5 - h p Lycoming piston engine, the VS-300 was lifted by a single rotor whose torque reaction was counteracted by a small tail rotor.

Left: The main rotor head of a modern helicopter is a conceptually simple but practically complex assembly.

Friedrich von Doblhoff, an Austrian, made his mark with the first jet-propelled helicopter, the Doblhoff WNF 342. This introduced the unusual concept of feeding compressed air and fuel into combustion chambers at the tips of the rotor blades, where the vapour mixture was burned to provide thrust. The generation of power at the rotor tips rather than in the fuselage avoided torque problems and made the tail rotor unnecessary. Experimental models with this sort of propulsion have been tested ever since, but despite its clear advantages the type has never really caught on.

The helicopter's only major drawback in an urban environment has been its noisiness. At first this was not an acute problem, for the smaller engines used in the early 1950s were relatively quiet and the public was less concerned than later about the environment. Then the growing size and, perhaps more importantly, the increasing weight of helicopters required the use of more powerful and therefore considerably more noisy engines.

At the same time, improved control and rotors allowed the helicopter to undertake a wider variety of roles with an increasingly heavy payload.

This tendency was further increased by the development of a turbine engine suitable for helicopter installations. This is the turboshaft, which has a considerably higher power/weight ratio than the radial piston engine. In itself this has improved the helicopter's payload capability, but other important advantages of a turboshaft powerplant are greater fuel economy, relatively vibration-free running, increased reliability, reduced volume, and lighter weight. These last two factors have been particularly important, for they opened the way for the powerplant to be relocated from the fuselage to a position above the cabin and close to the rotor shaft: this made greater fuselage volume available for payload, and also resulted in a further lightening of the dynamic system by removing the need for long transmission shafts connecting any fuselage-mounted engine with the gearbox located at the base of the rotor shaft.

The United States had pioneered the practical helicopter, and this allowed American companies other than Sikorsky and Bell (most notably Hiller, Hughes, Kaman, Piasecki and Vertol) to develop a thriving international business as well as excellent sales within the United States.

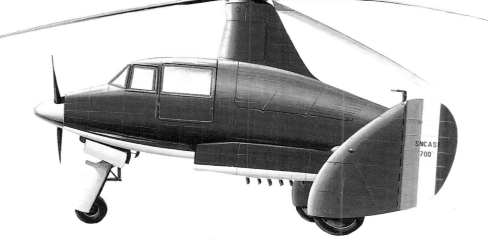

Below: The Sud-Est SE.20 was an experimental concept that led to no practical result.

Kaman concentrated on particular designs of twin-rotor helicopters, the first two on long-bodied machines with counter-rotating rotors at each end of the fuselage, and the last on short stumpy designs with an intermeshing arrangement of counter-rotating rotors.

By the 1950s several European companies had entered the arena of helicopter design and manufacture. Westland, Saunders-Roe and Bristol were early leaders in the United Kingdom, but by the 1960s

Below: The Flettner Fl 282 Kolibri preceded the Vought-Sikorsky VS-300 into the air, and was notable for its fully practical dynamic system with two intermeshing two-blade rotors.

Westland, licence-holders for Sikorsky designs, had become dominant. Sud-Est (later part of Aérospatiale) took most of the market in France, Bölkow in Germany and Agusta in Italy. Oddly enough, as the number of aircraft manufacturers declined in the 1960s and 1970s, that of helicopter manufacturers increased, especially in Latin America and Japan, although many of these produced only a few machines or just a single type before fading into obscurity.

The Mil design bureau has a virtual monopoly in the USSR, with some outstanding designs in several categories of medium single-rotor and heavy twin-rotor machines. The most important designer of naval helicopters, however, has been the Kamov bureau, which concentrates on helicopters of compact design through the use of a co-axial arrangement of two contra-rotating rotors.

After the United States, the USSR was the next major country to produce a helicopter of its own design. The Mil Mi-1 'Hare' entered production in 1948 as a light transport type, but was soon supplanted by the Mi-2 'Hoplite' that was also built in large numbers. A year later the American Stanley Hiller introduced his Hiller 12 series of light utility helicopters, of which eventually more than 2,000 were built. Helicopters as small as these represented the only early designs which could not readily be adapted for other uses, as their payloads were so small.

Training, observation and light communications were the only tasks that could be undertaken with any real efficiency. The helicopter thus began to come into its own only during the early 1950s, partly as a result of the celebrated successes of American 'choppers' in Korea. New production facilities were built in other countries and numerous helicopter designs appeared in the first half of the decade. Sud-Est, a French nationalized group, produced its first model in 1951. A utility helicopter, the Alouette (lark) then proved outstandingly successful and the most versatile helicopter designed in France: production variants were the Alouette II and enlarged Alouette III which were each developed in variants with the Turbomeca Artouste and later the Turbomeca Astazou turboshafts. The Yakovlev Yak-24 'Horse' appeared in the same year, and was the world's largest helicopter at the time. Intended as a military transport, the Yak-24 set a number of world rotorcraft records but was built only in small numbers because of intractable handling problems.

Most of the helicopters built up to the mid-1950s had a cruising speed of just under 100 mph (160 km/h) and a range of something like 250 miles (400 km). The main differentiating factor in their performance, therefore, had been the load they could carry. This was increasing rapidly in later types, and in the next generation of helicopters the performance also improved.

An indication of general improvement came in 1955 with the performance of the turboshaft-powered Alouette II: cruising speed rose to nearly 185 km/h (115 mph) and range to 645 km (400 miles), and the model sold widely to civil and military operators in many parts of the world. The same year saw the introduction of the first variants of the world's only really successful co-axial twin-rotor helicopter series, namely the Kamov Ka-15 'Hen' and Ka-18 'Hog'. These entered service with the Soviet army and navy, and were also used by Aeroflot, the Soviet airline organization. The performance of these two Kamov helicopters was inferior to that of the Alouette II, but their importance lies in the fact that they paved the way for the Ka-25 'Hormone'.

The most important helicopter adopted by the US forces up to that time appeared in 1956. This was the Bell Model 204, which was a nine-seat utility type that entered service as the HU-1 (later UH-1) Iroquois but is best remembered as the 'Huey' of the Vietnam War. In the basic model the continued improvement in helicopter performance was indicated by a cruising speed of 126 mph (205 km/h) combined with a range of 320 miles (515 km). The Model 204 variants were powered by variants of the Lycoming T53 turboshaft rated at between 770 and 1,100 hp, and these were followed by larger numbers of the Model 205 variants with accommodation for 15 men including the pilot, and an uprated T53 powerplant rated at between 1,100 and 1,400 hp. Variants of these two basic types were converted and developed in to a host of special combat roles, the most significant of which was the Model 209 HueyCobra armed combat helicopter. This was evolved for the close support of the troops landed from 'Huey' helicopters, and was in essence a narrow-fuselage derivative of the Model 204 with the dynamic system of the Model 205. Setting a pattern that has remained essentially unaltered in the intervening years, the fuselage accommodated the pilot above and behind the co-pilot/gunner: the pilot could fire the disposable armament carried on the four hardpoints under the HueyCobra's stub

Above: The Sud-Ouest SO.1220 Djinn was the first helicopter to enter production anywhere in the world with a rotor driven by the 'cold jet' principle of torqueless thrust by tip-mounted pressure jets.

Right: The Sud-Est (later Aérospatiale) Alouette II was the world's first helicopter to enter large-scale production with a turboshaft powerplant.

Below: The most important helicopter of the 1960s was the Bell H-1 Iroquois (almost invariably called 'Huey') series. This was produced in a large and bewildering assortment of marks as variants of the company's baseline Model 204, stretched and upengined Model 205, and twin-engined Model 212 helicopter family.

wings, but the primary weapon operator was the co-pilot/gunner who also handled the chin-mounted traversing turret with its elevating armament of one multi-barrel machine-gun and one grenade launcher. Quickly evolved and simply equipped, the HueyCobra was then evolved into more powerful variants with heavier and more versatile armament aimed with the aid of increasingly sophisticated avionics. The HueyCobra is still in widespread service in its latest AH-1S form (four subvariants). A two-engined version was developed for use by the US Marine Corps, and the original AH-1J SeaCobra has since been replaced by the upgraded AH-1T Improved SeaCobra and the AH-1W SuperCobra. All these Model 204, Model 205 and Model 209 variants retain the two-blade type of main rotor introduced on the original HU-1, but Bell is still continuing development of the narrow-fuselage marque and offers a much enhanced model with a four-blade main rotor.

The Soviet Mi-6 'Hook' of 1957 brought a new dimension to heavy-lift helicopter capabilities, setting world records with payloads of more than 20000 kg (44,092 lb). The Mi-6 was also the world's biggest helicopter of the time, and led to the Mi-l0 'Harke' flying crane helicopter of 1960. This later model was intended to carry heavy, bulky loads, and has a wide-spread landing gear arrangement under the fuselage so that a load can be brought up under the helicopter and attached to the lifting points.

More advanced ideas reached the hardware stage during the late 1950s, and in 1960 the important Sikorsky S-61 emerged from the experimental shops. The type soon entered service with the US Navy as the SH-3 Sea King with a powerplant of two General Electric T58 turboshafts. The Sea King was of great operational importance at the time of its introduction as the world's first all-weather helicopter effectively combining the submarine hunting and submarine killing roles that had previously required the efforts of two helicopters, one to hunt with sonar and the other to kill with depth charges and/or homing torpedoes; the US Coast Guard deploys a variant of the same basic type as a patrol and rescue helicopter. The US Air Force used the same basic airframe for transport missions and for rescuing aircraft and their crews, though these CH-3 and HH-3 Jolly Green Giant helicopters had a revised fuselage with retractable tricycle landing gear, a ventral ramp/door arrangement, and features such as armament and self-sealing fuel tanks. There were also two S-61 civil variants that secured modest but useful orders for the airliner and resources exploitation support industries.

In its land-based military role, the S-61 was supported by the 1961 Boeing-Vertol CH-47 Chinook medium-lift helicopter, which was particularly valuable in Vietnam for moving vehicles and artillery to the weight of 12,000 lb (5443 kg) into every combat area. The Chinook has stayed in production up to the present, the latest helicopters of this important type having enormously more power than their predecessors as

The Sikorsky VS-316 was the definitive development of the pioneering VS-300, and in 1944 became the world's first helicopter to enter full production when ordered by the US Army Air Forces as the R-4.

well as much enhanced avionics.

In 1962 the Americans finally produced a proper heavy-lift helicopter in the Sikorsky S-64, which bears a close resemblance to the Soviet Mi-10 and entered service as the CH-54 Tarhe. This also proved useful in Vietnam, where it was tested to the limits of its structural strength and versatility. The S-64, for example, was used for naval minesweeping and even to lift light naval vessels. France's only heavy-lift helicopter, the Aérospatiale Super Frelon (super hornet), appeared in 1962 after development with Sikorsky support in the development of the three-engined dynamic system and associated rotors, and was adopted by several other nations: the Israelis made good use of the type as a commando carrier, but the Super Frelon is very versatile and is currently operated by the French as a land-based heavy anti-submarine helicopter.

The Bell Model 209 HueyCobra of 1965 was the first helicopter gunship. The type's advent heralded the split of helicopter design into more specialized types. Although it suffered heavy losses in Vietnam, the HueyCobra soon proved itself a valuable weapon

Above: The Mil Mi-10 'Harke' was developed as a specialized flying crane helicopter with provision for a large load or a load-carrying platform to be installed between the straddling legs of the quadricycle landing gear.

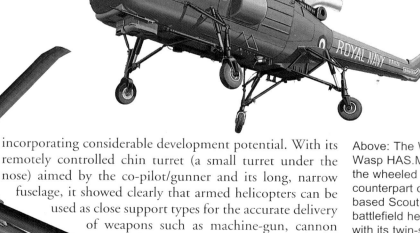

incorporating considerable development potential. With its remotely controlled chin turret (a small turret under the nose) aimed by the co-pilot/gunner and its long, narrow fuselage, it showed clearly that armed helicopters can be used as close support types for the accurate delivery of weapons such as machine-gun, cannon and grenade fire as well as unguided rockets and, in later variants, guided missiles such as the Hughes BGM-71 TOW

Currently the world's most advanced battle-field helicopter, the McDonnell Douglas AH-64 Apache is a very expensive but very capable type whose primary task is the detection and destruction of battle tanks.

Above: The Westland Wasp HAS.Mk 1 was the wheeled naval counterpart of the land-based Scout AH.Mk 1 battlefield helicopter with its twin-skid landing gear.

helicopters in inaccessible regions, and there is no reason why other nations should not also use them.

Whatever else helicopters may be used for, they remain ideally suited to the SAR role. Over the years helicopters have saved thousands of lives – people snatched from the tide on

Right: The Mil Mi-6 'Hook' heavy-lift helicopter could be fitted with substantial wings to offload he main rotor in forward flight.

secluded beaches, sailors rescued in storms or when their vessel has sunk, and the sick or critically injured lifted from ships and flown rapidly for treatment in hospital.

However, the helicopter and autogyro are not the only aircraft capable of vertical take-off. Several other varieties have been tried, but the only practical method other than the rotor seems to be the thrust of turbine engines. This has the advantage

wire-guided anti-tank missile; the HueyCobra can also carry a cannon pack. Although other helicopters had been fitted with armament (principally machine-guns firing from the side doors and a number of different light air-to-surface missile types) for use in the close support role, it was with the HueyCobra that the concept came to maturity.

Right: The PAH-1 is the German army's anti-tank derivative of the MBB BO 105 general-purpose helicopter, and carries on lateral outriggers anti-tank missiles that are guided via a stabilized sight let into the cabin roof.

The Hughes OH-6 Cayuse light utility helicopter, which appeared in 1966, also proved its qualities in Vietnam and has been adopted by several other countries. Part of its success derives from its advanced structural design, giving the OH-6 great strength and rigidity at a low weight, and a sleekly streamlined fuselage. The combination of these factors made the OH-6 agile for its size, although not aerobatic. Further development of the type by Hughes and then by McDonnell Douglas after it had bought the company, resulted in the Model 500 intended mainly for the civil market but also developed into the Model 500 Defender series with provision for many types of armament.

The oddest helicopter of

that once such an aeroplane has taken-off it can fly conventionally at high purely wingborne speed without the cumbersome drag of even the most advanced rotor systems.

The two most efficient systems of direct lift with jet engines are the vectored thrust used by the British Hawker Siddeley (now British Aerospace) Harrier close-support aeroplane, and the direct thrust of special engines as used in aircraft such as the West German

Right: The Westland Sea King HAS.Mk 1 was evolved in the United Kingdom as a more capable version of the Sikorsky SH-3 Sea King, and has since been developed further in this basic role as well as into variants optimized for the search-and-rescue, troop transport and even airborne early warning roles.

the 1960s was the Mil V-12 'Homer' of 1969. This did not enter production, but remains the largest helicopter yet built with a large inversely tapered braced wing each carrying at its tip a complete Mi-6 'Hook' dynamic system (powerplant and main rotor) for the carriage of payloads in the order of 40000 kg (88,183 lb).

The helicopter continues to flourish as a commercial vehicle, especially in the United States, and larger helicopters may in future be built specifically for the civilian market. The Soviets pioneered the use of heavy-lift

Dornier Do 31 experimental transport and EWR-Süd VJ 101 experimental combat aeroplane. In the British system, the exhaust nozzles of the centrally located engine can be swivelled downwards for direct lift, and then gradually turned back to the horizontal position to drive the aeroplane forward into increasingly rapid wingborne flight.

The only operational VTOL (Vertical Take-Off and Landing) aeroplane in the world in the late 1960s and early 1970s was the British Harrier, whose vectored-thrust lift/propulsion system was simple and light. From 1976, but on the other side of the 'iron curtain' another VTOL type entered service. Intended as a carrierborne attack aeroplane, this was the Yakovlev Yak-38 'Forger' which uses a fuselage-mounted powerplant of one vectored-thrust turbojet and two direct-lift turbojets.

In common with the rest of aviation, VTOL and STOL concepts and aircraft were hard hit by financial problems in the 1980s, and a new series of helicopter types proposed for service in the decade has been slow to enter service and find a market of economically acceptable size. Even the resources support market (such as the delivery or men, equipment and supplies to inhospitable land regions and to offshore oil and gas production platforms), which was a mainstay of helicopter sales in the 1970s, suffered even though the market has taken some quantities of more modern American types such as the Bell Model 212 (Twin Two-Twelve), Model 214 and Model 222; the Boeing-Vertol 234 civil version of the CH-47 Chinook twin-rotor military transport; the Sikorsky S-76 Spirit; and from France the Aérospatiale Super and Super Puma. The keynote of these machines is improved reliability (in both maintenance and operations) combined with better capability for all-weather operations thanks to upgraded avionics and systems designed to prevent the accretion of ice on the rotor blades (now largely of composite construction) and on the inlets for the twin-engine powerplant now almost universal for safety reasons. Further improvements in prospect are the increased use of composites to reduce structure weight and thus make possible greater payload or range on given power, and

better power/ weight ratios for a new generation of turboshaft engines, which will also have a lower specific fuel consumption and greater time between overhauls.

The VTOL concept has almost disappeared from the fixed-wing civil market, much greater emphasis being placed on STOL performance in a wide variety of small-capacity airliners such as the British Aerospace 146, the Aeritalia-Aérospatiale ATR-42 and the Saab 340 (all of which have much reduced airfield requirements), and on genuine STOL aircraft such as the turboprop-powered de Havilland Canada DHC-7 Dash 7 and DHC-8 Dash 8, and also the remarkable Antonov An-72 'Coaler' turbofan-powered machine which employs the same type of upper-surface blowing system as the YC-14 which, like the YC-15, has been abandoned as a military development.

Top: The Boeing Vertol CH-47 Chinook is the Western world's most prolific medium/heavy-lift helicopter, and has also been produced in the Model 234 version for the civil market.

Above: Two important light utility helicopters of Western origins are the AÈrospatiale Gazelle (above, in its SA 341 basic form) and the Bell Model 206 (above left, in its JetRanger civil form rather than OH-58 Kiowa military form).

Below left: The British Aerospace Harrier, seen here in its original Harrier GR.Mk 1 form, was the world's first operational VTOL warplane.

Below right: The Agusta A 109A is a successful general-purpose helicopter of Italian origins, and its notable for its sleek design with fully retractable landing gear.

Civil Aviation Enters the Age of the Mass Market

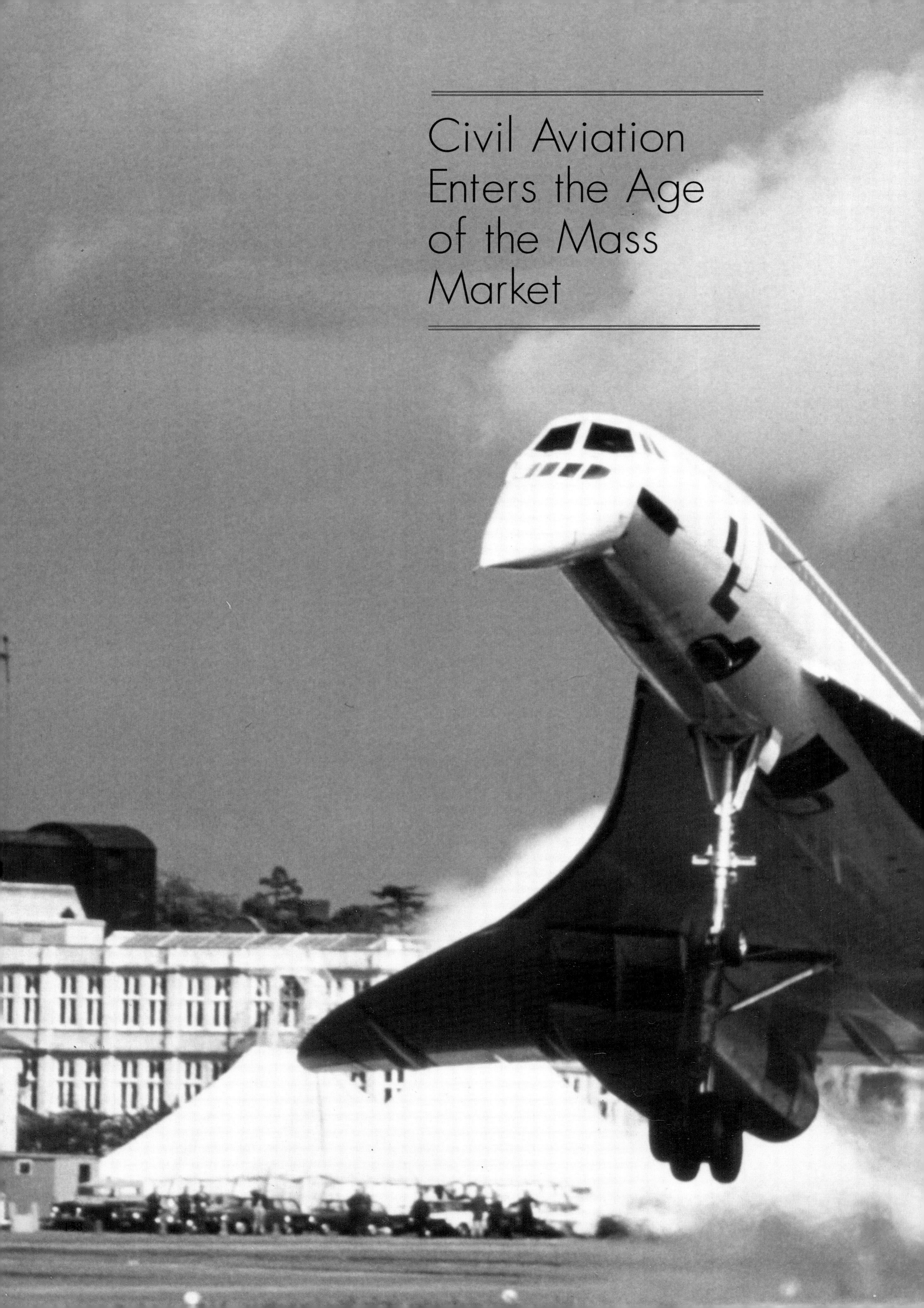

social reasons, World War II marked a decisive turning point in the history of civil aviation: the industry came to a virtually total standstill within Europe but continuing to grow, albeit at a reduced rate, within in the United States. Moreover, in the period of reconstruction that followed the end of the war, the Europeans in general and the British in particular were convinced, as they had been in the period leading up to the war, that airlines could survive only with government support: this feeling that civil aviation was in some manner inherently uneconomical bedevilled the recreation and initial development of all the European carriers.

This is not to deny that there really existed some basis for the apprehensions felt by the European airlines in the last years before 1939, for Europe enjoyed the advantages of excellent road and rail networks that offered strong competition to the airlines on the shorter routes. Even after the devastation resulting from the war, enough of these road and rail communications survived to pose a continued threat to air transport, especially as long as the Europeans were operating with pre-war airliners and hasty conversions of military aircraft. Neither of these types could realistically compete with the railways for speed on short routes, while trains additionally offered a higher level of comfort and a lower level of noise than those of post-war aircraft.

Thus the revived European carriers found themselves in the same difficult position as the American airlines of 1939: they were on the verge of technical competence and the exploitation of large markets but were not quite competent to grasp this commercially golden opportunity. The situation may therefore be summed up in the assessment that while the inclination was there, the real determination to develop this inclination was lacking. Most airlines were content to move ahead cautiously under the direct supervision of the governments which would subsidize

them in the event that they failed to return a profit on the minimal investment made in them. In these circumstances, therefore, it is hardly surprising that there was no surge forward into the new era by nationalized airlines such as the British Overseas Airways Corporation (ex-Imperial Airways) operating the long-haul intercontinental routes and British European Airways flying routes within the continent.

Many of the problems that beset the renascent European airline industry were unavoidable. At the end of the war the situation among the major nations was that Germany had effectively lost its industrial base, Italy was short of resources, and France faced great problems of reconstruction before it could turn to civil air transport. This meant that only the United Kingdom was in any sort of condition to start large-scale airliner projects, for it was the only European country with large-scale manufacturing capacity and some possibility of investment left.

Yet even the United Kingdom had to start virtually from scratch. Although several interesting projects incorporating the very latest technology had been under consideration during the last few months of peace, these had been abandoned during the war. Based on advanced engine and airframe technology, the Short and Fairey projects for long-range transports with a four-engined powerplant were ignored by the Brabazon Committee, which had been set up in 1943 to examine the needs of British civil aviation at the end of the hostilities.

In their approach to the planning and implementation of high-density, long-range operations, the Americans displayed an approach that was both more resolute and considerably more realistic. In this task, the Americans were greatly aided by their experience in World War II, in which the airlines had undertaken long-range operations for the armed forces such as the great route from the USA to North Africa via the South Atlantic crossing between Brazil and West Africa, and the air forces had operated difficult services such as the great airlift of supplies from India to China over the eastern Himalayas. Such experience had taught the Americans how to cost their operations with a nice exactitude, and also how to plan their services so that an adequate number of aircraft were serviceable at any given time to ensure that all route requirements could be met. The Americans also gauged the size and demands of the market half a decade in the future with astonishing

Left: The BAe/AÈrospatiale Concorde is currently the world's only supersonic airliner, and despite the age of its design still an extraordinarily impressive aeroplane.

159

superannuated types to hand. The Douglas DC-3 was very widely used as its performance and operating economics were well proved, and many thousands of the type were available at low cost from stocks of ex-military C-47 Skytrain/Dakota transports. Conversions and adaptations of wartime aircraft were numerous: BOAC, for example, used the Avro York transport derivative of the Lancaster and the Avro Lancastrian adaptation of the same bomber, as well as converted Vickers Warwicks and Handley Page Halifaxes to supplement the Short flying boats returned after wartime service with the RAF.

In the late 1940s BOAC received its first examples of the Avro Tudor, a type which had been ordered by the Brabazon Committee: the Tudor proved itself to lack the performance of its American rivals, and was also considerably less cost-effectiveness. At the same time BEA was using the twin-engined DC-3 and also a number of three-engined Junkers Ju 52/3m transports, the latter taken over from the Germans, for internal routes. In 1947 BEA received its first twin-engined Vickers Viking short/medium-haul airliners, which proved popular and successful in operation although even they could not match contemporary American airliners in either economy or performance.

By now there were more than 200 airlines in the world, and the aircraft of these operators could be seen at nearly 1,000 important airports. These airlines ranged from the American private-enterprise and European state-owned giants to small concerns with only a few aircraft, but the situation was far removed from that of the 1920s, with numerous small airlines in the most outlandish places. Many airlines continued to operate in backward regions, but the late 1940s saw the final triumph of the 'established' airlines, with countries taking pride in their national flag-carriers and making life difficult for the dubious operators with ever more stringent safety requirements in the air and on the ground. Small private operators, especially those using DC-3s, were left with the growing freight market in the world's more inhospitable and inaccessible regions.

The American supremacy in the new air transport market was immediately apparent. Although the American airlines still used conversions of wartime aircraft for freighting operations, and also the DC-3 for reliable and economical service on short routes, these operators had two excellent four-engined airliners available for longer-range routes and a replacement for the DC-3 was under development for medium-range routes. The two four-engined airliners were classic types: the strangely elegant and indeed beautiful Lockheed Constellation, and the more prosaic but no less successful Douglas DC-4.

A comparison of these two airliners with the best comparable British aircraft of the time, the Avro York, reveals the magnitude of the American technical lead. The DC-4 could carry a payload of up to 58 passengers at 245 mph (395 km/h) for almost 2,000 miles (3220 km) and the Constellation could carry a payload of about 100 passengers at 330 mph (530 km/h) for more than 2,400 miles (3860 km); the York, on the other hand, was capable of almost 300 mph (485 km/h) and possessed a range of 2,700 miles (4345 km) but could carry only 24 passengers. The inferiority of the York vis-à-vis the Constellation and DC-4 in terms of payload/range performance was further compounded by less numerically tangible

Above: The de Havilland Australia DHA-3 was designed for Australian bush operations, and was thus a rugged transport capable of carrying up to eight passengers or freight. It was unusual among aircraft designed after World War II in having a three-engined powerplant, and production totalled 20 aircraft.

accuracy. Operators such as Pan American, Trans World Airlines, National Airlines and American Airlines, who relied on profitable operations to stay in business, knew exactly what types of aircraft they needed, and made sure that manufacturers delivered the right types.

So the British were slowly developing aircraft that were wrong for the roles that were emerging or indeed conceived for tasks that were fast disappearing: typical of these types were the huge Bristol Brabazon intended for the low-capacity transatlantic route but cancelled after an eight-year development programme before it entered production, the Short Sandringham flying boat for which there was no large market, and the beautiful Saunders-Roe Princess flying boat also cancelled before it entered service. The Americans, on the other hand, were evolving and producing at moderately low cost several comfortable, high-performance transport aircraft for their many and continually growing number of continental and intercontinental routes: so successful were these new types, moreover, that the railways were soon losing a large proportion of their long-

Below: The Sud-Est SE.161 Languedoc resulted from a design appeared before World War II, and saw limited production and service as a medium transport after that conflict.

distance passengers. There was a growing demand for air freight. Today the railways in the United States carry only the heavy non-perishable freight that cannot be transported by aircraft, and passenger numbers are tiny.

What British operators failed to see, the American airlines grasped fully: this was the fact that the airliner had left behind it the days of its temperamental performance at medium altitudes and short ranges for the carriage of small number of high-paying passengers, and entered a new era of reliable performance at high altitudes and increasingly long ranges for the carriage of passengers and freight whose swelling numbers and weights opened the way to reduced fare rates.

Meanwhile, the lack of anything more advanced forced the European airlines to rely on the often

Below: First flown in 1943 as a four-engined development of the SM.75 tri-motor transport, the Savoia-Marchetti SM.95 entered service after the end of World War II for services on European routes, and was built only in small numbers.

factors such as the British airliner's considerably less comfortable passenger accommodation. Another factor that has to be borne in mind is that the York was the last stage in an evolutionary design process and could be improved no further without very extensive design, whereas the two American airliners were types were near the beginnings of their evolutionary lives. Development of the Constellation continued up to 1958, when it was still a marginally competitive design at a time when the first American-designed jet airliner was on the verge of entering service. The Douglas airliner, too, proved durable, and the same basic layout was kept in subsequent Douglas types, so that they were essentially enlarged DC-4s with full cabin pressurization, more powerful engines and improved performance in terms of speed, range and cruising altitude. Finally, both the American airliners used tricycle landing gear of the type that kept the fuselage level on the ground, while the York had obsolescent tailwheel landing gear.

The Convair CV-240 was inspired by a request from American Airlines for a DC-3 replacement, and first appeared in 1947. The CV-240 was in effect a postwar development of the DC-3 basic concept but incorporating all the latest technical developments, and capable of considerable development 'stretch'. From the CV-240 evolved the CV-340 and CV-440, of which useful numbers are still in service during the 1990s in their original piston-engined and later converted turboprop-powered forms.

In 1948 Douglas unveiled its DC-6. Essentially an improved DC-4 capable of carrying some 70 passengers at 280 mph (450 km/h) over intercontinental or transcontinental routes, the standard DC-6 was soon replaced by the larger DC-6B version, which was itself eventually superseded by the definitive DC-7 as the definitive model of Douglas' long-range airliner family. In the first half of the 1950s this Douglas airliner family was the most successful commercial aircraft in the world, and used by most of the long-haul operators.

The design and operation of such aircraft as the CV, DC and Constellation series confirmed the total professionalism of the American aviation business, which was notable for the success of its constituent airlines in ordering just the right number of the right aircraft at just the right time to meet the demands of a growing market. Some people may have argued that the romance had gone out of flying, but passengers were more than happy so the combination of speed, comfort and reliability offered by the airlines in the early 1950s at last meant that aircraft took over as the major form of long-haul transport in the United States.

The United Kingdom could not hope to match the volume of American air travel, or indeed the United States'

civil aircraft production capacity, but by the late 1940s British aircraft were beginning to equal and in some respects to excel their American rivals in performance. Among the civil types introduced in 1949 were the four-engined Handley Page Hermes in a fully developed form, the elegant twin-engined Airspeed Ambassador high-wing design for BEA's European routes, the four-engined turboprop Vickers Viscount medium-range airliner, and the four-engined turbojet de Havilland D.H.106 Comet.

The most important aeroplane of 1949, however, was undoubtedly the Comet that emerged as the world's first turbojet-powered airliner. Compared with the piston-engined of the day, which were characterized by straight wings carrying massive engines and their large propellers, the Comet appeared incredibly sleek as it possessed a beautifully streamlined nose with an unstepped cockpit, modestly swept wings, tricycle landing gear, and a powerplant of four turbojets installed in a low-drag installation in the wing roots. The only feature to mar the Comet's looks was the relative shortness of the fuselage, and this was a result of the type's origins in a mailplane project ordered by the Brabazon Committee. This defect also meant that the fuselage was able to accommodate only a very limited number of passengers, 36 in all. The prototypes and very first production aircraft were powered to a more than ample performance by four de Havilland Ghost centrifugal-flow turbojets, but later Comets switched to a more capable powerplant of four Rolls-Royce Avon axial-flow turbojets, which allowed a longer and more capacious fuselage to be combined with the existing high-lift wing.

By 1951 BOAC was training crews for the new airliner, and some of the proving flights were so impressive that several other operators decided that they must have the Comet for their prestige services or be left behind in a market in which passengers had now expressed a clear preference for high speed and modest comfort over modest speed and a higher level of comfort. In May 1952 the comet began commercial flights to South Africa and the type's future looked assured, especially as the model with a Rolls-Royce powerplant was now in production and orders were mounting. Passenger reports of the relative quietness of the Comet and its smooth flight helped reinforce the statistical evidence of the Comet's excellence.

Above: The Sud-Ouest SO.30 Bretagne was another European transport that had its origins in World War II and was built only in small quantities.

Below: The Ilyushin Il-14 'Crate' was evolved to replace the Il-12 'Coach', itself an unsuccessful attempt to supplant the Lisunov Li-2 'Cab' that was the Soviet licence-built version of the Douglas DC-3. The Il-14 was built in large numbers and is still operated by several third-world air forces.

Above: The Vickers Viscount was the world's first turboprop-powered airliner and, in terms of numbers built, was also the most successful British airliner ever produced.

1958, to be operated by BOAC on the North Atlantic route, which was really too long for effective service by an airliner originally intended for the British routes to Africa and the Far East.

Only one month after the Comet 4 had entered full revenue service, the death knell for the type on prestige high-density, high-speed routes such as that across the North Atlantic was sounded by the introduction of the superlative Boeing Model 707 turbojet-powered airliner. Bearing a distinct family likeness to the earlier Boeing B-47 Stratojet and B-52 Stratofortress turbojet-powered bombers, the Model 707 was far superior to the Comet as it was a later and therefore intrinsically more advanced airliner offering higher speed, greater payload and longer range. As it was a newer design, the type also had considerably more development potential, and many important lessons had already been learned during work on the B-47 and B-52 bombers.

Very shortly after this, British discomfiture was further increased by the appearance of a second American turbojet-powered airliner, the Douglas DC-8 that had been rushed through design and development to provide Douglas with a competitor to the Boeing offering. Produced in large numbers at a low unit cost in large and very efficient factories, the Model 707 and DC-8 immediately revealed the obsolescence of the Comet and soon outsold the pioneering British airliner by a very considerable margin. As has been the case with later types of turbojet-powered airliner, the Comet soon passed into the service of smaller airlines that did not face as high a level of competition, and to charter companies which could guarantee a full load every time the aeroplane took off and therefore were not so concerned about speed.

Turbojet-powered airliners had undoubtedly come to stay, and the Comet seemed well placed to secure a significant slice of the new market. Then disaster struck in 1954: two of the first production aircraft disappeared over the Mediterranean after taking off from Rome. Public anxiety was particularly intense because of the radical nature of the new airliner's design and powerplant. After a major effort in underwater recovery, wreckage was eventually brought up from the bottom of the Mediterranean and the investigators went to work. The cause of the problem was diagnosed as metal fatigue around the passenger cabin's square-cut window apertures, and a cure was swiftly devised

Above: The Douglas DC-4 was the civil counterpart of the C-54 Skymaster long-range transport, and with the Lockheed Constellation was instrumental in the rapid and successful development of international air services after World War II.

in the form of reinforcement panels around each aperture.

So great had been the psychological shock of the crashes, however, that this simple solution was not adopted and the whole Comet production programme was fatally delayed for the development of a new fuselage with rounded windows. The Comet's advantage over American rivals had been lost by the time the revised Comet 4 entered service in

Having persuaded itself that the future of long-haul flights lay with large turboprop-powered aircraft such as the Bristol Britannia, the British government had to revise its ideas in 1957 when BOAC suddenly became concerned about its possible elimination from the blue-ribband route across the North Atlantic. A quick programme to develop a rival to the Boeing and Douglas airliners led to the Vickers VC10, in many respects an outstanding aeroplane. Convinced that there was a large potential market for passengers wanting to fly between the smaller airports unwilling or unable to expand their facilities to the levels required for the Model 707 and DC-8, BOAC specified runway requirements significantly shorter than those of the American aircraft. Vickers therefore opted for a large wing, uncluttered by engines, to increase lift and reduce take-off/landing speed. So whereas the American airliners had comparatively small wings carried the engines in four pods pylon-mounted below and ahead of the leading edges, the British contender had its four engines installed in pods on each side of the rear fuselage, with the tailplane mounted on top of the vertical tail surface to keep it well clear of the engine exhausts.

The VC10 met BOAC's specification without difficulty, but the requirements themselves were based on the false assumption that most airports would be reluctant or unable to extend their runways and terminals to the standards required for the American airliners. When they did, allowing the American turbojet-powered transports to operate virtually everywhere in the world, the

Right: A type that appeared as the turboprop-powered airliner was approaching obsolescence, the Bristol Britannia was nonetheless a magnificent long-range transport that acquired an enviable reputation for reliability and quietness.

VC10 proved a relative failure since its large wing increased drag slightly, making the type uneconomical compared with the Model 707 and DC-8. This left the market open to the Americans, who built the Model 707 and DC-8 in enormous numbers in a number of variants matched to the requirements of airlines needing different passenger capacities, greater or lesser range, the capability to operate into and out of 'hot and high' airports, and the passenger, freight, quick-change passenger or freight, and mixed passenger/freight layouts. The original models carried some 175 passengers at 570 mph (917 km/h) for 3,075 miles (4950 km), while later models were able to carry some 190 passengers at 607 mph (977 km/h) for 6,160 miles (9915 km) with minimal alterations to the airframe except the lengthening of the fuselage.

The introduction of the turbofan helped to crystallize the differences among the airliners evolving to meet the growing market. In the 1950s, for example, there were two basic types of airliner, the short- and long-range types. The great majority of passengers travelled only short distances, for which turboprop-powered machines such as the Vickers Viscount, Vickers Vanguard (a development of the Viscount), Fokker F.27 Friendship, Lockheed Electra and Handley Page Herald were ideally suited. Routes of under 1,000 miles (1610 km) did not require the high speeds at which turbojets are economical, but for long-range routes a turbojet powerplant had enormous advantages.

Toward the end of the 1950s, the need for an intermediate-range airliner became apparent, and the French SNCASO group, more commonly known just as Sud-Ouest and now a component of Aérospatiale, took the opportunity thus offered and brought France into the international short- and medium-range airliner market with the delightful and classic Caravelle. In this useful type, a forward fuselage based on that of the Comet was married to a new and very efficient wing and a rear fuselage carrying two Rolls-Royce Avon turbojet engines in lateral pods, the first time such a mounting had been tried on a civilian airliner. After a slow start, the Caravelle caught on very quickly and proved successful not just as an airliner but also as an influence on the design of later aircraft of the same general type.

Designers in the 1960s felt that the turbofan powerplant was best suited for medium- and long-range airliners. Then the increasing efficiency of this sort of engine combined with the development of smaller engines of the same basic type models to make the turbofan applicable to all types of airliner during the early 1980s. As a result, the turbojet has all but disappeared from service with the world's airlines. On the other hand, advanced technology has turned the turboprop, which many considered obsolete on all but the smallest transports from the mid-1960s onward, into a highly competitive type, especially when fitted with the modern type of advanced propeller and a computerized control system of the type now universal on modern turbine-powered aircraft. The turboprop never faded entirely from the airliner scene, and from the early 1980s the type has undergone a considerable renaissance for airliners

such as the ATR-42, de Havilland Canada DHC-7 Dash 7 and DHC-8 Dash 8, EMBRAER EMB-110 Bandeirante and EMB-120 Brasilia, Fokker 50, Saab SF-340, and Shorts 330 and 360. Such airliners can carry up to 50 passengers over maximum-payload ranges of up to 1,000 miles (1610 km), their advanced turboprop powerplants allowing cruising speeds of up to some 500 km/h (311 mph) at a remarkably low specific fuel consumption.

Given that it was a large but relatively underdeveloped country with huge natural resources in many of its poorly accessed remoter areas, the USSR inevitably became a major exponent of heavy-lift aircraft for civilian use. The Western nations, with well developed rail networks, have more need for freight aircraft, a demand which can be met for the most part by converting airliners or producing freight-dedicated variants of standard airliners. Few alterations need normally be made beyond strengthening the fuselage floor and fitting larger doors so that bulky items can be loaded. A few such aircraft, such as the Canadair CL-44 version of the Britannia, have been built with a hingeing rear fuselage to ease the loading of long, wide loads.

Since the end of World War II, which proved that transport aircraft could be used effectively for more than the movement of special loads into inhospitable regions as had been the case in the 1920s and 1930s, there has been considerable development in the use of large transport aircraft for a host of applications. These are not military aircraft in any sense that they can be used for offensive military purposes, since they are not armed to any but the most limited defensive sense and then only in rare cases, but it is armed forces that use them to the greatest extent, with the United States leading the field. The technical developments that made them possible have also seen many other uses in the field of purely civil aviation.

In recent years the US Air Force's two main heavy transport models have been the large Lockheed C-141 StarLifter and the enormous Lockheed C-5 Galaxy, of

Above: The Lockheed Constellation series never overtook the Douglas DC-4 and its successors in terms of sales, but was a supremely elegant type that was very popular. The type underwent steady development in terms of performance and payload, and is here epitomized by the L-1049 Super Constellation.

Above: The Vickers Vanguard was designed as successor to the Vickers Viscount, but failed to match its predecessor's success.

Below: The Vickers Viking was the civil transport member of the family that also included the Valetta military transport and Varsity military trainer, and was an interim type that was rushed into effective service soon after the end of World War II.

United Kingdom. For medium-capacity operations over medium-range routes, de Havilland (already part of the Hawker Siddeley conglomerate and soon to be absorbed fully into it) produced the Trident with three engines in its tail. A very economical and safe aeroplane, the Trident was kin to the VC10 in pioneering the completely automatic blind landing device now standard in all modern airliners. The Trident was later stretched to accommodate twice as many passengers as the first models, and secured an enviable reputation on the longer European routes. Unfortunately, however, the Trident was initially sized to the particular but underestimated passenger requirement of BEA and never secured the commercial success it might have enjoyed if the first model had offered more passenger seats.

The Trident's relative lack of success in the export market was not mirrored by the sales of its American rival. Boeing replied quickly to this British lead by introducing its three-engined Model 727 medium-range transport in 1961. For the first time Boeing adopted the successful rear-engined formula, a tall T-tail to keep the elevators well above the engine exhausts, and full independence from ground services through the incorporation of a ventral airstair door and an auxiliary power unit. The company's vast production capacity soon saw the American airliner overtake its rival in sales and, although produced in only a few variants, the Model 727 went on to become the world's best-selling airliner that was overtaken in numbers only in the late 1980s by another Boeing transport, the Model 737.

The British had a greater lead with their new short-range jet airliner, the twin-engined British Aircraft Corporation One-Eleven high-capacity transport. BAC had been formed in 1961 by an amalgamation of the Vickers, Bristol and English Electric companies, later joined by Hunting, and the One-Eleven was developed from an earlier Hunting design. The type first flew in 1963 and immediately secured a number of orders both at home and abroad. The One-Eleven assumed the mantle of the Caravelle, and proved popular in service both with passengers and operators, being an economical and reliable aeroplane. Some 230 such aircraft were delivered from the British production line by the end of the 1970s, when the production rights were sold to Romania for the construction of a comparatively small number of additional One-Elevens.

The Americans were strangely slow to respond with their own short-range transports, but the Douglas DC-9, which resembles the One-Eleven in basic configuration and first flew in 1965, soon surpassed the One-Eleven in sales and has continued to the present in an active development and production effort that has seen the delivery of very large numbers of aircraft in a bewildering number of variants. Boeing was even later into the field with its Model 737, a twin-engined aeroplane like its two rivals. The Model 737 reverted to the traditional Boeing podded engine layout, however, although the two engine nacelles were attached directly to the underside of the wings without any intervening pylon. The

Top: The de Havilland Comet was the world's first turbojet-powered airliner, and is seen here in the form of a Comet 4 of the definitive model.

Above: The Hawker Siddeley (originally de Havilland) Trident pioneered the powerplant arrangement with three engines grouped at the tail, and might have enjoyed greater commercial success had it not been sized exactly to the requirement of British European Airways, which underestimated passenger demand.

which the latter was the world's largest aeroplane at the time of its introduction. These two long-range transports were complemented in the early 1980s by a modest number of the McDonnell Douglas KC-10 Extender dual-role tanker/transport derivative of the DC-10 airliner, and from the mid-1990s are to be supplemented by small quantities of another advanced military transport, the McDonnell Douglas C-17A Globemaster III. Outside the United States, both the United Kingdom and France developed large transports, but these were phased out of service by 1980. The British aircraft included the Blackburn Beverley and the Short Belfast, and the most notable French aeroplane of this category was the Breguet Sahara.

The most remarkable and versatile transport since the end of World War II, however, has been the Lockheed C-130 Hercules, a tactical airlifter powered by four turboprops. This has been adopted by a large number of air forces and has also seen widespread civilian use, and although it entered service in the first half of the 1950s is still in large-scale production and further development in the mid-1990s. The Hercules has excellent STOL (Short Take-Off and Landing) characteristics and has the ability, very useful in a machine of its size, to operate from rough airstrips.

It should be noted that the passenger traffic explosion of the 1960s, when the mass market really began to emerge once high-capacity aircraft of low operating cost had paved the way for package holiday flights and other elements of mass transport, demanded a new generation of short- and medium-range aircraft. First into this challenging field was the

Above: Operations in remoter parts of the world without sophisticated airports have always demanded special aircraft with a low-set fuselage but a high-set wing, and an Australian contender in this market was the Government Aircraft Factories Nomad.

Model 737 first flew in 1967, and has since that time been developed in a number of steadily more impressive variants that remain in production, and indeed in major development, right up to the present. The Model 737 has the extraordinary record of having secured more sales than any other airliner in history.

The late 1960s and early 1970s saw the emergence of a new market has proved increasingly lucrative for manufacturers as businessmen and other small parties need to get around the world ever more frequently at their own rather than at the airlines' convenience. The aircraft designed to meet this need is the 'bizjet' or executive jet (although there are a few turboprop examples), which has much the same range and speed performance as the big civilian airliners, but is designed for only about 10 passengers or less. Larger companies with international interests tend to keep one or more of these jets for high speed travel by their executives, and charter companies with a few such aircraft have sprung up all over the world to cater for the needs of smaller companies. Fitted out as comfortable flying board rooms or offices, executive jets have become part of the high-powered businessman's life.

Although the cost of developing such aircraft is high, most countries with an airframe industry have produced a model. In such a competitive market, not many designs have sold well, for buyers have a wide range of types from which to make their choice. The United States, with its powerful economy, large number of giant firms and scattered financial centres, has done best.

Most of the market in the pure-jet end of the range was captured initially by the 1963 Gates Learjet (later Learjet) 24, an extremely attractive and advanced looking aeroplane with twin jets podded at the rear of the fuselage, in the manner most commonly accepted in executive jets, and the 1966 Grumman American (later Gulfstream Aerospace) Gulfstream, another clean twin jet design. Both of these types proved to be just the beginning of a long line of related developments offering greater payload, higher speed and, in their later turbofan-engined variants, considerably greater range. Unusual for an executive jet, the Lockheed JetStar II has four engines, two in each of the rear fuselage pods. A later and highly successful contender in the American 'bizjet' market has been Cessna with a series of impressive rear-engined aircraft marketed under the name Citation.

For short-range operations in the United States, and for export to less developed countries, there are the Beechcraft Queen Air and King Air, and a number of other models which can be finished to the customer's own specifications. With the exception of the Queen Air, which has piston engines, these Beechcraft models are powered by turboprops. Several of the twin-engined cabin monoplanes built by Piper can also be delivered as executive aircraft.

The most successful British aeroplane of the executive type has undoubtedly been the de Havilland (Hawker Siddeley) 125, which was also adopted by the RAF as a liaison machine and navigational trainer. The first prototype of this twin-engined 'bizjet' flew in August 1962, and by March 1975 no less

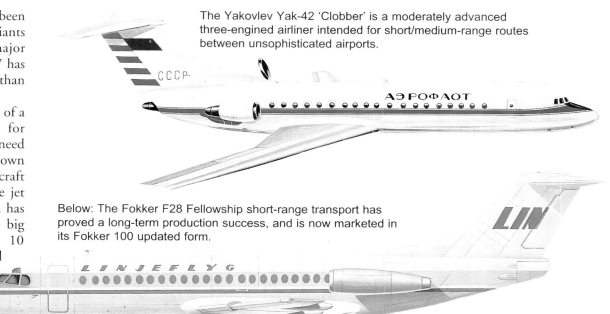

The Yakovlev Yak-42 'Clobber' is a moderately advanced three-engined airliner intended for short/medium-range routes between unsophisticated airports.

Below: The Fokker F28 Fellowship short-range transport has proved a long-term production success, and is now marketed in its Fokker 100 updated form.

than 336 examples had been sold, including 183 in North America. Continued production and development were undertaken by British Aerospace, created by a merger of Hawker Siddeley and BAC, and in early 1990s the marque was sold to Raytheon, an American industrial organization with great strength in the missiles and electronics fields.

Above: The Tupolev Tu-104 'Camel' was the world's second turbojet-powered airliner to enter service, and was developed both rapidly and cheaply as a derivative of the Tu-16 'Badger' bomber with a different fuselage.

Left: The AÈrospatiale (originally Nord) 262 twin-turboprop transport was a pressurized version of the Nord 260 unpressurized development of the Holste Super Broussard.

Below: Still serving in large numbers, the Tupolev Tu-134 'Crusty' twin-engined transport was designed as a much updated derivative of the Tu-124 for the USSR's short-range internal air services.

The French equivalent of the HS 125 is the basic Dassault Mystère/Falcon series. Based on the same airframe, the aircraft of this versatile twin-jet family can be finished as executive jets, small transports and light freighters. Like the HS 125, the Dassault executive has enjoyed surprisingly good sales in North America, which has also proved to be a major market for Dassault's larger and longer-ranged corporate transports, the Mystère/Falcon 50 and 900.

Light aircraft of the powered type have been produced in a bewildering number of types and sizes since the end of World War II, and about three-quarters of all the airframes, and almost all engines, are manufactured in the United States. The great prewar names such as Piper, Cessna and Beech emerged from the war with considerable production capacity, and a large market waiting for

the new generation of lightplanes. Since that time the American giants have enjoyed an almost unrivalled domination of the lightplane market, with their European competitors failing to secure more than a foothold.

The market for such aircraft continued to grow right into the mid-1980s, but the increasing sophistication and cost of the aircraft produced by the larger companies led to a certain disenchantment on the part of light plane enthusiasts. In the mid-1980s the rising cost of such lightplanes combined with increasing losses as a result of product-liability cases in the extremely active American judicial system, and the result was the virtual death of the American lightplane industry as Beech, Cessna and Piper all trimmed their product lines and production totals. Sales continue at a much reduced level, but the tendency of such aircraft has been to become small airliners or aerial family saloons rather than enthusiasts' flying machines. This has led to a split in the market, with the large companies continuing as before but an ever increasing number of amateurs entering the market with small aircraft of the 'experimental' type. These can normally be built from plans, using simple materials and tools, by anyone with a modicum of basic skill, and have restored what is called 'seat of the pants' flying.

Rapid progress in the development of advanced passenger aircraft was well under way when the oil crisis that started with the Arab-Israeli war in October 1973 led to a world financial slump. The rate of growth in passenger traffic, which had been increasing quickly ever since the end of World War II, suddenly slowed and in some cases even went into reverse, and airlines were hard pressed to make ends meet with the aircraft they already had, and as a result temporarily abandoned their plans to order the new and considerably larger machines that were becoming available.

For the manufacturers, it made little difference whether the airlines were in private or national ownership. If the airline was privately owned, new aircraft were out of the question for financial reasons, and the threat of a large number of failures hung over both the airline business and manufacturing companies. If the airline was state owned, new aircraft sales were still out of the question, but at least the companies were unlikely to go out of business. Some sales were still made by the manufacturers, but their number was severely reduced and several companies in the United States, notably Lockheed, resorted to bribery in an effort to secure sales for military and also civilian aircraft.

The American manufacturers had become accustomed to enjoying the largest proportion of the world airliner market, and were now caught in a very difficult situation. They continued to expand, on the assumption that the market would continue to grow at the previous rate, so that they would not be caught without marketable new aircraft. They then faced the prospect of a slump hitting them before they could sell enough machines to recoup their development and production costs.

The civilian aircraft involved in the bribery scandals were for the most part the new generation of wide-bodied airliners, developed to carry the maximum number of passengers (according to their critics, the maximum number

Top and top centre: The Boeing Model 707 was the airliner that introduced the era of mass air transport, and must therefore rank as one of the most important aircraft ever designed.

Bottom centre: The Douglas DC-9 was designed to rival the Boeing model 737 in the short-haul market, and though it never overtook its rival in overall terms it has been a ommercial success that is still in development and production.

Left: Sold in larger numbers that any other British-designed transport, the Britten-Norman Islander offers modest purchase and operating costs for operating requiring a small-capacity transport providing STOL capabilities to and from unprepared airstrips.

Left: The Fokker F27 Friendship twin-turboprop transport has been a considerable success, and is now offered in its Fokker 50 updated form. These are two military derivatives, namely the Maritime Enforcer patrol aeroplane with anti-ship and anti-submarine capabilities, and the Sentinel electronic intelligence gatherer.

Below: Just as the Tu-104 transport was evolved from the Tu-16 bomber, the Tupolev Tu-114 'Cleat' long-range transport was evolved from the Tu-95 'Bear' bomber.

of passengers in the maximum discomfort). With the technology it had developed while producing and planning large aircraft for the US Air Force, Boeing was ready in 1965 to start work on a new airliner capable of carrying a very large number of passengers over very long routes. The mammoth Model 747 was introduced in 1968 and 1969, and Boeing was so certain of success with the design that it did not bother with a prototype but ran development tests and certification trials on the first production aeroplane.

The Model 747 was inevitably dubbed the 'jumbo jet' and can carry a maximum of 500 passengers in a high-density seating layout, although a more typical load is 385; the airliner's maximum speed is 610 mph (980 km/h), and its range is 6,200 miles (10,000 km). In its initial form, the Model 747 was powered by four podded Pratt & Whitney JT9D turbofans each capable of developing a static thrust of 43,500 lb (19732 kg), though the type was later developed in variants with still more powerful engines produced by General Electric and Rolls-Royce as well as Pratt & Whitney. Seen from a distance, the aeroplane appears quite ordinary, and it is only when the observer gets close to the machine that he begins to gain a realistic impression of the

Above: The Ilyushin Il-62 'Classic' long-range transport was clearly inspired by a British airliner, the Vickers VC10.

Left: The BAC One-Eleven pioneered the concept of a powerplant of two turbofans pod-mounted on the sides of the rear fuselage under a T-tail, and was a successful type that did not quite gain the commercial success that was perhaps its due.

Bottom left and right: The Boeing model 737, seen here in the form of a model 737-200 airliner and its flightdeck, has been the world's most successful airliner and is still is full development and production.

Below: The success of the DC-9 short-range transport found Douglas without the production facilities or the financial resources to meet demand, and was a primary reason for the merger of the manufacturer with the cash-rich McDonnell to create McDonnell Douglas.

huge size of the aeroplane, which in its initial Model 747-100 form is 231 ft 4 in (70.51 m) long and 63 ft 5 in (19.33 m) high with a wing spanning 195 ft 8 in (59.64 m). Although the Model 747 is expensive, it is economic in service and most of the larger airlines have found it ideal for their long routes. To suit the requirements of airlines operating under particular circumstances, Boeing has also produced the 'jumbo jet' in a number of variants suiting the aeroplane to short 'fat' routes demanding maximum payload capacity over modest ranges, and long ' thin' routes calling for modest payload over long ranges; there are also mixed passenger/freight and all-freight variants.

The success of the Model 747 was rapid, for this pioneering 'wide-body' airliner proved beyond doubt that the era of mass air transport had arrived with a vengeance despite the considerable runway and terminal facility demands of the 'jumbo jet'. The Model 747 was an immediate sales success, and this brought it home to

Above: The AÈrospatiale (originally Sud-Est) Caravelle was the second European turbojet-powered airliner to enter service, and was the most successful French transport ever built.

manufacturers and operators alike that the more passengers carried in a single airframe, the greater would be the profits, and companies all over the world considered the development of wide-bodied

Right and bottom: To match the American giants of the aerospace world, Europe created the Airbus consortium that is here represented by its first product, the A300 that was the world's fourth wide-body airliner to enter service.

aircraft in an effort to cash in on the mass transport boom. In the United States Lockheed during 1969 and 1970 developed the TriStar, with three Rolls-Royce RB211

turbofan engines each developing 42,000 lb (19051 kg) static thrust; two of the engines were installed in pods pylon-mounted under the wing leading edges and the third engine was mounted in the tail. Up to 400 passengers can be carried over ranges of 4,500 miles (7240 km).

McDonnell Douglas (form by the 1967 amalgamation of the flourishing McDonnell and problem-hit Douglas) also entered the fray with its DC-10. This has its engines disposed in the same basic fashion as the TriStar, and these engines are General Electric or Pratt & Whitney turbofans each generating 45,000 lb (20412 kg) static thrust. Accommodation and performance are comparable with those of the TriStar, but the DC-10 suffered adverse criticism as a result of an imperfectly designed baggage door in the fuselage. This caused what was at the time the world's worst air crash when a DC-10 of Turkish Airlines crashed near Paris, killing more than 375 people.

In Europe, too, there were plans for a locally designed wide-bodied airliner. As the costs of developing such an aircraft are so high, France and Germany decided to collaborate, with Britain's Hawker Siddeley building the wings as a private venture and smaller elements of the programme entrusted to CASA in Spain and Fokker in the Netherlands. Power for the A300, which was the first product of Airbus Industrie, is provided by two General Electric CF6 turbofans, each rated at 51,000 lb (23134 kg) static thrust. By the standards of twin-engined airliner, the A300 carries a considerable number of passengers, up to a maximum of 375 but generally 267, but is intended only for short- and medium-range operations. The type entered service in 1974.

The most notable feature of all these wide-bodied aircraft, as their name implies, is the width of the fuselage. This allows the passengers to be seated in long transverse rows divided by two longitudinal aisles separating the seats into groups and giving easy access to the aircraft exits and facilities. Also notable is

the use of the new generation of very high-powered turbofans built by General Electric, Pratt & Whitney and Rolls-Royce, and using many advanced structural techniques and materials.

With the resurgence of air travel by holiday makers and other mass travellers, these wide-bodied aircraft soon became the norm for high-density routes where speed is not absolutely necessary. Keeping drag down to acceptable limits in aircraft with such large fuselages was inevitably difficult, and called for the utmost skill on the part of designers. Newly developed high-lift devices were of great use, for in the sophisticated forms used on the wide-bodied aircraft and new military aircraft such devices permitted the wings to be cut down to a minimum span and area but still provide more than adequate slow-speed landing and take off characteristics.

With such aircraft, civil aviation reached the highest subsonic speeds practical without very expensive airframes and unacceptably high fuel consumption, for which a slightly reduced journey times would not compensate. The market for supersonic airliners remains hazardous, for it has yet to be established that there are enough passengers to make the production of SSTs (Super-Sonic Transports) worthwhile in economic terms. Inevitably demand lies with people, such as businessmen, to whom time is money. But only on long distances does the time saved by supersonic flight make such travel worthwhile. This was only one of the problems, for the development of SSTs was also littered with severe technical difficulties.

By the mid 1950s designers in France, the United Kingdom and the United States were all considering SSTs: the first two directed their efforts toward a transport capable of cruising at a upper speed of Mach 2.2 so that there would

be no need for special and expensive alloys to cope with the high temperatures generated by high-speed flight, while the last proposed a Mach 3 aeroplane making extensive use of the new temperature-resistant alloys and metals such as titanium. For political as well as economic reasons, the French and British governments decided in the early 1960s that a collaborative project would be a good idea.

The agreement between the United Kingdom and France was signed in 1962, and by 1963 the designers of this first major international aerospace venture had settled on the basic design of a 130-seat Mach 2.2 airliner with the range to operate on the air routes across the Atlantic. The development of the aeroplane, which eventually became the BAe/Aérospatiale Concorde, was thorny and complicated at many levels but was highly successful in its overall terms and also helped to iron out some of the difficulties likely to be met in other collaborative projects. The first prototype flew in 1969, and the Concorde entered service with Air France and British Airways simultaneously in January 1976.

The future of the Anglo-French SST remained uncertain a year later. Political decisions, based on environmental concerns and perhaps a suspicion that the Europeans had pulled a fast one on the Americans, whose own SST project had been cancelled in 1970, had prevented the Concorde from operating on the route for which it was designed, namely that to New York from Paris and London. The project had already suffered many delays, and proved so much more costly than estimated, that it faced much political opposition in both parent countries. In the long run, though, the Concorde entered full and operationally profitable service on the Atlantic routes, though the project as a whole was a commercial failure as only a very small number of the aircraft were built. The type has also proved exceptionally popular in service, and remains a valued component of the fleets operated by Air France and British Airways (ex-BOAC and BEA).

The USSR was not to be outdone by the Western bloc, and also developed the Tupolev Tu-144 as an SST remarkably similar to the Concorde. There were serious problems with the design and development of this Soviet type, however, and considerable structural revision was required before the type could be considered for service. Progress was further hampered, moreover, by the unaccountable crash of a prototype during the 1973 Paris Air Show. During the late 1970s and very early 1980s the Tu-144 saw limited freight and passenger service within the USSR, but was withdrawn from service in the light of intractable technical problems, generally assumed to be associated with the engines.

During the early part of the 1980s the airline business underwent a traumatic period of economic adjustment as the major operators began to come to grips with the financial realities of virtually no seat-mile growth at a time of much enhanced fuel costs and capital outlay on new aircraft. Yet better times for the airlines were imminent with a resurgence of confidence in the desirability of air transport, a fall in the price of fuel, and the emergence of aircraft that were either entirely new or much developed forms of the best machines from the current generation.

Below: Despite the fact that it fell victim to political and environmental pressures, and was therefore built only in very small numbers for Air France and British Airways, the BAe/AÈrospatiale Concorde supersonic airliner was a magnificent creation that still returns a useful operating profit on its transatlantic services.

Below left: The Aero Spacelines Super Guppy was evolved as a conversion of the Boeing C-97 Stratofreighter transport with an immensely bulged upper fuselage lobe for the carriage of outsize loads. Four of the aircraft are used to transport major assemblies from various parts of Europe to the Airbus assembly line in Toulouse.

Designed as an air-superiority fighter with exceptional climb performance, the McDonnell Douglas F-15 Eagle is the successor to the same company's F-4 Phantom II and has matured into a truly exceptional multi-role type able to deliver a large and diverse weapon load with considerable accuracy.

Through the Present and into the Future

Through the 1970s and into the early 1980s the world of aviation moved, albeit with a fair degree of unsteadiness, past an important turning point that was possibly as important as any in its short but momentous history. This turning point had two major and intricately connected causes: the world recession of the period, and the enormously increased cost of all aviation fuels. This latter factor was readily discernible in the lack of real commercial success by the BAe/Aérospatiale Concorde supersonic airliner: when it was being designed in the early 1960s, this potentially world-beating Anglo-French transport was planned for operations on the basis of the current price of jet fuel, which was about 12 US cents per US gallon (3.79 litres), but by the time the Concorde entered service in 1976 the price had risen steeply to over US $1 per US gallon and in the next few years after 1976 the price continued its meteoric climb. The Arab countries, which were then the world's primary oil producers, felt themselves forced into the use of the 'oil weapon' by Western support for Israel in the Arab-Israeli wars of 1967 and 1973, and

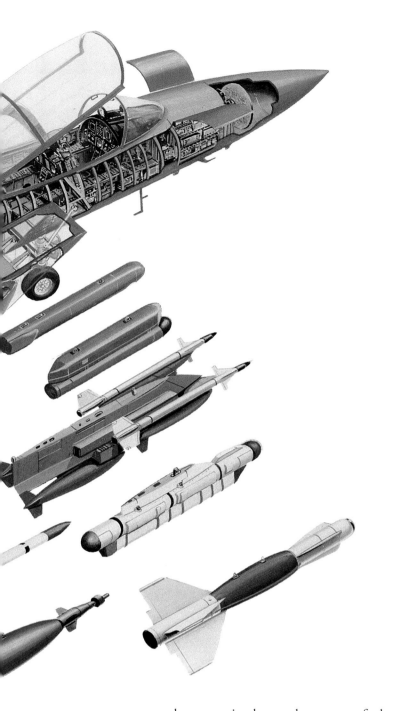

then remained acutely aware of the weapon's potency during an era of increased demand but also of escalating fears of stock exhaustions within the foreseeable future. The world recession of the period was partially attributable to the general rise in fuel prices resulting from the use of the 'oil weapon', and both the recession and the increase in fuel prices directly affected the development of aviation in general and civil aviation in particular: four important families of wide-bodied civil transport aircraft entered service in the 1970s to cater for the steady growth in passenger seat demand, and at first secured great success. Then the combination of recession and greater airline costs, passed on to the passenger in the form of higher prices, severely curtailed this growth during the early 1980s and in turn jeopardized the future of many airlines and the several aircraft manufacturers who depended for their economic stability on the twin factors of growth and a consistent purchasing policy by the airlines.

Such was the cost of engine development in the 1980s continuing into the early 1990s that all major manufacturers plan their engines in families matched or matchable to several aircraft in service or under development. In this way costs can be kept down slightly, but engines are still the single most expensive item in any major aircraft. The three Western companies that dominate the market for civil and military turbofans in the West are General Electric and Pratt & Whitney in the United States, and Rolls-Royce in the United Kingdom. During the late

1980s and early 1990s, however, a slight supplement to the efforts of these major players was created by the growing involvement of engine manufacturers from France, Germany and Japan, often in alliance with one or more of the major companies for the design, development and production of engines matched to a niche in the airliner market requiring engines of less power than those developed by the large companies.

It is to be anticipated that the steady progress of the late 1980s and early 1990s will be maintained with the continued development of engines along the lines evident above, with further improvements in all aspects of 'conventional' engine technology to reduce specific fuel consumption and increase the ease with which engines can be maintained. This latter can be achieved in part by the improved manufacture of key components such as compressor blades, using advanced industrial processes to ensure high accuracy and unflawed basic materials (including single crystals, carbon fibre, graphite, boron and ceramics, all of which are becoming increasingly common in the latest generations of aircraft); and in part it can be achieved by the greater use of modules in the basic construction of the engine. This latter means that a suspect or time-expired module (a complete compressor stage, for example) can be removed as a unit and replaced by a similar unit while the original is repaired, overhauled or merely examined. The use of modular construction on a larger scale also opens the way to increased accuracy, so that high-speed rotating assemblies such as compressor stages can be balanced after construction and then 'plugged' into the relevant engine without the need for the entire unit to be rebalanced. This saves time and money in itself, and also benefits the operator's economics by reducing the quantity of spares and servicing equipment he needs to hold.

Another aspect of powerplant development that has become increasingly important in the 1980s and early 1990s is the computerized control of the aircraft's engine in flight by means of full-authority digital systems. These small software-controlled 'black box' systems are designed to operate the engines at maximum safety and economy levels. Inputs from the flightcrew, air data sensors, flight-management system and the engines themselves are all assessed continuously by the computer to provide optimum and constantly updated control settings for the engines given all the ambient conditions, and to monitor the performance of the engines, displaying information to the flightcrew only when the data necessary for a decision are not instantly derivable from the computer's programming. The fine control of the engines by such a system has been found to offer very significant improvements in overall engine management and hence in fuel economy, and despite their cost such digital control systems became standard in almost all civil and military aircraft from the late 1980s.

Although most dependent on engine performance and basic aerodynamic design for operating economy, modern aircraft are also very susceptible to commercial lack of profitability as a result of excessive structure weight. Whereas military aircraft are generally designed to the safe-life principle in which components are proved by testing to have a statistically established life expectancy before failure, civil aircraft conform to the fail-safe design principle in which the system can withstand any failure, usually by the provision of redundant components, systems or even structures. A fail-safe design is inevitably safer than a safe-life design, but generally suffers from a higher structure weights, and any extra weight in the aeroplane's structure or systems means less payload and, as a result of this, less revenue. It is very important for the design team, therefore, to pare airframe weight down to a minimum commensurate

Above: The single most important fighter currently serving with the US Air Force and the air arm of a number of American allies is the General Dynamics (now Lockheed) F-16 Fighting Falcon multi-role air combat and attack fighter.

Top: The Grumman E-2 Hawkeye is the US Navy's carrierborne counterpart to the US Air Force's Boeing E-3 Sentry in the AWACS (Airborne Warning And Control System) role. Though it has lower performance and endurance than its turbofan-powered land-based partner, the turboprop-powered Hawkeye is still a superb 'force multiplier' that has gained useful export orders.

Centre: The US Air Force's latest bomber is the Northrop B-2A Spirit, which is to be produced only in small numbers but which will provide the USAF with the ability for 'stealthy' and therefore undetected penetration of enemy air space for the delivery of strategic weapons.

with the fail-safe design philosophy. By the 1970s this philosophy was very well developed, but it had inevitable disadvantages.

For a given maximum take-off weight, it was possible to calculate a fail-safe structure of optimum weight: but to fix this weight at the proposed maximum for the initial model precluded increases in later models, for structural reasons; while to allow for future growth could penalize the initial model with too heavy an airframe. Designers thus had to juggle with the ratio between these two factors to arrive at a sensible solution. Then there came the concept of active controls, opening up the possibility of considerably higher weights without the need for a significantly strengthened structure, especially in the wing roots where alterations are always expensive in terms of money and weight. The problem with increased weight (in this particular application) is that it increases the bending moment on the wing, and thus worsens the structural problems resulting from transient but nonetheless highly significant gust and manoeuvring loads. For economic and safety reasons it is undesirable to resort to the alternatives of reduced speeds and reduced manoeuvring parameters as a means of reducing 'g' so the idea of active flight controls for dealing with the increased bending loads associated with higher weights was particularly attractive. So far only Lockheed has used such a system, in the case of its three-engined L-1011-500 TriStar wide-body transport, designed to carry smaller numbers of passengers over longer routes than earlier versions of the TriStar. To reduce induced drag it .was desirable to increase span by some 9 ft (2.74 m), with great benefits to range performance. But only the use of active controls on the wings could prevent unacceptably high bending moments with the original root structure: thus the L-1101-500 is provided with three sets of accelerometers to measure vertical accelerations; the inputs from these sensors are processed by the onboard automatic flight-control system computer to control the ailerons. In short, the sensors tell the computer the moment a gust strikes the aeroplane in such a way as to cause an upward bend in the wings, whereupon the computer instructs the outboard ailerons to move symmetrically upward thereby cancelling the upward bending movement initiated by the gust. The system thus negates the aerodynamic feature of the wing's higher aspect ratio, which tends to move the lift distribution outward from the roots and so increase bending moment, by artificially shifting the lift distribution inboard at critical times. The net effect of this theoretically simple but practically fairly complicated feature is greater aerodynamic efficiency and less drag, with a resultant decrease of 3% in fuel consumption. Though this may appear an insignificant saving, it should be appreciated that it is equivalent to just under 950 US gal (791 Imp gal/3596 litres) in the case of the L-1101-500's maximum fuel capacity of 31,642 US gal (26,348 Imp gal; 119778 litres), which would represent a very useful fuel saving over one year s high utilization of such airliners.

Lockheed in 1982 decided to drop out of the commercial airliner market after current orders for the TriStar had been fulfilled in 1985, so there seems little immediate chance for active tail controls to be introduced as had been hoped. An active tailplane, for example, would have permitted smaller control area, allowing the slab tailplane to be reduced in size with a saving in weight of 1,680 lb (762 kg) and a further 3% cut in fuel consumption.

The key to the active control concept is provided by the combination of sensor and computer as a key element in the control loop, and these two factors have become increasingly dominant in aviation. They are already significant, forming as they do the heart of the AFCS

(Automatic Flight-Control System) that manages the operation of most modern airliners, providing a flight-management capability that allows excellent optimization of the flight profile to take account of all foreseeable operating and ambient conditions. This in itself makes for significant operating economies, and also relieves the flightcrew of an appreciable portion of its workload by undertaking the routine tasks of navigation and the monitoring of systems such as the powerplant, flight controls and high-lift devices, communications, environmental control system etc. This factor has allowed the standard flightcrew of even a long-range airliner to be reduced to a mere two pilots in most aircraft, whereas airliners of the previous generation required an aircrew of four or five including a flight engineer, navigator and, in some cases, a radio operator. This reduction in manning requirements clearly possesses instant attractions for the airlines as they need fewer aircrew, and has longer-term implications in permitting the reduction of the size of the flightdeck and crew rest station, with advantages in reduced structure weight and cost etc.

Coordinating the talents of an autopilot, INS (Inertial Navigation System) or other advanced navigation system such as GPS (Global Navigation System), and meteorological system into one computer-controlled package, the AFCS allows the flightcrew to concentrate on the important decision-making and vital-level monitoring functions without detriment to safety. At a considerable increase in capital cost, therefore, the new breed of airliner reduces the operator's running costs by cutting back fuel consumption, trimming crew salary requirements and easing the burden of maintenance. The AFCS is a remarkably versatile system, and allied to it, either individually or collectively, are several other computer-directed systems, such as the CSAS (Command and Stability Augmentation System), the INS which measures the aeroplane's three-dimensional accelerations and integrates these in time to determine the position of the aeroplane relative to the predetermined starting point, and VOR (VHF Omni-Range) which is a ground-located navigation aid usable only when the aeroplane is flying along predetermined airways.

The latest generation of airliners' flightdeck revolution is not confined to the computer-controlled management of the entire airliner as a system, but has also embraced the very manner in which the flight crew are kept informed of the flight parameters whose variations vitally affect the course and nature of any flight. Up to recent times, the flightdeck of even a simple aeroplane was generally a complex of dials, gauges, attitude indicators, several other species of information-imparting paraphernalia, and controls for the flying surfaces and their auxiliaries as well as for the engines, landing gear, radio and radar equipment. Now the information revolution has led to a total flightdeck revolution

This the newer civil aircraft (Airbus Industrie A310, A320, A330 and A340, the Boeing Model 757, Model 767 and Model 777, and the McDonnell Douglas MD-11 upgraded version of the DC-10) each incorporates a flightdeck layout based on a small number of multi-function displays of the CRT (Cathode Ray Tube), LED (Light-Emitting Diode) or liquid-crystal types replacing most of the earlier airliners' vast array of dials and gauges. On these displays, generally of the full-colour type, the flightcrew can call up any information they need, presented in specially devised digital forms for ease of assimilation, and can also use the screens for display of computer-integrated information from several sources. At the same time the AFCS can override the standard information

Above: The Antonov An-72 'Coaler' and its later An-74 derivative provide the CIS (previously the USSR) with a turbofan-powered STOL transport able to operate even in the direst of geographical and climatic conditions.

shown on the screens to warn the crew of anything beyond the capabilities of the computer and therefore demanding a human decision. These visual warnings are generally accompanied by some type of aural warning to ensure that the flightcrew takes immediate notice of information required for their rapid arrival at a decision that may have

Above: The McDonnell Douglas F/A-18 Hornet is a dual-role fighter and attack warplane evolved from the Northrop YF-17 land-based prototype as a carrierborne machine for use by the US Navy and Marine Corps.

safety implications.

The effect of this transformation of the cockpit is that a crew of two can undertake with ease the work that previously needed the attention of three, four or even five men. As it deals automatically with the routine matters that previously required constant attention through the watching of apparently innumerable dials and gauges, the AFCS also

Above: The BAe 146 is unique among modern short-range transports in offering virtual STOL capability through the use of advanced high-lift devices and a powerplant of four turbofans.

Top: The most advanced version of the McDonnell Douglas F-15 Eagle currently in service is the F-15E, a highly developed strike and interdiction variant with a second crew member to manage the advanced avionics.

Top, centre and above: The Lockheed F-117 Skyknight precision attack warplane owes its angular appearance to the dictates of 'stealth' design. Intended to reach and destroy key targets without being detected and therefore intercepted, the F-117 has a shape designed to reflect the enemy's radar emissions in any and all directions except that back to the radar's receiver. The type also has shielded engines to reduce its thermal signature.

offers the two members of the flightcrew a less congested working environment whose greater ergonomic sophistication is conducive to improved operational efficiency.

In the short term, the market seems to be incapable of supporting more than the two current giants, which are Airbus Industrie and Boeing. It became notably evident during the 1980s how Airbus, a multi-national European grouping, has come to challenge Boeing for domination of the market for wide-body airliners then dominated by products such as the Model 737, Model 747 and Model 767. To maintain this challenge Airbus had to expand its product range so that it could compete with Boeing across the whole spectrum of the civil market.

Equally notable has been the eclipse of Lockheed and McDonnell Douglas in the airliner world. Its fingers burned to the tune of almost US $2.5 billion by the TriStar programme, Lockheed decided to end its commitment to the civil market. McDonnell Douglas fared better with the DC-10, which also spawned the KC-l0A Extender military derivative for the US Air Force, but its MD-11 updated version has not secured a flood of orders, and the longer-term future of the MD-80 and MD-90 upgraded versions of the venerable DC-9 series are failing to match the latest versions of the truly great Model 737 series in terms of sales. McDonnell Douglas remains committed to the civil transport market, however, and a number of concepts have been prepared under the MD designation that replaced DC from 1983.

It seems likely, therefore, that the only two major manufacturers of large civil transports in the foreseeable future will be Airbus and Boeing, which both concentrate on advanced-technology aircraft for the mid- and upper portions of the market spectrum for passenger and freight aircraft. It is worth noting, however, that while there appeared to be little demand for the 'jumbo' size of airliner, with seating for some 500 passengers, during the first half of the 1980s, Boeing kept its Model 747 in production and thereby gained considerable benefit when the market for high-capacity transports revived later in the decade. Boeing has also devoted considerable effort to the continued development of the Model 747, which has profited from the introduction of improvements and updated models in terms of increased orders. The resurgence of airline demand for high-capacity transports also persuaded Airbus to enter this commercially dangerous but potentially lucrative market with the A330 and A340 half-brothers. Both aircraft can carry up to 440 passengers, although 375 is a more standard layout, and are aimed at the medium/long- and long-range markets respectively. The two types share an essentially similar airframe, but whereas the A330-300 baseline model has a powerplant of two General Electric

Below and below centre: The Rockwell Orbiter is the key element of the American Space Shuttle Transportation System, and is an aerospaceplane that is boosted into space with the aid of strap-on boosters before undertaking a gliding return to a conventional runway.

CF6-80E1A2 turbofans each rated at 67,500 lb (30618 kg) static thrust but replaceable by similarly rated Pratt & Whitney PW4000 or Rolls-Royce Trent turbofans for the carriage of a typical payload over a range of 8765 km (5,446 miles), the A340-300 baseline model has a powerplant of four CFM International (General Electric/SNECMA) CFM56-5C2 turbofans each rated at 31,200 lb (14152 kg) static thrust for the carriage of a typical payload over a range of 13250 km (21323 km). Both aircraft entered service in the mid-1990s, and are offered in a number of variants typical of the current trend to attract orders through the availability of models optimized with different engines, weights, fuel capacities and seating layouts.

Further down the capacity spectrum, several of the medium-capacity airliners from the 1960s and 1970s were still in gainful production during the 1980s during the early and mid-1980s, but a major portion of this market has also fallen to Airbus and Boeing, the former offering the wide-body A310 as a short/medium-range transport for a maximum of 255 passengers, and the latter bracketing the target market the narrow-body Model 757 as a short/medium-range transport for a maximum of 223 passengers and the wide-body Model 767 as a medium-range transport with seating for a maximum of 289 passengers. Accommodation for about 250 passengers seems to be the capacity required by the airlines for service from the 1980s into the 1990s, and with the exception of the narrow- and wide-body fuselages all three aircraft are variants of the same basic design philosophy: a low-set wing characterized by moderate sweep and nicely calculated high-lift devices, a swept tail unit with a low-set tailplane, and a powerplant of two high-efficiency turbofans installed in pods pylon-mounted below and ahead of the wings.

The first part of the 1980s was marked by considerable airline and manufacturer enthusiasm for smaller airliners, it being widely accepted that the growing demand for seats on the world's short- and medium-range routes demanded the

Left: Much of the concept and technology for the SSTS was proved by the North American X-15 experimental aeroplane, a rocket-powered type that was launched from a converted Boeing B-52 Stratofortress bomber.

Left: The USA devotes considerable resources to research, and this Lockheed c-141 StarLifter military transport was modified to carry a 36-in (91.4-cm) telescope for NASA.

Above: The Vought-Hiller-Ryan XC-142 was an experimental type to validate the concept of the tilting wing for VTOL capability. Carrying four turboprops each driving a large-diameter 'proprotor', the wing was pivoted so that it could be raised to the vertical position, in which the proprotors delivered vertical thrust to lift the machine straight off the ground, and then gradually lowered to the horizontal position, in which the proprotors delivered forward thrust for wingborne flight. A vertical landing was achieved by reversing this process. The XC-142 proved fully practical, but the tilting wing concept has yet to find its way into a production aeroplane.

creation of a new airliner based on the latest technology and providing accommodation for up to 150 passengers. The role seen for the new type was replacement of venerable airliners such as the classic three-engined Boeing Model 727, two-engined Boeing Model 737 and two-engined McDonnell Douglas DC-9. But these three designs continued to sell well during the early 1980s, but the Model 727 was taken out of production in 1983. The two twin-engined designs remained in full-scale production and indeed in further development, but gradually the Model 737 eclipsed the DC-9 to become the best-selling airliner of all time in succession to the Model 727. The fortunes of the DC-9 and its upgraded MD-80 and MD-90 derivatives have continued to wane, though the type still secures orders and remains a profitable manufacturing proposition, but the position of the Model 737 in its niche remains unassailable, and is likely to remain so as Boeing develops new variants with longer fuselages, more modern engines and advances such as a 'glass' flightdeck to exploit the sub-niches of a market more than eager to exploit the capabilities of a type that combines a low-cost airframe of proven profitability with the very latest in cost-cuttings technologies.

Most airlines were therefore happy in their current resources-strapped condition not to order a new high-risk aeroplane before it has flown, while the airframe and engine manufacturers were unwilling to commit scarce capital to projects which had attracted no genuine customer commitment. Much of the initial work for such a project has been undertaken, however, notably the design of a new breed of engines, epitomized by the Anglo-Japanese RJ.500 turbofan. This multi-national approach to aircraft design has now become an established norm among all but the largest American aerospace corporations, for the complexity (and hence the cost) of modern aircraft programmes is beyond the resources of most companies, and indeed of most single countries. The situation of the 1980s continued into the 1990s, and in the middle of this decade there appears to be no real likelihood that a completely new medium-range, medium-capacity airliner will be designed in the immediate or even intermediate future.

At the smaller end of the air transport market, low-capacity airliners continued to sell with modest vigour during the 1980s as the deregulation of the American air transport industry allowed a number of small airlines to spring up as feeders for the main operators or to service the requirements of smaller communities wanting air links to major cities. This tendency, albeit on a smaller scale, spread to other parts of the world during the late 1980s and early

1990s, and have ensured the continued production of well-established machines such as the twin-turboprop Fokker F.27 Friendship and twin-turbofan Fokker F.28 Fellowship. Indeed, such was the continued success of its two types during the 1980s that Fokker developed updated versions as the Fokker 50 and Fokker 100 respectively, and although the airline industry's downturn in the early 1990s adversely affected sales, both types are selling moderately well and are being developed into slightly more capacious variants to cater for the enlargement of this segment of the air transport market.

Still further down the capacity spectrum, the 1980s witnessed a small but significant boom in commuter airliners, and here against a background of smaller (but not negligible) commercial risk there is a growing number of new aircraft that entered service in the later 1980s. The three most ambitious contestants in this hotly contested marketplace were the Aeritalia/Aérospatiale ATR-42 and ATR-72, the Saab-Fairchild SF-240 (changed in 1987 to Saab 340 after Fairchild's 1985 withdrawal from the programme) and the de Havilland Canada DHC-8 Dash 8. This is a market niche in which the superiority of the turboprop is well established, and it is indicative of the future anticipated for small airliners of this type that the major engine manufacturers (notably General Electric, Pratt & Whitney and Rolls-Royce) have developed or are all proposing a new generation of turboprops, using core turbines which can also be used in a small turbofan family, where previously the field had been dominated by older engines and by specialized manufacturers offering turboprops such as the Turbomeca Bastan and Astazou from France, and the Pratt & Whitney Aircraft of Canada PT6A.

There were signs of uncertainty in the third-level/commuter market in the mid- and late 1980s, and companies showed a natural reluctance to take risks in such circumstances. Even so, there appears to be a steady if unspectacular place for the cheapest commuterliners such as the Shorts 360, de Havilland Canada DHC-7 Dash 7, Let L-410 Turbolet, Dornier Do 228, CASA C-212 Aviocar and various offerings (notably the EMB-110 Bandeirante and EMB-120 Brasilia) of the Brazilian EMBRAER concern, whose inroads into the American market caused much concern to the troubled Swearingen firm, taken over by Fairchild in 1981. The American company overcame its problems, and during the early 1990s its Metro series began to enjoy a revival of fortune.

The longer-term future of the commuterliner now seems assured by the steady expansion of the market, whose upper level has moved into the regional transport niche with aircraft offering both high performance and greater passenger capacity than the pure commuterliners. Typical of this new breed are the EMBRAER/FMA CBA-123, Canadair Regional Jet development of the CL-601 Challenger corporate transport, Dornier Do 328, Airtech CN-325, Saab 2000, and British Aerospace ATP.

In the 1950s there were strong suggestions that the combined capabilities of the computer and various sensors would make the manned aircraft a thing of the past, especially in military service: with the pilot eliminated, it was confidently expected, fuselage cross-sections could be reduced, paving he way for other improvements such as reduced structure weight, less powerful engines and smaller fuel tankage. Such aircraft would be cheaper to build and maintain, allowing the production of more aircraft (this in turn reducing unit cost considerably and thus permitting further purchases); these unmanned aircraft would also permit far higher 'g' loadings to be attained, so that the machines could be thrown about the sky in much tighter manoeuvres. In the event such hopes proved drastically premature, and it seems clear that even if the state of the avionics art now permitted the creation of such aircraft, they would not be built on a production basis except in missile form. (The cruise missile, for example, is essentially

Left and below: The Grumman X-29 is a fascinating research aeroplane intended to explore the forward-swept wing concept. This offers advantages over the conventional swept wing in several aspects of the transonic and supersonic flight regime, and was made technically possible by the development of composite materials that permit the construction of a very stiff yet light wing not prone to divergent oscillation that could tear a wing off an aeroplane of conventional structure.

an unmanned aeroplane and has constituted a major portion of the United States strategic nuclear deterrent since the late 1980s). The reason is simple: in civil aircraft the crew is essential for psychological purposes, as few passengers would permit themselves to be flown by a 'robot', no matter how well programmed; in military aircraft the presence of a pilot (at least) offers an unrivalled decision-making capability that may never be matched by a computer unless true intelligence can be created artificially. Only in this event would it be possible to do away with manned military aircraft, for there will always be situations in which lack of concrete data will call for the flexible responses of human judgement, or even the use of intuition.

Thus the manned aeroplane is here to stay within the foreseeable future. The flexibility offered by humans is nowhere better attested than in the control of the strategic nuclear deterrents of the two superpowers up to the time of the USSR's collapse in 1989. The USA and USSR each had large numbers of surface- and underwater-launched ballistic missiles, but nevertheless still felt the need to retain comparatively small but nonetheless significant manned bomber forces that could be retargeted after 'launch', could be recalled, could undertake a variety of approaches to the target, and could undertake other missions with the aid of additional or different equipment. The Soviets' most important such assets, which are still operated by some of the USSR's successor states in the Commonwealth of

Independent States such as Russia and the Ukraine, are the Tupolev Tu-22M 'Backfire' and the Tu-160 'Blackjack' variable-geometry bombers. The form is a radical development of the disappointing Tu-22 'Blinder' fixed-wing bomber, while the latter bears a striking conceptual likeness to the Rockwell B-1 Lancer, the American type designed as successor to the Boeing B-52 Stratofortress. The B-52 was designed for long-range subsonic missions carrying free-fall nuclear weapons, but in its last B-52G and B-52H variants was revised for the low-level penetration of Soviet airspace with two North American AGM-28 Hound Dog air-to-surface supersonic cruise missiles later replaced by 12 or more examples of the Boeing AGM-86 air-to-surface subsonic cruise missile offering far higher penetration capability than the AGM-28 as a result of its extreme targeting accuracy and relative immunity to interception as a result of its very low-level cruise altitude and 'stealthy' design. The B-1A was designed for high supersonic performance at high altitude, but the growing sophistication of the Soviet air-defence capability led to the type's cancellation, though it was later reinstated as the B-1B with lower overall performance but superior capabilities in the penetration role with a large complement of cruise missiles and/or free-fall nuclear weapons. In simple financial terms it is hard to see how the B-1B programme could be justified as truly cost-effective, but in strategic and political terms there can be no doubt that the type provides the United States with important capabilities in the power-projection role that demands extreme operational flexibility right up to the moment of weapon release.

The B-1B is an exceptional illustration, inasmuch as the cost and complexity of a single-role aeroplane makes such

HYDROGEN
JETTISON-VEN

Above: The North American X-15 remains the aeroplane that has flown fastest and highest, and was of enormous benefit in the development of several important technologies appropriate to modern aircraft.

types rare in modern air forces, where single-role aircraft are generally dedicated to specialized reconnaissance as exemplified by the Lockheed SR-71 and the TR-1 updated version of the classic U-2 in American service, or the Myasishchyev M-17/55 'Mystic' entering Russian service in the mid-1990s, or to control as exemplified by the Boeing E-3A Sentry developed from the Model 707 transport and by the Ilyushin A-50 'Mainstay' developed from the Il-76 'Candid' transport. These extremely costly aircraft have good survival chances as they are not intended for operations in the combat zone.

The SR-71 'Blackbird' has already been mentioned. This was retired from first-line service in the early 1990s but is still in limited use for experimental tasks. The SR-71 is a truly remarkable aeroplane, and remains the current holder of the world absolute speed and altitude records. Its origins are still veiled, but it is clear that the type was planned as the launch platform for supersonic reconnaissance drones, developed into the YF-12A experimental interceptor and then turned into the SR-71 strategic reconnaissance platform. The 'Blackbird' is a massive delta-wing machine with the fuselage contours faired laterally into a lifting shape, and is powered by two afterburning bleed-turbojets running on special low-volatility fuel. Prodigiously expensive to build and to maintain, the SR-71 fleet provided the US forces with a mass of reconnaissance information after Mach 3+ flights at exceptionally high altitudes.

For the control of its armed forces, the United States deploys two types modified from civil airliners. As noted above, the Boeing E-3 Sentry is an adaptation of the Boeing 707 with a large rotodome above the fuselage containing

the antenna for the very capable Westinghouse APY-1 radar. Operating at high altitude on long patrols, the E-3 can monitor all air activity within a radius of 250 miles (402 km) at whatever altitude, while an onboard tactical team uses computers to assess data from this radar and other sources (provided by secure data link), and then controls friendly forces to deal with the threats revealed. The United States planned a fleet of 40 Sentries but in fact ordered just 34 such aircraft, while later purchasers were NATO with 18, Saudi Arabia with five, France with four and the United Kingdom with seven. The USSR's first such aeroplane was the considerably less sophisticated Tupolev Tu-126 'Moss', but from the early 1990s this was replaced by the A-50 'Mainstay' derivative of the Il-76 'Candid' transport mentioned above. These AWACS (Airborne Warning And Control System) aircraft are marvellously complex yet efficient adjuncts to the tactical control of air power: they are really airborne command posts, generating data for themselves but also receiving inputs from other aircraft, satellites and surface forces. In fact, each aeroplane is capable of controlling the entire range of air activities in a complete theatre of war.

The operational capability of the E-3 is partnered at the national level by the Boeing E-4. This is based on the Model 747 airliner, and though six such aircraft were originally planned, the final total is just four. These are the most expensive single aircraft yet built, but provide the United States with the means of controlling the entire national war effort from a single airborne, and therefore relatively invulnerable, aeroplane. Designated the ABNCP (Air-Borne National Command Post), the E-4 is crammed with computers and communications gear, making each aeroplane the third possible 'war emergency capital' of the United States with the National Military Command Center and Alternate National Military Command Center, which are both ground-based and therefore more vulnerable even if buried below the surface.

The control of tactical air operations has also become increasingly important, and the world's most successful exponent of this art is the Grumman E-2 Hawkeye, which was developed for carrierborne use by the US Navy and has proved itself particularly effective, especially during the

and therefore rely on the extensive use of podded ECM equipment located on underwing hardpoints otherwise dedicated to the carriage of weapon and/or drop tanks. There is little doubt, however, that the increased survivability of combat aircraft carrying ECM pods more than offsets their reduced disposable warload. ECM pods are standard on the combat aircraft of all air forces with any claim to modernity of equipment.

Both the United States and, before its 1989 dissolution into the CIS, the USSR have introduced new combat aircraft over the last few years, as have the Western Europeans. The most important of these, so far as the 1980s were concerned, are the Mikoyan-Gurevich MiG-23 'Flogger' variable-geometry tactical fighter, the MiG-27 'Flogger' attack fighter derivative of the MiG-23, the Sukhoi Su-24 'Fencer' variable-geometry strike and attack aeroplane, and the Su-25 'Frogfoot' close-support and anti-tank aeroplane for the Warsaw Pact forces; the Fairchild Republic A-10 Thunderbolt II anti-tank aeroplane, the General Dynamics F-16 Fighting Falcon air-combat and multi-role fighter, the Grumman F-14 Tomcat carrierborne multi-role fighter with a variable-geometry wing platform,

Israeli invasion of Lebanon during early 1982. The E-2 was still in production during the mid-1990s for the US Navy, which had ordered just under 200 such aircraft by that time, and other current purchasers of this highly effective yet affordable 'force multiplier' platform include Egypt, France, Israel, Japan, Singapore and Taiwan.

This type of aeroplane is extremely expensive but can make the use of combat aircraft much more efficient, hence the description of such aircraft as 'force multipliers'. It is probable, therefore, that AWACS in not ABNCP aircraft are likely to figure prominently in the future plans of the major air forces. But there is another side to the AWACS coin, for if it is desirable to make full use of one's own AWACS aircraft, it is just as desirable to prevent the enemy from making full use of his. It therefore seems likely that the role of ECM (Electronic Counter-Measures) aircraft will be extended from its already prominent position. The US Air Force pioneered the modern use of such aircraft over Vietnam in the 1960s and early 1970s, and they have proved themselves valuable aids to combat aircraft, jamming the radar of enemy ground and air missiles and hampering the use of early warning systems.

As with AWACS aircraft, the electronics for such machines are very costly and make the purchase of such aircraft a subject for major consideration. Such is the pace of electronic development, moreover, that ECCM (Electronic Counter-Counter-Measures) are soon developed for the ECM equipment, and this requires that the ECM equipment requires constant updating to keep abreast of enemy advances in radar and other electronic technologies. Yet the overall importance of such EW (Electronic Warfare) equipment was amply confirmed during the 1973 Arab-Israeli war, in which only the arrival of ECM equipment from the United States saved the Israeli air force from an even heavier mauling by Soviet-made missiles.

The deployment of EW aircraft thus increased considerably during the 1980s, largely in the USA. Few other countries can afford to purchase single-role aircraft with the extraordinary capabilities of the US Navy's Grumman EA-6 Prowler all-weather type, which has capabilities at the strategic, operational and tactical levels,

Below: Not all military aircraft are designed for high speed. The Lockheed TR-1 tactical reconnaissance aeroplane, for example, is really a turbojet-powered sailplane that cruises comparatively slowly at very high altitude. The type was evolved from the U-2 series of 'spyplanes', and in the early 1990s was redesignated as the U-2R.

Above: Another firmly subsonic type is the Fairchild Republic A-10 Thunderbolt II anti-tank and battlefield close support aeroplane, which was designed for long loiters before making low-level, jinking attacks for the firing of its devastating 30-mm cannon (firing depleted uranium projectiles) or the release of weapons that can range between free-fall bombs and AGM-65 Maverick guided missiles.

Right: The shape of modern military aircraft is undergoing a major change to wring the utmost out of the agility made possible by the development of 'fly-by-wire' control systems. Typical of this trend toward canard aircraft, with the longitudinal control surfaces relocated from the tail to the forward fuselage, is the Dassault Rafale under development for entry into French service at the beginning of the next century.

the McDonnell Douglas F-15 Eagle air-superiority fighter, and the McDonnell Douglas/Northrop F/A-18 Hornet carrierborne dual-role fighter/attack aeroplane for the United States; the Dassault-Breguet Mirage F1 and Mirage 2000 for France; and the variable-geometry Panavia Tornado multi-role combat aeroplane for Italy, the United Kingdom and West Germany, which became Germany with the 1990 reunification of the previous separate countries of East Germany and West Germany.

The United States and the United Kingdom are collaborating in an investigation of the possibilities for a supersonic STOVL combat aeroplane, and the only other contender in this major but wholly underestimated field has been the USSR (now Russia). Here the VTOL/STOVL torch is carried by the Yakovlev design bureau, whose first operational aeroplane of this type has been the Yak-38 'Forger' carrierborne attack aeroplane. From the late 1990s the bureau has been involved in he evolution of the Yak-141 'Freehand' as a supersonic successor, but a number of crashes and an acute shortage of funding have jeopardized production to the production stage.

The performance plateau reached with current military aircraft results from reliance on aluminium alloys as the primary structural medium, and this precludes sustained speeds in excess of Mach 2.25. Titanium is used in special cases where heat is likely to be extreme, but the cost of this metal prohibits its use on a large scale. Composite materials of various kinds became commoner during the 1980s, but again their costs are high and their applications were somewhat specialized. Later in the decade, however, continued development of aeronautical materials made feasible the larger-scale employment of composite materials

for load-carrying structures and also of advanced alloys of lithium and aluminium. The gradual acceptance of these high-technology materials did not indicate any desire for higher performance, however, but rather the desire to reduce weight without any sacrifice of strength, and to simplify the production and maintenance of complex structures not readily buildable in conventional materials.

Russia is still actively involved in the development of advanced combat aircraft, but is beset by political as well as financial problems, and is therefore unlikely to emerge as a realistic successor to the USSR in terms of military power. The country inherited the bulk of the USSR's military machine, with lesser portions going to the Ukraine and the other ex-Soviet republics that now constitute the Commonwealth of Independent States, and is hard pressed to maintain its current strength without investing heavily in advanced weapons for a future that is unlikely to see any real military threat to the CIS or its components.

It was the threat of the USSR that spurred the development of other modern weapons for the Western bloc. So far as aircraft are concerned, these range from light multi-role tactical fighters such as the Italian-originated by now Italo-Brazilian AMX International AMX to advanced tactical combat aircraft such as the Dassault Rafale (squall) for the French air force and naval air arm, and the Eurofighter 2000 for the British, German, Italian and Spanish air forces. The AMX has entered service, and the Rafale and Eurofighter 2000 are due to enter service at the beginning of the next century, although the reduced level of the threat for which they were designed has already led to the curtailment of certain of the programmes' most advanced elements and a scaling down of both the urgency and planned procurement of the two types. It is worth noting that the Rafale and Eurofighter 2000, together with the JAS 39 Gripen (griffon) that is further advanced toward production for the Swedish air force, are of the 'modern' configuration with canard foreplanes and an aft-mounted delta wing controlled via a 'fly-by-wire' system for extreme agility and the capability to fly at very high angles of attack. This last has been shown to offer superior combat capabilities, and is a notable feature of the MiG-29 and Su-27. All three Western types are inherently 'stealthy', have advanced powerplants offering a very high power/weight ratio in afterburner, and have electronics based on a digital databus system for the maximum exploitation of active and passive sensors, advanced computers, and the very latest in disposable weapons. These are all features of the combat aircraft currently being delivered or under development for service in the next century.

So far as performance is concerned, the upper limits reached in the mid-1970s are likely to remain for some time, for there appears to be no pressing need for the higher speeds and ceilings that are possible. Instead greater emphasis has been placed on increasing utility within the current performance limits, and thus in making the new generation of aircraft more cost-effective. Only in range is improvement both desirable and likely, and this applies both to military and to civil machines. The ultimate in range performance, it should be noted, was not secured by either a military or commercial aeroplane, but by an extraordinary record-breaker in the mould of the private-enterprise machines of the 1920s. Designed by Burt Rutan and flown by Dick Rutan and Jeanna Yeager, the twin-piston engined Rutan Voyager covered a nonstop distance of 24,986.67 miles (40212.1 km) as it flew round the Earth in nine days on 14/23 December 1986.

Civil aircraft are unlikely to change radically, although 'fly-by-wire' control systems are becoming increasingly common and there will probably be a sharp increase in the numbers and perhaps the types of STOL 'taxi' aircraft and medium-capacity airliners intended for short-range routes. The real future of civil aircraft, however, lies with improvements in operating economy through the development of structurally and aerodynamically advanced wings (based on aerofoils of supercritical section and carrying tip-mounted winglets for more economical high-speed cruise capability), high-lift devices, and control surfaces used in conjunction with 'fly-by-wire' control systems and electronic flight-management systems. This will make it much easier to keep down the size of airports and enable aircraft to be operated with less power.

This second factor is of growing importance from both the economic and the public relations points of view. People all round the world are increasingly disturbed by aircraft noise, especially during take-off and landing at municipal airports. More efficient wings will enable lower power settings to be used, thus reducing noise. The airline operators will be further aided by the development of much

quieter engines, which was well under way in the 1980s, and the aircraft will also have greater range, for lower power requirements give the added bonus of increased distance for a given quantity of fuel.

Supersonic flight on a fairly widespread basis is unlikely before the end of the millennium. This would be especially useful for long routes, where the reduction in journey times can be considerable, but environmental objections currently make the development of new-generation SSTs (Super-Sonic Transports) highly unlikely. It is almost certain, however, that the SST does have a longer-term future, so the next generation of SSTs must surely be based on variable-geometry wings, advanced engines and supercritical aerodynamics. Such aircraft could fly nonstop between major cities much more than just 2,500 miles (4000 km) apart, which is the range for which the BAe/Aérospatiale Concorde was designed. Improved ceilings could help to reduce the problem of 'sonic boom', while improvements in the technology of supersonic turbofans will lower the noise and pollution levels.

Aviation so far has been concerned almost exclusively with flight within the earth's atmosphere. The years to come, however, will see the first operations by aircraft designed to work equally well in space. The origin of such machines can be traced back to the Bell X-1 experimental aeroplane built by the Americans just after the end of World War II. Launched from a parent aeroplane and landing on a small landing gear arrangement, the rocket-powered X-1 was the first aeroplane in the world to break through the 'sound barrier', reaching 670 mph (1078 km/h) at 42,000 ft (12800 m) on 14 October 1947. At the height it was flying, the X-1 had reached Mach 1.015.

The aircraft of the X-series achieved successively higher speeds and altitudes until the North American X-15 reached the limits of 'atmospheric' flight in the 1960s, touching 4,534 mph (7297 km/h) or Mach 6.72 and climbing to an altitude of 350,000 ft (106700 m) towards the end of the decade. While the X-1 had been dropped by a B-29 at 30,000 ft (9145 m), the much larger and very considerably heavier X-15 had to be launched by a B-52 at some 35,000 ft (10670 m) before igniting its rocket engine and climbing into the upper reaches of the atmosphere.

Below: Whatever else aviation has achieved or may get achieve, it is perhaps the joy of flight which is most important in spiritual if not financial terms. There can be little that is more uplifting in this respect than the superb flying of aerobatic teams such as the Royal Air Force's Red Arrows, seen here in their BAe Hawk trainers.

Index